Perception is basic to knowledge, and self-perception is basic to self-knowledge. It is through *ecological* self-perception that we are aware of our immediate situation: of where we are and what we are doing. Through *interpersonal* self-perception we are aware of our ongoing social interactions: of who we are with and what is going on. These modes of perception, which appear very early in infancy, are the foundation on which more conceptual forms of self-knowledge are later established.

In this fifth Emory Symposium in Cognition, a distinguished interdisciplinary group of scholars analyzes both forms of self-perception from a wide range of viewpoints. The discussion is framed by Ulric Neisser's argument that there are five distinct forms of self-knowledge: ecological and interpersonal perception, conceptualization, memory, and private experience. This framework holds together topics ranging from infant perception to the control of movement and from early social and emotional development to the philosophy of dialogue.

Emory Symposia in Cognition 5

The perceived self

The Emory Symposia in Cognition

Series editor: Ulric Neisser

Neisser, U. (Ed.) *Concepts and conceptual development: Ecological and intellectual factors in categorization* (1987)

Neisser, U., & Winograd, E. (Eds.) *Remembering reconsidered: Ecological and traditional approaches to the study of memory* (1988)

Fivush, R., & Hudson, J. A. (Eds.) *Knowing and remembering in young children* (1990)

Winograd, E., & Neisser, U. (Eds.) *Affect and accuracy in recall: Studies of "flashbulb" memories* (1992)

Neisser, U. (Ed.) *The perceived self: Ecological and interpersonal sources of self-knowledge* (1993)

The perceived self

Ecological and interpersonal sources of self-knowledge

Edited by

ULRIC NEISSER
Emory University

Published by the Press Syndicate of the University of Cambridge
The Pitt Building, Trumpington Street, Cambridge CB2 1RP
40 West 20th Street, New York, NY 10011–4211, USA
10 Stamford Road, Oakleigh, Melbourne 3166, Australia

© Cambridge University Press 1993

First published 1993

Printed in the United States of America

Library of Congress Cataloging-in-Publication Data
The perceived self : ecological and interpersonal sources of self
knowledge / edited by Ulric Neisser.
   p. cm. – (Emory symposia in cognition ; 5)
Papers from two conferences in the Mellon Colloquium on the Self
at the Emory Cognition Project : the Conference on the Ecological
Self, held at Emory University in May 1989, and the Conference on
the Interpersonal Self held in May 1990.
Includes index.
ISBN 0-521-41509-8 (hard)
1. Self – Congresses. 2. Self-perception – Congresses. 3. Self-
Knowledge, Theory of – Congresses. 4. Environmental psychology –
Congresses. 5. Interpersonal relations – Congresses. 6. Self –
Social aspects – Congresses. I. Neisser, Ulric. II. Series.
BF697.5.S43P47 1994
155.2–dc20   93–7500
                                                  CIP

A catalog record for this book is available from the British Library.

ISBN 0-521-41509-8 hardback

Contents

v

Preface

This fifth Emory Symposium in Cognition is both like and unlike its predecessors. It resembles them in its recognizably ecological emphasis, as well as in its attempt to integrate the study of adult cognition with that of development. Unlike them, however, its scope is not defined by a traditional field like "memory" or "categorization." Instead, it is delineated by a more fundamental distinction, that between the self and everything else. William James said it best: "Each of us dichotomizes the Kosmos at a different place" (1890: 290). As perceivers and thinkers, all human beings learn things about both sides of that dichotomy. We perceive, remember, and think about the world around us, but also about ourselves. This book, the first of three projected volumes, deals with perceiving. It focuses on two forms of self-perception, the *ecological* and the *interpersonal.* A companion volume on the remembering self follows soon; a third, still in preparation, will focus on self-concepts.

The self may be a new topic for cognitive psychologists, but not for everyone. Philosophers and psychologists of various persuasions have written about it for many years with considerable insight. Those contributions have been so diverse, spanning so many years and disciplines, that it is hard to keep track of them all. Even more striking than their diversity, however, is their unanimity on one critical point. All have been chiefly concerned with *intellectual* forms of self-awareness: with self-concepts and self-understandings and self-narratives. But although these are surely important (our next two volumes will be devoted to them), they are not the earliest or the most basic forms of self-knowledge. Perception comes first, and is most certain. So (I believe) it must be the right place to start.

It was James J. Gibson who first insisted that perceiving the self is a necessary concomitant of perceiving the environment. They go together, he said, "like the two sides of a coin." This point is elaborated in the first part of the present volume, especially in chapters 1 and 2. Once this concept is understood, earlier theories of the self seem increasingly inadequate. To ignore self-perception is, in Freud's phrase, like playing *Hamlet* without the Prince of Denmark. In the mid-1980s, I began to think seriously about the self from this perspective. How is the "ecological self" (my term, but essentially Gibson's idea) related to the selves described by other psychologists and philosophers? The first step was to establish some definitions, which

I tried to do in a 1988 paper called "Five Kinds of Self-Knowledge." Each form of self-knowledge gives rise to something almost like a different "self." As it turned out, two of those selves were perceptual: Not only ecological but also interpersonal perception provides critical information about the self. The conceptual, remembered, and private selves are quite different. They do not depend on perception but on taking oneself as an object of thought.

A generous grant from the Mellon Foundation funded a series of five conferences based on these ideas. The series as a whole was called *The Mellon Colloquium on the Self at the Emory Cognition Project.* It began with the Conference on the Ecological Self, held at Emory in May 1989: Chapters 2–7 are based on presentations given on that occasion. The remaining chapters (8–16) are from the Conference on the Interpersonal Self, held in May 1990. Papers from the three later conferences will appear in subsequent volumes of this series.

I am deeply grateful to the contributors whose work appears here – for their significant contributions, for taking my own ideas so seriously and criticizing them so carefully, and also for their patience. It has taken a long time to get this book out. I believe, however, that it was worth the wait. I am also grateful to the Mellon Foundation and to Emory University for making the colloquium – and hence these volumes – possible. Special thanks go to the many colleagues and students who helped organize and coordinate the conferences, too many to list here. I do particularly want to acknowledge the work of David Jopling, Mellon postdoctoral fellow at the Emory Cognition Project, who contributed to the colloquium at every level.

The Colloquium on the Self has been a wonderfully stimulating enterprise. I hope that this volume and its successors will, to some extent, enable readers to share in the excitement of these meetings and the ideas that were presented. There was a sense that however difficult the problem of the self may be, we were making a real start on it. I believe, indeed, that we did so; readers must decide for themselves.

Ulric Neisser

Contributors

ROSS BUCK is professor of Communication Sciences and Psychology at the University of Connecticut in Storrs.

SONDRA HORTON FRALEIGH is director of the graduate dance program and professor of dance at the State University of New York at Brockport.

ELEANOR J. GIBSON is the Susan Linn Sage Professor of Psychology Emerita at Cornell University.

MARJORIE GRENE is Honorary Distinguished Professor at Virginia Polytechnic Institute and State University.

JAMES M. GUSTAFSON is the Luce Professor of Humanities and Comparative Studies at Emory University.

R. PETER HOBSON is senior lecturer in the department of child and adolescent psychiatry, Institute of Psychiatry, University of London.

MARC JEANNEROD is director of the INSERM Laboratory of Neuropsychology and professor at the University of Lyon.

DAVID JOPLING is assistant professor of philosophy at York University.

DAVID N. LEE is reader in psychology at the University of Edinburgh.

KATHERINE A. LOVELAND is associate professor in psychiatry and pediatrics at the Mental Sciences Institute, University of Texas at Houston.

ULRIC NEISSER is the Robert W. Woodruff Professor of Psychology at Emory University and director of the Emory Cognition Project.

SANDRA PIPP is associate professor of psychology, University of Colorado.

FRANKLIN C. SHONTZ is professor of psychology at the University of Kansas.

DANIEL N. STERN, a psychoanalyst, is professor at the University of Geneva, Switzerland.

MICHAEL TOMASELLO is professor of psychology at Emory University.

COLWYN TREVARTHEN is professor of child psychology and psychobiology at the University of Edinburgh.

Part I

Introduction

1

The self perceived

ULRIC NEISSER

This book brings new ideas to bear on an old problem. The old problem is that of self-knowledge and the self; the new ideas are based on analyses of ecological and social perception. James J. Gibson (1979) was the first theorist to insist that perceiving the self is an inevitable counterpart of perceiving the environment. Gibson's ideas are basic to the notion of an *ecological self*, which will be elaborated in this chapter. But the view of perception to be presented here is not simply ecological; it is social as well. Face-to-face interaction between individuals establishes a sense of an *interpersonal self* that is very different from anything the inanimate environment can offer. Both forms of self-perception appear very early in life, and both give rise to the experience of effective agency that is such an important component of self-awareness. They are the foundation on which other, more intellectual aspects of the self are built.

Because the term *self* has more than one meaning, it is best to begin with definitions. Distinctions among various kinds of self have been proposed for more than a century: William James's (1890) contrast between the "I" and the "me" was only the first of many such contrasts. A few years ago I contributed to this tradition with a cognitive analysis, that is, one that focuses on forms of information (1988). In my view people have access to five basically different kinds of information about themselves. Each kind specifies a different aspect of the individual and thus implicitly defines a different sort of self. This volume, the first of several based on that analysis, focuses on ecological and interpersonal forms of self-knowledge. These are the first forms of self to develop in early infancy. Other forms – the remembered, private, and conceptual selves – are also important but arise only later. The ecological and interpersonal selves are also unique in being *perceived*: They need not be recalled, imagined, constructed, or conceptualized.

One very different meaning of self must be set aside before we begin. Much folk psychology and many religious traditions postulate an inner self of some kind, a "real me" who is (or should be) ultimately responsible for behavior. That hypothesis is rejected here. None of the five selves in my scheme are homunculi of this sort; rather, it is the *whole person* who perceives, acts, and is responsible. On this point the ecological approach is in full agreement with most contemporary philosophy (e.g., Dennett, 1991a), as well as with neuroscience (e.g., Churchland & Sejnowski, 1992). The brain

3

is not organized by any Cartesian flow toward and from some inmost center but by richly parallel processing and modular subdivision. Daniel Dennett makes this point with characteristic flair.

Searching for the self can be somewhat like [this]. You enter the brain through the eye, march up the optic nerve, round and round in the cortex, looking behind every neuron, and then, before you know it, you emerge into daylight on the spike of a motor nerve impulse, scratching your head and wondering where the self is. (1991b, p. 355)

In the argument to be presented here, a self is not a special part of a person (or of a brain); it is a whole person considered from a particular point of view. The ecological self, for example, is the individual considered as an active agent in the immediate environment. Such agents perceive *themselves*, among other things: where they are, how they are moving, what they are doing, and what they might do, whether a given action is their own or not. The interpersonal self is the same individual considered from a different point of view: namely, as engaging in face-to-face interaction with others. These interactions are perceived too, just as positions and movements are. We can see and hear and feel what we are doing, both ecologically and interpersonally.

It is not only adults who perceive themselves in these ways; babies do too. Modern research leaves no doubt that young infants perceive their environments, their conspecifics, and themselves. They see what is within their reach, maintain a specific awareness of things that have gone out of sight, and distinguish their own actions from those of other individuals. They engage in lively social interactions with other people and are aware of the extent to which they control those interactions themselves. The fact that these achievements appear in the first weeks and months of life makes self-perception especially important: It is the first and most fundamental form of self-knowledge.

Perception may be the first form of self-awareness, but it is by no means the only one. A brief account of the others, and of the aspects of the self that they establish, is appropriate at this point. Perhaps most important, all human beings subscribe to a wide array of beliefs and assumptions about themselves. Taken together, these beliefs constitute the self-concept or *conceptual* self (Neisser, 1988). In its mature form, the conceptual self leans heavily on cultural forms. My own self-concept, for example, includes such categories as "professor," "husband," "father," "American," and "cognitive psychologist." Each of these roles – and I have many more – brings expectations, evaluations, and obligations in its train. The evaluations are especially important: I may think of myself as smart or stupid, good-looking or ugly, praiseworthy or worthless. The key phrase here is "think of myself." These aspects of the self are not directly perceived; as forms of reflective self-consciousness, they appear only when I *think* about myself or my situation.

Evidence from developmental psychology suggests that the conceptual self appears near the end of the first year. Younger infants have active ecological and interpersonal selves, but they do not take themselves as objects of thought. The ability to think explicitly about oneself probably begins with the realization that someone else is doing so already – that is, on becoming aware that one is the object of another person's attention. That awareness is not possible until about the tenth month, when shared attention (to events and objects) begins to be a common mode of parent–child interaction (Bruner, 1983; Tomasello, 1988). Only then does the child begin to understand what other people are attending to or talking about. On some occasions, what they are attending to is the child in question. Only when this is understood can the self-concept begin. (For a more detailed account of this development, see Michael Tomasello's chapter 9.)

Then there are life narratives. It seems likely that all adults in all cultures occasionally recount their experiences to others and to themselves as well. Such stories establish a version of the self-concept that transcends the present moment: a *temporally extended* self. This remembered self appears much later in childhood than the self-concept, per se. Even the most talkative young children live chiefly in the present, with little to say about the past or the future. Two-year-olds can recall something about prior experiences when asked (Fivush, Gray, & Fromhoff, 1987), but they do not swap stories about old times; more generally, they do not think of themselves as having life narratives. Such narratives, along with the skills of producing them, are acquired only in the third year or later (Fivush & Hudson, 1990; Neisser & Fivush, in press).

Because it is based on memory and reconstructions, the self remembered does not have the same claim to accuracy as the self perceived. Often, the way we remember things is not the way they really were. The fallibility of memory has led some contemporary theorists to argue that the self is nothing but a constructed narrative, and a self-serving one at that. This argument must be rejected. The ecological and interpersonal selves are directly perceived rather than constructed, and they are in place long before the self-narrative begins.

A further source of self-knowledge must also be considered. The inner quality of conscious experience – of thoughts and images, pains and dreams, "raw feels" and feelings – is unique to each individual. Because these experiences are intrinsically private, they are often thought to define the self in an essential way. I believe, however, that the uniqueness of conscious experience is not equally important to everyone. The *private self* is a focus of attention for some people – Jung (1921/1971) called them "introverts" – but not for others. In any case, the fact that consciousness is uniquely private is probably discovered rather late. Although 2-year-olds surely have conscious experiences, they do not focus on the fact that those experiences are theirs alone. The privacy of mental life becomes salient only later in development, perhaps in connection with the "theories of mind" that seem to mature around age 4 or 5 (e.g., Astington, Harris, & Olson, 1988).

The remainder of this chapter deals with various aspects of self-perception. We begin with the ecological self: first with location and movement, then action and agency. Then we consider social perception and the interpersonal self. Finally, we turn to early development: the ecological self in infancy and the beginnings of interpersonal experience.

The ecological self: Location and movement

In my view, the claim that we perceive ourselves is coherent only in the framework of a particular theory of perception: James Gibson's (1966, 1979) ecological approach. (Earlier attempts to understand self-perception were largely unsuccessful; see Franklin Shontz's chapter 5 for a historical review.) In that theory perception has a special status. Gibson often called it "direct," meaning that the perceptual systems pick up information that invariantly specifies an objectively existing state of affairs. Unlike other forms of knowing, perception is not constructive or inferential. The rich information normally available to vision, for example, enables us to see the environment and our own actions as they really are.

This approach assumes that the perceptual systems of animals evolved to take advantage of objectively existing information. The aim of the study of perception is to identify that information, to discover what it specifies, and to determine how it is picked up. Such an enterprise must begin naturalistically, with perceivers in free movement through the ordinary environment. That analysis soon reveals something that earlier theories had ignored: The available information specifies a lot about perceivers themselves as well as about their environments. "Egoreception accompanies exteroception, like the other side of a coin. . . . One perceives the environment and coperceives oneself" (Gibson, 1979, p. 126).

As you walk across a room, many kinds of information enable you to perceive your own movement and its trajectory. There is kinesthetic feedback from joints and muscles, as well as detection of acceleration in the vestibular organs; there are the echoing sounds of your footsteps, and especially the systematic changes of optical structure available to your eyes. Vision is perhaps the most important of these for the ecological self. To understand why, we need another Gibsonian concept: the *optic array*. The room through which you are walking (like any space in any illuminated environment) includes an infinite number of potential points of observation. Each point is surrounded by a "shell" of optical structure; that is, light is reflected to it from all directions. Consider, for example, the point at which your right eye is now located. One sector of the structure available there consists of light from the right-hand wall; another sector (embedded in the first) of light is perhaps reflected from a picture on that wall; other sectors are from the ceiling, the lamp, the book, and so on. Now consider that every shift to a new viewing point must change that optical structure. Movement of the observer always gives rise to a systematic *optic flow*, which precisely specifies the movement that produced it. It is optic flow, more than anything else, that enables you to see your own path of motion through the environment.

Several different kinds of optic flow can be distinguished analytically. As you move parallel to a wall, for example, every contour and texture element in the corresponding sector of the array streams backward. Under evolutionary conditions, this kind of flow uniquely specified movement of the observer; it did not occur otherwise. Unsurprisingly, then, artificially established parallel flow is enough to produce the experience of egomotion. This phenomenon is easily studied with the aid of a "moving room" (Lee, 1980; Lishman & Lee, 1973). A person standing on the (motionless) laboratory floor will sway in gentle synchrony as the surrounding walls are moved slightly back and forth. With larger displacements, subjects have a compelling experience of egomotion even though they are actually standing still.

Another important source of information for the ecological self is *occlusion*. The direction of your line of sight toward any stable object (except one exactly straight ahead) must change as you move forward. For that reason, objects that are fully visible from one position may be shifted behind other ("occluding") objects during the course of the motion. This specifies the relative positions of the objects: The occluded one is always farther away than the one that hides it. Even without actual occlusion, the changing visual directions of various objects ("differential motion parallax") specify your own path of motion precisely.

Another kind of optic flow, *looming*, occurs whenever an object moves toward you. The corresponding sector of the optic array gets larger and larger; just before contact, it may fill the entire visual field. The rate of this magnification is especially informative; with fixed velocity, it specifies the time of the impending collision (Lee, 1980). This means that the optic array specifies aspects of the future as well as the present, giving you what Lee (see his chapter 3) calls "prospective control" over your actions and their consequences. Taken together, these various forms of optic flow specify the position and movement of the ecological self quite precisely.

The self is specified in other modalities as well, including vestibular proprioception, somatic proprioception, and touch. Hearing too: bats depend on the *acoustic array* established by reflected sound. Despite this difference, bats' sense of where they are in the environment is entirely comparable to ours (cf. David Lee's chapter 3 on this point). Blind people also make use of information in the acoustic array, though not so sensitively as bats. Indeed, blind persons using "facial vision" (which, despite its name, is actually based on sound) can perceive the layout of the near environment surprisingly well (Hull, 1990).

The ecological self: Action and agency

The ecological self is a doer: We are just as aware of our actions and their effects as of our movements. This awareness, too, concerns the future as well as the present. As Gibson (1979) pointed out, any given situation affords some actions and not others. Right now, for example, the floor of my study affords walking and its door affords passage. What this means is simply that I can walk across the room and go out the door if I want to. Other examples: I can pick up a pencil from the desk and write with it; I can also throw it across the room, use it to press a computer key, or drop it in the wastebasket. Every situation offers infinitely many such *affordances*, of which only a few are perceived and even fewer realized in action. They depend on the individual as well as the situation, varying from species to species and person to person.

Recent research has shown that affordances are accurately perceived. We see at a glance whether objects are within reach (Carello, Grosofsky, Reichel, Solomon, & Turvey, 1989), doors are wide enough to walk through (Warren & Whang, 1987), or chairs are the right height to sit on (Mark, 1987). Such perception is necessarily "body-scaled" (Warren, 1984) – that is, the distance that matters for reaching is not measured in inches but in relation to our own bodily dimensions and capabilities. Partly for this reason, the perception of affordances is subject to constant learning and recalibration. A floor that afforded only crawling to a baby at 11 months affords walking a few weeks later; a fence that afforded leaping when I was 30 may afford only clambering when I am 60; the affordances of a pond change dramatically when one learns to swim.

It would be a fact that the pencil affords throwing, even if doing so had never occurred to me. By insisting on the objective existence of affordances, Gibson broke with a long-established tradition. Although phenomenologists often note that the world and the self are perceived in terms of possible action, they typically assign such possibilities to some nonphysical realm: to the "phenomenal field," for example, or the "behavioral world." As Gibson defined them, however, affordances are in the *real* world. They are discovered rather than invented. Indeed, they must be discovered if the individual is to survive.

Once an affordance has been perceived and the appropriate action initiated, that action must be appropriately controlled. In the view of most contemporary action theorists, such control depends in part on motor programs or schemata. Although Gibson did not share this view (he was suspicious of all mental models and structures), it seems inescapable to me. As Marc Jeannerod points out in chapter 4, "It is hard to conceive of motor devices that would be entirely driven by external events." (The schemata do not control every detail of every movement, however. Other determinants include the inertial properties of body parts and the couplings between them; cf. Kelso, 1982; Turvey, 1990.) One convincing argument for the existence of motor schemata is that many rapid actions are fully planned in advance. In catching a ball, for example, the last 200–300 ms of movements are executed independently of visual feedback (Whiting, Gill, & Stephenson, 1970). Yet even in such "open-loop" movements, we are aware of what we do; the activity of the control schemata gives rise to a kind of awareness.

Sometimes the precise direction of an upcoming movement is established only after a critical stimulus has appeared. Under these conditions the time needed to shift the focus of the control schema to a new environmental target can be measured. Georgopoulos and Massey (1987) have done just that. Stimuli were presented in a timed reaching task, but the subjects did not reach directly toward the stimulus. Instead they had to reach in a direction offset from the stimulus by a predefined angle (say, 35° clockwise). Reaction times increased linearly with the amount of offset, suggesting that the subjects had to shift their conrol schemata ("imagined movement vectors," p. 361) across the field before beginning the reach itself. M. J. Wraga and I (Neisser & Wraga, 1992) have obtained similar results in a key-pressing paradigm. In my view, these rapidly changing, quasi-conscious motor intentions are aspects of the ecological self. In particular, they are responsible for the sense of agency that is so central to ecological self-awareness.

All of us are aware when we have done something ourselves. When I slap my hand on the desk, for example, I see and hear and feel the consequences of my action. The optic and acoustic and mechanical effects occur just when and as they should, given the control schemata that initiated the movement. A very different experience occurs if I passively allow *you* to pick up my hand and bang it on the desk for me. The sensory consequences may be quite similar, but the coincidence with my own intention is missing. In this context, *intention* refers to the activation of particular movement control structures. We perceive actions as our own if and only if their consequences are appropriate to the schema by which they were generated. Dancers, athletes, and others skilled in bodily motion are especially sensitive to that fit. (In chapter 6, Sondra Horton Fraleigh examines dance from this point of view.)

In summary, we perceive our movements and actions veridically, because they are specified by information – especially optic flow information – that is available to the perceptual systems. Personal agency – the fact that we have carried out an action ourselves – is specified by the degree to which the consequences of a movement match the schemata by which it was generated in the first place. Thus the perceived ecological self includes an awareness of where we are, what we are doing, and what we have done.

The interpersonal self: I and Thou

Human beings are social creatures. In many societies people spend most of their waking lives within sight and earshot of one another. Even in cultures where one is often alone, the most meaningful occasions involve communication with others. That communication may be based on close physical contact, as when we embrace; on acoustical signals, as when we speak to one another; on visual information, as when we smile or exchange gestures; and perhaps on other modalities too. Often, it involves several modalities at once. We value this communication, and would hardly be human without it. William James puts the case eloquently:

No more fiendish punishment could be devised, were such a thing physically possible, than that one should be turned loose in society and remain absolutely unnoticed by all the members thereof. If no one turned round when we entered, answered when we spoke, or minded what we did, but if every person we met "cut us dead," and acted as if we were non-existing things, a kind of rage and impotent despair would ere long well up in us, from which the cruellest bodily tortures would be a relief; for these would make us feel that, however bad might be our plight, we had not sunk to such a depth as to be unworthy of attention at all. (1890, vol. I, pp. 293–294)

People do, usually, turn round when we enter and answer when we speak. We do the same for them. Mutuality of behavior is the rule, not only among humans but for many other species as well. Crickets call to crickets, frogs to frogs; dogs and apes and monkeys encounter each other in systematic, species-specific ways. Every such exchange brings something new into existence: a series of reciprocated behaviors occurring at a particular time and place. Those behaviors are *perceptible*. What is perceived is not merely the other's behavior, but its reciprocity with one's own. Both participants are engaged in a mutual enterprise, and they are aware of that mutuality.

Considered as a participant in a shared communicative activity, each member of such a dyad is an *interpersonal self*. Where the ecological self is an active agent in the physical environment, the interpersonal self is an agent in an ongoing social exchange. That self, too, is perceived: We see ourselves as the target or focus of the other person's attention and as cocreator of the interaction itself. Gibson's claim about ecological perception, quoted earlier, transposes naturally to the social case: "Egoreception accompanies alteroception like the other side of a coin. . . . One perceives the other and coperceives oneself" (modified from Gibson, 1979, p. 126). This is true whether we are returning an embrace or just maintaining eye contact, improvising in a jazz group or just taking turns in a conversation.

Human beings confirm one another's selfhood in so many ways that it is impossible to list them all. Almost every personal encounter is mutually regulated: A directs behavior toward B, and B to A, in a reciprocal pattern that both establish together and both perceive. This pattern exists objectively and observably. It depends on communication – especially on what Ross

Buck (see chapter 12) calls "spontaneous communication," which he distinguishes from symbolic and linguistic processes. Nevertheless, my argument is not the same as Buck's. For him, communicative behaviors are important mainly because they transmit information about the participants' inner states. Buck conceives of such behaviors – facial expressions, for example – as messages from a sender to a receiver; the receiver then treats the messages as information about the sender's motives and emotions. Although this may often happen, it is not essential to interpersonal exchange as defined here. In my view, patterns of reciprocated behavior exist in their own right. A mutual embrace is a perceptible fact, whatever the true feelings of the embracing participants and whatever they may believe about each other. The interpersonal self is not an inner state to be communicated, or chiefly a detector of such states in others; it is simply a person engaged in a social exchange.

To be sure, we do often perceive the feelings of others in a very immediate way. This is possible because, as Solomon Asch (1952) noted many years ago, there is a natural congruence between feelings and their expressions. The gestures that express anger exhibit the same focused force as the feeling of anger itself, and a loving touch has just the tender quality of the mood that produced it. Under ideal conditions, then, expressive behaviors fit their emotions perfectly. Nevertheless, it is unwise to define social perception in terms of awareness of other people's feelings. For one thing, social perceiving begins at an age where this would be quite implausible. Although infants engage in "protoconversations" (Bateson, 1975) a few weeks after birth, they do not think of others as having specific mental states until about age 4 (Astington et al., 1988). For another, perceiving or inferring other people's feelings from their expressions is a very uncertain process. The relation between behaviors and inner states is culturally modulated; in addition, it can be deliberately altered or suppressed. What *is* certain, in contrast, is perception of the gestures themselves in relation to one's own behavior. You may be mistaken about your partner's thoughts but not about the fact that she is maintaining eye contact; about her real feelings but not about the touch of her hand. Assessing feelings is a chancy business, but actual social behavior is easily perceived. So, too, is the target of that social behavior, the interpersonal self.

Some ecological psychologists have described interpersonal relations in terms of *social affordances* (see Loveland and Buck, this volume; Walker-Andrews, 1986). Just as the body-scaled size and position of a stick constitute information about its graspability, so, too, does your partner's facial expression constitute information about her receptivity to your social behavior. Indeed, effective social action requires that both kinds of affordances be perceived. Gibson made this point in one of his "Rules for the Visual Control of Locomotion":

To kiss someone, magnify the face-form, if the facial expression is amiable, so as almost to fill the field of view. (It is absolutely essential for one to keep one's eyes open so as to avoid collision. It is also wise to learn to discriminate those subtle invariants that specify amiability.) (1979, p. 233; italics in original)

Like its ecological counterpart, the interpersonal self is an active agent in a real environment. Social actions, too, are executed under the control of internal schemata. You are aware of your own interpersonal activity and of what its result should be. You then perceive its actual result, the appropriate (or perhaps inappropriate) response of your partner. As in the nonsocial case, the fit between intentions and outcomes establishes a strong sense of personal effectiveness.

In emphasizing the similarity of the ecological and interpersonal selves, I must not overlook a significant difference between them. The movement-produced information that specifies the activity of the ecological self is based on universal principles of optics. Those principles are the same for everyone: Parallel optic flow means "I am moving" to any animal with a developed visual system. Patterns of interpersonal behavior, in contrast, are species-specific. Horses do not value eye contact as we do, and cats do not hold hands. The dominant male stare so important for primates has no counterpart among spiders, probably not even among rabbits. These behavior patterns are consequences of natural selection (just as perceptual systems are), but they are very different in different groups. The form that interpersonal behavior takes among primates, for example, is critical for the characteristic patterning of their social life; and among humans, for the development of culture (Tomasello, Kruger, & Ratner, in press).

Is social perception really a special case? In chapter 7, Marjorie Grene argues to the contrary. For her, all knowledge ultimately derives from ecological perception. Gibson would probably have agreed with Grene, but my view is different. The social seems just as basic as the nonsocial, and it originates independently. Without the special contribution of interpersonal experience, normal human forms of knowing could not exist. This is not a new argument. It has been made (in other ways) by such thinkers as Vygotsky (1978) and G. H. Mead (1934).

A particularly powerful formulation is that of the theologian Martin Buber (1923/1955). Buber distinguished two primary modes of human existence, which he called I–It and I–Thou. The I–It relation involves the manipulation of something or someone. (*Manipulation* here includes intellectual analysis.) The encounter with Thou is quite different: Free of manipulation, it involves only direct engagement and commitment. Superficially at least, there is a parallel between Buber's distinction and the present argument. The I of I–It is something like an ecological self, whereas the I of I–Thou is an acutely interpersonal one. But Buber's categories are deeper than this: One can have an objectifying relation (I–It) not only with objects but also with persons. (This is quite different from encountering them as Thou.) We can even objectify mental entities – our own ideas, for example. This means, I think, that Buber would have taken not only the ecological self but also the remembered, private, and conceptual selves as examples of what he derisively called "It, always It" (1923/1955, p. 5). On the other hand, he describes the encounter with Thou as deeply mysterious. For him, Thou characterizes not only the relations one sometimes achieves with other individuals but those with the divine.

The relation of Buber's ideas to those presented here (and in Neisser, 1988) is discussed by James Gustafson in chapter 15. Gustafson also considers the work of Mead (1934), including Mead's famous concept of a "generalized other." Like Mead and unlike Buber, the present approach takes "a basic stance that is 'scientific' in a modern North American sense – the external observer seeking to provide a genetic or causal explanation of the emergence of self and mind" (Gustafson, chapter 15, p. 281). But even in such a cognitively oriented enterprise, the special status of interpersonal experience and social feeling must not be overlooked. That experience begins very early in life, and the emotions that accompany it are unique. Awareness of interpersonal engagement does not depend on anything else in experience: not on inference, not on reflection, not even on ecological perception. Thou cannot be reduced to a category of It.

The notion that there is something unique about interpersonal encounter can be extended still further. In the last chapter of this volume David Jopling shows how the "philosophy of dialogue," as set out by Buber and Emmanuel Levinas, challenges basic Cartesian assumptions. Perhaps the deepest of those assumptions is that of the interiority of the mind: Consciousness is somehow inside, the world outside. This assumption gives rise to the so-called "problem of other minds." Because each person's experience is private, how can we know what anyone else's inner life is like? The philosophy of dialogue avoids this problem because it does not begin with private experience. The encounter with the "other" is primary instead; no self and no life experience exist before that encounter. If we take social interaction itself as the basic event, the problem of other minds disappears.

I believe that this is a valuable insight, but only half the story. It is true that direct face-to-face interaction establishes a preconceptual form of knowing: knowledge of the "other" and of the self as engaged with that other. But it is not the only such form of knowing: Ecological knowledge, obtained through interaction with the physical environment, is equally direct. Both forms of perception are present from early infancy, long before the more sophisticated conceptual forms of self-knowledge begin to appear. The remainder of this chapter focuses on those early achievements.

The ecological self in infancy

Perception is the most fundamental source of self-knowledge, in two different senses. In one sense, it is fundamental because we can rely on it: Whatever we may be wrong about, we at least perceive our immediate ecological and social situation as it really is. In another sense, it is fundamental simply because it is first (Neisser, 1991). Even very young infants, still many months away from having a self-concept, are keenly aware of themselves as active agents in real physical and social settings.

That awareness has not always been obvious. Throughout most of psychology's history, from Locke to James to Freud to Piaget, the mental life of infants was regularly described as no better than a buzzing confusion. Where we (as adults) see real and persisting objects, babies were believed to see only blurs of visual sensation; where we experience ourselves as distinct individuals, they were thought to experience only "oneness" with their mothers. Realistic perception was described as a late intellectual achievement, based on the slow accumulation of memories and associations. For the most part (Piaget being the exception), these views were not based on empirical observation. Instead, philosophers simply tried to imagine what primitive perceiving must be like. The results of modern infant research suggest that they didn't get it right.

The richest relevant data concern environmental perception and the ecological self. *Looming* is a well-studied example. Many investigators (e.g., Ball & Tronick, 1971) have shown that young infants will flinch from an expanding optical display. (This behavior has also been demonstrated in a wide range of animal species.) Their perception of these displays is apparently much like ours – that is, they see a rapidly approaching object. Interestingly, their defensive flinch is not a simple reflex. They do not move away from a looming aperture, such as a framed window; instead, they lean forward to see what it may reveal (Carroll & Gibson, 1981).

Parallel flow in the optic array specifies movement of the ecological self to young children, just as it does to adults. This was first shown by Lee and Aronson (1974) in the moving room. A slight movement of the room's walls is enough to make standing 12-month-olds falls down. (They fall in trying to brace themselves against the illusory egomotion.) Butterworth and Hicks (1977) have shown that parallel flow affects the posture of 6-month-old infants, and Butterworth (1990) cites work that extends this finding back to 2 months. Based on these and related findings, Butterworth (1990, 1992) has independently developed an argument similar to that presented here, that the beginnings of self-perception are based on the kinetic structure of the optic array.

The case of *occlusion* is especially interesting, because it bears on Piaget's concept of "object permanence." When one object goes behind another, its visible surface gradually disappears from the optic array. This "texture deletion at an edge" specifies that the object is moving behind a barrier, which is exactly what we see (Gibson, Kaplan, Reynolds, & Wheeler, 1969). When all its surface is gone, the object has moved completely behind the barrier; we see that too. Thus the fact that objects continue to exist when they go out of sight can be perceived; it need not be inferred (Gibson, 1979). But do babies see things this way too? The accepted view in developmental psychology has long been just the opposite: that the permanent existence of objects is not understood until about the end of the first year. This view was based on Piaget's classic finding that infants do not search for hidden objects: When an attractive toy is covered with a cloth, 6-month-olds make no attempt to retrieve it. Doesn't this mean that it no longer exists for them – that out of sight means out of mind?

Apparently not. More recent experiments, testing for object permanence in a different way, have supported Gibson's analysis rather than Piaget's. The subjects of these studies first see an object go behind a barrier and are then shown a further event that would be impossible if the object were still there. A wooden block may be placed behind a screen, for example; the screen then folds down flat onto the table through the space where the block should be (Baillergeon, Spelke, & Wasserman, 1985). Four-month-olds exhibit great surprise on seeing such displays. Appropriate controls show that they are surprised for the same reason that we would be: What they have just seen is impossible! Infants evidently have a realistic grasp of the layout of the local environment. Instead of being restricted to a meaningless blur of sensations, as was once supposed, they are ecologically located selves. (Eleanor Gibson reviews other evidence on this point in chapter 2.)

Infants can also see what actions that layout may afford. The perception of *affordances* in infancy is particularly interesting because infants' capacities for action change so rapidly (Adolph, Eppler, & Gibson, 1993). At 3 months of age they can flinch from something that looms up; at 6 months they reach for and grasp nearby objects; at 9 months they can usually crawl; some months after that, they begin to walk. Their perception of affordances keeps pace with these changes. By 15 weeks, if not earlier, they distinguish objects within arm's reach from those too far away: They reach for the former but not the latter (Field, 1976). As crawlers, they crawl onto surfaces that will support them but not over the edges of cliffs (Gibson & Walk, 1960); as walkers, they do not try to walk on the unreliable surface of a gently agitated waterbed (Gibson et al., 1987). Infants, like adults, are effective perceivers of what the environment affords for them.

There is, however, at least one situation in which infants' self-perception is quite different from that of older children and adults: when they look into a mirror. Although 1-year-olds are very interested in their reflection – they may touch it, smile at it, look behind the mirror for the child who

appears in it – they don't seem to know that it is a representation of themselves. The best evidence for this comes from the "rouge test" (Amsterdam,
1972; Gallup, 1970). After a spot of rouge has been covertly applied to their
foreheads, subjects are allowed to look in the mirror. If this leads them to
explore their foreheads manually, or to try to wipe off the mark, they must
know that the rouge-marked face in the mirror is their own.

This test has been extensively used with various species of monkeys and
apes as well as with children. Chimpanzees and orangutangs usually pass
it (i.e., they grope for the spot on their own foreheads), whereas other
nonhuman primates do not (Mitchell, in press). A systematic study by Lewis
and Brooks-Gunn (1979) showed that children begin to pass the rouge
test between 15 and 21 months of age. What can we say about their understanding at earlier ages, when their mirror behavior does not yet indicate
recognition? Do they have no sense of self? That interpretation has occasionally been made not only for young infants but also for the nonhuman
primates that fail the test too (Gallup, 1970). From an ecological point
of view, it must be mistaken. As we have seen, infants are aware of themselves as active agents virtually from birth. Like other primates (including
those that fail the rouge test), they know where they are, what they can
do, and what they have done. Whatever they may lack, it is surely not
an ecological self.

Nevertheless, the results of the rouge test seem to demand explanation.
If infants have a sense of self, why don't they recognize their mirror images
as we do? At least two plausible interpretations suggest themselves. For one
thing, they may not understand the optics of mirrors. As Loveland has
pointed out (1986; see also chapter 13), mirrors offer a very special view
of the environment. Affordances are not specified in the same way as in
normal vision: To grasp an object seen in the mirror, one may have to reach
backward rather than forward. Failure to understand these distinctive optics
would make it difficult to use reflected images for any purpose at all. The
relation between such general mirror skills and self-recognition proper is
not yet fully resolved (Loveland, 1986; Mitchell, in press).

A more social explanation must also be considered. Perhaps what develops
after 15 months is an increased awareness of the face and of its importance
for personal relations. Without some such awareness, why should one care
about a spot of rouge on one's forehead? The fact that embarrassment and
other forms of evaluative self-consciousness appear at about the same age
(Hart & Fegley, in press) lends some plausibility to this hypothesis. In my
view, such an "evaluative self-consciousness" is a further, more sophisticated
development of the conceptual self. Although the self-concept begins to
appear as early as 9 months of age (with the realization that one can be
the object of another person's attention), it may take another year to
understand that others' evaluations are partly related to one's personal

appearance and to one's face. Thus, even though the ecological and inter-personal selves are both established much earlier, the rouge test may still index a significant point in social development.

The interpersonal self in infancy

The evidence for the early appearance of the interpersonal self is rich indeed. Even neonates are interested in faces (Johnson, Dziurawiec, Ellis, & Morton, 1991) and imitate facial gestures shortly after birth (Meltzoff & Moore, 1977, 1983). By 6 or 8 weeks of age, babies engage in active protoconversations (Bateson, 1975) with their mothers. They return em-braces, maintain eye contact, and exhibit the beginnings of reciprocal vocalization. Such exchanges often include what Daniel Stern calls "vitality affects": surges of feeling that are closely coordinated with analogous surges in the partner (Stern, 1985; see also chapter 11). These sustained and motivated behaviors are clear cases of the interpersonal self in action. As Colwyn Trevarthen has argued (see chapter 8), they testify to a strong innate readiness for emotional relationships with other persons.

An experiment by Murray and Trevarthen (1985) illustrates the activity of the interpersonal self with particular clarity. The subjects of the experi-ment were mothers and their 6- to 8-week-old infants interacting over closed-circuit television. Each partner saw a life-size, full-face image of the other and heard the other's voice as well. Under these conditions their exchanges were entirely natural: The babies smiled and goo-gooed at their mothers, who happily responded in kind. After a few minutes of this, real-time communication was interrupted. Now, the baby was shown a videotape of its mother, which had been recorded during the successful interaction a few moments earlier. The results were dramatic. The previously happy babies became miserable. They looked away from the TV monitor, fidgeted, and generally seemed to wish that they were somewhere else. This happened even though they were seeing the very same visual and auditory display that had given them so much pleasure before.

This time, however, they had no sense of efficacy or agency. Videotapes do not return gestures, maintain eye contact, or respond to vocalizations. The infants' unhappiness in the videotape condition helps us understand what they were enjoying during the earlier and more natural interchange: their own sense of participation in what was going on. Like the rest of us, infants are interpersonal selves. They know when they are actively engaged with another person and when that person is reciprocally engaged with them.

The fact that personal encounters occur so early in infancy may explain why they often seem beyond rational comprehension. Those encounters are our first experiences with Buber's Thou occurring at a time of life when we do not yet understand either the nature of the "other" or the limits of her resources. That must make such encounters essentially mysterious. It is not surprising, then, that interpersonal relations often seem mysterious even in later life! (That sense of mystery may attach itself to other relations as well, including those with the supernatural.) Understandable or not, these relations are among the most valuable forms of human experience. We may count ourselves fortunate if our adult lives continue to include encounters with Thou, not merely with It – that is, if our lives genuinely engage the interpersonal self.

Although the existence of interpersonal feeling in the infant is incontrovertible, there is still much we do not know. Just how much young children are aware of in their social partners, and in themselves, remains largely unexplored. (Sandra Pipp reports some relevant data in chapter 10.) One intriguing possibility is that there may be specific pathologies of the interpersonal self, conditions that interfere with the normal development of face-to-face social interaction. Infantile autism is an obvious candidate. Autistic children are notorious for their unnatural social behavior, and it is often suggested that some innate deficit in emotional responsiveness may be responsible. In chapter 13, Loveland describes this syndrome from an ecological point of view: Autistic individuals have problems in perceiving social affordances. In chapter 14, Peter Hobson extends the analysis to include the congenitally blind as well as the autistic. If face-to-face behavior is really important for the normal development of the interpersonal self, we would expect the blind to be at a disadvantage: One major source of information is not available to them. Hobson's evidence suggests that this disadvantage is quite real, though it can be overcome.

In summary, perception provides us with two distinct kinds of self-knowledge. The ecological self is located here and now in the environment: We can see (and hear and feel) where we are and what we are doing, what we might do and have done. Always, since before we can remember, we have been active agents in the extended and tangible world. In addition, we see and feel and hear our ongoing interactions with others and are keenly aware of our own contributions to those exchanges. Each of us has been an interpersonal self just as long as – perhaps longer than – an ecological one. These two forms of perceptually given knowledge are examined further in the following chapters.

REFERENCES

Adolph, K. E., Eppler, M. A., & Gibson, E. J. (1993). Development of the perception of affordances. In C. Rovee-Collier & L. Lipsett (Eds.), *Advances in Infancy Research* (Vol. 8, pp. 51–98). Norwood, NJ: Ablex.

Amsterdam, B. (1972). Mirror self-image reactions before age two. *Developmental Psychobiology, 5,* 297–305.

Asch, S. (1952). *Social psychology.* New York: Prentice Hall.

Astington, J. W., Harris, P. L., & Olson, D. R. (1988). *Developing theories of mind.* Cambridge University Press.

Baillergeon, R., Spelke, E. S., & Wasserman, S. (1985). Object-permanence in five-month-olds. *Cognition, 20,* 191–208.

Ball, W. A., & Tronick, E. (1971). Infant responses to impending collision: Optic and real. *Science, 171,* 818–820.

Bateson, M. C. (1975). Mother–infant exchanges: The epigenesis of conversational interaction. In D. Aaronson & R. W. Rieber (Eds.), *Developmental psycholinguistics and communication disorders. Annals of the New York Academy of Sciences* (Vol. 263). New York: New York Academy of Sciences.

Bruner, J. (1983). *Child's talk.* New York: Norton.

Buber, M. (1923/1955). *I and Thou.* New York: Scribners.

Butterworth, G. (1990). Self-perception in infancy. In D. Cicchetti & M. Beeghly (Eds.), *The self in transition: Infancy to childhood.* Chicago: University of Chicago Press.

Butterworth, G. (1992). Self-perception as a foundation for self-knowledge. *Psychological Inquiry, 3,* 103–111, 134–136.

Butterworth, G., & Hicks, L. (1977). Visual proprioception and postural stability in infancy: A developmental study. *Perception, 6,* 255–262.

Carello, C., Grosofsky, A., Reichel, F. D., Solomon, H. Y., & Turvey, M. T. (1989). Visually perceiving what is reachable. *Ecological Psychology, 1,* 27–54.

Carroll, J., & Gibson, E. J. (1981). *Differentiation of an aperture from an obstacle under conditions of motion by three-month-old infants.* Paper presented at Society for Research in Child Development, Boston.

Churchland, P. S., & Sejnowski, T. J. (1992). *The computational brain.* Cambridge, MA: MIT Press.

Dennett, D. C. (1991a). *Consciousness explained.* Boston: Little, Brown.

Dennett, D. C. (1991b). The origins of selves. In D. Kolak & R. Martin (Eds.), *Self and identity: Contemporary philosophical issues.* New York: Macmillan.

Field, J. (1976). Relation of young infants' reaching behavior to stimulus distance and solidity. *Developmental Psychology, 12,* 444–448.

Fivush, R., Gray, J. T., & Fromhoff, F. A. (1987). Two year olds talk about the past. *Cognitive Development, 2,* 293–410.

Fivush, R., & Hudson, J. A. (1990). *Knowing and remembering in young children.* Cambridge University Press.

Gallup, G. (1970). Chimpanzees: Self-recognition. *Science, 167,* 86–87.

Georgopoulos, A. P., & Massey, J. T. (1987). Cognitive spatial-motor processes. I. The making of movements at various angles from a stimulus direction. *Experimental Brain Research, 65,* 361–370.

Gibson, E. J., Riccio, G., Schmuckler, M. A., Stoffregen, T. A., Rosenberg, D., & Taormina, J. (1987). Detection of traversability of surfaces by crawling and walking infants. *Journal of Experimental Psychology: Human Perception and Performance, 13,* 533–544.

Gibson, E. J., & Walk, R. D. (1960). The "visual cliff." *Scientific American, 202,* 64–71.

Gibson, J. J. (1966). *The senses considered as perceptual systems.* Boston: Houghton Mifflin.

Gibson, J. J. (1979). *The ecological approach to visual perception.* Boston: Houghton Mifflin.

Gibson, J. J., Kaplan, G. A., Reynolds, H. N., & Wheeler, K. (1969). The change from visible to invisible: A study of optical transitions. *Perception and Psychophysics, 5,* 113–116.

Hart, D., & Fegley, S. (in press). Social imitation and the emergence of a mental model of self. In S. Parker, M. Boccia, & R. Mitchell (Eds.). *Self-awareness in animals and humans.* Cambridge University Press.

Hull, J. M. (1990). *Touching the rock.* New York: Pantheon.

James, W. (1890). *Principles of Psychology.* New York: Holt.

Johnson, M. H., Dziurawiec, S., Ellis, H., & Morton, J. (1991). Newborns' preferential tracking of face-like stimuli and its subsequent decline. *Cognition, 40,* 1–19.

Jung, C. G. (1921/1971). *Psychological types.* In *Collected works of C. G. Jung* (Vol. 6). Princeton, NJ: Princeton University Press.

Kelso, J. A. S. (1982). *Human motor behavior: An introduction.* Hillsdale, NJ: Erlbaum.

Lee, D. N. (1980). The optic flow field: The foundation of vision. *Philosophical Transactions of the Royal Society of London, B290,* 169–179.

Lee, D. N. , & Aronson, E. (1974). Visual proprioceptive control of standing in human infants. *Perception and Psychophysics, 15,* 529–532.

Lewis, M., & Brooks-Gunn, J. (1979). *Social cognition and the acquisition of the self.* New York: Plenum.

Lishman, J. R., & Lee, D. N. (1973). The autonomy of visual kinaethesis. *Perception, 2,* 287–294.

Loveland, K. (1986). Discovering the affordances of a reflecting surface. *Developmental Review, 6,* 1–24.

Mark, L. S. (1987). Eyeheight-scaled information about affordances: A study of sitting and stair-climbing. *Journal of Experimental Psychology: Human Perception and Performance, 13,* 361–370.

Mead, G. H. (1934). *Mind, self, and society: From the standpoint of a social behaviorist.* Chicago: University of Chicago Press.

Meltzoff, A. N., & Moore, M. K. (1977). Imitation of facial and manual gestures by human neonates. *Science, 198,* 75–78.

Meltzoff, A. N., & Moore, M. K. (1983). Newborns imitate adult facial gestures. *Child Development, 54,* 702–709.

Mitchell, R. W. (in press). Mental models of self-recognition: Two theories. *New ideas in psychology.*

Murray, L., & Trevarthen, C. (1985). Emotional regulation of interactions between two-month-olds and their mothers. In T. M. Field & N. A. Fox (Eds.), *Social perception in infants.* Norwod, NJ: Ablex.

Neisser, U. (1988). Five kinds of self-knowledge. *Philosophical Psychology, 1,* 35–59.

Neisser, U. (1991). Two perceptually given aspects of the self and their development. *Developmental Review, 11,* 197–209.

Neisser, U., & Fivush, R. (in press). *The remembering self.* Cambridge University Press.

Neisser, U., & Wraga, M. J. (1992). Shifting attention across the field before making a directed reach. Poster presented at the Psychonomic Society, St. Louis, MO.

Stern, D. N. (1985). *The interpersonal world of the infant.* New York: Basic Books.

Tomasello, M. (1988). The role of joint attentional processes in early language development. *Language Sciences, 10,* 69–88.

Tomasello, M. , Kruger, A. C., & Ratner, H. H. (in press). Cultural learning. *Behavioral and Brain Sciences.*

Turvey, M. T. (1990). Coordination. *American Psychologist, 45,* 938–953.

Vygotsky, L. S. (1978). *Mind in society.* Cambridge, MA: Harvard University Press.

Walker-Andrews, A. (1986). Intermodal perception of expressive behaviors: Relation of eye and voice? *Developmental Psychology, 22,* 373–377.

Warren, W. H. (1984). Perceiving affordances: Visual guidance of stair climbing. *Journal of Experimental Psychology: Human Perception and Performance, 10,* 683–703.

Warren, W. H., & Whang, S. (1987). Visual guidance of walking through apertures: Body-scaled information for affordances. *Journal of Experimental Psychology: Human Perception and Performance, 13,* 371–383.

Whiting, H. T. A., Gill, E. B., & Stephenson, J. M. (1970). Critical time intervals for taking in flight information in a ball-catching task. *Ergonomics, 13,* 265–272.

Part II

The concept of an ecological self

2

Ontogenesis of the perceived self

ELEANOR J. GIBSON

To perceive the world is to coperceive oneself.

J. J. Gibson

"The stage is set, enter the hero of the play. . . . We take a new step, long deferred and often anticipated, and introduce the Ego" (Koffka, 1935, p. 319). So begins the second half of a book that played an important role in my early education as a psychologist. This was Kurt Koffka's way of introducing his treatment of action. The ego he considered a field object, segregated from other objects, and also the "executive" in control of behavior.

There are many other ways of discussing the ego (see Neisser, 1988). I am going to refer to the "self," as Neisser did, rather than the ego, because the term carries less literary and moral baggage. My aim is to show the way in which the self is rooted in perception. "You" are an object in a world of other objects, and I perceive you as such. So, indeed, am "I," and just as surely I perceive myself as an object in the same world of things and events that I locate you in. There is ample information to specify these objects, including myself.

The view of the self that I describe is centered in the ecological approach to perception (J. J. Gibson, 1979), a systems approach in which an animal and its environment constitute a system marked by a relation of reciprocity. Within this dynamic, interactive system the animal is constrained by its environmental niche and the niche is fitted to and acted upon by the animal. Within the system the self is a kind of interface between the animal and its environment. It is present potentially at birth and it develops as life goes forward.

The self that I am concerned with is not an image or a representation of anything. It is a perceived object separate from all other objects in the world, one that has its own functions and relations with other objects. It is truly perceived, because there is information that specifies the self in arrays directly available to observation by the animal. It is essential for effective survival, unlike any other self that might be conceived of.

This chapter will present arguments and evidence for the reality of the perceived self, stressing the information that specifies a self. It is organized around five topics, each focusing on a kind of information for the self that is perceived. For each topic the argument for the cogency of the information specifying the self will be presented, and following that, the evidence for its pickup by a human being early in life. Attention will be given to the time in development when the information becomes effective, as that time may be associated with important developmental landmarks. I begin with the most critical topic, how a person is able to differentiate himself from the external world of objects and events.

Differentiation of self from world

Information for perception is contained in an ambient array of energy. In the case of visual perception, we refer to this as an ambient optic array. Energy in this array is structured as light is reflected from surfaces in the environment. An animal positioned in this array can actively use its perceptual systems to detect information specifying the surfaces and events around it. At the same time there is information in the optic array as structured by the body of the perceiver for the self as a unique segment of the array.

There is information in a stationary optic array that specifies the perceiver, because from a fixed point of observation, the body of the perceiver conceals a portion of the environment around him uniquely, in a way that is *propriospecific* (Gibson, 1979, p. 112). Ernst Mach pointed this out, with a drawing of his view of himself, which he referred to as his "visual ego." The eyebrows, nose, eyeglasses, mustache, and so on frame the visible vista, and the rest of the world is temporarily hidden.

Fortunately for our knowledge about the world, we are movable animals. What a fixed view conceals at one moment is revealed as we move our heads and bodies around so as to achieve a continuous and connected view of the environment. Information for the self as a unique and separate object is not lost as we move around, because optic flow in the ambient array is created as the person engages in locomotion. A flowing array as a person moves forward has a focus of continuous expansion, and the focus of this flow specifies the direction toward which the moving perceiver is heading, a perfect invariant specific to himself. The unmoving persisting world is continuously being revealed in this streaming vista, the moving self and the unmoving world being reciprocal aspects of the same perception. The cases of the stationary observer and the moving observer both exemplify Gibson's statement that "to perceive the world is to coperceive oneself."

In both cases, information specifying the self is available even to an infant (although its stubby nose does not provide a striking feature of its stationary view). Despite a neonate's relative immobility, she is at times carried or wheeled around with a resulting focus of expansion. How early infants detect these sources of information and use them to differentiate themselves from other objects we do not know. But experimental evidence is available for a related differentiated perception, the differentiation of self motion from object motion.

What is the importance of such a distinction for perception? If the information for all movement were simply displacement across the retina, there could be no way of distinguishing an apparent displacement of something resulting from one's own movement from displacement resulting from a change in position of the object itself. When objects move, they move with reference to a stationary layout of other objects. The displacement is a relative one, and a local one. But when the observer engages in movement of the head or her whole body, there results a flow of the entire optic array. J. J. Gibson pointed out this neat information for a distinction between self and object motion many years ago:

The retina may be stimulated by motion, or more exactly, the retinal image may undergo motion, in two general ways. The first and simplest is relative displacement. In this case the image corresponding to an object is displaced in relation to the image corresponding to the rest of the world, i.e., the image of the background against which the object-image is located. This is the stimulus that exists when an object in the visual scene moves. The relative displacement is the same whether the eyes follow the moving object or not. The second may be called deformation. In this less familiar type of stimulation, the image is distorted as a whole; it stretches or expands or contracts rather than merely being transposed. This sort of change obviously does not occur in real objects, or at least solid objects, but it happens all the time to our retinal images – especially to the image of the terrain or background. The fact to be especially noted is that the retinal image over the whole retina, the image representing the entire visual field, may undergo this kind of motion, i.e., may flow at different rates in different parts.

– The general rule may be formulated that whenever the *observer himself* moves, the retinal image corresponding to the whole visual field undergoes deformation.

– When *objects* move, the corresponding object-images within the retinal image of the field undergo relative displacement (and may also undergo deformation if the objects move toward or away from us) but the retinal background image of the whole field does *not* undergo deformation. –

– When both the observer and objects move in a three-dimensional space, there occurs both deformation of the retinal background-image, and displacement of the retinal object-images. Both the observer's own movement and the movement of objects are perceived simultaneously, under normal circumstances, without any interference between the two kinds of perception.

The importance of these distinctions lies in the fact that deformation of the retinal background-image yields not only the perception of subjective motion but provides a powerful stimulus for space perception. Different aspects of this deformation are specific not only to the direction of one's motion and to the velocity of one's motion, but also to the angle of inclination of the surface at which one is looking, to the distance of all points of the surface, and in fact to the distance of all stationary objects in one's field of vision. (1947, pp. 219–220)

Gibson later dropped references to the retina, describing information entirely in terms of the optic array, as in the following paragraph:

A transformation of the whole optic array specifies a movement of the observer. It is propriospecific. Invariants under transformation of the whole optic array specify invariants of the layout of the environment. They are exterospecific. The separation of the information about the world from the information about the observer's *movement* in the world, the isolation of the invariants from the motions, is something that a visual system does in its dual role of being both exteroceptive and proprioceptive. (1966, p. 201)

Evidence is available that infants perceive movement of an object relative to the unmoving background layout rather early. Harris, Cassel, and Bamborough (1974) observed infants 8 to 28 weeks old tracking a moving target object. The object either moved alone against a stationary background or the background moved with it, in the same direction and at the same speed. For subjects of all ages, tracking was disrupted when the target and the background moved together. In another condition, the background moved in the opposite direction from the target, without any disruption of tracking the object. The essential condition for tracking object movement was evidently relative displacement of the object with reference to the background layout.

An even more apt experiment is one in which both object and observer move at the same time, and yet the infant subject shows differentiation of his own movement from the object's (as in the third case cited by Gibson above). Kellman, Gleitman, and Spelke (1987) performed an experiment with 4-month-olds in which an infant observed a vertical rod moving back and forth behind a small screen that concealed the middle portion of the rod. Earlier experiments had demonstrated that when the rod moves in this situation, it is perceived as complete, despite the partial occlusion. When presented as stationary, it is not perceived as a complete rod but rather as two separate pieces. In the experiment, the baby sat in a movable seat that made partial revolutions conjoined to the rod's movement, so that the rod moved with the infant. When conjoint movement occurred, the baby still perceived the rod as complete, but not when he moved himself and the rod was stationary. Furthermore, babies looked much longer at a moving rod than at a stationary one, regardless of whether or not they themselves were moving.

The attention babies paid to a moving object in this situation is characteristic of their attentive focus on events occurring in the world around them, especially events involving movement. This external focus suggests strongly that they are differentiating between self and world. Hofsten (1982) carried out studies on infants when they were observing and reaching for a target moving in an arc around them. Newborn infants, although incapable of actually reaching and catching the target, showed more frequent arm extensions while fixating on the moving object. There was a tendency for those extensions to be clustered in the direction of the target, and the extension movement slowed down as it came near the object. Hofsten thought the function of these early fixated reaches was attentional rather than manipulative, and that the looking and the reaching were part of the same orienting response toward the object. "The focus of the exploratory systems," he said, "is external from the very beginning of life" (1982, p. 246).

One further kind of information for differentiation of oneself from external objects and events exists in multimodal specification of an object or an event via more than one receptor system. Perceiving that multimodal information is actually specifying the *same thing* is an argument for existence of that thing as an external object, outside one's own body. There are psychologists (and many philosophers in the past) who maintained a "separatist" position in this respect – that is, they argued that visual, aural, tactile, and other modal experiences resulting from stimulation by the same object were always specific to the receptor system and simply resulted in a "polysensory complex" (Piaget's term). The experiences were subjectively different and had to be made to cohere eventually by way of repetition and associative learning. But from the ecological view, multimodal specification of an event or object is evidence for its being something unique and external. Whether infants do perceive multimodal information resulting in a coherent experience of a single event is thus a question of importance (E. J. Gibson, 1984), and it has received considerable investigation.

One kind of experiment that illustrates coordinated information for a unique event located in the world was first performed by Wertheimer (1961). He sounded a clicking instrument at one side of the head of his newborn daughter, and noted that she turned her head and gazed at the sounding object. This experiment has been repeated systematically many times. Results vary somewhat with the kind of sound presented and the state of the infant, but replications attest to its basic validity. Eye and ear are coordinated in attending to something external (much as the eye and the extended arm were in Hofsten's case).

A different kind of evidence for perceiving a coherent multimodally specified object is given in an experiment in which bimodal dynamic information specifies a property of some object or surface, like elasticity. Gibson and Walker (1984) let infants (4 weeks old) mouth an object that was either rigid or spongy so as to obtain haptic information for rigid or deforming movement. Following mouthing, the infants watched a display of two identical objects, one moving in a deforming pattern and one in a rigid pattern. Preferential looking resulted, with the infants fixating more on whichever was the novel movement for them. Both haptic information from mouth movement and dynamic information in the optic array specified the same property of an object (rigid or elastic) in this case, although they were not synchronized in a single event. Other experiments show that preferential looking occurs when optical and acoustic information specify, in synchrony, the same event (Spelke, 1976; Walker, 1982). It is perceived as one event, "out there."

Specification of the self as a place

Objects in the world are separable bounded units and they occupy a space uniquely. Because only one object can occupy a space at a given time, an object is localizable; it has "its" space. This is true of the self, like other objects. Where is the self, then? According to Koffka, it is localized in the space between the front and the behind. "Here, between the 'in front' and the 'behind,' is that part of the behavioral world which I call my Ego." This object is "functionally different from all others, inasmuch as it determines fundamental space aspects" (1935, p. 322). Left and right, which are relative to oneself, would be such aspects, besides front and behind.

Koffka's view of the ego as a region in behavioral space differs from an ecological view, which does not hypothesize two worlds, one a behavioral one, subjective and peculiar to an individual, and one geographic or physical. Certainly the self always occupies a place, a real place in the layout. If it is stationary, it also has a unique view from its station point, not quite the same as any other view. But this circumstance alone would not provide information for the self as an object in the world external to it. The world might simply be perceived as part of it, or one with it (as Piaget believed it is for a long period early in life). But animals are movable objects, and the world can be viewed from many perspectives. The changing perspective is continuous and flows as we move. Wherever we are, it is our perspective on the world that is a localizable place. It is this fact that is reflected in language, in the personal pronouns "you" and "I." "I" is a name for everyone, peculiar only to the speaker, who is "here." In a sense, we carry some special information for this distinction around with us, emanating from our noses, always with us, always visible and always "here."

It is an interesting fact that blind children, even when progressing normally otherwise in language acquisition, are years behind seeing children in learning the proper usage of these terms. They have the words "you," "I," "me," "mine," and "yours," but they are applied inappropriately. Why should this be the case?

As Fraiberg (1977) and her colleagues have made clear, mobility is greatly retarded in blind children. They have no view of a changing vista with shifting flow patterns in an optic array that clearly specifies a ground under them, or of objects going in and out of view in an orderly fashion, or of a continuously expanding pattern when they go forward, with a nonmoving focus specifying exactly where they are going. This kind of changing array with movement of the self provides information for a continuous surface of support for objects localized on the surface with respect to oneself and each other and for changing perspectives on the layout that bring things in and out of view.

It is this kind of information – changing perspectives, continuity of flow, predictable occlusion and disocclusion – that allows a seeing child to learn during the first 2 years of life about changing perspectives on the world, that things and the layout persist at the same time that one moves with respect to them. I believe that sighted babies begin to learn these things at once, as they watch things move (people, feeding bottles, pets), but independent locomotion brings superb opportunities for learning about perspectives.

Here is Fraiberg's description of the kind of external world that can be perceived by a blind infant:

In this world without pictures, persons and things manifest themselves in random fashion, emerging from the void as transient tactile-auditory experiences, returning to the void as they remove themselves, or as they are removed from the near space which is his "space." Sounds and voices register from "out there," but sound is discontinuous, intermittent, and the behavior of the blind baby in the first six to nine months tells us clearly that sound does not yet connote a person or thing "out there."

In contrast to the usual panorama, the endless spectacle of sensory pictures which furnish the sighted child's world from the moment he opens his eyes, the blind child's space is empty or sparsely furnished. In fact, to our perception as seeing persons his space may be richly furnished, but the toy we see in his crib or playpen is "not there" to him unless he makes accidental contact with it. (1977 p. 158)

Fraiberg says further: "It is a *conceptual* problem for the blind infant: he must infer the identity and substantiality of an object 'out there' when only one of its attributes, sound, is given. The sighted baby, who reaches for and attains an object 'on sight' at four and a half months, does not *need* a concept of the object for this coordinated task" (p. 159, italics in original).

It is not only the objects that are not well specified for the blind child; it is equally the layout – a continuous ground, solid, without holes or dropoffs – and the obstacles and apertures in the layout that can be approached from any angle. The advantage given by information in flow patterns produced by movement, with opening of vistas or occlusion resulting from approached or approaching obstacles, is incalculable.

What has this learning about changing perspectives on the layout to do with perceiving oneself, other than making it possible to attach the word "I" appropriately to a given speaker-perspective? It provides a basis for perceiving the self as *this* object, moving around or stationed *here* in a persisting environmental layout. In this sense, the perceived self is identified as a place, a locus, with respect to which all other objects can be localized as it moves about.

Piaget and Inhelder (1956) called our attention to the fact that children learn that people have different views of the world, ones that they eventually can predict. This accomplishment is sometimes referred to as "taking perspectives." A further step in Piagetian stage theory is the "coordination of perspectives," that is, welding all the various perspectives together so as to construct an objective, nonegocentric world in which the self is located.

I do not think we need hypothesize these stages (unless the blind child is forced to some such laborious expedient). Evidence for an external world is available and used by neonates. Moving around in it yields direct information for where one is in a persisting layout. There is no reason to suppose that an infant is egocentric and eventually constructs a nonegocentric world. The information for vistas extending ahead and for changing patterns of occlusion is directly available, and detection of affordances of the layout in relation to oneself and where one is or is going can begin in early infancy, automatically providing information for oneself as a moving entity in a persisting layout. A static "wedge" or stationary perspective on the world is a rare occurrence whose significance is apt to be learned quite late in childhood, perhaps only when a child is taught to draw in perspective.

Perceiving affordances

My third argument for direct perception of the self has to do with perceiving affordances for acting in the world. "The affordance of anything," J. J. Gibson said (1977), "is a specific combination of its substance and its surfaces taken with reference to an animal." As Warren (1984) put it, this is a "dynamic animal–environment fit." Notice that there are two halves involved in this "fit": what the environment offers and the animal that is the potential user. For an affordance to be activated appropriately, the layout and objects in the world must be perceived in a scale relative to the animal, to its anatomy and its capacities for action. For example, if some object is to offer the affordance of a tool for an animal, it must be scaled so as to fit the animal's body and appendages and its capacities for operating the object, and it must be possible for the animal to perceive whether or not that is the case.

This raises a most pertinent question for self-perception: whether and how an animal perceives environmental supports on a scale relevant to itself, both dimensional and dynamic. To seek evidence for this question, we look for research that investigates perception of affordances: studies that analyze both the information for the affordance and whether it is perceived and acted on appropriately. Describing the information that underlies perception of an affordance is no simple matter, for both aspects of the affordance must be considered – the environmental supports for the affordance and the capacities for action of the animal. Furthermore, how does the animal go about detecting the properties of the supports offered with respect to their "fit" for itself? What is the information for a fit and how does the animal obtain it?

It seems to me that, for the most part, human infants have to learn to perceive affordances. Perceptual learning is involved, a kind of learning consistent with the undeveloped action system of the neonate. Action systems are exercised as they become available, however. The neonate is equipped from birth with two useful exploratory systems, the visual system and the mouth–haptic system. Visual exploration is especially useful in early perceptual learning about the world and what it affords, as the infant observes events occurring. There are the flow patterns in the optic array induced by objects (such as faces) moving toward it or away from it, and occlusion and disocclusion going on as objects move in front of other objects and then away again. An example of perceiving and acting appropriately with respect to an affordance is an infant's response to a "looming" object – something moving toward it on a collision course, producing a pattern of accelerating expansion and occluding other objects as it draws near. Infants respond to a looming object (or a rapidly expanding shadow simulating the optical information) by pulling the head backward and extending arms or hands, a kind of avoidance action. But a window (aperture) moving toward the infant at a similar rate and on a similar course does not produce such an action (Carroll & Gibson, 1981). The occlusion information is different: A vista is being opened up and the infant looks into it as the view through it expands.

Infants cannot pass through apertures on their own, but adults can. Do adults perceive a doorway as the right size for them, as an affordance theory predicts? Warren and Whang (1987) performed an experiment addressing this question. Does a person perceive dimensions of the layout in accordance with the dimensions of his own body? If so, how? The dimensions would need to be scaled in units relative to the body and the appropriate action. Warren and Whang found that there was a constant for a critical aperture width, the aperture–shoulder ratio. They varied aperture widths, had subjects of varying body size walk toward them, and measured shoulder rotation. In another experiment subjects made visual judgments of whether or not they could walk through an aperture without shoulder rotation. Even when there was no absolute information for size and distance judgments, the subjects could do this. Warren and Whang concluded that intrinsic information given by eye height allowed scaling of objects in the environment directly in terms relative to the perceiver's body dimensions. Other experiments investigating perception of optimal riser height for stair climbing (Warren, 1984) and chair height for sitting (Mark, 1987) confirm the ability of adults to perceive affordances offered by objects in a metric relevant to body size – in short, to themselves.

It is difficult to perform research with infants and young children when we are asking detailed questions about scale of environmental supports and body fit. We have to pursue our investigations with them on a coarser level, because preverbal children are unable to give precise psychophysical judgments as adults can. But we can watch what they do when appropriately varied opportunities are presented to them. A small amount of research of this kind exists, and so far it confirms the hypothesis that even infants detect approximate relationships between dimensions of their bodies, such as arm length and shoulder width, and environmental opportunities like an object to be reached for. For example, Field (1976) investigated reaching in 3- to 5-month-old infants and found that as early as 15 weeks babies do not reach for objects that are too far away to be touched. Now that we know better what questions to ask, studies such as this one can profitably be extended to investigate when finer distinctions precisely related to body measurements can be made, and how such competence develops.

As infants grow and new action systems such as grasping, crawling, and walking emerge, the new systems instigate exploratory activity with two important results:

1. Exploratory activity has perceptible consequences that inform the child about potential environmental supports and their affordances for the new activity.
2. It also has the effect of testing the child's capacities, especially dynamic ones that less active observation would not reveal. For many activities, like lifting, walking, and jumping, this kind of exploration is essential for yielding information for the self and its potential and for providing a means of attaining greater skill in perceptually guided action.

Research at Cornell University on perceiving affordances for traversability of surfaces presented to crawling and newly walking infants illustrates these two points (Gibson et al., 1987). Newly walking infants were compared with crawling infants not yet walking on surfaces that presented different affordances for locomotion. A walkway was constructed so as to be fitted with variable surfaces that provided different affordances for locomotion. A surface traversable for bipedal walking should be extended, flat, and, above all, firm and rigid. A firm, rigid surface was constructed of plywood and covered with an opaque geometrically patterned fabric. Another surface was constructed of a waterbed covered with the same material. It could be gently agitated so as to deform visibly. Needless to say, it offered poor walkability. Babies were placed on a wooden starting platform, with their mothers at the opposite end of the walkway, and their behavior was videotaped. The tapes were later coded for latency to embark on the experimental surface, for accumulated time spent in both visual and haptic exploration, and for time spent in displacement (that is, activities other than attending to the surface, the mother, and the task of crossing to her). The walkers had a longer latency to leave the starting board when the waterbed surface was in place than when the rigid surface stretched before them. They spent more time in visual and haptic exploration of the waterbed surface than the rigid one, and also more time in displacement, often turning away from the surface and their waiting mother. The crawling infants, on the contrary, plunged ahead onto the surface, crawling off without testing it and showing little displacement activity. Most convincing, none of the walkers attempted to walk over the waterbed surface, although many walked over the other surface.

That the young walkers must have gained information about the waterbed surface from their exploratory activity is confirmed by another study. Young walkers were presented with the same rigid and waterbed surfaces, this time covered with plexiglass so that both surfaces were actually firm and rigid, although the deforming waterbed was still visible. This time, there was no difference in latency to embark on the two surfaces, nor was more time spent in displacement. Furthermore, just as many infants walked over the waterbed as over the standard rigid surface. Evidently, they were learning something about the two surfaces and their powers of negotiating them upright – that is, what the surfaces afforded.

Exploratory activity of this kind has the adaptive result of teaching infants to control their own activity, in this case locomotion. Exploratory activity with manipulable objects may result in another kind of control: control over environmental change.

Controlling the environment

It has been emphasized that the relation between the self and the environment is one of reciprocity. The self has dimensions that are perceived in relation to dimensions of the environment, and the dimensions and properties of the environment constrain what activities the animal can perform. An animal can also apply energy to objects and surfaces of the environment so as to produce changes in them. Not only are there environmental consequences that can be observed; at the same time, the action provides information for the *self as a causal agent*. Perceiving oneself as an agent, a source of control, the possessor of causal efficacy, is the epitome of perceiving oneself.

This fact was noted by W. Preyer more than a century ago, and described in a famous chapter called "Development of the Feeling of Self."

Another important factor is the *perception of a change produced by one's own activity* in all sorts of familiar objects that can be taken hold of in the neighborhood; and the most remarkable day, from a psychogenetic point of view, in any case an extremely significant day in the life of the infant, is the one in which he first experiences the *connection of a movement executed by himself with a sense-impression following upon it*. The noise that comes from the tearing and crumpling of paper is as yet unknown to the child. He discovers (in the fifth month) the fact that he himself in tearing paper into smaller and smaller pieces has again and again the new sound-sensation, and he repeats the experiment day by day and with a strain of exertion until this connection has lost the charm of novelty. At present there is not, indeed, as yet any clear insight into the nexus of cause; but the child has now had the experience that he can himself be the cause of a combined perception of sight and sound regularly, to the extent that when he tears paper there appears, on the one hand, the lessening in size; on the other hand, the noise. The patience with which this occupation – from the forty-fifth to the fifty-fifth week especially – is continued with pleasure is explained by the gratification at being a cause, at the perception that so striking a transformation as that of the newspaper into fragments has been effected by means of his own activity. (1890, p. 191)

Other examples of similar activities are given, followed by the conclusion that

the satisfaction they afford must be very great, and it probably has its basis in the feeling of his own power generated by the movements originated by the child himself (changes of place, of position, of form) and in the proud feeling of being a cause. (p. 193)

After Preyer's time, an infant's discovery of the possibility of controlling external events was documented and discussed by Piaget, and later became the subject of research in American laboratories. Piaget observed and described many instances of discovery of control in his own children. My favorite is the story of Laurent discovering that a string attached to his wrist, when the wrist was turned or jerked, set in motion a rattle attached to the other end.

The next day, at 0;2 (25) I connect his right hand to the celluloid balls but leave the string a little slack in order to necessitate ampler movements of the right arm and thus limit the effect of chance. The left hand is free. At first the arm movements are inadequate and the rattle does not move. Then the movements become more extensive, more regular, and the rattle moves periodically while the child's glance is directed at this sight. There seems to be conscious coordination but both arms move equally and it is not yet possible to be sure that this is not a mere pleasure reaction. The next day, same reactions.

At 0;2 (27), on the other hand, conscious coordination seems definite, for the following four reasons: (1) Laurent was surprised and frightened by the first shake of the rattle which was unexpected. On the other hand, since the second or third shake, he swung his right arm (connected to the rattle) with regularity, whereas the left remained almost motionless. Now the right could easily move freely without moving the rattle, the string being loose enough to permit Laurent to suck his thumb, for instance, without pulling at the balls. It therefore seems that the swinging was intentional. (Piaget, 1952, p. 161)

Laurent's pleasure in feeling himself the agent of this event was attested to by repetition and facial expressions of growing interest. When Piaget attached the string to the other wrist, the one previously activated remained still and the other was pulled at once and deliberately.

We see not only the discovery of the affordance of a simple tool in this case but at the same time discovery of the efficacy of one's own action, again illustrating the reciprocity of animal and environment. Fortunately, this phenomenon that so impressed Preyer and Piaget has in recent years been the topic of a body of research, albeit coming from a theoretical view that would have astonished them. The view was that of Skinnerian behaviorism, and the research was referred to as a demonstration of "contingent reinforcement" or "instrumental conditioning." The reinforcement, however, was not related to any bodily need such as hunger or thirst but was the occurrence of some environmental event that could be seen or heard or both. Siqueland and DeLucia (1969) used high-amplitude non-nutritive sucking in an experiment with very young infants (3 weeks and up) to demonstrate learning to control presentation of a succesion of slides of cartoon figures and pictures of human faces. The same activity was later used in experiments on infants' differentiation of phonemes (Eimas, Siqueland, Jusczyck, & Vigorito, 1971). Infants learned in a few minutes to suck at high amplitude to produce a speech event, a voice repeating a single syllable such as "ba." What could possibly be interesting about such an event? It seems obvious that the infants engaged in repeated production of it solely because of its predictability and the consequent feeling of control, of effecting a "happening" in the world.

A more interesting event was produced, again by means of high-amplitude sucking, in an experiment by Kalnins and Bruner (1973). Infants 3 months of age or less sucked at high amplitude to produce clearing of focus of a movie being presented to them. When sucking reduced blur of the picture, amplitude rose quickly to a peak. When the focusing mechanism was disconnected, sucking was almost immediately discontinued. When the experiment was reversed, so that infants had to cease sucking to reduce blur, no learning resulted. Nonnutritive sucking is an exploratory activity, and when its activation results in clear viewing of something interesting, infants learn to control the event at will.

A variation of this method, reminiscent of Piaget's observations of Laurent maneuvering the string attached to his wrist, is so-called conjugate reinforcement as described by Rovee-Collier (Rovee & Rovee, 1969; Rovee-Collier & Gekoski, 1979). Rovee-Collier tied strings to the ankles of 4-month-old infants, the other end attached to a mobile hanging over the baby's crib. As a baby kicked, the mobile twirled, and the harder the kicks, the faster the twirling. Numerous experiments on this pattern have shown very rapid establishment of kicking, with every appearance of interest in controlling the mobile's motion. Sullivan (Sullivan & Lewis, 1989; Lewis, Sullivan, & Brooks-Gunn, 1985) performed similar experiments, adding observations of emotional expressions of the infants. A cord attached to the infant's wrist activated a projector when pulled, showing a slide of a smiling face and starting a tape playing music from "Sesame Street." The infants were videotaped throughout the experiment, and the tapes were coded at critical points during the session. Pulls of half the subjects were contingent with the appearance of the slide and music; the other subjects received the same program of slides and music, but these events were not contingent on their pulls (thus, the babies in this case were not controlling the slides and music). Emotional expressions differed for the two groups. The noncontingent group indulged in a great deal of fussing, whereas the contingent group exhibited excitement, enjoyment, and high interest and vocalization at the peak of activity.

Discovering one's causal efficacy, as illustrated in these experiments, is the basis for perceiving oneself as an agent; to use a traditional term, it is the foundation for the "will." In current terminology we may think of it as underlying "intention." Behavior, including perception, is intentional, not a response to a stimulus but initiated by the perceiver-actor. Information for perception is actively sought, not passively accepted by a helpless recipient. Behavior is goal-directed, and the observations of infant behavior that we have just cited lead us to think that it is intentional, in the sense that even fairly young infants obtain and use information for themselves as agents.

When infants come to perceive objects that are means to an end as tools, there is further informational basis for the self as agent. The nipple provided by the experimenter for nonnutritive sucking to produce a picture show and the string attached to an ankle or wrist that activates a toy are indeed tools. But infants may not differentiate them at once as means to an end, even while using them and detecting their own efficacy in producing external events and change in the environment. Still, Piaget's observation of transfer of action from one limb to another when the string was moved suggests differentiation of tool from self. It has been pointed out by some persons working in artificial intelligence that a typical failure of robots is the inability to recognize activation of an event by a differentiated self. Human infants, on the contrary, show ability to detect this fact, in a primitive way at least, before the end of the first half year. Better knowledge of causal relations will come later, but self-control is already testimony to a perceived self.

The self and representation

Discussion so far has centered on what it is that specifies the perceived self. The answer, in a nutshell, is that events in the world do, as for all perception. Information for perceiving the self has to come from interaction with the environment. Resilience of a surface when stepped on, for example, specifies the power of the self when exerting pressure on the surface. There is continuous proprioceptive information for the self, from postural changes alone, as when one sits up or leans against the wind, to changes in flow patterns in the optic array when one moves. There is information from many sources for one's body, but that is not the same thing as a "body image" or any kind of image of one's self.

But are there not actual images of oneself, not only imagined representations, that can be perceived, such as a mirror image or a photograph? Certainly a representation of oneself, such as a mirror image or a photograph, can be perceived, but the information for perception of oneself in these cases seems different from the kind of information we have been discussing. The specification of the self in a representation is indirect.

Research on young children's recognition of themselves in a mirror has long been cited as a major source for studying genesis of self-perception. Typically, children show signs of self-recognition in a mirror between 15 and 20 months of age, not merely by indentifying themselves by name, but with simpler means such as fingering a temporary facial blemish like a spot of rouge on the nose (see Loveland, 1986, for a review). Earlier, they may treat the mirror image as a social object, another child, and somewhat later be puzzled by it, touch it, and look behind it. It has been a matter of great interest to many psychologists that chimpanzees (and possibly other great apes) appear to recognize themselves in the mirror, whereas monkeys and other primates, excepting humans, do not.

How does a child come to recognize the mirror image as herself? The suggestion has been, from the baby biographies to the present, that she observes the synchrony between movements she is executing – waving an arm, grimacing, and the like – and the attendant reflected events in the mirror. This is a contingency dependent on one's own action, similar to the contingencies we noted in the research on control, but it has the added feature that the contingent event bears a peculiar similarity to the controlling action. This arm waves, and so does the reflected one. Thus there is information for agency, or control of an event, and also featural similarity in the consequences that are observable. They are not always observable in the same mode, however. The toddler grimacing at herself in the mirror cannot see her face directly. No, but she can *feel* it, feel herself "making a face." There is intermodal, or bimodal, specification of the act, haptic and visual.

Whether perception of intermodal specification actually plays a role in mirror recognition has been investigated by Bahrick and Watson (1985). Actually, their research was conducted with videotapes of the infant subjects rather than with mirrors. The babies watched videotapes of themselves in a perfectly contingent live display, presented side by side with a display of a peer or a noncontingent display of themselves made earlier. In this situation, babies 5 months old showed a consistent preference for watching the noncontingent display, whether of themselves or another infant. They were thus aware of the contingency at an early age. Bahrick and Watson screened off the infants' views of their own kicking legs so that visual comparison of the actual self-motions and the video displays could not underlie detection of the contingency. They were able to conclude, therefore, that the perceived contingency was based on the "invariant intermodal relationship between proprioceptive information for motion and the visual display of that motion" (p. 963). It would seem, then, that contingency of the sort provided by the mirror is detected long before children notice featural information, such as an unusual facial blemish, in a mirror. The perception of contingency, as in the experiments on control, is directly perceptually based. But feature recognition constitutes a different case.

Photographs provide a medium for study of feature recognition in which dynamic contingencies resulting from action are eliminated. Infants' recognition of themselves in photographs comes later than mirror recognition (Zazzo, 1948; Lewis & Brooks-Gunn, 1979), with age varying depending on the measure of recognition and the choice set of alternative photos offered the infant being tested. Pictures of oneself are likely to be differentially responded to by 21 to 24 months of age (Lewis & Brooks-Gunn, 1979). This contrast with detection of dynamic contingency at 5 months clearly demonstrates that recognition of oneself in static pictorial representations is a very different phenomenon than perceiving oneself directly on the basis of information given in action and its consequences.

It seems conclusive that representations, either imaginal or conceptual, do not underlie direct perception of the self, nor do they need to for self-perception to be achieved very early in life.

Conclusion

The ecological self is a bounded object, separate from other objects and discriminated from them early in life. It can be localized in space with respect to a few constant features of the environmental layout (e.g., ground and horizon), but it is movable, and its movement provides excellent information for where one is going and where one is with respect to other objects in the surrounding layout. It differentiates its own movement from movement of other objects. It has anatomical dimensions and dynamic competences that are detected through exploratory activity that permits the self to scale the environment and what it affords in relation to itself. It can act so as to control changes in the environment, and it perceives the consequent events as caused by its own action, in distinction to events otherwise controlled. Multimodal information contingent on its actions specifies both control of these actions and unity of the self as perceiver and actor.

None of the information specifying the ecological self is representational; rather it is directly perceivable. Representations of bodily features of the self do occur in mirror images and photographs and coincide with such idiosyncratic features as body size, shapes of parts, and coloration that are directly perceptible to others. These representations may eventually be related to the ecological self, but they do not define it and recognition of them is biologically quite unnecessary. Neither is the ecological self defined by images or by reflections about itself leading to a self-concept. The ecological self is the rock-bottom essential self that collects information about the world and interacts with it.

What we perceive is the world – its layout, the things and events therein, and what they afford. These are specified for our perceptual systems by information in ambient arrays of energy, such as an optic array, acoustic array, or biomechanical array. How, then, to return to our original question, is it that we perceive ourselves? We do because each of us *is* an object in the world, and information exists to specify the self for each of us as we act in the world. We may call it proprioceptive information, as distinguished from exteroceptive information, but both are available to the active observer, at the same time. I conclude, as I began, with the same quotation from J. J. Gibson: "To perceive the world is to coperceive oneself."

REFERENCES

Bahrick, L. E., & Watson, J. S. (1985). Detection of intermodal proprioceptive–visual contingency as a potential basis of self-perception in infancy. *Developmental Psychology, 21*, 963–973.

Carroll, J., & Gibson, E. J. (1981). *Differentiation of an aperture from an obstacle under conditions of motion by three-month-old infants.* Paper presented at Society for Research in Child Development, Boston.

Eimas, P. D., Siqueland, E. R., Jusczyk, P. W., & Vigorito, J. (1971). Speech perception in infants. *Science, 171*, 303–306.

Field, J. (1976). Relation of young infants' reaching behavior to stimulus distance and solidity. *Developmental Psychology, 12*, 444–448.

Fraiberg, S. (1977). *Insights from the blind.* New York: Basic Books.

Gibson, E. J. (1984). Development of knowledge about intermodal unity: Two views. In L. S. Liben (Ed.), *Piaget and the foundations of knowledge.* Hillsdale, NJ: Erlbaum.

Gibson, E. J., Riccio, G., Schmuckler, M. A., Stoffregan, T. A., Rosenberg, D., & Taormina, J. (1987). Detection of the traversability of surfaces by crawling and walking infants. *Journal of Experimental Psychology: Human Perception and Performance, 13*, 533–544.

Gibson, E. J., & Walker, A. S. (1984). Development of knowledge of visual–tactual affordances of substance. *Child Development, 55*, 453–460.

Gibson, J. J. (1947). *Motion picture testing and research* (AAF Aviation Psychology Research Report No. 7). Washington, DC: U.S. Government Printing Office.

Gibson, J. J. (1966). *The senses considered as perceptual systems.* Boston: Houghton Mifflin.

Gibson, J. J. (1979). *The ecological approach to visual perception.* Boston: Houghton Mifflin.

Harris, P. L., Cassel, T. Z., & Bamborough, P. (1974). Tracking by young infants. *British Journal of Psychology, 65*, 345–349.

Hofsten, C. von (1982). Eye–hand coordination in the newborn. *Developmental Psychology, 18*, 450–461.

Kalnins, I. V., & Bruner, J. S. (1973). The coordination of visual observation and instrumental behavior in early infancy. *Perception, 2*, 307–314.

Kellman, P. J., Gleitman, H., & Spelke, E. S. (1987). Object and observer motion in the perception of objects by infants. *Journal of Experimental Psychology: Human Perception and Performance, 13*, 586–593.

Koffka, K. K. (1935). *Principles of Gestalt psychology.* New York: Harcourt, Brace.

Lewis, M., & Brooks-Gunn, J. (1979). *Social cognition and the acquisition of self.* New York: Plenum.

Lewis, M., Sullivan, M. W., & Brooks-Gunn, J. (1985). Emotional behavior during the learning of a contingency in early infancy. *British Journal of Developmental Psychology, 3,* 307–316.

Loveland, K. (1986). Discovering the affordances of a reflecting surface. *Developmental Review, 6,* 1–24.

Mark, L. S. (1987). Eyeheight scaled information about affordances: A study of sitting and stair climbing. *Journal of Experimental Psychology: Human Perception and Performance, 13,* 361–370.

Neisser, U. (1988). Five kinds of self-knowledge. *Philosophical Psychology, 1,* 35–59.

Piaget, J. (1952). *The origins of intelligence in children.* New York: Norton.

Piaget, J., & Inhelder, B. (1956). *The child's conception of space.* New York: Humanities Press.

Preyer, W. (1890). *The mind of the child.* New York: D. Appleton.

Rovee, C. K., & Rovee, D. T. (1969). Conjugate reinforcement of infant exploratory behavior. *Journal of Experimental Child Psychology, 8,* 33–39.

Rovee-Collier, C., & Gekoski, M. J. (1979). The economics of infancy: A review of conjugate reinforcement. In H. W. Reese & L. P. Lipsitt (Eds.), *Advances in child development and behavior* (Vol. 13, pp. 195–255). New York: Academic Press.

Siqueland, E. R., & DeLucia, C. A. (1969). Visual reinforcement of nonnutritive sucking in human infants. *Science, 165,* 1144–1146.

Spelke, E. S. (1976). Infants' intermodal perception of events. *Cognitive Psychology, 8,* 553–560.

Sullivan, M. W., & Lewis, M. L. (1989). Emotion and cognition in infancy: Facial expressions during contingency learning. *International Journal of Behavioral Development, 12,* 221–237.

Walker, A. S. (1982). Intermodal perception of expressive behaviors by human infants. *Journal of Experimental Child Psychology, 33,* 514–535.

Warren, W. H. (1984). Perceiving affordances: Visual guidance of stair climbing. *Journal of Experimental Psychology: Human Perception and Performance, 10,* 683–703.

Warren, W., & Whang, S. (1987). Visual guidance of walking through apertures: Body-scaled information for affordances. *Journal of Experimental Psychology: Human Perception and Performance, 13,* 371–383.

Wertheimer, M. (1961). Psychomoter coordination of auditory and visual space at birth. *Science, 134,* 1692.

Zazzo, R. C. (1948). Image du corps et conscience de soi. *Enfance, 1,* 29–43.

3

Body–environment coupling

DAVID N. LEE

Like all animals, we exist by virtue of coupling our bodies to the environment through action. Inadequate coupling, whether it be on the perceptual side, as when driving in fog, or on the movement side, as caused by muscular dysfunction, can be a prescription for disaster. Perception is necessary for controlling movement just as movement is necessary for obtaining perceptual information. Perception and movement compose a cycle that is action.

Action in the environment is the root of the ecological self (Neisser, 1988). As Neisser has so neatly put it in this volume: We are what we do. Therefore, to understand the self, we need to understand how actions can be geared to the environment. The first point to note is that control has to be prospective. If we see a person or animal going around bumping into things, we think something clearly must be wrong – so much do we take prospective control for granted. For to avoid colliding with objects, the consequences of continuing one's present course of action (such as heading in a particular direction, braking with a particular force) must be perceived and evasive action taken in time. However, collisions are not necessarily to be avoided. In fact, getting around the environment depends on bringing about collisions of the feet with the ground, the hands with a branch, and so on. These collisions have to be carefully controlled if they are to secure the required propulsive force for locomotion while avoiding injury to the body. Making physical contact with people, animals, or objects likewise requires controlling collision, whether it be to make harsh or gentle contact. In all cases, precise prospective control is needed. The where, when, and how of the collision must be perceived ahead in time and the body prepared for it. Therefore, a crucial aspect of body–environment coupling is predictive perceptual information. How such information is available in the input to the perceptual systems is the concern of this chapter.

Though vision is probably the richest source of information, and the one about which most is known, it is by no means the only source of information. For example, using echolocation in place of vision, bats fly with the finesse of a bird and blind people can get around tolerably well. Because different forms of perceptual input inform about the same things, serving the common function of coupling the animal to the environment, they must share invariant features. By analyzing different types of perceptuo-motor control – guidance by vision, echolocation, and touch – this chapter

43

describes invariants in sensory input that make control possible and thus underpin the ecological self.

Optic flow

Prospective control of action in the environment depends on the availability of information about the position, orientation, and movement of the organism as a whole and its parts relative to surfaces in the environment. Because control requires making contact with some surfaces while at the same time avoiding others, information must be simultaneously available about surfaces lying in different directions. Furthermore, because *movement* has to be controlled, the information must have a temporal component. In short, the information must constitute a spatiotemporal flow field.

J. J. Gibson first formulated the concept of the optic array in his classic paper on ecological optics (1961). Since then, the concept has been further refined, and mathematical descriptions of the optic flow field (the changing optic array resulting from movement) have been developed. This has led to a number of empirical studies (e.g., Gibson, 1966, 1979; Koenderink & van Doorn, 1977; Lee & Young, 1986). In this section I present a brief description of the optic flow field and the information it provides for gearing action to the environment.

Light reflected from surfaces makes possible visual perception of the world. Surfaces are generally covered with textural elements (facets, patches of different pigmentation, and so on) that have stepwise different light reflecting properties from their neighbors. The light reflected from a textural element normally radiates over a wide angle, and so at any point of observation in the environment where an eye may be placed light will be incident from many different textural elements. The light from each element to the point of observation forms a thin optic cone, with the base of the cone on the element and the apex at the point of observation. The set of cones constitutes the optic array at the point of observation. Because at each point of observation there is a unique array, whenever the head is moving relative to the environment, as it normally is, the optic array at the moving point of observation is continuously changing, giving rise to an *optic flow field*.

Various ways have evolved for registering the direction and composition of the light in the optic flow field, from the several forms of chambered vertebrate eye with their lenses and retinas (Walls, 1967) to the omatidia of insects, which resemble a radial bundle of light guides. It is worth pausing to contemplate the insect eye, because it dispels the common misconception that vision depends on having a retinal image.

The optic flow field is of fundamental importance in understanding visual perception because it stands outside particular visual systems. It is the input available to each and every one of them. The job of a visual system is to pick up the information in the flow field, and this, inter alia, involves scanning the flow field for detail by turning the eyes and/or head. Because the pickup of detailed visual information is essential for proper visual control of movement, it is not surprising that head–eye coordination in scanning the optic flow field develops early in human infants (Daniel & Lee, 1990).

The optic flow field that results when the point of observation moves along a linear path through a rigid environment is illustrated in Figure 3.1. The radial bundle of optic cones coming from surface elements ahead opens up about the central optic cone, which corresponds to the line of movement of the point of observation. The resulting *linear optic flow field* has the invariant property that the optic cones (approximated as lines) fan out, each cone remaining in a particular plane through the line of movement of the point of observation.

In general, more than one optic cone will be moving in a particular plane [e.g., the cones with bases H(ut) and T(ree) in figure 3.1]. This leads to the second invariant property of the linear optic flow field: When an optic cone [e.g., T(ree)] catches up with a slower optic cone [e.g., H(ut)] moving in the same plane, it envelops and replaces it. This is because the faster moving cone corresponds to a nearer environmental texture element, which therefore occludes the farther one.

These two invariant properties are of central importance, for it has been shown (Lee, 1974) that an optic flow field with these properties necessarily constitutes a linear optic flow field that is *specific to* a particular linear movement of the self relative to a rigid environment with a particular layout. The linear optic flow field therefore provides information about the movement of the self and about the layout of the environment. Thus, for example, if a person is presented with a linear optic flow field by moving the visible surroundings as a unit, this specifies movement of the self relative to rigid surroundings. As a consequence, the person's balance can be optically manipulated. This is illustrated in Figure 3.2. A person stands on a fixed floor while the walls and ceiling of a surrounding "room" are, for example, moved forward. This produces a linear optic flow field that provides information that the head is moving backward. Therefore the person adjusts posture and sways forward. Balance in toddlers can be powerfully visually driven by optic information, and they can be literally bowled over (Lee & Aronson, 1974). The more powerful optic information normally comes from the periphery of the linear flow field where the flow is usually faster, and this has greater effect on balance than the central field both for toddlers and adults (Stoffregen, 1985; Stoffregen, Schmuckler, & Gibson, 1987). Adults' balance can also be visually driven, but normally they just sway and do not fall. This is apparently because they get better information through their feet about how they are moving with respect to the environment than do toddlers. If that information is rendered less precise, for example, by

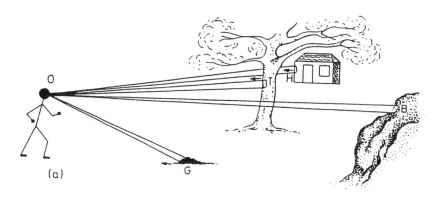

(a)

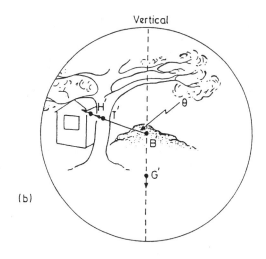

(b)

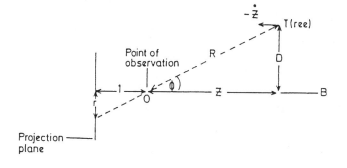

(c)

Figure 3.1. The linear optic flow field. (a) From each small surface texture element facing the point of observation *O*, light is reflected to *O*, forming a narrow optic cone. Only a few optic cones are illustrated, but in general there will be a densely packed radial bundle of optic cones converging on *O* to form an optic array. As the point of observation moves in the direction of the surface element *B*, on the boulder, the radial bundle of cones opens out about the central cone *OB*, which lies along the path of locomotion, to form a *linear optic flow field*. The flow field has the invariant property that each optic cone, which may be approximated as a line, fans outward from *OB* remaining in a particular plane through *OB*. A second invariant property is that when two optic cones, which are moving in the same plane, coincide, the faster moving one envelops and replaces the slower. This is illustrated by optic cones *OT*(ree) and *OH*(ut). They are fanning out in the same plane through *OB*, but, because surface element *T* is nearer than *H*, optic cone *OT* is fanning out faster than *OH*. As *OT* catches up with *OH*, it will envelop it, because then surface element *T*(ree) will be occluding *H*(ut).

(b) Another way of visualizing the linear optic flow field – a section through the flow field perpendicular to line *OB*, which is equivalent to a movie taken from *O* with the optical axis of the camera pointing at *B*. Arrows indicate direction of motion of image elements. Image of *B* is *B'*, etc. Note that *T'* and *H'* are moving outward from *B'* along the same radial flow line at angle θ to vertical.

(c) A section through the linear optic flow field containing the line *OB* and surface element *T*, approximated as a point: also showing projection onto a plane. *Z* is the distance, along *O*'s path of motion, from the present point of observation to the point of *O*'s nearest approach to *T*. $-\dot{Z}$ is the rate of change of *Z*. *R* is the length of line *OT*, with rate of change $-\dot{R}$. This notation is used throughout the text.

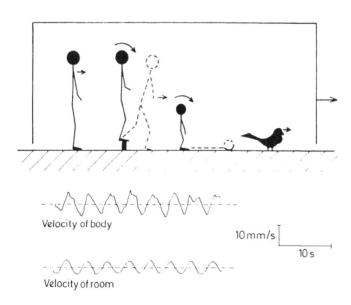

Velocity of body

10 mm/s

10 s

Velocity of room

Figure 3.2. Vision in balance control. See text for details. (From Lee & Young, 1986.)

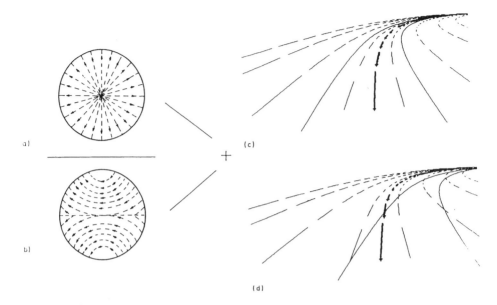

Figure 3.3. Linear, rotary, and combined optic flow fields on a flat surface, as in Figure 3.1b. (a) Linear optic flow field, with radial flow lines. (b) Rotary optic flow field brought about by rotation of the frame of reference of the optic array about a vertical axis through the point of observation. Flow lines are elliptical; they are the projections of circles centered on the axis of rotation. (c) and (d) Combined optic flow field resulting from movement of the point of observation along a circular path. Flow lines (shown broken) are hyperbolic; they are the projections of circles centered on the center of curvature of the path of locomotion. The central heavily drawn flow line is the *locomotor flow line*, which specifies the future course of the point of observation if the current circular path were maintained. Solid lines depict the edges of a road along which the point of observation is moving. In (c), the course lies safely along the road, in (d), the course leads off the road to the left. (Modified from Lee & Lishman, 1977.)

balancing crossways on a narrow beam where the feet can tip, then adults, too, can be bowled over (Lee & Lishman, 1975).

The eye is very sensitive to head movement. As shown by the graphs in the lower part of Figure 3.2, an adult's body sway was visually driven by anterior–posterior sinusoidal oscillations of the room of amplitude 3 mm (Lee & Lishman, 1975). Larger oscillations cause a standing dove to bob its head to keep the head locked to the room for short periods of time. If the bird is yoked to a (small) room so that the room moves with the bird, then it does not bob its head because the head is already locked to the visual surroundings (Friedman, 1975).

The other fundamental optic flow field is the *rotary optic flow field*, which results when the frame of reference of the optic array rotates about an axis through the point of observation (e.g., during a head turn). The form of the rotary optic flow field is illustrated in Figure 3.3b. Because the head is often turning and moving linearly at the same time, the optic flow field is generally a composite of a linear and a rotary flow field. The two component flow fields are perceptually separable (Warren & Hannon, 1990) and so information can be obtained from each. Because the rotary optic flow field does not provide information about the layout of the environment but only about rotation, it is normally kept at low amplitude by controlling head and eye movements in order to facilitate pickup of information from the much richer linear optic flow field.

However, this is not to say that the rotary component of an optic flow field always should or can be eliminated entirely. The curvilinear, linear-plus-rotary optic flow field, in fact, provides information for prospective control of steering on a curve, as illustrated in Figures 3.3c and 3.3d (also see Lee & Lishman, 1977, and Warren, Mestre, Blackwell, & Morris, 1990). A crucial aspect of the curvilinear flow field is the locomotor flow line, the heavily drawn broken line in Figures 3.3c and 3.3d. The line specifies the course the vehicle will follow if the steering angle is kept fixed. The driver's task is to maintain the locomotor flow line within the flow lines corresponding to the edges of the road, as in Figure 3.3c. If the locomotor flow line should ever intersect the road-edge flow lines (as in Figure 3.3d), then the vehicle is at risk of leaving the road at that point unless steering is adjusted. In other words, the driver's current program of action is, in effect, optically mapped onto the environment, running ahead of the vehicle. Actual collision is avoided by seeing prospective collision.

Acoustic flow

Let us now consider acoustic information about the environment. Imagine you are in a park and a band is playing. Sound from the trumpets will be reaching you from one direction, sound from the clarinets from another, and so on. If you stand still and close your eyes, you will be able to point quite accurately at whichever instrument you choose. (In laboratory experiments, Oldfield and Parker [1984] found pointing accuracy [mean absolute error] of about 5° to acoustic targets in the frontal field, even when the head was immobilized. Accuracy of pointing to corresponding visual targets was about 2°. If you now walk toward the band, still with eyes closed, your direction of pointing will continuously change, matching the changing direction of the particular instrument. At any instant, you could switch to pointing to another instrument. In fact, the heard directions of all the instruments would be continuously changing in the same way that the seen directions would be changing if you were to open your eyes. The ability to point in this way using hearing demonstrates both the acoustic flow field and the capability of picking up information from it.

Picking up information from the acoustic flow field requires registering the direction and characteristics of sounds. The human auditory system is capable of registering the direction of a sound by a variety of means – time and intensity differences at the two ears, changes in the spectral composition of the sound due to multiple reflections in the pinnae and head shadow effects, and the changes in all these that result when there is movement of the head or sound source (see Moore, 1989, for review). The same is true in bats, which have exquisitely sensitive systems for registering acoustic flow.

Blind mobility

Blind people have used echolocation for a long time, but it used to be called "facial vision" because they reported experiencing pressure on the face when they approached obstacles. Sounds such as tapping a stick, clicking the tongue, or whistling are used to illuminate the nearby environment with broadband sound. Nearly 50 years ago, experiments by Supa, Cotzin, and Dallenbach (1944) established that facial vision was, in fact, echolocation. Kellog (1962) found that blind subjects could detect objects subtending an angle of as little as 3.5° and could discriminate changes in distance and in area of the order 20% and 30%, respectively. Some materials could be discriminated with very high accuracy (e.g., velvet and plain wood 99.5% of the time); discrimination was generally good between soft and hard materials. Rice (1967) found that a circle, square, and triangle of the same area could be distinguished by some subjects.

However, regrettably little research has been done on human echolocation over the last 20 years, and most of that research has been on the use of head-mounted or hand-held ultrasonic aids. Because the wavelengths of sounds audible to humans are longer than those used by bats in echolocation, the potential for spatial resolution of surface detail is less. The purpose of ultrasonic aids is to overcome this limitation of human hearing by emitting ultrasound, picking up the ultrasonic echoes by microphones, and then translating these sounds electronically into audible sounds fed to the ears through headphones. Though such devices can enable the user to discriminate surface textures, they have not been very successful as mobility aids (Dodds, 1988). A possible reason is that the devices do not allow full natural hearing to access the ambient acoustic flow field. In particular, the pinna of the ear – that highly developed structure used in picking up direction of sound in humans, bats, and most other animals – is put out of action by the use of headphones. Most hearing aids do the same, which is possibly one reason why the wearer finds hearing particularly difficult in a "cocktail party" situation, where directional hearing is important for focusing on a speaker.

Bats

When it comes to understanding the potential of acoustic flow, much can be learned from studying bats. The sonar world of an echolocating bat is based on reflections of its cries off surrounding surfaces. The remarkable ability of bats to use sonar to steer themselves around obstacles was studied by Griffin and colleagues (Griffin, 1958; Griffin, Novick, & Kornfield, 1958; Grinnell & Griffin, 1958) some 35 years ago. Bats (*Myotis lucifugus*) can, for example, almost perfectly avoid vertical wires of only 0.3 mm diameter when flying at 3–4.4 m/s (Griffin, 1958, p. 357). Most later research has concentrated on narrow-field abilities like object discrimination. These studies have revealed the fine discriminating power of bats' echolocation, for example, with respect to object size and small movements like the fluttering of insect wings (e.g., Simmons, 1989) Neurophysiological studies have shown how such abilities are reflected in elegant brain architecture (Suga, 1988).

Notwithstanding these considerable advances, the central question remains: How is echolocation used to navigate, negotiate obstacles, and land on surfaces – in short, to get around in the world? In what follows, I set out a speculative (and incomplete) answer to the question in the hope that it might stimulate empirical research.

In summarizing the experiments on bat locomotion, Webster (1967) concluded that the bat behaves as though its sonar system provides a wide-angle view of the environment, while, at the same time, the bat is apparently capable of rapid shifts of focus and attention to pick up relevant detail. How is this possible? Suppose a bat is flying through foliage chasing an airborne insect, as many bats do. The bat makes high-frequency cries, and the sound is reflected back from different directions from the surrounding surfaces. Because the flow field of reflected sound is all the bat has to go on to avoid colliding with branches and to capture its prey, the acoustic flow field must provide information for guidance that is on a par with what would be available in the optic flow field. Now, for a flow field to provide information, it must be structured. The optic flow field is structured because of the differing light-reflecting properties of the surrounding surfaces. Likewise, the acoustic flow field is structured by the differing sound-reflecting properties of the surfaces. Thus the acoustic flow field can be conceived as a bundle of differentiable acoustic cones analogous to the optic cones constituting the optic flow field.

Bringing out the full sound-reflecting properties of surfaces requires broadband sonic illumination, just as broadband light is necessary for bringing out the color of surfaces. When the visual world is seen under the narrow spectrum of sodium street lamps, it is monochrome and much impoverished. So, too, would the world appear to a bat if it were to emit sounds only over a narrow frequency range. In fact, all known species of bat illuminate the environment with broadband, "white" sound, which would make it possible for them to perceive the timbre of surfaces (that is, the reflectance x frequency profile). This would give them the auditory equivalent of color vision and so richer information. To what extent bats can perceive the timbre of surfaces needs to be investigated.

The acoustic flow field is not, in general, isomorphic with the optic flow field: Acoustic texture elements of the surfaces (facets and patches of different sound reflectance) do not necessarily coincide with optic texture elements. However, the important point is that the basic form of the acoustic flow field is the same as the optic flow field, and therefore it could provide similar information about the movement of the animal and the layout of the environment. In principle, the theory of available information described earlier for the optic flow field applies equally to the acoustic. Other information-bearing properties of acoustic flow are described in a later section, but for the present let us consider another form of sensory flow.

Haptic flow

A blind person is walking down a city street holding a long cane. The tip of the cane touches the ground a constant two step lengths ahead and is swept from side to side in time with the step cycle. The cane thus zigzags over the ground joining prospective footfalls two ahead. What the person is doing is generating a (delimited) haptic flow field to obtain information for prospective control of walking. Insects use their antennae in a like manner. The haptic flow field is similar in essential respects to the optic and acoustic flow fields in that the stimulation is spatially and temporally ordered. The haptic flow for the blind person is not as rich in information as normal optic flow, but it somewhat resembles the optic flow available when picking one's way down a rough track in the dark using a flashlight to illuminate the ground ahead.

Another type of delimited haptic array, which has its optic counterpart, is gained by circumscribing an object being investigated. One can gain information about an object both by looking at it and by running the hands over it. Numerous experiments attest to the greater informational content of the optic flow field over the static optic array (see, e.g., Gibson, 1979). In a similar vein, Gibson's (1962) elegant cookie-cutter experiment revealed the richness of information in the *changing* haptic array compared with the static array. In the experiment, blindfolded subjects were better able to identify the shapes of the cookie cutters when they could actively handle them as opposed to having the shapes passively pressed on the palms of their hands. When the cutter was passively rotated on the palm, thus creating imposed haptic flow, identification performance was intermediate. It is worth noting that in the active handling case, the pattern of stimulation was by far the most complex when described in physical terms, involving changing articulations of the fingers and changing pressures and shear forces on the skin of the fingers and palm. Yet active handling provided the best information. Thus, the body acts by different principles than we do when describing the physical world.

The parallel between haptic flow and optic flow is well illustrated by the "feelies" experiment of Caviness and Gibson (Gibson, 1963). Subjects were given 10 smooth, irregularly sculptured objects to handle and had to match them to a replica set they could see in front of them. After brief practice with the unfamiliar forms, matching the haptic and visual information was accomplished with little error. Another example of the parallel between haptic and optic flow is a system for converting an optic input, picked up by a TV camera, into a haptic display of vibrators applied, for example, to a person's back. After very little training, subjects were able to recognize common objects and describe their arrangement in three dimensions (White, Saunders, Scadden, Back-y-Rita, & Collins, 1970). Movements of batting a ball, walking and pointing to a target, and slalom walking can also be guided with reasonable precision by means of such a device (Jannson, 1983).

Haptic–somatic system

Like the visual system, the system of mechanoreceptors in the joints, muscles, and skin provides *exterospecific* information about the relation of the body to the environment (as with the blind person using a stick), *exterospecific* information about the form of objects, and *propriospecific* information about the relation of one part of the body to another (Lee, 1978). The three types of information are normally available concurrently. Thus the mechano-receptors are components not solely of a haptic system that provides information through touching and holding but of a broader *haptic–somatic* system that also provides essential propriospecific information about the body. When handling an object, for example, information is obtained through stimulation of the receptors in the skin. Nevertheless, without additional information about how the fingers are configured, the haptic array would be incompletely defined and so information about the object would be imprecise. Similarly, perceiving the direction of something relative to the body visually or acoustically depends on adequate information about the orientation of head on shoulders and of eyes in head.

Though accurate propriospecific information is available visually, it is not always possible or convenient to use vision for this purpose. The haptic–somatic system is most important because it *constantly* provides proprio-specific information. The information is, however, subject to drift (e.g., Harris, 1965) and needs to be kept in tune with vision (Lee, 1978).

Optic information for timing

Suppose you are at the roadside deciding whether to cross before the next vehicle arrives. It is often suggested that perceiving the time to contact of something with us, or of us with something (to take the driver's view), requires perceiving distance away and speed of approach. However, this is not necessarily so. Temporal information is, in fact, primary, and information about distance and speed is derivable from it. If this sounds strange, consider perception of acceleration. Because we think of acceleration as rate of change of velocity (which indeed it is), it is natural to suppose that perceiving acceleration requires first perceiving velocity. However, the vestibular system registers acceleration of the head directly, not via detecting velocity. Thus our way of thinking about acceleration would have led us to misconstrue vestibular function. Likewise, the traditional way of thinking about time to time contact could lead us to misconstrue visual function.

The tau function

Let us look at the linear optic flow field in more detail. Consider an arbitrary surface texture element in the environment, such as H in Figure 3.1. The cone of light from H to the point of observation O and the line of movement of O define a plane represented in Figure 3.1c. Because O is moving, the distances Z and R are decreasing over time, whereas angle ϕ is increasing. D remains constant. Denoting rate of change over time of Z and R by $\dot{Z}$ and $\dot{R}$, we can show that

$$Z/\dot{Z} = R/\dot{R} \ \cos^2\phi \tag{3.1}$$

We now introduce the *tau function*, a central feature in describing the timing and spatial information available in sensory flow fields. Tau (τ) of quantity X is defined as X divided by the rate of change of X – that is, $\tau(X) = X/\dot{X}$. Therefore, Equation 3.1 can be written

$$\tau(Z) = \tau(R) \ \cos^2\phi \tag{3.2}$$

If we consider now the optic cone from a surface texture element H to O and the small angle α subtended at O by H in the direction perpendicular to the plane of movement HOC, then it can be shown that

$$\tau(Z) = -\tau(\alpha)\cos^2\phi \tag{3.3}$$

Thus the tau function of distance Z is specified by the tau function of optic angle. Other optical specifications of $\tau(Z)$ are given in Lee, Reddish, and Rand (1991).

The tau function Z, $\tau(Z)$, is important information for an organism. The negative of $\tau(Z)$ is the time it would take the surface element H to reach the nearest position to the point of observation under constant velocity. This

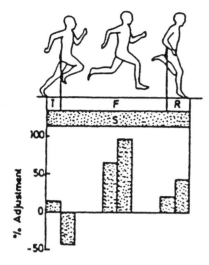

Figure 3.4. Possible parameters to vary to adjust step length *S* when running to secure footing: *T* = trailback; *F* = flight distance; *R* = reach forward. Histograms show, for two runners, the percentage of the adjustment in *S* that was found to be attributable to each of the parameters. Flight distance is what was principally varied. Further analysis showed that this was a result of varying flight time. See text for further details. (From Lee & Young, 1986.)

time has been termed the *tau-margin* (Lee & Young, 1985). The tau-margin is, for example, the type of information needed for regulating step size when locomoting over irregular ground. Two empirical studies bear on this: how long jumpers visually guide themselves onto the takeoff board (Lee, Young, Reddish, Lough, & Clayton, 1983) and how runners negotiate stepping-stones (Warren, Young, & Lee, 1986). The data of both studies indicate that control is basically a problem of timing as opposed to distance judgment: that optic information about the tau-margin is used to regulate the flight duration of the next step rather than distance information being used to regulate spatial aspects of the step such as trailback on takeoff or reach forward on landing (see Figure 3.4). Another example of the use of optic information about the tau-margin is catching a moving object, an ability that infants develop remarkably early (Hofsten, 1980).

Timing interceptive actions

Interceptive acts frequently have to be timed under conditions where approach velocity is not constant. Catching something that is falling, landing from a jump, and a predator seizing a dodging prey are some examples. If the approach is accelerative, as under gravity, then, strictly speaking, the tau-margin to the approach surface is an overestimate of the time to contact with the surface. However, with normal accelerations, the overestimate is

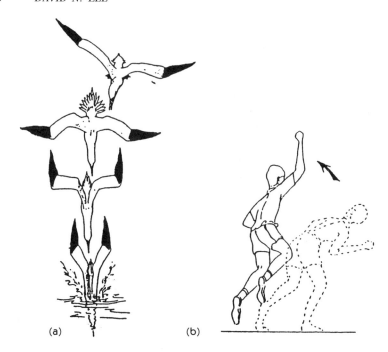

(a)   (b)

Figure 3.5. Visual timing of interceptive actions under accelerative approaches. (a) Gannet plunge diving into the sea. (b) Person leaping to punch a falling ball. See text for details of experiments.

negligibly small when the time to contact is less than about 300 ms (Lee et al., 1983). Thus, providing the value of the tau-margin is perceptually monitored up to within 300 ms of contact, the tau-margin provides sufficiently accurate information for timing.

Furthermore, the tau-margin would be simpler to pick up than actual time to contact. Indeed, even in principle, the latter could be accomplished only if the acceleration were predictable, which is, of course, a situation preys seek to avoid. Because simple robust mechanisms are, in general, preferable to more complex ones, it is likely that perceptual mechanisms for timing interceptive actions have evolved to use the tau-margin rather than to engage in computations involving estimates of acceleration.

Experiments indicate that the tau-margin is indeed used in timing actions during accelerative approaches. One experiment (Lee & Reddish, 1981) studied the behavior of the gannet (*Sula bassana*). This large seabird fishes by plummeting vertically into the sea at speeds up to 60 mph. As it approaches the water, with wings half-open for steering, it needs to see when to streamline its body so that it can slice into the water without injury (Figure 3.5a). Because it is accelerating under gravity, the tau-margin, $-\tau(Z)$, for the water (Z = height above water), which gives time to contact under constant velocity, overestimates the actual time to contact. Does the bird perform a complex visual computation, taking into account acceleration, or does it adopt the simpler more robust strategy of starting to streamline when the tau-margin reaches a certain trigger value? If it were to do the latter, then it would start streamlining sooner before contact the longer the dive. This is because a higher velocity is reached in a longer dive and so, as the bird approaches the water, gravity does not produce as large a proportionate increase in velocity as it does with a shorter dive. Therefore, time to contact is closer to the tau-margin the longer the dive. Data from film analysis of dives were consistent with the hypothesis that the tau-margin is used by gannets in timing streamlining.

Another experiment (Sidaway et. al, 1989) was a human version of the gannet study. The difference was that people dropped feetfirst from different heights onto the floor instead of headfirst into water, and the timing of preactivation of the leg muscles to act as shock absorbers took the place of timing of wing closure for streamlining. It was found that the timing of muscle preactivation was based on the value of the tau-margin for the floor.

In another experiment (Lee et al., 1983), an object was moving rather than the person. A soccer ball was dropped from different heights to someone standing below who had to leap and punch it back up (Figure 3.5b). Records of how the angles at the person's knee and elbow changed as they set up for the punch indicated that the sequencing of those movements was geared to the changing value of the tau-margin for the ball as it approached.

Primacy of timing information

It has been shown that it is not necessary, in principle, to pick up information about distance or speed in order to register the tau-margin, as it is directly specified in the optic flow field (Equation 3). It is not necessary in practice either, as has been shown in experiments where time to contact is judged from displays consisting of dilating images that simulate approaching objects but contain no information about the distance or velocity of the objects (Schiff & Detwiler, 1979; Todd, 1981). Furthermore, human infants and many species of animal have been shown to be sensitive to the visual information about impending collision given in such displays (Bower, Broughton, & Moore, 1970; Ingle & Shook, 1985; Schiff, 1965; Yonas & Granrud, 1985).

In natural situations, when information about distance and velocity is presumably available, might not time to contact be computed from perceived distance and velocity? It is hard to see what would be the advantage of such a computational method. In the first place, computing the tau-margin from distance and velocity, however they were perceived, would introduce two sources of error and these would compound to give greater error in the estimate of the tau-margin. Second, information about distance and velocity

58   *DAVID N. LEE*

has to be scaled in terms of body–action dimensions. It turns out that this requires registering the tau-margin (or its equivalent) from the optic flow field, as we will now see.

Consider leaping a ditch. In a certain sense, information about the width of the ditch is needed, but it is not information about its width in meters or any other arbitrary unit of measure. What is required is information specifying the magnitude of leg thrust needed to clear the ditch. In general, things need to be perceived in terms of the type and magnitude of action that could or is to be applied to them; that is, of their *affordances* (Gibson, 1979). (*Describing* the ditch is, of course, a type of action, and this may require perceiving the width of the ditch in terms of meters, but we will concentrate here on more fundamental actions.)

With these points in mind, let us consider the spatial and kinematic information available in the optic flow field. Refer to Figure 3.1 and Equation 3.3, for an arbitrary surface element *H*:

$$\tau(Z) = Z/\dot{Z} \tag{3.4}$$

$$D = Z \tan \phi \tag{3.5}$$

Now the tau-margin, $-\tau(Z)$, is optically specified (Equation 3.3), and so is ϕ. Therefore, we have three unknowns (Z, $\dot{Z}$, and D) and two equations; and so if one unknown is specified, the equations are solvable for the other two. *Specifying an unknown quantity in terms of a known quantity X, thus making the equations soluble, is to scale the information in units of X.* The following are some units in which scaling might be achieved.

Scaling units

Locomotor cycles. Natural locomotor activity is generally cyclical, whether on the ground, in water, or in the air. The frequency of strides, wingbeats, or tailbeats tends to be regular but can be changed to fit the demands of the environment. Suppose that an animal is moving linearly at a constant speed with a constant locomotor period *T*. If at the start of a locomotor cycle the tau-margin for a surface element is $\tau(Z)$, then the distance *Z* of nearest approach to an element is $\tau(Z)/T$ locomotor cycles. The size of objects can likewise be expressed in units of locomotor cycles.

Visual regulation of gait to hit the takeoff board in the long jump run-up (Lee, Lishman, & Thomson, 1982) and when running over irregularly spaced stepping-stones (Warren et al., 1986; see Figure 3.4) are nice examples of the use of this type of information. In both cases, the runner adjusts cycle time, by regulating the vertical impulse applied to the ground, in order to control where the foot strikes the ground.

Head acceleration. Suppose an animal is traveling in a straight line at a constant speed and accelerates its head forward. Pigeons do this when they are coming in to land on a perch (Davies & Green, 1988). Suppose the acceleration is A. Then, for any surface element in the environment, differentiating Equation (3.4) with respect to time gives

$$\dot{Z} = A\tau(Z) \; / \; [\dot{\tau}(Z) - 1] \tag{3.6}$$

Thus $\dot{Z}$ (and also Z and D, from Equations (3.4 and 3.5) are specified in terms of head acceleration and $\tau(Z)$. The acceleration could be registered by the vestibular system, in which case Equation 3.6 applies even when the body is accelerating, and A is then the combined head and body acceleration. Alternatively, acceleration might be registered in terms of the action of the neck muscles. These different possibilities need to be tested empirically.

Head velocity. Suppose an animal is stationary, preparing to leap to something, and makes a head movement. Cats, for example, frequently do this in a very obvious way, bobbing their heads up and down. Then the velocity $\dot{Z}$ of the environmental surface elements relative to the point of observation will be determined solely by the head movement. $\dot{Z}$ is thus specified in terms of the action with the head. Hence, from Equations 3.4 and 3.5, the spatial coordinates Z and D of each surface element are also specified in terms of the head action and the optically specified quantities tau-margin $(-\tau(Z))$ and ϕ. It is reasonable to suppose that head action could be intrinsically related to leaping action, and so distance would be specified in terms of leaping action, but this needs to be tested.

Eye height. As a person runs, walks or simply sways on level ground, the D coordinate of every point ahead on the ground beneath the path of movement of the eye (e.g., point G in Figure 3.1) is equal to the eye height. Thus, applying Equations 3.4 and 3.5 to any such element yields a solution for $\dot{Z}$, the speed of movement, in terms of eye height. Furthermore, because $\dot{Z}$ is the same for all environmental surface elements, the spatial coordinates of each are specified in terms of eye height. If a person were to scale speed and distance in terms of eye height, then artificially lowering eye height, unbeknown to a person, should make speed, distances, and sizes appear larger. The principle was used to singular effect in the movie *The Incredible Shrinking Man* (1957). By placing the camera – yielding both the character's and the audience's eye view – close to the floor in a doll's house, the house was made to look the size of a normal house and a cat peering in the window appeared enormous. The effect has been studied experimentally (e.g., Warren & Whang, 1987). Standing subjects viewed a variable width doorway through an aperture that prevented them from seeing that the floor on which the doorway stood was higher than the one on which they stood. The result was that the subjects perceived the doorway to be wider than it actually was. Manufacturers of sports cars presumably benefit from the enhancing effect on perceived speed of lowering eye height.

Controlling collision

In all the ways of scaling, the optic information is solely about the tau-margin and its time derivative, together with the direction angles to surface elements. The optic variables specifying the tau-margin and tau-dot (the time derivative) are thus seen to be fundamental variables yielding information about distance, size, and velocity, as well as about time. It therefore makes sense to formalize the optic flow as two superimposed fields: a tau-margin field and a tau-dot field. That is, to each element (corresponding to a particular environmental surface element) in an optic flow field is associated a pair of angular coordinates (θ, ϕ) (see Figures 3.1b and 3.1c), a tau-margin value, $-\tau(Z)$ and a tau-dot value, $\dot{\tau}(Z)$. $\tau(Z)$ is optically specified by Equation 3.3, $\dot{\tau}(Z)$ by the derivative of that equation.

We have seen some of the spatial and temporal information provided by the tau-margin field. The tau-dot field affords direct information for controlling collision, on which many activities depend, as will now be shown. For more details on some aspects of what follows, see Lee (1976).

Suppose the point of observation is moving linearly with respect to a rigid environment. Consider an arbitrary surface element in the environment. By Equation 3.4

$$\tau(Z) = Z/\dot{Z}$$

and differentiating

$$\text{tau-dot} = \dot{\tau}(Z) = 1 - Z\ddot{Z}/\dot{Z}^2 \tag{3.7}$$

Now, if forward acceleration $-\ddot{Z}$ were to remain constant, then the "collision velocity," $-\dot{Z}_c$, with the element (i.e., the velocity at nearest approach) is given by

$$\dot{Z}_c^2 = \dot{Z}^2 - 2Z\ddot{Z}$$

and so from Equation 3.7

$$\dot{Z}_c^2/\dot{Z}^2 = 2\dot{\tau}(Z) - 1 \tag{3.8}$$

From this equation three situations may be distinguished:

No collision. If tau-dot $= \dot{\tau}(Z) < 0.5$, then $\dot{Z}_c^2/\dot{Z}^2 < 0$ and so no collision will ensue. Thus, in decelerating to avoid colliding with something, all that is necessary is to keep $\dot{\tau}(Z) < 0.5$. There is no requirement for explicit information about distance, velocity, or deceleration in order to stop without

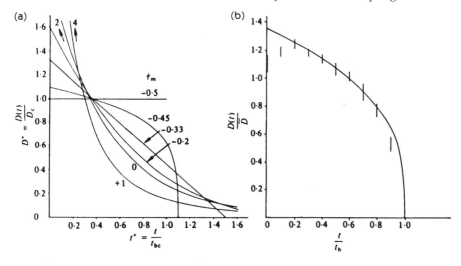

Figure 3.6. (a) Predicted patterns of deceleration if tau-dot were kept constant. Curves for different constant values of tau-dot ($\dot{\tau}_m$) are shown. Normalized deceleration (in terms of constant deceleration D_c required to stop) is plotted against normalized time (in terms of time to stop t_{bc} under constant deceleration). Note how deceleration monotonically decreases for all values of tau-dot except 0.5, where deceleration is constant. (b) Deceleration data (standard deviation bars) of a test driver stopping at a nominated point from various speeds up to 100 km h^{-1} (62 m h^{-1}). The data are plotted in dimensionless form: $D(t)$ is the deceleration at time t after starting to brake; $\bar{D}$ is the mean deceleration during the stop; t_b is the stopping time. The curve is that one of the theoretical set in (a) that best fits the empirical data. The fit is good from the initial peak in deceleration onward (how deceleration is built up initially is not taken into account in the theory). The tau-dot value for the best fitting curve is 0.425. Thus the test driver was braking just below the level of 0.5 that would have required constant deceleration to stop. (From Lee, 1976.)

collision. Once a deceleration is set such that $\dot{\tau}(Z) < 0.5$, then maintaining this deceleration guarantees stopping before collision. Obviously, the larger the deceleration, the more the organism will stop short of the obstacle.

Just reaching. This can be achieved by regulating deceleration so that tau-dot, $\dot{\tau}(Z)$ maintains a constant value not greater than 0.5. To achieve a constant value of 0.5, the deceleration needs to be kept fixed. To achieve a constant value less than 0.5, the deceleration has to be monotonically decreased during the approach to the obstacle (see Figure 3.6a). Data from test drivers (Lee, 1976) indicate that they use the second strategy (Figure 3.6b). It is a procedure that not only would work if nothing unforeseen happened (e.g., brake fade when driving) but also has a built-in margin for error, as the procedure entails progressively slackening off the brakes, thus always leaving some braking power in reserve.

Collision. If tau-dot = $\dot{t}(Z) > 0.5$, then collision will ensue. As we discussed earlier, collision is not always to be avoided because it is necessary for most activities, from striking and thrusting from the ground in walking and running to touching an object in order to grasp it. However, it is crucial that the collision be controlled so as to avoid injury. When the body collides with something immobile, the kinetic energy of the body has to be converted into another form of energy. For example, when a person or animal jumps or steps down from a height, the kinetic energy at impact has to be converted mainly into elastic energy in the muscles, tendons, and ligaments. This is accomplished by stretching them. If the kinetic energy of impact is too great, however, the stretching force will be too great and there will be rupturing – unless other action is taken, such as converting the kinetic energy of impact into kinetic energy of forward movement, as when walking or running down slopes or stairs, or into kinetic energy of rotation, by going into a roll as parachutists sometimes do. On the other hand, even if the kinetic energy at impact is not too great to be absorbed by muscle action, if the muscles are not sufficiently tensed (and the limbs adequately flexed) prior to impact, they will not be able to deal with the shock of landing, and balance may be lost or even bones broken.

Thus, in controlling collision, it is essential to have action-scaled information about the kinetic energy of the body in order both to control the kinetic energy during the approach – for example, by braking, if this is possible – and to set the body up to receive the shock of impact. Relevant information is provided by the value of tau-dot, $\dot{t}(Z)$. In particular, because kinetic energy is proportional to velocity squared, Equation 3.8 states that

$$\text{kinetic energy at collision} / \text{current kinetic energy} = 2\dot{t}(Z) - 1 \qquad (3.9)$$

Therefore, the shock-absorbing action of the muscles (which is effectively their combined elastic constant) that is required to maintain balance and avoid injury in the forthcoming collision is specified in units of the muscular action required to accommodate the current kinetic energy. Expertise about the latter would require experience with the type of action concerned – for example, jumping or stepping down from different heights – and information about current velocity, and hence kinetic energy, which could be registered by one of the ways of scaling described earlier.

It is apparent, therefore, that walking or running down stairs or slopes can pose a considerable control problem. Even toddlers appear quite aware of the problem. They balk at trying to walk down slopes that they have little hesitation in attempting to walk up (Adolph, Gibson, & Eppler, 1990).

Registering tau-dot

Tau-dot is a dimensionless quantity, defined in terms of distance, velocity, and acceleration (see Equation 3.7). However, as we have shown, tau-dot is optically specified without the need for information about distance, velocity, or acceleration. Thus, in principle, tau-dot should be registerable even in an artificial situation where information about distance, velocity, and acceleration is excluded. An experiment by Kim, Turvey, and Carello (1989) shows that this can indeed be achieved. Subjects were able to reliably judge from computer displays whether a simulated approach of a surface with tau-dot held constant would result in a "soft" (tau-dot less than 0.5) or a "hard" (tau-dot greater than 0.5) collision.

Acoustic information for timing

Because the acoustic flow field has the same form as the optic flow field, it also provides timing and spatial information in terms of the tau function $\tau(\alpha)$, as in Equation 3.3. In addition, in echolocation there are two other acoustic tau functions that provide the same information as $\tau(\alpha)$:

1. *Tau function of echo delay.* Echo delay d – the time interval between the sound pulse being emitted and the echo returning from a surface element – is proportional to the distance of the element. Using reasoning similar to the derivation of Equation 3.3 (see Lee, van der Weel, Hitchcock, Matejowsky, & Pettigrew, 1992, for details), it can be shown that

$$\tau(Z) = \tau(d) \cos^2\phi \tag{3.10}$$

It should be noted that $\tau(d)$ is defined within a pulse–echo pair, which means that timing and spatial information can in principle be derived from a single sound pulse and its echo.

2. *Tau function of intensity.* The other acoustic tau function is $\tau(I)$, where I is the intensity of the echo at the point of observation. Assuming a sound pulse of constant intensity, I is proportional to the inverse of the square of the distance R of the surface element reflecting the sound. Using reasoning similar to the above, it can be shown that

$$\tau(Z) = -2\tau(I) \cos^2\phi \tag{3.11}$$

As in the case of echo delay, $\tau(I)$ is defined for a single echo, which, therefore, in principle provides timing and spatial information.

There have been no reported experimental investigations of timing of actions using echolocation, and so these ways of timing need to be tested. However, a study by Schiff and Oldak (1990) is relevant. They presented sound films of approaching trucks, cars, and speaking people, using the sound only, the picture only, and both picture and sound. The film was turned off at a variable time during the approach, and the subject had to indicate when the vehicle or person would have made contact with them. For time to contact up to 4 s, judgments with sound only were as accurate as with picture only or with both picture and sound. Because the sound was recorded and played back through a single channel, interaural time or intensity differences could not have informed about time to contact. Thus the information the subjects were using must have been available monaurally. A likely candidate is the tau function of intensity, for Rosenblum et al. (1987) found that intensity change is the most effective information for locating moving sound sources.

Self in control

The theme of the chapter has been the prospective gearing of actions to the environment through predictive sensory information. This fundamental ability of every mobile organism is, I have suggested, the basis of the ecological self – the self in control.

Actions can be geared to the environment through different types of perceptual input, and so there must be properties of the input that are invariant across perceptual systems. In an attempt to discover such perceptual invariants, researchers have analyzed different forms of input. The changing pattern of light or sound reflected from environmental surfaces and incident on a moving organism composes a flow field. It has been shown that the optic and acoustic flow fields have important common properties for constraining action. First, the potential future course of the organism, which is essential information for controlling steering, is, in effect, mapped onto the environment in the flow field. Second, the tau-margin – the time to nearest approach to a surface under constant approach velocity – is specified by the tau function of each of several optic and acoustic variables. I have shown that the tau-margin is potent control information for a wide range of activities, including timing interceptive actions, regulating magnitude of movement, and controlling collision.

Could it be that the tau-margin is specified by the tau function of input to haptic, electric, chemical, and other perceptual systems, too? I have outlined some similarities between haptic and optical flow fields, but more work is required in the little–researched haptic area. The same applies to research on all perceptual systems other than vision and audition. Thus, how general the tau function is remains an open empirical question. It is easy to show, however, that for the tau-margin to be specified by the tau function of a perceptual input variable, it is necessary and sufficient that the input variable be a power function of distance from a surface. This mathematical constraint could aid the search for general perceptual invariants.

ACKNOWLEDGMENTS

I thank Claes von Hofsten and Vincent Hope for their helpful critical comments on the manuscript. The research was supported by grants from the Medical Research Council and the U.S. Air Force European Office of Aerospace Research and Development.

REFERENCES

Adolph, K. E., Gibson, E. J., & Eppler, M. A. (1990). Perceiving affordances of slopes: The ups and downs of toddlers' locomotion. Emory Cognition Project Report No. 16. Atlanta: Emory University Psychology Department.
Bower, T. G. R., Broughton J. M., & Moore, M. K. (1970). Infant responses to approaching objects: An indicator of response to distal variables. *Perception and Psychophysics, 9*, 193–196.
Daniel, B. M., & Lee, D. N. (1990). Development of looking with head and eyes. *Journal of Experimental Child Psychology, 50*, 200–216.
Davies, M. N. O., & Green, P. R. (1988). Head bobbing during walking, running and flying: relative motion perception in the pigeon. *Journal of Experimental Biology, 138*, 71–91.
Dietz, V., & Noth, J. (1978). Pre-innervation and stretch responses of triceps bracchii in man falling with and without visual control. *Brain Research, 142*, 576–579.
Dodds, A. (1988). *Mobility training for visually handicapped people.* London: Croom Held.
Dyhre-Poulsen, P., Laursen, A. M., Jahnsen, H., & Djorup, A. (1980). Programmed and reflex muscular activity in monkeys landing from a leap. In J. E. Desmedt (Ed.), *Spinal and Supraspinal Mechanisms of Voluntary Motor Control and Locomotion. Progress in Clinical Neurophysiology, 8*, 323–329.
Friedman, M. B. (1975). Visual control of head movements during avian locomotion. *Nature, 255*, 67–69.
Gibson, J. J. (1961). Ecological optics. *Vision Research, 1*, 253–262.
Gibson, J. J. (1962). Observations on active touch. *Psychological Review, 69*, 477–491.
Gibson, J. J. (1963). The useful dimensions of sensitivity. *American Psychologist, 18*, 1–15.
Gibson, J. J. (1966). *The senses considered as perceptual systems.* Boston: Houghton Mifflin.
Gibson, J. J. (1979). *The ecological approach to visual perception.* Boston: Houghton Mifflin.
Griffin, D. R. (1958). *Listening in the dark.* New Haven CT: Yale University Press.
Griffin, D. R., Novick, A., & Kornfield, M. (1958). The sensitivity of echolocation in the fruit bat, *Rousettus. Biological Bulletin, 115*, 107–113.
Grinnell, A. D., & Griffin, D. R. (1958). The sensitivity of echolocation in bats. *Biological Bulletin, 114*, 10–22.
Harris, C. S. (1965). Perceptual adaptation to inverted, reversed, and displaced vision. *Psychological Review, 72*, 419–444.
Hofsten, C. von (1980). Predictive reaching for moving objects by human infants. *Journal of Experimental Child Psychology, 30*, 369–382.
Ingle, D. J., & Shook, B. L. (1985). Action-oriented approaches to visuo–spatial brain functions. In D. J. Ingle, M. Jeannerod, & D. N. Lee (Eds.), *Brain mechanisms and spatial vision.* Dordrecht: Nijhoff.

Jansson, G. (1983). Tactile guidance of movement. *International Journal of Neuroscience, 19*, 37–46.

Kellog, W. N. (1962). Sonar systems of the blind. *Science, 137*, 399–404.

Kim, N.-G., Turvey, M. T., & Carello, C. (1989). Optical information for the prospective control of contacts with surrounding surfaces. *Perception Action Workshop Review, 4*, 6–9.

Koenderink, J. J., & van Doorn, A. J. (1977). How an ambulant observer can construct a model of the environment from the geometrical structure of the visual inflow. In G. Hauske & E. Butenandt (Eds.), *Kybernetik 1977.* Munich: Oldenburg.

Lee, D. N. (1974). Visual information during locomotion. In R. B. McLeod & H. L. Pick (Eds.), *Perception: Essays in honor of James J. Gibson.* Ithaca, NY: Cornell University Press.

Lee, D. N. (1976). A theory of visual control of braking based on information about time-to-collision. *Perception, 5*, 437–459.

Lee, D. N. (1978). The functions of vision. In H. L. Pick & E. Saltzman (Eds.), *Modes of perceiving and processing information.* Hillsdale., NJ: Erlbaum.

Lee, D. N., & Aronson, E. (1974). Visual proprioceptive control of standing in human infants. *Perception and Psychophysics, 15*, 529–532.

Lee, D. N., & Lishman, J. R. (1975). Visual proprioceptive control of stance. *Journal of Human Movement Studies, 1*, 87–95.

Lee, D. N., & Lishman, J. R. (1977). Visual control of locomotion. *Scandinavian Journal of Psychology, 18*, 224–230.

Lee, D. N., Lishman, J. R., & Thomson, J. A. (1982). Visual regulation of gait in long jumping. *Journal of Experimental Psychology: Human Perception and Performance, 8*, 448–459.

Lee, D. N., & Reddish, P. E. (1981). Plummeting gannets: A paradigm of ecological optics. *Nature, 293*, 293–294.

Lee, D. N., Reddish, P. E., & Rand, D. T. (1991). Aerial docking by hummingbirds. *Naturwissenschaften, 78*, 526–527.

Lee, D. N., van der Weel, F. R., Hitchcock, T., Matejowsky, E., & Pettigrew, J. D. (1992). Common principle of guidance by echolocation and vision. *Journal of Comparative Psychology A, 171*, 563–571.

Lee, D. N., & Young, D. S. (1985). Visual timing of interceptive action. In D. J. Ingle, M. Jeannerod, & D. N. Lee (Eds.), *Brain mechanisms and spatial vision.* Dordrecht: Nijhoff.

Lee, D. N. & Young, D. S. (1986). Gearing action to the environment. In H. Heuer & C. Fromm (Eds.), *Generation and modulation of action patterns.* Heidelberg: Springer Verlag.

Lee, D. N., Young, D. S., Reddish, P. E., Lough, S., & Clayton, T. M. H. (1983). Visual timing in hitting an accelerating ball. *Quarterly Journal of Experimental Psychology, 35A*, 333–346.

Moore, B. C. J. (1989). *An introduction to the psychology of hearing.* London: Academic Press.

Neisser, U. (1988). Five kinds of self–knowledge. *Philosophical Psychology, 1*, 35–39.

Oldfield S. R., & Parker, S. P. A. (1984). Acuity of sound localization: A topography of auditory space. I. Normal hearing conditions. *Perception, 13*, 581–600.

Rice, C. E. (1967). Human echo perception. *Science, 155*, 656–664.

Rosenblum, L. D., Carello, C., & Pastore, R. E. (1987). Relative effectiveness of three stimulus variables for locating a moving sound source. *Perception, 16*, 175–186.

Schiff, W. (1965). Perception of impending collision: A study of visually directed avoidant behaviour. *Psychological Monographs, 79* whole number 604.

Schiff, W., & Detwiler, M. L. (1979). Information used in judging impending collision. *Perception, 8,* 647–658.

Schiff, W., & Oldak, R. (1990). Accuracy of judging time to arrival: Effects of modality, trajectory, and gender. *Journal of Experimental Psychology: Human Perception and Performance, 16,* 303–316.

Sidaway, B., McNitt-Gray, J., & Davis, G. (1989). Visual timing of muscle preactivation in preparation for landing. *Ecological Psychology, 1,* 253–264.

Simmons, J. A. (1989). A view of the world through the bat's ear: The formation of acoustic images in echolocation. *Cognition, 33,* 155–199.

Stoffregen, T. A. (1985). Flow structure versus retinal location in the optical control of stance. *Journal of Experimental Psychology: Human Perception and Performance, 11,* 554–565.

Stoffregen, T. A., Schmuckler, M. A., & Gibson, E. J. (1987). Use of central and peripheral optical flow in stance and locomotion in young walkers. *Perception, 16,* 113–119.

Suga, N. (1988). Parallel–hierarchical processing of biosonar information in the mustached bat. In P. E. Nachtigal & P. W. B. Moore (Eds.), *Animal sonar: Processes and performance.* New York: Plenum.

Supa, M., Cotzin, M., & Dallenbach, K. M. (1944). "Facial vision": The perception of obstacles by the blind. *American Journal of Psychology, 57,* 133–183.

Todd, J. T. (1981). Visual information about moving objects. *Journal of Experimental Psychology: Human Perception and Performance, 7,* 795–810.

Walls, G. L. (1967). *The vertebrate eye and its adaptive radiation.* New York: Hafner.

Warren, W. H., & Hannon, D. J. (1990). Eye movements and optical flow. *Journal of the Optical Society of America, A7,* 160–169.

Warren, W. H., Mestre, D. R., Blackwell, A. W., & Morris, M. W. (in press). Perception of circular heading from optical flow. *Journal of Experimental Psychology: Human Perception and Performance.*

Warren, W. H., & Whang, S. (1987). Visual guidance of walking through apertures: Body-scaled information for affordances. *Journal of Experimental Psychology: Human Perception and Performance, 13,* 371–383.

Warren, W. H., Young, D. S. & Lee, D. N. (1986). Visual control of step length during running over irregular terrain. *Journal of Experimental Psychology: Human Perception and Performance, 12,* 259–266.

Webster, F. A. (1967). Some acoustical differences between bats and men. In R. Dufton (Ed.), *International conference on sensory devices for the blind.* London: St. Dunstan's.

White, B. W., Saunders, F. A., Scadden, L., Bach-y-Rita, P., & Collins, C. C. (1970). Seeing with the skin. *Perception and Psychophysics, 7,* 23–27.

Yonas, A., & Granrud, C. E. (1985). The development of sensitivity to kinetic, binocular and pictorial depth information in human infants. In D. J. Ingle, M. Jeannerod, & D. N. Lee (Eds.), *Brain mechanisms and spatial vision.* Dordrecht: Nijhoff.

4

A theory of representation-driven actions

MARC JEANNEROD

The aim of this chapter is to develop the idea that an important part of human action is driven by internal rather than external factors. The basic postulates are that internally driven actions result from autonomous processes, that they are based on representations that anticipate the effects of interaction of the self with the external milieu, and finally, that they play an important role in structuring the self. The first part of the chapter presents a brief historical account of the notions of intention and representation as envisioned in the context of the generation and control of actions. A second part is devoted to exploring the field of mental imagery, which represents a new approach to representational phenomena. Finally, the third part deals with the nature of representational systems that may account for producing voluntary action.

The neurophysiological correlates of intention

What are the respective roles of stimulus-driven and representation-driven actions in structuring our knowledge about the external world? The issue is at the core of a long-lasting debate between two schools of thought. I will call *centralist* the school that holds that experience and knowledge grow from actions that are the expression of a mental content. This view is usually accompanied by a nativist view of learning, and is mostly heralded by modern cognitive psychologists. I will call *peripheralist* the school that holds that behavior is structured by the incoming flow of information, and that learning results from association between external stimuli or events. The peripheralist view can be traced back to classical empiricism, but its modern version arose as a consequence of behaviorist psychology.

The two theories disagree not only on how action is generated and controlled but also (and mainly) on how, and to what extent, it contributes to structuring the self. The centralist view holds that action has such a structuring role if and when it arises from a representation. Representations can be seen as "anticipatory schemata" that steer action to a predefined goal. They are hypotheses made by the subject about the external world; and the consequences of action can either reinforce or infirm these hypotheses. As Neisser (1976) puts it, in speaking of perception: "By constructing an anticipatory schema, the perceiver engages in an act that involves information from the environment as well as his own cognitive mechanisms. He is changed by the information he picks up" (p. 57). I suggest that what Neisser calls the "perceptual cycle" is probably more likely to be a "perceptual-motor cycle."

An apparently intermediate view envisages that the subject is not merely reacting to the environment but, rather, is actively seeking information. According to this view (e.g., Gibson, 1966) perception would be a generalized form of proprioception, in the sense that information pickup would be contingent on the subject's activity. In Gibson's terms, information would be "obtained" by subjects rather than imposed on them. This conception, however, in spite of introducing the subject as an agent in the perceptual process, still pertains to the peripheralist school. Gibson's subject is an "ecological self," with little or no autonomy with respect to the external world, as opposed to the "representational self" of the centralist theory.

A brief history of the neurophysiological concepts relevant to centralist and peripheralist theories

Historically, one of the first formulations of the opposition between the supporters of peripherally controlled and centrally controlled models of behavior can be found in the discussion about the origin of muscle sense and its contribution to knowledge of our own movements and the positions of our body parts (see Scheerer, 1987). This discussion is a critical one for the theory , because it deals with how we become aware of our own actions. The fact that we unambiguously feel ourselves the authors of our actions is obviously an essential condition for envisioning action as a factor in structuring the self.

A quotation from a paper by Charles Bell written in the first years of the nineteenth century sets the terms of the debate: "At one time, I entertained a doubt whether this [the sensation of the positions of our limbs, or "muscle sense"] proceeded from a knowledge of the conditions of the muscles or from the consciousness of the degree of effort which was directed to them in volition" (quoted by Phillips, 1986; see also Jones, 1972). The philosopher F. P. Maine de Biran, in 1807, had clearly assigned the main role in the knowledge of our movements to consciousness of the degree of effort. We know our movements, he said in substance, through both the intimate feeling of the productive cause of our effort and the sensation that corresponds to muscular contraction. However, according to Maine de Biran, the sensation of muscular contraction alone, without being associated with a feeling of effort, would lead only to a vague impression or remain unperceived, as in the case of heartbeats (see Jeannerod, 1983; Scheerer, 1987). The cause of the movement must be distinguished from its effect, in spite of the fact that the two coexist in voluntary action.

Physiologists of the time, however, were faced with the problem of polarization of nerve transmission. For most of them, nervous activity was a centripetal phenomenon that originated from sensory organs; sensations, therefore, could only be of peripheral origin. Support for this theory (an early peripheralist formulation) came from Charles Bell himself, who had established that each muscle was innervated by a motor and a sensory nerve. "Between the brain and the muscle there is a circle of nerves, one nerve conveys the influence from the brain to the muscle, another gives the sense of the condition of the muscle to the brain. If the circle be broken by the division of the motor nerve, motion ceases; if it be broken by the division of the other nerve, there is no longer a sense of the condition of the muscle" (Bell, 1826). The true physiological status of this function of sensory nerves arising from muscles would only be disclosed 80 years later by Sherrington, when the sensory organs within the muscles were discovered. Proprioception then assumed its role as a dominant theory concerning the origin of position sense. This origin was peripheral, and the propagation of nervous information was, therefore, in the centripetal, "orthodromic," direction.

The opposite conception, that of a central origin of position sense and muscular feelings, was mainly heralded by J. Muller's school in Germany, where the notion of "sensations of innervation" was developed. These were sensations from a central origin, no longer of a peripheral origin, transmitted by motor nerves, not by sensory nerves, by which subjects could feel the motor impulses emitted by their brain toward their muscles. This theory was soon supported by an increasing number of people, not only in Germany. As Bain stated in 1855: "The sensibility accompanying muscular movement coincides with the *outgoing* stream of nervous energy, and does not, as in the case of pure sensation, result from any influence passing inwards by incarrying or sensitive nerves" (quoted by Lewes, 1879, p. 23). Bain thought that there was a feeling of the exerted force and that this feeling was the "concomitant of the outgoing current by which the muscles are stimulated to act."

This point was clearly formulated by Lewes (1879), who introspectively distinguished between the "motor feeling" accompanying the active contraction of a muscle and the "sensation" generated by this contraction. Lewes thus considered that the complex experience arising from a voluntary movement was the sum of both the "sense of effort" and the "sense of effect." In an even more polemical way, Waller (1891) claimed that muscle sense, "in the sense of centripetal process *from muscle* is not supported by any direct proof, and so long as the alternative hypothesis of expended energy in 'motor' centres is not disproved, it is not possible to admit that the feeling is entirely of peripheral origin, nor that the muscular contribution is the predominant factor among its peripheral constituents" (p. 243).

The most influential arguments used by the German school to demonstrate the reality of the sensations of innervation were derived from obser-vations of eye movements. J. E. Purkinje noticed that, whereas we perceive the world around us as stable when we move our eyes and sweep the surrounding objects on our retina, passive displacement of one eye (by a slight pressure exerted on the outer edge of the eyeball) produces the impression of a movement of the surrounding objects (see Grüsser, 1984). How, then, do we distinguish a real displacement of the visual world from a displacement of our retina across the visual world? This was obviously quite an ancient question, first raised by Aristotle (Grüsser, 1986). For Purkinje, and later on for von Helmholtz (1867), the difference between the voluntary movement of the eye, where the world seems stable, and the passive dis-placement of the eyeball, where the world seems unstable, was that only in the first case is the movement due to an intention, an effort.

This hypothesis can be verified by a third condition, in which the voluntary effort is not associated with movement. This may happen when one eye muscle is paralyzed. In this case, as observed clinically by von Graefe, objects in the surrounding world seem to move in the direction of the intended movement (see Grüsser, 1986). In such patients the direction of visual objects is also misjudged whenever eye movements are attempted in which the paretic muscle is involved (see Perenin, Jeannerod, & Prablanc, 1977). Helmholtz concluded: "These phenomena prove conclusively that our judgements as to the direction of the visual axis are simply the result of the effort of will involved in trying to alter the adjustment of the eyes" (1867, pp. 245–246). Wundt summarized Helmholtz's observations by stating that, because sensations originating from the act of will are normally fused with those arising from muscles during the movement, they would only be observed separately when a paralysis abolishes the movement and preserves the will to make it (see Ross & Bischof, 1981). Indeed, such a situation seemed to fulfill Maine de Biran's quest for a pure sensation of effort, uncontaminated by peripheral sensations.

Besides the observations of eye-muscle palsy, several clinical conditions reported in the literature come close to this ideal. Among these are the self-observations reported by people experiencing pathological paralysis. The physicist Ernst Mach (1906), for example, described his own impres-sions after he experienced hemiplegia due to a stroke. At first, when paralysis of his arm was complete, Mach noted that the acts of will he made to move it, although clearly perceptible, were not accompanied by any real sensation of effort. Later, after recovery had begun and the paralysis was less dense, each act of will was accompanied by the sensation of having the hand or foot held down by enormous weights. The sensation of effort was perceived as a sensation of heaviness or resistance that opposed movement. More recently, a similar self-observation was reported by A. Brodal. While attempt-ing to move his paralyzed limb, he experienced that "it is as if the muscle was unwilling to contract, and as if there was a resistance which could be overcome by very strong voluntary innervation. . . . This force of innervation is obviously some kind of mental energy, which cannot be quantified or defined more closely" (Brodal, 1973).

A similar dissociation between efferent and afferent sensations during movement, observed in subjects with complete anesthesia of one limb (including the loss of sensations generated by passive displacement) but still able to produce voluntary movement with that limb, can also be interpreted within the same framework. According to Duchenne de Boulogne (1855), these patients still have "muscular consciousness," although they lose muscular sense, that is, sensations generated by muscular activity. Duchenne was led to the interesting conclusion that muscular consciousness could exist independently of muscular sensations. Cases of this sort were abundant in the literature and several were quoted by William James in the chapter on "Will" in his *Principles of Psychology* (1890). When intending to move their anesthetized limb, patients clearly had the impression of having executed the movement, even if the limb was actually blocked by the observer. When the movement was effectively executed, its actual direction or extent often did not correspond to their intention.

Finally, the impressions of movement of a phantom limb in amputated patients, though more controversial, are relevant to this point. An editorial note appearing in 1875 (unsigned, but attributed to H. Jackson) suggested that some of the writer's patients had very precise sensations of the movements of positions of the phantom hand. Patients stated: "My hand is now open, it is closed. . . . I touch the thumb with the little finger. . . . It is now in the writing position." Jackson concluded that "the volition to move a certain part is accompanied by a mental condition which represents the quantity of movement, its force, an idea of a change in position of these parts in the consciousness" (p. 462). It was shown later that sensations of phantom limb movements were accompanied by muscle contraction in the stump. If these contractions are blocked by drugs, the sensations of movement disappear (Henderson & Smyth, 1948).

The theory of sensations of innervation underwent a long eclipse during the first part of the twentieth century. This was partly due to James's arguments against the theory. According to him, sensations of innervation represented superfluous and cumbersome mechanisms, unnecessary for understanding the observed effects of paralysis. Moreover, there was no clear demonstration of these sensations. The intense feeling of effort that the paralyzed subject felt could be explained in a very simple manner: In forcing himself to contract a paralyzed muscle, the patient in fact contracted other, healthy muscles. It was this contraction that, via the centripetal pathway (the normal parthway for sensation), gave him the notion of his effort. In the case of the paralyzed eye (the example used by Helmholtz to establish the theory), it was the movements of the other, normal eye that produced the effects felt by the subject. James (1890) ironically concluded: "Beautiful and clear as this reasoning (postulating the sensations of innervation) seems to be, it is based on an incomplete inventory of the afferent data." Hence his "disbelief" in the sensations of innervation and his "presumptions" against them. However, in the alternative explanation he proposed – that "all our ideas of movement, including those of the effort which it requires, . . . are images of peripheral sensations" (pp. 492–493) – James conceded that these sensations might be "remote," that is, built on memorized sensations rather than on the sensations generated by the movement itself. Thus, his critique was directed more toward the type of material with which the motor image was built rather than the existence of such an image.

The centralist theory, postulating the importance of motor acts in visual perception (or, more generally, in sensorimotor integration), reappeared in the literature from the field of ethology. Uexkull, for example, explicitly stated that the "world of action" (the motor commands) had to be integrated with the sensory world (see Grüsser, 1986). He postulated that this integration could be realized by a direct influence of the motor commands on the sensory centers. This statement may have prompted the revival 40 years ago of a neurophysiological theory compatible with the notion of sensations of innervation. In 1943, Sperry observed that fish with inverted vision caused by surgical 180° eye rotation tended to turn continuously in circles when placed in a visual environment. In a later paper (1950) he interpreted this circling behavior as the result of a disharmony between the retinal input generated by movement of the animal and a compensatory mechanism for maintaining the stability of the visual field.

The mechanism postulated by Sperry for this stability was a centrally arising discharge that reached the visual centers as a corollary of any excitation generated by the motor centers and normally resulting in movement (hence the term *corollary discharge,* used by Sperry to designate this mechanism). In this way the visual centers could distinguish the retinal displacement related to a movement of the animal from the displacement produced by moving objects. Visual changes produced by movements of the animal were normally "canceled" by a corollary discharge of a corresponding size and direction, and had no effect on behavior. If, however, the corollary discharge did not correspond to the visual changes (e.g., after inversion of vision), these changes were not canceled and were read by the motor system as having their origin in the external world. The animal then moved in the direction of this apparent visual displacement.

Based on similar observations in insects, Holst and Mittelstaedt (1950) independently came to the same conclusion. They postulated that every time the motor centers send a command for a movement, they also send a copy of this command (the "efference copy") to the visual centers. Holst and

Mittelstaedt further postulated that information reaching from the retina has a plus sign, and the efference copy has a minus sign. If the two signals are congruent, they cancel each other, so the visual information is not taken into account by the system. Corollary discharge and efference copy thus represent two nearly identical formulations of the fact that the nervous system can inform itself about its own activity.

Recent research on sensations of innervation

Research on sensations of innervation has been continuing almost without interruption since their rediscovery under different names by Sperry and Holst. These sensations have been studied both in patients with complete or partially recovered paralysis and in normal subjects during transient neuromuscular block or during fatigue.

In studying patients with paralysis of central or peripheral origin, Gandevia (1982) replicated some of Mach's self-observations. In conformity with these earlier findings, hemiplegic patients reported that attempts to move completely paralyzed limbs produced no feeling of heaviness. When ability to move began to return, their attempts were accompanied by a feeling of intense heaviness. Finally, the sensations of heaviness decreased as movements became easier and regained strength. By contrast, in patients with paralysis of peripheral origin, attempts to move the paralyzed limbs were always associated with sensations of heaviness.

Experiments involving transient paralysis in volunteer subjects have led to more ambiguous results. Several authors using ischemic block or local injection of curarizing agents to produce paralysis of one hand failed to observe sensations of effort during attempts to move (Laszlo, 1966; McCloskey & Torda, 1975). However, another less direct, but more objective, way to test the perception of efferent activity is to ask subjects to indicate the *amount* of effort they had to exert to achieve a given task. Gandevia and McCloskey (1977) asked subjects to press a lever with one thumb (the "reference" thumb) in order to produce a reference tension, displayed visually on an oscilloscope screen. With the other thumb, they pressed another lever to match, without visual control, the muscular contraction or effort produced by the reference thumb. During partial curarization on the side of the reference thumb, the subjects could still produce the reference tension by putting more effort into the action in order to overcome the partial neuromuscular block. Accordingly, with their other thumb, they indicated a much larger muscular effort than normally required to produce the same tension.

The same authors also used the perceived heaviness of weights as a measure of muscular effort. The same matching technique was used, that is, subjects chose weights with one arm until the heaviness perceived with that arm matched the reference weight lifted by the other arm. During partial paralysis the subjects chose exaggerated weights, indicating an increase in the heaviness perceived with the weakened arm. The same result was obtained by muscular fatigue instead of partial paralysis. McCloskey, Ebeling, and Goodwin (1974) showed that after the reference arm supported the weight for some minutes and became fatigued, weights heavier than the reference weight were chosen to match it. These results fit Holmes's general statement that forces exerted by weakened muscles are overestimated (Holmes, 1922; Holmes observed this fact in patients with unilateral cerebellar lesion and found consistent overestimation of weights by the asthenic cerebellar arm). This is because subjects have to produce more force centrally to overcome the muscle weakness. If judgment about force relied only on information directly related to the actual muscular tension (as the proprioceptive hypothesis implies), no overestimation should occur; on the contrary, subjects should underestimate the generated force.

Other aspects of sensations of innervation (their temporal organization) can also be measured by using purely introspective methods. These aspects can be inferred from judgments that subjects make about when they release the command to move a limb. In an experiment by McCloskey, Colebatch, Potter, and Burke (1983), subjects were instructed to perform a test movement at will. The instructions also implied that they should disregard the movement and concentrate on their commands to the limb ("Think about when you tell it to move"). Finally, they were given a reference stimulus that occurred at a variable delay with respect to the onset of their movement (as judged from EMG records). It was found that the reference stimulus had to be given about 100 ms prior to onset of EMG activity in order to be judged as coincident with onset of the motor command. In order to avoid possible cues arising from contracting muscles, the same experiment was repeated under ischemic block of the arm. In that case, where no muscle contraction occurred, the efferent volleys were recorded from the nerve upstream with respect to the block. Again, the reference stimulus had to precede the nerve volleys significantly to be felt as coincident with the subjective central command.

These experiments demonstrate that subjects can identify the neural signals related to their central commands, and that they can distinguish these signals from those arising from muscles at the time of the movement itself. Several arguments demonstrate that the command-related sensations are unlikely to have arisen from the muscle. The sensations occur in advance of the relevant EMG activity and persist under ischemic block. In addition, muscle spindles, which might represent a possible source of signals for these sensations, do not seem to discharge during isometric muscle contraction prior to the movement (Vallbo, 1973).

The problem that remains to be solved is the precise nature of these "sensations" related to "expended energy." Are they real sensations? Alternatively, are they cognitive judgments, direct revelations of consciousness, the "birthright of the soul," as Lewes once stated (1879)? Gandevia (1982) proposed an interpretation of the sensations of effort reported by subjects with weakened muscles (by neuromuscular blockade, fatigue, or other ways), as well as of their perception of increased heaviness as measured psychophysically. He suggested that neural traffic in motor corticofugal paths might be read off and used as the relevant signal for the observed illusions. Indeed, complete paralysis following pyramidal lesions at the cortical level is not accompanied by sensations of increased effort or heaviness, precisely because no traffic occurs in the motor pathways after such lesions. Sensations reappear during partial recovery of movements, when neural traffic is reestablished. The same hypothesis would account for permanence of sensations of effort in all cases of distal paralysis, where corticofugal pathways are not altered.

More recently (1987) Gandevia proposed that the discharge responsible for these sensations does not arise directly from the corticofugal pathway, because transcranial electrical stimulation of this pathway does not produce a sensation of effort. Instead, the subject experiences a passive movement. This observation conforms with Penfield's observations during direct electrical stimulation of the cerebral hemispheres in conscious patients: When such stimulations produced a movement, the patient invariably experienced having been moved passively by the experimenter with no sensation of having been the author of the movement (Penfield & Boldrey, 1937). It can be suggested therefore, that the relevant discharges for the sensations of innervation arise from structures such as premotor cortex or basal ganglia, which subsequently impinge upon primary motor cortex and on the descending pathway.

Motor images as clues to central motor mechanisms

Sensations of innervation and related phenomena (sense of effort, felt will, etc.) are difficult to measure because they are so fleeting. By comparison, the study of another subjective counterpart of action, the explicit mental representation of intended movements (motor images), may offer an easier approach to the central determinants of action. In this section I make two assumptions: first, that the content of motor images is an overt counterpart of the normally covert phenomena that account for preparing and programming an action; and second, that these overt and covert phenomena share the same neural mechanisms.

Mental manipulation of motor images

The first assumption relies on a large body of experimental work on the use and manipulation of representational information. Results obtained in the field of visual imagery can be mentioned first. The classic Shepard and

Metzler experiments provide evidence that the information stored in visual images preserve the metric spatial properties of the represented objects. In these experiments pairs of three-dimensional shapes were shown to the subjects. One of the shapes was rotated by an angle that differed at each presentation; subjects had to compare it with the one shown in the canonical orientation and decide whether they were the same or different. The time taken by subjects to respond increased with the angle of rotation of the target shape. This relation was interpreted by the authors as due to mental rotation of the target by the subject until it matched the orientation of the other shape (Shepard & Metzler, 1971; see also Paivio, 1978). In other words, the represented shapes were mentally manipulated just as if they were real three-dimensional objects.

In a more recent experiment based on the same premises, Georgopoulos and Massey (1987) explored the time needed by subjects to prepare movements at various angles from the actually shown direction of a visual target. This procedure implied that the subjects had to build up a representation of the direction of the mental target before performing the movements. It was found that the reaction times for these movements increased proportionally with the size of the angle. The authors' interpretation was that subjects mentally rotated the movement vector until the angle of rotation corresponded to the size required, before executing the reaching movement. They estimated the rate of rotation to be around 400°/s.

Interestingly, Georgopoulos, Lurito, Petrides, Schwartz, and Massey (1989) successfully transposed this paradigm to monkeys. In animals trained to move a handle at given angles with respect to the direction of a target light, they recorded from a category of neurons located within primary motor areas, the discharge of which was known to increase prior to goal-directed movements in a given direction. Each of these neurons can be characterized by a preferred vector along which its discharge is maximum. Georgopoulos et al. computed the population vector (by summing the individual vectors encoded by several neurons) in relation to movements directed at visual targets, including the condition where the monkey had to make movements in a direction different from that of the visual target. In the latter condition they found that the direction of the population vector changed in advance of the movement itself. The vector progressively rotated from the direction indicated by the visual target to the direction of the intended movement.

These results demonstrate that the time to process mentally a change in the direction of a movement is a function of the amplitude of the change. This relation is similar to other temporal relations that have been formalized under the heading of Fitts' law, which predicts the duration of a movement as a function of the difficulty of the task (Fitts, 1954). Fitts' law was once considered an effect of temporal constraints on the processing of reafferent visual feedback during movements. In fact, more recent interpretations stress the fact that Fitts' law is already embedded into the action-generation mechanisms and that it pertains to central rather than peripheral stages of the motor process (Meyer, Smith, Kornblum, Abrams, & Wright, 1990). Thus, if imagined and real actions are effectively governed by the same principles, the temporal relations found during actual execution should also be found during motor imaging and motor preparation. An experimental test of this prediction is proposed here later on.

Further interest in the mental manipulation paradigm as a tool for investigating mechanisms of action preparation arose from chronometric studies by Kosslyn, Ball, and Reiser (1978). These researchers asked subjects to memorize complex visual stimuli (e.g., a map of an island) and to generate mental images of these stimuli. Then they instructed the subjects to travel mentally on the map between landmarks. They found that travel time (as inferred from the times when subjects reported that they had "arrived" at the prescribed point) increased linearly with the distance to be mentally scanned. This result, like those of the mental rotation experiments, suggests that processes underlying mental movements within visually represented space might be similar to those underlying actual movements in physical space. In a replication of the Kosslyn et al. experiment, Denis and Cocude (1989) found that the time taken to travel mentally between landmarks on the memorized map was closely similar to the time taken to actually scan between the same landmarks on the real map.

The similarity of timing between mental and actual performance seems to be generalizable to many different types of actions. Earlier, in 1962, Landauer had compared the time taken by the subjects for reciting the alphabet (or a series of numbers) aloud and for thinking it to themselves. He found that overt and implicit recitations took almost the same time. Landauer concluded that "it seems that one does not think words and numbers appreciably faster than one can say them aloud, suggesting that the two behaviors may involve much the same central processes," (p. 646). Decety and Michel (1989) reached the same conclusion in comparing actual and mental movement times in a graphic task. The time taken by right-handed subjects to write their signature (or a piece of text) was the same whether the task was executed actually or mentally. The same temporal invariance was found, although overall movement duration was increased, when subjects used their left hand. Another interesting finding was that it took the subjects the same time, both actually and mentally, whether they wrote the test in large letters or in small letters. This behavior conforms, in the case of real movements, to the so-called isochrony principle (see Viviani & Terzuolo, 1980). It is thus important for the theory that the same organization principle was maintained in the case of mental movements. The time limitation in motor performance, especially in complex tasks like reading or writing, is apparently not due to execution factors; instead, it is related to the mental phase of the process.

Involvement of common neural mechanisms in motor imagery and motor preparation

The second assumption is that the similarity of motor preparation and motor images reflects a similarity of neural mechanisms. This assumption is supported by results of neurophysiological experiments in the field of visual perception and visual imagery. Studies of evoked potentials or mapping of brain metabolic activity in normal subjects have shown quite convincingly that the distribution of brain activation during visual imagery is the same as during visual perception. Observations in patients have shown that brain lesions affecting perceptual processes also affect imagery in the same modality (for a review, see Farah, 1989). In the motor domain confirmatory arguments can be drawn from experiments using functional mapping of regional cerebral blood flow (rCBF). This technique has shown cortical motor areas to be activated during a mentally imagined sequence of movements. The pattern of cortical activation, which includes the premotor areas and the supplementary motor area, is strikingly similar to that observed during actual execution of the same sequence of movement. The only marked difference between the two situations is that the primary motor cortex is activated only if movements are actually executed (Roland, Skinhoj, Lassen, & Larsen, 1980).

In a recent experiment Decety, Sjöholm, Ryding, Stenberg, and Ingvar, (1990) demonstrated that, in addition to cortical areas, the cerebellar metabolism also increased by about 20% during motor imagery. This result suggests that many of the structures that are normally involved in generation of motor output are activated during motor imagery. It could be that this activation has a "priming" function for the motor pathways, in anticipation of their use during real execution. This hypothesis might explain the success of the mental training methods that have been used empirically for more than 10 years, particularly in sports (e.g., Mendoza & Wichman, 1978; for a review, see Decety & Ingvar, 1990; and Swets & Bjork, 1990). Mental practice seems effective in improving physical performance, and its advantages are enhanced if physical and mental practice are interspersed.

A partial experimental verification of the hypothesis

These assumptions lead to several specific predictions. First, in accordance with some of the foregoing results, the time to travel mentally to places in memorized space and the time to travel physically to the homologous places in actual space should be similar. This prediction was tested in an experiment in which we compared the durations of movements actually performed with those of the same movements mentally represented. A simple walking task was used: Blindfolded subjects were asked either to walk or to imagine themselves walking to previously inspected targets. A second prediction is that one should be able to identify, within motor images, parameters that are normally encoded in motor programs. To test this prediction, a second experiment using the same walking task was performed. In this case, however, an extrinsic constraint was imposed on execution of the task. Subjects carried a heavy load while they walked, both actually and mentally, so that they had to produce a greater amount of force to perform the task.

The subjects in these two experiments were university students in physical education selected for their imaging ability. Different tests were given prior to the experimental sessions to evaluate the subjects' imagery ability, for example, the Movement Imagery Questionnaire (Hall, Pongrac, & Buckholz, 1985). All subjects scored as good imagers.

The first experiment (Decety, Jeannerod, & Problanc; 1989) was conducted on a running track in an outdoor stadium. Three white marks, 5 m apart, were traced on the ground with white chalk. Subjects' starting position on the track was such that their distance from these targets could be either 5, 10, or 15 m. Starting position was varied from trial to trial. At the beginning of each trial, subjects were allowed to look for 5 s at one of the targets. After being blindfolded, they were instructed to construct a mental representation of the track and the target. Finally, after another 5-s delay, they were asked either to walk at a normal pace to the target and to stop when they thought they had reached its location (actual walking condition) or to imagine themselves walking to and stopping at the target (mental walking condition). Conditions and target distances were randomly distributed in order to avoid block effects. Walking times were measured in both the actual and the mental walking conditions. Subjects held an electronic stopwatch in their right hand. They switched the stopwatch on when they started to walk (actually or mentally) and off when they stopped. Walking time was read directly from the stopwatch by the experimenter. Subjects were given no information on their spatial or temporal errors.

In the actual walking condition, walking times increased with the distance covered. In the mental walking condition, walking times were very close to those in the actual walking condition (for the same subjects and corresponding distances). The similarity of the two distributions of walking times was confirmed statistically. When the mean values of travel time for the actual and mental walking conditions were plotted against each other for each target, intrasubject linear correlation coefficients ranged between $r = .89$ and $r = .99$. The first prediction, namely, that actual and walking times should be within the same range, was thus supported. The fact that walking times increased with target distance, in both the actual and the mental walking conditions, replicated and expanded the results obtained by Denis and Cocude (1989) in their visual scanning experiments.

The fact that walking times were invariant across actual and mental conditions raises an important question. By analogy with the arguments of several authors (e.g., Pylyshyn, 1973; see also Mitchell & Richman, 1980;

Richman, Mitchell, & Reznick, 1979), it might be suggested that the subjects had tacit knowledge of what *should* happen when they walked mentally for longer distances, namely, that duration of the action should increase. If this were the case, the observed temporal invariance would be due simply to a strategy of the subjects (i.e., to replicate in the mental condition the temporal sequence registered in the actual condition). One possible way to answer this question is to introduce an external constraint on the motor task, so that the subjects would have to produce a greater effort to execute it. If time is the only variable represented in the motor image, this external constraint should not affect the duration of the imagined action. If, on the other hand, other variables, like muscular force, were represented, then the durations of the imagined and the actually executed movements should differ, because the constraint would exert its effect only in the actual condition and not in the mental condition.

A second experiment was thus performed with the same subjects and the same setup as the first. A 25-kg weight was placed on the subjects' shoulders in a rucksack. Subjects were placed on the track and were instructed to look at one of the targets for 5 s. Then they were blindfolded and were requested either to walk and reach the target location (actual walking condition) or to imagine themselves walking to it (mental walking condition).

Walking times in the actual walking condition with the 25-kg load were in the same range as those measured in the same subjects in the actual walking condition of the first experiment. By contrast, travel times in the mental walking condition with the load were significantly increased (by 30% or more) in all subjects and for all target distances. Finally, it is interesting to note that subjects spontaneously reported in the mental walking condition a strong *sensation of effort* that they felt to increase with the distance of targets.

The results of this second experiment showed a clear disssociation between actual and mental walking times. It took longer to carry mentally a 25-kg load to the target than to actually perform the task. Because actual walking times remained virtually the same as without the load (as shown by comparing data from the same subjects in the two experiments), the difference between actual and mental times was entirely due to an increase in the mental time. This result validates the ensemble of results obtained in the two experiments. The similarity of actual and mental walking times obtained in the first experiment disappeared in the second one, showing that subjects were not merely replicating the durations they had experienced in the actual walking task.

These results raise the issue of the relation between motor images and the mechanisms subserving actual execution. In the first experiment the time needed to perform the task mentally was the same as that needed to actually execute it. This seems to suggest that there is no discontinuity between the mechanisms responsible for mental performance and those for physical execution. Executive movement structures would thus be subordinate in the hierarchy to a higher level at which every preplanned action sequence is represented. The content of these higher-level mental structures should logically be the same whether the executive structures are activated or not. The results obtained in the second experiment, however, seem to conflict with this model. In carrying a load, the mental walking times were found to be longer than the actual walking times. How are we to account for this difference?

When the subjects carried the load, they may have centrally programmed a greater force to overcome the resistance. In the actual walking task this increase in force resulted in maintaining the same speed as without load. In the mental walking task, however, the increase in encoded force was not used to overcome any resistance because subjects did not actually walk. The exaggerated sensation of effort that they reported may have been the subjective correlate of this increased force specified by the program. This interpretation does not yet account for the increase in subjective movement *duration* when the load was present; the link between encoded force and encoded time is still missing. It may simply be that subjects "read" the increase in felt force as an increase in felt movement duration. Whatever the final explanation, this finding stresses the fact that not only time but also other parameters related to the force of the action are represented in motor imagery.

Other findings, showing changes in vegetative functions during motor imagery, seem to support this interpretation. Decety, Jeannerod, Germain, and Pastene (1991) reported that vegetative variables related to effort (e.g., heart rate, total ventilation) increase during motor imagery. This increase was proportional to the mentally represented effort. This effect can be considered as a response pertaining to the normal pattern of activation that occurs during motor programming. The central programming structures evidently anticipate the need for energetic mobilization required by the planned movement, just as they anticipate the amount of activity needed in the motor pathways for producing the movement (see Goodwin, Mc-Closkey, & Mitchell, 1972).

Possible models for central representational systems

Having shown some of the implications of a centralist theory of action generation for the structuring of the self, I now want to discuss the nature of the representational systems from which action originates. The main point at this stage is to determine the degree of autonomy of the central part of a physiological system that generates movements of an endogenous origin. Several modalities of functioning for such systems will be examined, ranging between complete "closed" systems without autonomy of the central stage and "open" systems with different degrees of independence with respect to the external milieu (see Jeannerod, 1990).

Motor representations as references

It is hard to conceive of motor devices that would be entirely driven by external events. Even the simplest feedback regulation models seem to imply a minimal amount of representation of their internal state. This notion was already familiar to engineers (if not to biologists) in the early part of the nineteenth century. Regulation of steam engines (by governors) implied a reference state that the system was supposed to reach and maintain. Later, biological systems were also described in terms of this mode of functioning. C. Bernard, in his lessons published in 1878, made the point that systemic regulations were circular mechanisms aimed at maintaining constancy of the internal milieu. Regulation of blood glucose, for instance, was based on constancy of glycemia (the reference state) at a level corresponding to metabolic needs. When glycemia dropped below this level, processes were activated to restore the reference state. This mode of regulation can be schematized as based on a (genetically) predetermined representation activated by receptors and controlling effectors.

This idea of self-regulation (inherent in the later concept of homeostasis) was used to explain many different physiological functions. It was Pfluger who first expressed the idea that even reflexes in spinal animals were "purposive," in the sense that they were apparently organized so as to preserve the integrity of the animal organism in response to aggressions (see Jeannerod, 1983). It is now well established that such reflexes as pupillary response to light, postural reactions, the vestibulo-ocular reflex, and others are produced by self-regulating systems; they are compensatory responses to discrepancy between their reference state and their input stage.

It is a matter of discussion whether this mode of control, which seems valid for reflexes, can also apply to individual voluntary movements. Bernstein (1967) considered that, in actions like prehension, a required position of the limb was established by the command apparatus and compared during execution to its actual position as detected by the sensory receptors. The error between the actual and the required values was used as a driving signal to the muscles until the system self-stabilized. This model was similar to that which Craik (1947) had designed for actions like tracking a moving target by hand. In such situations, according to Craik, the human operator behaved as an intermittent correction servo, where errors with respect to the reference were corrected by small ballistic movements.

It is common sense, however, that voluntary movements should be relatively independent of feedback signals and should be directed at individual goals rather than governed by fixed global references. The terms *goal* and *reference* are used here tentatively to express different degrees of teleonomic involvement and to indicate that, whereas reflex movements are clearly executed in fulfillment of a supraordinate function, voluntary movements have a greater autonomy with respect to biological needs and, therefore, with respect to external or internal stimuli. I wish to make a radical distinction between two types of representational systems. A first category would be systems with low-level representations (or references), limited to self-regulating mechanisms. The functioning of such systems is based on automatic correction of errors with respect to their central reference, as is the case for reflexes. Another category would be systems with higher-level representations (or goals), endowed with self-organizing properties. Their functioning is based on endogenous generation of goals for action. The final section of this chapter is devoted to discussion of models that could fit this definition.

Motor representations as autonomous processes

The concept of self-organizing systems postulates that motor representations are autonomous mental constructs. The nature of such constructs is, admittedly, still a matter of speculation. Hierarchical structures similar to those of computer programs are often used to conceptualize action plans. Actions are represented as sequences of steps involving tests and operations (see Miller, Galanter, & Pribram, 1960). Norman and Shallice (1980), for instance, assume that specification of the components of actions is carried out "by means of numerous memory schemas, some organized into hierarchical or sequential patterns, others in heterarchical or independent parallel (but cooperating) patterns" (p. 5). In this concept, any given action sequence is represented by an organized set of schemas, with one – the source schema – serving as the highest-order control and activating the other component schemata for the individual movements of that action. When a given source schema has been selected, component schemata are controlled by horizontal and vertical processing threads. Horizontal threads determine the order of activation of the component schemata and thus specify the structure for the desired action sequence (although vertical threads determine activation values for these schemata). Activation values involve attentional control, motivational factors, and so on.

The problem, however, is more with the nature of the representations than with their implementation. By analogy with the classic computational model that has been used in other domains of cognitive functioning, one could tentatively say that the content of motor representations (the action goals) is available in symbolic form. Action would then consist in retranslating the symbols contained in this representation. Accordingly, it has long been assumed that mental images are abstract propositional entities, neutral with respect to stimulus modality and response systems. This theory implies that there should be no difference in how perceptually based and verbally based information is represented and, therefore, that mental images would be best described as "sentencelike" expressions (for a discussion of this point, see Paivio, 1986). However, the arguments put forward by the supporters of the computational approach – for example, the fact that images can be generated by verbal description or can be described verbally by the subject who experiences them – are not sufficient to imply that these images are built in the same way as linguistic propositions.

An alternative view is that mental images (and, by extension, representations) derive from delayed interaction with the external world and are built from perceptual-motor experience. This implies that the information represented in mental images should be modality-specific, instead of amodal as is assumed by the computational theory. Mental images could be conceived as analog (as opposed to digital) representations, isomorphic with perceptual information (see Paivio, 1986). This would account for the proximity of mechanisms of motor images and motor programs that has been postulated in this chapter, and, in addition, would preserve the notion of an autonomy of representational systems with respect to direct influence of the external milieu.

The discussion here concerning the role of representation-driven actions in structuring the self would, therefore, fit into the classic motor theory of cognitive structure, a theory "which maintains that movement or its sensory consequences are a constituent element of a mental process, such that the process would not exist or would have different qualities, had the motor component been absent" (Scheerer, 1984, p. 77). Because actions stem from a preorganized (even if relatively rudimentary) system of representation, they impose their structure on afferent information created by the movement. Afferent information, in turn, will reinforce the representation from which the movement originated. Classic experiments, such as that of Held and Rekosh (1963), have lent support to this theory, by showing that shape adaptation (compensation for curvature produced by prisms) is contingent on active involvement of the subject during the perceptual process (for a discussion, see Gyr, Willey, & Henry, 1979). This result provides the missing link between neural contingencies, such as afferent information, sensory consequences of movement, and motor engrams, and the representation that the self builds and maintains about the external world. Elucidating the content of the initial representation and the rules that govern its expression is a fascinating prospect for future research.

REFERENCES

Bell, Ch. (1826). On the nervous circle which connects the voluntary muscles with the brain. *Philosophical Transactions of the Royal Society of London, 116,* 163–173.

Bernard, C. (1878). *Leçons sur les phénomènes de la vie.* Paris: Baillère.

Bernstein, N. (1967). *The coordination and regulation of movements.* Oxford: Pergamon.

Brodal, A. (1973). Self-observation and neuro-anatomical considerations after a stroke. *Brain, 96,* 675–694.

Craik, K. J. W. (1947). Theory of the human operator in control systems. I. The operator as an engineering system. *British Journal of Psychology, 38,* 56–61.

Decety, J., & Ingvar, D. H. (1990). Brain structures participating in mental simulation of motor behavior. A neuropsychological interpretation. *Acta Psychologica, 74,* 13–34.

Decety, J., Jeannerod, M., Germain, & Pastène, J. (1991). Vegetative response during imagined movement is proportional to mental effort. *Behavioral and Brain Research, 42,* 1–5.

Decety, J., Jeannerod, M., & Problanc, C. (1989). The timing of mentally repre-sented actions. *Behavioral and Brain Research, 34,* 35–42.

Decety, J., & Michel, F. (1989). Comparative analysis of actual and mental movement times in two graphic tasks. *Brain & Cognition, 11,* 87–97.

Decety, J., Sjöholm, H., Ryding, E., Stenberg, G., & Ingvar, D. (1990). The cerebellum participates in mental activity: Tomagraphic measurements of regional cerebral blood flow. *Brain Research, 535,* 313–317.

Denis, M., & Cocude, M. (1989). Scanning visual images generated from verbal descriptions. *European Journal of Cognitive Psychology, 1,* 293–307.

Duchenne de Boulogne, G. B. A. (1855). *De l'électrisation localisée, et son application à la pathologie et à la thérapeutique.* Paris: Baillère.

Farah, M. (1989). The neural basis of mental imagery. *TINS, 12,* 395–399.

Fitts, P. M. (1954). The information capacity of the human motor system in controlling the amplitude of movement. *Journal of Experimental Psychology, 47,* 381–391.

Gandevia, S. G. (1982). The perception of motor commands or effort during muscular paralysis. *Brain, 105,* 151–159.

Gandevia, S. G. (1987). Roles for perceived voluntary motor commands in motor control. *TINS, 10,* 81–85.

Gandevia, S. G., & McCloskey, D. I. (1977). Changes in motor commands, as shown by changes in perceived heaviness, during partial curarization and peripheral anaesthesia in man. *Journal of Physiology, 272,* 673–689.

Georgopoulos, A. P., Lurito, J. T., Petrides, M., Schwartz, A. B., & Massey, J. T. (1989). Mental rotation of the neuronal population vector. *Science, 243,* 234–236.

Georgopoulos, A. P., & Massey, J. T. (1987). Cognitive spatial-motor processes. *Experimental Brain Research, 65,* 361–370.

Gibson, J. J. (1966). *The senses considered as perceptual systems.* London: Allen & Unwin.

Goodwin, G. M., McCloskey, D. I., & Mitchell, J. H. (1972). Cardiovascular and respiratory responses to changes in central command during isometric exercise at constant muscle tension. *Journal of Physiology, 226,* 173–190.

Grüsser, O. J. (1984). J. E. Purkinje's contribution to the physiology of the visual, the vestibular and the oculomotor system. *Human Neurobiology, 3,* 129–144.

Grüsser, O. J. (1986). Interaction of efferent and afferent signals in visual perception. A history of ideas and experimental paradigms. *Acta Psychologica, 63,* 3–21.

Gyr, J., Willey, R., & Henry, A. (1979). Motor-sensory feedback and geometry of visual space: An attempted replication. *Behavioral Brain Sciences, 2,* 59–94.

Hall, C., Pongrac, J., & Buckholz, E. (1985). The measurement of imagery ability. *Human Movement Science, 4,* 107–118.

Held, R., & Rekosh, J. (1963). Motor-sensory feedback and the geometry of visual space. *Science, 141,* 722–723.

Helmholtz, H. von (1867). *Handbuch der physiologischen Optik.* Leipzig: Vos.

Henderson, W. R., & Smyth, G. E. (1948). Phantom limbs. *Journal of Neurology; Neurosurgery, and Psychiatry, 11,* 88–112.

Holmes, G. (1922). The Croonian lectures on the clinical symptoms of cerebellar disease and their interpretation. *Lancet.* Reprinted in C. G. Phillips (Ed.), *Selected papers of Gordon Holmes* (pp. 186–247). Oxford: Oxford University Press, 1979.

Holst, E. von, & Mittelstaedt, H. (1950). Das Reafferenzprinzip. Wechselwiskungen zwischen Zentralnervensystem und Peripherie. *Naturwissenschaften, 37,* 464–476.

Jackson, H. (attributed to). (1875). Psychology and the nervous system. *British Medical Journal, 2,* 462–463.

James, W. (1950). *Principles of psychology.* London: MacMillan. New edition, New York: Dover, 1950.

Jeannerod, M. (1983). *Le cerveau-machine. Physiologie de la volonté.* Paris: Fayard. English translation, *The brain machine: The development of neurophysiological thought.* Cambridge, MA: Harvard University Press, 1985.

Jeannerod, M. (1990). The representation of the goal of an action and its role in the control of goal-directed movements. In E. L. Schwartz (Ed.), *Computational neuroscience* (pp. 352–368). Cambridge, MA: MIT Press.

Jones, E. G. (1972). The development of the "muscular sense" concept during the nineteenth century and the work of H. Charlton Bastian. *Journal of the History of Medicine and Allied Sciences, 27,* 298–311.

Kosslyn, S. M., Ball, T. M., & Reiser, B. J. (1978). Visual images preserve metric spatial information: Evidence from studies of image scanning. *Journal of Experimental Psychology: Human Perception Performance, 4,* 47–60.

Landauer, T. K. (1962). Rate of implicit speech. *Perceptual and Motor Skills, 15,* 646.

Laszlo, J. (1966). The performance of a simple motor task with kinaesthetic sense loss. *Journal of Experimental Psychology, 18,* 1–8.

Lewes, G. H. (1879). Motor feelings and the muscular sense. *Brain, 1,* 14–28.

McCloskey, D. I., Colebatch, J. G., Potter, E. K., & Burke, D. (1983). Judgments about onset of rapid voluntary movements in man. *Journal of Neurophysiology, 49,* 851–863.

McCloskey, D. I., Ebeling, P., & Goodwin, G. M. (1974). Estimation of weights and tensions and apparent involvement of a "sense of effort." *Experimental Neurology, 42,* 220–232.

McCloskey, D. I., & Torda, T. A. G. (1975). Corollary motor discharges and kinaesthesia. *Brain Research, 100,* 467–470.

Mach, E. (1906). *Die Analyse der Empfindungen und das Verhältniss des Physichen zum Psychischen* (5th ed.). Jena: Fischer.

Maine de Biran, F. P. (1807). De l'aperception immédiate (mémoire de Berlin). J. Echeverria (Ed.). Paris: Vrin, 1963.

Mendoza, D. W., & Wichman, H. (1978). Inner darts: Effects of mental practice on performance of dart throwing. *Perceptual and Motor Skills, 47,* 1195–1199.

Meyer, D. E., Smith, J. E. K., Kornblum, S., Abrams, R. A., & Wright, C. E. (1990). Speed-accuracy tradeoffs in aimed movements. Toward a theory of rapid voluntary action. In M. Jeannerod (Ed.), *Motor Control and Representation, Attention and Performance, XIII* (pp. 173–226). Hillsdale, NJ: Erlbaum.

Miller, G. A., Galanter, E., & Pribram, K. H. (1960). *Plans and the structure of behavior.* New York: Holt.

Mitchell, D. B., & Richman, C. L., (1980). Confirmed reservations: Mental travel. *Journal of Experimental Psychology: Human Perception Performance, 6*, 58–66.

Neisser, U. (1976). *Cognition and reality: Principles and implications of cognitive psychology*. San Francisco: Freeman.

Norman, D. A., & Shallice, T. (1980). Attention to action: Willed and automatic control of behavior. *Human information processing Technical Report No. 99*, San Diego: University of California. Reprinted in G. E. Schwartz & D. Schapiro (Eds.), *Consciousness and self-regulation*. New York: Plenum, 1986.

Paivio, A. (1978). Comparison of mental clocks. *Journal of Experimental Psychology: Human Perception Performance, 4*, 61–71.

Paivio, A. (1986). *Mental representations: A dual coding approach*. Oxford: Clarendon.

Penfield, W., & Boldrey, E. (1937). Somatic motor and sensory representation in the cerebral cortex of man as studied by electrical stimulation. *Brain, 60*, 389–443.

Perenin, M. T., Jeannerod, M., & Prablanc, C. (1977). Spatial localization with paralysed eye muscles. *Ophthalmologica, 175*, 206–214.

Phillips, C. G. (1986). *Movements of the hand*. Liverpool: Liverpool University Press.

Pylyshyn, Z. (1973). What the mind's eye tells the mind's brain: A critique of mental imagery. *Psychological Bulletin, 80*, 1–24.

Richman, C. L., Mitchell, D. B., & Reznick, J. S. (1979). Mental travel: Some reservations. *Journal of Experimental Psychology: Human Perception Performance, 5*, 1, 13–18.

Roland, P. E., Skinhoj, E., Lassen, N. A., & Larsen, B. (1980). Different cortical areas in man in organization of voluntary movements in extrapersonal space. *Journal of Neurophysiology, 43*, 137–150.

Ross, H. E., & Bischof, K. (1981). Wundt's view on sensations of innervation: A review. *Perception, 10*, 319–329.

Scheerer, E. (1984). Motor theories of cognitive structure: A historical review. In W. Prinz & A. F. Sanders (Eds.), *Cognition and motor processes*. Berlin: Springer.

Scheerer, E. (1987). Muscle sense and innervation feelings: A chapter on the history of perception and action. In H. Heuer & A. F. Sanders (Eds.), *Perspectives on perception and action* (pp. 171–194). Hillside, NJ: Erlbaum.

Shepard, R. N., & Metzler, J. (1971). Mental rotation of three-dimensional objects. *Science, 171*, 701–703.

Sperry, R. W. (1943). Effect of 180° rotation of the retinal field in visuomotor coordination. *Journal of Experimental Zoology, 92*, 263–279.

Sperry, R. W. (1950). Neural basis of the spontaneous optokinetic response produced by visual inversion. *Journal of Comparative Physiology and Psychology, 43*, 432–489.

Swets, J. A., & Bjork, R. A. (1990). Enhancing motor performance: An evaluation of "new age" techniques considered by the US army. *Psychological Science, 1*, 85–96.

Vallbo, A. B., (1973). Muscle spindle afferent discharge from resting and contracting muscles in normal human subjects. In J. E. Desmedt (Ed.), *New developments in electromyography and clinical neurophysiology: Vol. 3. Human reflexes, pathophysiology of motor systems, methodology of human reflexes* (pp. 152–262). Basel: Karger.

Viviani, P., & Terzuolo, C. (1980). Space-time invariance in learned motor skills. In G. E. Stelmach & J. Requin (Eds.), *Tutorials in motor behavior* (pp. 525–533). Amsterdam: North-Holland.

Waller, A. D. (1981). The sense of effort: An objective study. *Brain, 14*, 179–249.

5

The ecological self in historical context

FRANKLIN C. SHONTZ

This chapter relates the concept of the ecological self, as described in Ulric Neisser's "Five Kinds of Self-Knowledge" (1988), to research and theory on the perceptual and cognitive aspects of body experience, particularly as these concern self-awareness. By and large, the relationship is established by adopting a historical perspective, describing a context and line of continuity that integrate that corpus of research and theory with many of the topics discussed in this volume.

Two ecological psychologies

J. J. Gibson

According to Neisser, "The ecological self is the self as perceived with respect to the physical environment: 'I' am the person here in this place, engaged in this particular activity" (1988, p. 36). The concept of ecological selfhood has its origins in the theory promulgated by J. J. Gibson, that systematic flow patterns in the visual field contain sufficient information to specify the situations that give rise to them. These ideas were first proposed to explain visual perception (Gibson, 1950). They evolved into a more general ecological psychology that assigns objective existence to information that arises from the external world (Gibson, 1979; Neisser, 1990). Animals have evolved visual systems that take advantage of this "omnipresent veridical information" (Neisser, 1988, p. 37).

The optic flow field, along with contributions from touch and hearing, are said to be sufficient to localize the perceiving entity as an embodied observer, or ecological self. The embodied observer is also capable of bringing about changes in the environment. Consequently, the observer's awareness of existence is specified by what the observer sees of itself, what the observer feels, and what the observer is capable of doing when acting on the environment as a causal agent.

The ecological self is not to be thought of in phenomenological terms (Neisser, personal communication, October 25, 1990), presumably because informational flow fields are apprehended directly, without intermediation. Therefore, the ecological approach to understanding selfhood forgoes subjectivity. It does not advocate trying to see the world as the perceiver sees

89

it, from within. Rather, it seems to advocate examining the entire process of perception all at once. Thus, the concept of the ecological self makes the agent-observer a component of perceptual activity as a whole, and the object of theoretical interest seems to be the whole of that activity. What most obviously marks the approach as ecological is its insistence that the way to begin the study of psychology (not only of perception or selfhood) is to examine what takes place in the environment and not what takes place in the observer's head.

R. G. Barker

Roger Barker (1968), whose ideas were later elaborated by Schoggen (1989), developed a different kind of ecological psychology. Barker's form is concerned with understanding the influence of the natural environments, or settings, within which human behavior takes place. The all-important concept of environment is treated in molar fashion. Barker acknowledges that the environment contains physical and geographic features, but it "includes also the objectively observable *standing patterns of behavior* of people – that is, specific sequences of people's behavior that regularly occur within particular settings" (Schoggen, 1989, pp. 1–2; italics in original). Examples of settings that contain standing patterns of behavior are church services and baseball games. This form of ecological psychology is not concerned with the "I," with selfhood, or with awareness. The experiences of individuals are of no particular interest. Instead, the properties of the environmental settings within which stable patterns of behavior occur occupy the investigator's full attention.

Obviously, Barker's ecological approach to explaining behavior is more closely allied to social psychology than to the study of perception or cognition. On a metatheoretical level, it appears to resemble the Gibsonian approach in several ways, but the similtarities and differences between the two ecological psychologies have yet to be spelled out in detail.

Body schemata

H. Head

Many of the functions that Neisser attributes to the ecological self are similar to those that the neurologist Henry Head (1920, 1926) assigned decades ago to a hypothetical set of *body schemata* that presumably reside somewhere in the brain. Using analogies appropriate to the times, Head maintained that a body schema operates like a meter in a taxi. It does not function by inference, whether conscious or unconscious, but mechanically, in the way that a meter in a taxi converts miles into dollars and cents. Similarly, a body schema transforms or translates physical stimulation into perceptions of positions of body parts or locations of stimuli on the body surface automatically (i.e., without the mediation of thinking). When and if body perception comes into awareness, it is already charged with meaning.

As noted earlier, the theory of ecological knowledge of selfhood includes the idea that what a person sees and does contributes to the perception of the embodied self. In contrast, Head did not theorize about the self. He referred most perceptual and action functions to postural and topographic schemata. These schemata are somewhat like blueprints or diagrams of the body, but they are also responsive to situational changes. The operations of body schemata therefore account for perception of both the static positions and dynamic movements of the body and its parts in space.

Head provided a specific metaphor to describe intraorganismic activity. In the concept of the ecological self, however, the way in which environmental information is processed within the observer is not (or at least not yet) a topic for speculation. It is simply taken for granted. The Gibsonian approach, from which the idea of the ecological self was derived, has been criticized along those lines for being only a stimulus analysis (albeit a superb one), and for not specifying how stimulus information is used by organisms (Haber, 1985, p. 256). From an ecological standpoint, this criticism may miss the point because it artificially treats stimulus, organism, and presumably responses as well, as separate or separable entities.

M. Scheerer

Head trod the conventional path and theorized about what goes on within the observer. However, his theoretical approach was more neurological and mechanistic than cognitive or psychological. Martin Scheerer (1954) corrected this neurological bias by applying to the concept of body schemata, and to other similarly operating cognitive-perceptual processes, the term *silent organization*. Scheerer borrowed the phrase silent organization from Gestalt psychology, and he acknowledged the functional similarity of silent organizations to Head's concept of schemata. Scheerer did not claim that silent organizations are either neurological or mental. He characterized them as being "transphenomenal," but he presumably believed that they exist inside the person rather than in the environment. He typically argued either that the principles of cognition are transcendent to the mind–body distinction or that they are, in a phrase borrowed from Wilhelm Stern (1938), "psychophysically neutral."

Scheerer was a holistically oriented, field-theoretical, Gestalt psychologist who, in collaboration with Kurt Goldstein, spent years studying the functional adaptations of persons with central nervous system damage. Many of his theoretical ideas were inspired by his observations of the ways in which these persons adapted to their abnormal neurological states. Neisser dismisses pathological cases, such as phantom limbs and syndromes consequent to brain damage, because they are relatively rare and therefore presumably of little theoretical interest. This near indifference to pathology is consistent with the general tendency in the Gibsonian approach to stress the normal functioning of the adequate organism. Like Scheerer, however, many neurologists have tended to regard such syndromes as being paticularly important. These clinical investigators have often tried to arrive at a description of the structure and properties of the perceptual process, if not of the self. They have not typically been directly interested in observing intact perceptual systems operating within arrays of environmental information.

Heider's mirror analogy

The clinical neurological strategy seems consistent with the logic of an analysis of the perceptual situation published in 1930 by the psychologist Fritz Heider. In that analysis Heider, who was also a Gestalt psychologist, likened the perceptual apparatus (which he regarded as being one component of the more inclusive perceptual–environmental system) to a mirror. He argued that, as long as this mirror copies the environment exactly, it does not give information about its own properties, "only where the mirror distorts E [the environment] can one get information about properties of P [the perceptual apparatus] from the mirror image. This means that only when our perception is mistaken, only when it does not correctly reproduce the objects, can one obtain useful data for the study of the properties inherent in the system" (Heider, 1930/1959, p. 50). Heider's analysis sounds simplistic and mechanistic now because it refers to "apparatuses" rather than systems, processes, feedback loops, or programs, but only a few substitutions of more modern language would be required to bring it up to date.

Failure of the perceptual system to reproduce objects accurately often occurs in cases of central nervous system pathology. It also occurs in unusual perceptual situations, such as those that generate optical illusions, and in certain kinds of experiments in which personal states or environmental surrounds are constructed to isolate and manipulate a particular element or property of the perceptual process. Many neurologically inclined investigators have apparently accepted the idea that the incorrect reactions, which are given as responses to relatively simple stimuli by persons with impairments of the nervous system, reveal more about how the perceptual system functions than do responses to the same stimuli given by persons without impairments. Perhaps a dedicated Gibsonian would prefer to study the ecological conditions of normal perception first, but it is difficult to understand how an appreciation of selfhood, perception, or action can be complete without at some point taking a close look at the internal operations of organisms. According to Heider's logic, and apparently that of clinical investigators as well, the study of pathological cases is one important way that that can be accomplished.

It is not clear where or whether the self or self-awareness can be fit anywhere into Heider's analysis. Heider did not theorize much about the self, as such, nor was he concerned with the influence of pathology on perception. He was, I think, more concerned with describing the processes that could, in principle, be studied in the laboratory with experiments or demonstrations carried out on normal subjects.

The problem of veridicality

One problem with Heider's otherwise appealing reasoning is that it takes for granted the investigator's ability to recognize when the mirror is doing its job properly – that is, when a perception or judgment is veridical (accurate or correct) and when it is not. Many investigations, most notably those that deal with perceptual illusions, have amply demonstrated that even normally functioning perception does not always mirror the physical properties of objects or events accurately, or at least not univocally.

The very idea of veridicality seems to imply the possibility of finding an unequivocal standard of accuracy that is independent of the opinions of observers. If Heider's views were followed uncritically, certain lines of evidence might lead to the conclusion that, in situations where judgment and environment do not agree, something has gone wrong with the perceptual apparatus, that it is no longer behaving like a good mirror. The difficulty with this conclusion is that unequivocal criteria of perceptual accuracy are not as easy to come by as is often supposed. That is because the standard of physical accuracy, for which the mirror analogy is appropriate, is easily confused with the standard of cognitive adequacy, for which the mirror analogy is not appropriate.

It is one thing for an investigator to judge whether a response is accurate according to some easily measured physical standard such as length. It is another to judge whether a response is normal or abnormal in a statistical sense, pathological or healthy in a clinical sense, adaptive or maladaptive in an evolutionary sense, or functional or nonfunctional with respect to a specific purpose such as achieving rehabilitation goals for a patient with a stroke. Gibson's and Neisser's approaches evidently take the adequacy of perception by normal organisms in their environments for granted. Neither attempts to look at the objects, independently of the flow of information the environment as a whole produces. It is as if these approaches were willing to treat all bona fide responses of normal organisms as being accurate – as if they disregarded ordinary physical standards of veridicality, preferring normative standards or regarding all responses as being completely determined by the properties of the optic flow field without the possibility of error. Suppose that a person is provoked to fall down by a looming array of stimuli that poses no objective danger. Differences in definitions might enable some who follow the ecological approach to treat this as a veridical response (i.e., one that is truthful and not illusory), but others might not accept this interpretation.

If everyone actually behaved in the same way in the same situation, it might not be amiss to say that a perceptual or overtly behavioral response is veridical simply because it occurs. But even in contrived experiments, where observers are exposed to optic flow fields that are similar for every subject, individual differences are bound to appear and beg to be explained. Persons with certain forms of pathology, especially to the central nervous system, can be counted on to increase intersubject response variability greatly in almost any situation. If such persons are regarded as being too rare to be relevant, the aberrant data they yield are likely to be treated as outliers and discarded even before results are analyzed. Such procedures would do nothing to increase knowledge of the ecological self.

The embedded self

With regard to self-perception, Neisser acknowledges that we do not perceive ourselves as perceivers or as isolated selves, but "as embedded in" the environment and as acting with respect to it. Fritz Heider's ideas are consistent with that view. One of Heider's main points was that one's frame of theoretical reference must be broad enough to encompass the scope and complexity of the perceptual–environmental system as a whole. It is equally important to recognize that experimentation on isolated variables is inadequate, because such experiments limit investigators to studying only one component of the system at a time. Perhaps Heider did not emphasize strongly enough the idea that this traditional way of carrying out experiments is inadequate to the task of examining the perceptual process as a whole. A primary principle of Gestalt psychology, and of the later systems approach, has always been that taking an element out of context, so that it may be examined in isolation, is like studying an organ in vitro rather than in vivo. Disembedding, or disembodying, an element for study does not merely isolate it but alters both it and the entire system within which it normally functions. There is reason to question whether studies of the functioning of units of artificially isolated or disconnected brain tissue (even if it is not pathological) reveal how those segments function when the brain is whole.

In general terms, the issue is whether research on separated elements provides a suitable model of self-experience in extralaboratory, so-called real-life settings. The answer is, probably not. The study of pathologies, as such, is similarly limited in its power to yield an adequate model of healthy functioning. However, as the contributions of Goldstein and Scheerer have demonstrated, holistic study of the functioning of *persons* who have patholo-gical conditions (which is quite a different topic) can be highly informative.

Awareness of self

Neisser states that the ecological self is not ordinarily conscious, or at least that it is not an object of thought. Once again, this is more than a little reminiscent of Scheerer's concept of silent organizations as hypothetical cognitive entities. If a silent organization were experienced, it would no longer be silent. If only part of it were experienced, the rest would be altered immediately by that act of perception. It is perhaps fair to regard the silent organizations of the body schemata as being components of a more inclusive perceptual field, which is equivalent to the whole system of the organism in the environment. Certainly, silent organizations should not be regarded as part of the environment or of the media that come between environ-mental things and perceptual responses.

Scheerer would not have been sympathetic with the strategy of developing experimental–analytical ways to study body schemata by manipulating in-dependent variables or by isolating parts or elements for investigation. Like Goldstein, he would have opted for examining the experiences of human beings naturalistically, in the conduct of their everyday affairs. Gibson and Neisser would perhaps agree with this approach.

Affect and motivation

Another feature of the concept of the ecological self is its complete omission of any consideration of the influence of affect. Also Neisser makes no men-tion of the dreaded "*m* word," *motivation*. He does mention affordances but does not note that, whatever the affordances may be in a given situation, those that are sought out by an animal that is hungry will differ greatly from those that the same animal seeks out during the rutting season. The affor-dances that are acted on by a person under the influence of lower-level moti-vations (physiological drives, safety needs) will certainly be different from those that are sought out by someone in search of love, esteem, or beauty of self-expression (Maslow, 1970).

Research on the perception of the body, the environment, or even more importantly, the self should not be carried out without remembering that among human beings, at least, perception, cognition, and behavior are usually engaged in for some reason. Often the reason is to satisfy some need, and that need is as much a part of the organism as are its perceptual and cognitive apparatus. Even if the topic of motivation is covered under the heading of some other kind of self-knowledge, its influence on the ecological self must be accounted for at some point in a comprehensive theory of selfhood.

Body image

Although no one knows exactly what the body image is, considerable interest has been shown in studying phenomena that presumably influence or are influenced by body-image variables. In summarizing recurrent themes that appeared in their edited volume on the subject, Pruzinsky and Cash (1900, p. 340) noted that one important idea appeared in practically every chapter of their book. It was that body-image experiences intertwine with feelings about the self. They also observed that body image is not a single cohesive entity but multiple, hence the use of the plural "body images" in the title of their book. In some discussions, they seem to use the singular and plural forms interchangeably. As a result the reader is left uncertain whether body image is to be thought of as a single entity with many facets, as many more or less independent agencies that work cooperatively together, or in some other entirely different way.

Perhaps the problem of understanding what body images are arises from an all too common tendency for psychological theorists to multiply hypothetical mental constructs when they learn that research outcomes have failed to come together in a simple way. Nearly all of the contributions to the volume edited by Cash and Pruzinsky show that the properties ascribed to the body image are determined mainly by the types of information the investigator has chosen to collect. Perhaps the understanding of body image might be enhanced if it were approached more in the way ecological psychology approaches selfhood. Someday an article may be written with the title "X Kinds of Knowledge of the Body Image." Perhaps X may turn out to equal five, and these kinds of knowledge may turn out to be similar to those proposed by Neisser regarding selfhood. Certainly the effort seems worth a try.

Some parallels

A cogent example of a possible parallel between body image theory and self theory appears in the way Neisser relates the ecological to the interpersonal self. Neisser notes that intimate personal contact may cause the ecological selves of the participants to go unnoticed. That idea calls to mind one of Seymour Fisher's ideas about the body image, that it serves within the personality as a boundary between self and environment (1986). It also calls to mind the psychoanalytic notion that the body image of one person may on certain occasions expand to incorporate the body image of another (Schilder, 1935).

Along similar lines, the contention that the private self is essentially independent of the ecological self fits well with a comment by Seymour Fisher and Sidney Cleveland (1958). In a study using Rorschach inkblots to study body boundary experiences (an aspect of the private self), they had been so strongly impressed by the influence of personality dynamics that they had virtually taken the physical body out of body image entirely. A review of Fisher's 1986 book added that they had apparently removed the image from it as well (Shontz, 1989). In any case, an extensive research project in the 1960s failed to reveal any reliable correlations between judgments of distances on the personal body and responses to a variety of tests of personality (Shontz, 1969). This project is described in the next section.

Judgments of distances on the body

Even when considered separately from the concept of body image, the experience of the personal body as an object in space with geometric pro-perties is particularly relevant to the ecological self. The personal body is the source of a flow of information that contains both variant and invariant properties. From this flow, as it relates to information with its source in the environment, emerge important components of knowledge of the embodied self.

A series of experiments on perception of distances on the personal body illustrates what may be learned by applying systematic methods to the study of even a limited aspect of body experience (Shontz, 1969). (An excellent summary of much of this research is available in Fisher, 1986, pp. 161–170.) The primary question was whether estimates of distances on the personal body display the same characteristics as estimates of the sizes or lengths of nonbody objects.

Most of the experiments used an apparatus on which subjects provided estimates of distance or length by adjusting the size of the opening between two movable "collars" that slid along a horizontal rod, placed at approxi-mately eye level. Estimates were produced using both descending (collars initially as far apart as possible) and ascending (collars initially touching at the center of the rod) procedures. Subjects, who were typically college students, were covered by a drape so that they could not see their own bodies. They estimated straight-line distances between designated points on their bodies. The standard stimuli were head width (straight through, from temple to temple), forearm length, hand length, foot length, and waist width (straight through at the belt line, as it would be seen in a mirror). Subjects also estimated the lengths or designated dimensions of nonbody objects. These were usually pieces of wood doweling, but some experiments used more complex stimuli, such as masks or pieces of plywood cut out to simulate the shapes of body parts, or stuffed cloth objects that were shaped like body parts. The dependent measure in all experiments was the ratio of estimated size to actual physical size (expressed as a percentage).

Estimates of distances on the body differed from estimates of the sizes or lengths of nonbody objects in several ways. Estimates of the body were more sensitive to starting position: Differences between estimates under descending and ascending conditions were consistently greater for distances on the body than for nonbody objects. Moreover, distances on the body were usually overestimated, whereas lengths of nonbody objects were usually underestimated. However, given the finding that all estimates were smaller under some conditions (e.g., ascending procedures) and larger under others (e.g., descending procedures), "overestimate" and "underestimate" have only relative meaning.

In percentage terms, variability was consistently higher among estimates of a set of body parts than among estimates of a range of simple nonbody objects. In general, responses to distances on the body were also less accurate. Typical scores for body-part size estimates showed errors of 10% to 20%, whereas typical scores for simple nonbody objects showed estimate errors of about 5%.

Percent error in estimates of the lengths of nonbody objects was systematically and negatively correlated with length. A negative correlation of this type could result if subjects made errors of about the same absolute size, regardless of stimulus length. No such correlation appeared in estimates of body-part size. Instead, these scores exhibited a consistent pattern that has not yet been satisfactorily explained. Regardless of experimental conditions, head width and forearm length were nearly always overestimated more (or underestimated less) than were hand length and foot length. Estimates of waist size were highly variable; in several experiments, though not all, women were found to overestimate waist size more than men.

Many additional experiments were carried out to determine the stability of these distinctive characteristics of body perception. The familiar pattern of error scores appeared regardless of the posture of the subject (standing or sitting), whether body parts were identified verbally or by touch, whether subjects could or could not see their bodies, and whether the apparatus was actively manipulated by the subject or was manipulated for the subject by the examiner (eliminating kinesthetic feedback). Nonbody stimuli that more closely approximated the sizes and shapes of body parts than did lengths of doweling were used in attempts to reproduce the distinctive error pattern for estimates of body part sizes, but these attempts were unsuccessful.

Two broad conclusions were drawn from this series of investigations. The first was that people are relatively less certain about the geometric properties of their own bodies than about the geometric properties of nonbody objects. This was a bit surprising. One might expect people to be highly familiar with their own bodies, because exposure to one's own body is virtually constant throughout life. The second conclusion was that perception of the personal body is driven more by central processes (e.g., body schemata) than by data provided by the contemporaneous stimulus situation. This conclusion seems to imply that recognizing an object as being a body part activates internal processes that are powerful enough to alter normal perceptual activity.

Fate of the recognition hypothesis

In later experiments (Shontz & McNish, 1972), subjects judged distances on their own bodies, on mirror images of their bodies, on the bodies of other persons, and on life-size drawings. These experiments supported the idea that the distinctive characteristics of estimates of distances on the personal body could be elicited by almost any optical input that the person consciously recognized as being human. This possibility was partially confirmed by Predebon (1980a, 1980b). However, it was given a new twist by a more systematically controlled experiment, which used stimuli that were deliberately constructed to appear relatively more or less human (Shissler, 1985). The stimuli were three 174-cm drawings that looked more or less like saguaro cactuses. The first drawing looked entirely like a cactus, the second was ambiguous, and the third looked much like a person. Subjects estimated "standard body distances," which were marked on the stimuli, and some estimated distances on their own bodies. It was expected that greater stimulus similarity to human features would produce correspondingly greater similarity of responses to those typically elicited by human figures. However, most of the typical features of personal body perception were evident in responses to all three stimuli, whether or not they were described or consciously recognized by subjects as human.

These findings seem to imply that, irrespective of recognition, the human organism is prepared to respond similarly to any optical arrangements with geometric properties that are minimally similar to those of a whole human being (not merely to a part of a human being). The person's responses are less consciously thoughtful and apparently more automatic than had been supposed by the first version of the recognition hypothesis. What remains to be determined are the essential features of the geometric arrangements that initiate this reaction. Perhaps this is a "Gibsonian" type of problem. Certainly, it seems relevant to an understanding of the ecological self.

Conclusion

It does not beg the question to say that every contributor to this volume agrees that body experience is important to self-knowledge. The ideas in Neisser's 1988 paper provide an excellent framework by which much of the work that has already been done by others on body experience can be organized. At the same time, a closer look at some of the ideas that have emerged from that work may well suggest beneficial refinements, expansions, and modifications of Neisser's views. Much more remains to be done at the levels of both theory and research.

REFERENCES

Barker, R. G. (1968). *Ecological psychology: Concepts and methods for studying the environment of human behavior.* Stanford, CA: Stanford University Press.

Cash, T. F., & Pruzinsky, T. (1990). *Body images: Development, deviance and change.* New York: Guilford.

Fisher, S. (1986). *Development and structure of the body image* (Vols. 1 and 2). Hillsdale, NJ: Erlbaum.

Fisher, S., & Cleveland, S. E. (1958). *Body image and personality.* Princeton, NJ: Van Nostrand.

Gibson, J. J. (1950). *The perception of the visual world.* Boston: Houghton Mifflin.

Gibson, J. J. (1979). *The ecological approach to visual perception.* Boston: Houghton Mifflin.

Haber, R. N. (1985). Perception: A one-hundred-year perspective. In S. Koch & D. E. Leary (Eds.), *A century of psychology as a science* (pp. 250–281). New York: McGraw-Hill.

Head, H. (1920). *Studies in neurology* (Vol. 2). London: Oxford University Press.

Head, H. (1926). *Aphasia and kindred disorders of speech.* Cambridge University Press.

Heider, F. (1930). Die Leistung des Wahrnehmungssystems. *Zeitschrift fur Psychologie, 114,* 371–394. Reprinted as The function of the perceptual system. In G. S. Klein (Ed.), *Psychological issues.* New York: International Universities Press, 1959.

Maslow, A. H. (1970). *Motivation and personality* (rev. ed.). New York: Harper & Row.

Neisser, U. (1988). Five kinds of self-knowledge. *Philosophical Psychology, 1,* 35–59.

Neisser, U. (1990). Review of James J. Gibson and the psychology of perception. *Contemporary Psychology, 35,* 749–750.

Predebon, J. (1980a). Length judgments of body parts. *Psychological Reports, 51,* 83–88.

Predebon, J. (1980b). Effect of body recognition on judgments of lengths of component parts. *Perceptual and Motor Skills, 51,* 879–882.

Pruzinsky, T., & Cash, T. F. (1990). Integrative themes in body-image development, deviance and change. In T. F. Cash & T. Pruzinsky (Eds.), *Body images: Development, deviance and change.* New York: Guilford.

Scheerer, M. (1954). Cognitive theory. In G. Lindzey (Ed.), *Handbook of social psychology* (pp. 91–142). Reading, MA: Addison-Wesley.

Schilder, P. (1935). *The image and appearance of the human body.* London: Kegan, Paul, Trench and Trubner.

Schoggen, P. (1989). *Behavior settings: An extension of Roger G. Barker's "Ecological psychology."* Stanford, CA: Stanford University Press.

Shissler, L. C. (1985). *The recognition hypothesis of body perception: Use of an ambiguous stimulus figure.* Doctoral dissertation, University of Kansas, Lawrence.

Shontz, F. C. (1969). *Perceptual and cognitive aspects of body experience.* New York: Academic Press.

Shontz, F. C. (1989). Review of S. Fisher. *"Development and structure of the body image. Volumes 1 and 2."* Psychoanalytic Psychology, 6, 503–507.

Shontz, F. C., & McNish, R. D. (1972). The human body as stimulus object: Estimates of distances between body landmarks. *Journal of Experimental Psychology, 95,* 20–24.

Stern, W. (1938). *General psychology from the personalistic viewpoint* (H. D. Spoeri, Trans.). New York: Macmillan.

6

Good intentions and dancing moments: Agency, freedom, and self-knowledge in dance

SONDRA HORTON FRALEIGH

The title of this chapter may seem like an assemblage of disparate terms, but I hope to show that they are all interrelated. My method of analysis is phenomenological – that is, it seeks to unravel the structure and values of a phenomenon, in this case, self-knowledge in dance, through reductive analysis. In order to avoid being sidetracked with an explanation of phenomenology, I will simply say that phenomenology is a descriptive method; it is also philosophical. Once embarked upon a phenomenological description, one is obligated to pursue the essence of the phenomenon, the thing in itself. Phenomenology aims to describe and define through a distillation of consciousness. In this sense, it is reductive. In focusing on self-knowledge in terms of dance, agency and freedom arise as important experiential values. They are intrinsic values in dance, aspects of the dancer's knowledge of, or perception of, *self*. Agency and freedom are interrelated aspects of dancing moments (those times when our intentions are realized in dance), and dancing moments are the basis for self-knowledge in dance. I will utilize the psychological concept of the "ecological self," from Ulric Neisser, the self directly perceived as it moves through, acts upon, and experiences its immediate environment. I have said nothing yet about the "good" in "good intentions." This will arise along the way, as I present brief arguments for the above.

Good intentions and dancing moments

First, I will pose several related questions that will guide my thinking. Do dancers engage in special actions that will lend them unique impressions of themselves? If so, who is a dancer, and when is dance happening? Should all people who engage in dance activities be called dancers? In my 20 years of teaching dance, I've had hundreds of students in dance classes – modern dance, jazz dance, social dance – and they ranged from novices to advanced dancers. Were all of them dancers? A few are now performing with professional companies. But how about the many others? I thought of them all as dancers, because they were giving attention to themselves as dancers.

Can we safely call some people dancers and other people non-dancers? A recent fashion trend dresses women on the streets in leotards and men

102

in jazz shoes, as though everyone wanted to look like (and maybe to be) a dancer. And why not? The image of the dancer once rejected through puritanical modesty is now acceptable for emulation. Dancers represent overt and often covert sexiness and sensuality, and easy fluidity of body, an expressive body both strong and graceful, but above all aesthetically vital (given various cultural preferences), sometimes mysterious and enigmatic, charged with energy and life. Who wouldn't want to have such a body image, self-image? Actors have it, with emphasis on a dramatic-emotional body image. And athletes have it too, given emphasis on strength and "can-do," mastering bodily tests and contests. But dancers face thin air. They hold no bats and balls. Unlike athletes, their movement does not serve competitive values. There will be nothing to win, nothing to lose. And, unlike actors, dancers don't express themselves through words. Dancers expect their bodies to speak imaginatively, metaphorically, through motion.

Who, then, is a dancer, when is dance happening, and how do we know ourselves through dance? We are aware that some people are more talented dancers than others. These are the people who come to epitomize dancing, and so we call them dancers, notwithstanding, that to dance, to move free of every care and encumbrance, is the birthright of all. I want to argue that dancing depends on realization of intent. Even professional dancers have moments when they say the dance happens or it doesn't. "I really dance," Josephine Endicott told me in an interview about her solo in Pina Bausch's *Rites of Spring*: "I really dance in 'Sacre,' I dance until I die" (Fraleigh, 1987). Dancers also have moments when they say: "It just isn't there," or "I can't feel it, I'm not getting it." They know something is missing, namely, the dance. All the moves are there, but the ingredients that turn movement into dance aren't realized. I may intend to dance but not fulfill that intent; something interferes with my good intentions. The subtle energy that "allows" the dance to happen is blocked. I go through the motions, but where is the dance?

Here is the crux of the problem: What we can know of ourselves through dance depends on the fulfillment of our intentions in movement, on whether something occurs in the dancing according to intent that we recognize as dance. For intending to dance is intending to do something more than just move. Dance is more than movement. It is movement done with an aesthetic intent. Aesthetic intent is also apparent in form sports such as diving, gymnastics, and figure skating, but is subordinated to competitive and testing intentions (except when sports movement is removed from competition and done purely for pleasure). To value movement aesthetically is to value it for itself, its intrinsic affective qualities. Dance movement has its own reasons for being, intrinsic to the dance and its purpose: theatrical, ritual, social, and the like. I realize that the term *aesthetic* has no currency in many cultures, but the principle of the intrinsic value of movement in dance does exist cross-culturally when fully understood. Most basically, the aesthetic refers to the affective, the entire realm of feeling and sentience. All dance pays attention to movement and its affective power.

The following is a summary description of the intentional basis of dance, stated phenomenologically (in terms of self-evidence):

When I dance, I am subtly attuned to my body and my motion in a totally different way than I ordinarily am in my everyday actions. That is, I seldom take notice of my ordinary comings and goings. I'm either in a rush, just getting things done, or maybe couch potatoing, trying to get going. The point is, I'm not really paying much attention to my movement. I'm just doing it (or not, as the case may be). But when I dance, I am acutely aware of my movement, I study it, try out new moves, study and perfect them, until I eventually turn my attention to their subtleties of feeling, and meaning. Finally, I feel free in them. In other words, I embody the motion. When I make any movement truly mine, I embody it. And in this, I experience what I would like to call "pure presence," a radiant power of feeling completely present to myself and connected to the world. This could also be described in other ways, but I think dancing moments can be named. These are those moments when our intentions toward the dance realized.

Self-knowledge in dance

Such moments provide the basis for a certain kind of self-knowledge, immediately perceived knowledge, an awareness that can nevertheless be described as something known by the dancer through experience. The self known in dance is the self perceived through kinesthetic flow with respect to intent, the self present in its immediate environment, the self oriented in present time, or the "ecological self" as psychologist Ulric Neisser has defined this aspect of the self. This is the self alive to the moment, the self that sees, feels, and knows its own motion. Of the five perspectives on self that Neisser has established, the ecological self directly pertains to the immediately perceived self known in the context of action and its effectiveness. This self is "an embodied actor as well as an observer, it initiates movements, perceives their consequences, and takes pleasure in its own effectivity" (Neisser, 1988, p. 39). Because dance movement is aesthetic (done for itself and its intrinsic values), the dancer is aware of her movement: She initiates it, perceives its consequences, and takes pleasure in her own effectiveness as she moves. She is directly attuned to *agency* as an avenue of self-knowledge. The experience of a "controllable body" is a principal aspect of the ecological self (Neisser, 1988, pp. 39–41).

Intention and agency

Of a particular performance, professional dancer Laura Glenn stated: "I just remember feeling powerful. I had a sense of being at one with the space around me" (Salem, 1988). One of the values of dance (dancing moments) is the experience of being in control of one's body. Or, stated more in tune with the nondualistic concern of phenomenology for the unity of self and body: The dancer is not simply in control of his body; when his intent is fulfilled, *he is his body*. He is an agent. The dancer is one with his body-of-action when intent is fulfilled. The nondualistic perspective of phenomenology is that intention does not precede movement, it is part of it. This view is explained most succinctly in Gilbert Ryle's *Concept of Mind*, (1963). I am speaking of intention in terms of actions undertaken, not of those purely mental processes (intentions to do something in the future) that may or may not happen. I refer to intention as it applies to intentional motion.

Paul Ricoeur is the phenomenologist who has best explained the nature of intentional motion. In his *Freedom and Nature* (1966), he explains that intention signals decision and consent, as well as motion. Moreover, these are not separate phases. When I move my body, I decide to do so, and I consent in the motion. I am not divided against my own action. I consent in it. I move "in good faith" with my intentions. Decision and consent are assumed in intentional motion; they are aspects of intention. This is so even in those times when I am awkward, when my intentions are not fulfilled, when something interferes with the kinetic flow of my motion, my consent in the flow, or my good intentions toward it.

In dancing, I open myself to feelings of being inept and to feelings of agency. But it is the latter, the experience of agency, that characterizes dancing moments. These are moments of controlling, or I would rather say "owning," one's body, of feeling completely at home in the world, as surroundings meld with bodily sensations of belonging. In dance, I feel and pay attention to my own movement, as I articulate it, directing and allowing its emergence. Urgency, or even the faintest flutter of motion are both mine, as I experience my powers of movement expression. I come to know the space – time of my dance, exactly where it goes in space, the length of its phrases, its pulses, its stretching, coiling, windings and unwindings. I know its stillness, its barely thereness, as well as its explosions. I own all of the feelings that these motions and stillnesses create in me, as I own my self in motion, moving as I intend to.

When I move in good faith with my intentions, I am fully alive to my powers of motion. I am powerful in dancing moments, because I move with finite, yet gentle, control. The power and the control are the result of the right investiture of my energies in accord with intent. At this point, I am released from needing to control; control has been internalized, the movement made easy through practice. I no longer need to think about my movement, where it is going, what I am doing. I own my movement. (A curious thought, for how could I *not* own my movement? As a matter of consciousness, however, this is possible. I can sense that the movement doesn't feel right, is not really mine.)

Agency and freedom

Movement agency, given a gentle and not an ironfisted discipline, leads to something still more important to dance. The more the dancer experiences agency in motion, the more she is able to *let* rather than make the motion happen. In the broadest sense, to dance is to be free, to feel free and at ease in motion. The dancing moment connotes freedom; it appears when grace appears. Without grace, or we might also call this freedom, there is no dance. Grace appears and freedom is experienced in context of intention. Grace and freedom are not assigned to particular movement in dance, as is sometimes assumed to be the case. It is not the kind of motion that matters but, rather, the fulfillment of intention. The dancer who intends to drop suddenly to the floor can be just as free and graceful in that motion as the dancer who lets an arm float upward.

Grace in dance has been mistakenly limited in Western thought to the antigravitational grace of ballet, especially as this has been represented by the romantic ballerina who seems to float ethereally above the earth, escaping the physical earthly body. Likewise, the classical ballerina whose general orientation is upward and outward in her elevated toe shoe displays these classical qualities with a grace that Selma Jean Cohen defines as "effortless, seamless flow" (1982, p. 129). If grace were defined only on balletic terms, then earthbound barefoot dancing and percussive dancing, including much of African and East Indian dance, could never be called graceful. And neither could modern and postmodern dance. These genres have demonstrated that "grace and gravity are not antagonists" (Fraleigh, 1987, p. 99) and that grace may exist along a continuum of effort, from the understated elegance in the matter-of-fact efforts of Yvonne Rainer's *Trio A* to the acrobatic explosions and tumblings of the new Canadian aesthetic in such companies as O Vertigo and La La Human Steps.

It would be wrong, however, to assume that grace has no constancy across dance forms. I agree with Heinrich von Kleist, who portrays grace as absence of self-consciousness and movement from a gravitational center (1983, pp. 178–184), and with Henri Bergson, who describes the dynamic and temporal qualities of grace as ease of motion, "mastering the flow of time." The graceful dancer seems in control – therefore, in control of time and with it the future (Bergson, 1910, pp. 11–13). She is centered in the present but fully cognizant of the future, as one movement dissolves into the next. Ease in performance of any kind of movement (strong or light, angular or curvilinear) and mastery of time flow or the achievement of *spontaneity* when intention is fulfilled constitute the metaphysic (grace) of dancing moments (Fraleigh, 1987, p. 99).

There is a curious metaphysical intersection of agency and freedom in dance. Movement we call dance is certainly not "out of control" except in rare cases where this may be an intentional expressive device. But much so-called dance stops short of freedom and rests solely on the point of agency and control. Dance is free of deliberate doing. When we are dancing, we are moving "ourselves," and we "ourselves" are being moved. We have initiated an interaction between ourselves as we are immediately present in the motion and ourselves as we may be given to the motion, given up. That is, we may forget ourselves, get lost; the motion consumes the mover. The dance becomes larger than its controllable bodily elements. There can be a joyful release from the self and the perception of oneself as a finite limited body. This can provoke laughter or tears, and it doesn't matter whether the dancing itself is floating, finger snapping, foot stamping, slow and meditative, or fast and gyrating.

What matters to the dance is the release, as it takes on a life of its own, moving beyond boundaries of agency and control – exhilarating and enlightening – freeing the dancer from the limitations of self and self-control. The dance exists at this point of freedom, when the motion is *allowed* to emerge, not made to happen. This evaporation of the self is the central point of both art and religion, a point many artists are explicitly aware of. For instance, Butoh dancer Natsu Nakajima stresses "killing the self," or loss of self in her work (Nakajima, 1988). She strives "not toward art, but toward love."

To answer the original question: Yes, dancers do engage in special actions that will lend them unique impressions of themselves. In dancing moments, those times when the dancer moves in tune with intention, in good faith with the dance, he experiences the ecstasy of belonging to himself and being at home in his surroundings. The universe is his, for he does not feel at odds with it. His movement becomes an easy extension of space–time, for he is not divided against his own motion but has found the center of its kinetic flow. He experiences the satisfaction of personal bodily powers. Finally, he feels free. "Dancing freely," says the founder of Butoh, Kazuo Ohno, "means giving up the notion of oneself, reverting to the original memory of the body" (quoted in Masson-Sekine & Viola, 1988, p. 22). Freedom in dance is a metaphysical point in time when the dancer no longer dances the dance, but in a very Zen sense, the dance dances him.

Though this happening is intrinsic to dance as the dance and the dancer coincide, I believe the same phenomenon occurs in other activities. Csikszentmihaly (1988) refers to it in play, work, and creative activities as "flow." Certainly a writer's idea may overtake him, or an architect's design begin to direct his total vision, carrying him beyond his expectations. But in dance, as nowhere else, the person is engaged with her whole bodily being, moving through and with space–time for no other purpose than the aesthetic (affective) power of the motion. She moves for the moving; she dances for the dancing. The dancer experiences agency and metaphysical freedom in motion. She experiences bodily powers as pure powers, and is released from the limits of "self." She forgets herself and lives purely in the dancing moment.

Pure presence: Problems of imagination and interpretation

But is it quite this simple? How about the imaginative-metaphorical level of the dance? Does it complicate this purity, as dance is more than movement? It engages us in full gestalts of movement meanings: literal and nonliteral, ranging from the dramatic to the abstract. Dancing connects us imagistically and psychophysically to a larger universe of movement and meaning, one we can see and feel and one we can richly imagine. It extends from an immediate presence of perceptual awareness (call this physical) to a level of meaning that involves the imagination (call this mental), and reminds us of the inextricable link between them, a theme taken up by Mark Johnson in his book *The body in the mind* (1987). I like Trisha Brown's way of stating the connection between the physical body and the imagined in dance: "I have bones, and they hang down from my imagination" (1988). She acknowledges the operation of imagination in her dances, even though they are not symbolically imagistic, only vaguely referential, as is the case in post-Cunningham dance, which points to the intrinsic value of movement. All dance, whether nonreferential or symbolically denotative is imagistic, as it stems from our ability to give movement a visible form, a visible image.

The real movement we see and feel in dance has been created through an extension of the imagination. From all the possibilities arising in the making of a dance, the particular configuration of the dance arises: unique, distilled, and chosen, even if the method of choreography involves chance elements or improvised choices occur. The final version connects us to the choreographer's movement choices, his incorporation of creative imagination, whether the movement is carefully designed or spontaneously rendered. The manner in which imagination is inscribed in dance indeed connects us with the choreographer's entire aesthetic perspective or worldview. The dancer embodies and interprets the intentions of the choreographer and orients her own intention toward the act of dancing. I want to argue that the dancer experiences something of a dialogue between herself and the dance, including its imagistic-metaphorical level. And as she realizes her own intentions (that is, when she can do the dance as she interprets it), she experiences an exhilarating presence or freedom that might aptly be called "pure presence."

Let's consider this through a problem case. What happens when a dancer performs dramatic roles with values contrary to the experience of freedom? For instance, Martha Graham's solo figure in *Errand into the Maze* faces the "creature of fear"; she confronts the monster representing her own fears and emerges triumphant. There is a struggle toward freedom. In the process, much of her movement is anguished and restricted. Is it possible in such a dance that the dancer can still experience the satisfaction of "becoming the dance" and being free amidst the conflict?

To believe that the dancer is bound in her own consciousness to the struggle she embodies would be to subscribe to the self-expression theory of dance, that the dancer undergoes the emotions she portrays *realistically*, a theory now largely discredited in aesthetic theory and refuted in terms of dance theory by Adina Armelagos and Mary Sirridge (1977, pp. 13–24). Isn't the performer's problem to be both inside and outside the emotional elements of the dance? This is well understood in Japanese traditional theater (Kabuki and Nō, especially in the case of the onnagata when the actor denies his maleness to take on a female role). The performer denies self or moves beyond the specific self in order to be conscious of a difference between himself and his role (Hoff, 1985, p. 6). It could be argued that when the dancer-actor identifies completely with emotional elements, he is no longer portraying emotion but is living the emotion. The logical consequence of this is loss of control, breakdown. In awareness of portrayal, and in interpretation, lies artistry. This entails control and skill, much more than simple emotional outpour.

I believe that it is in this area of control and skill that the dancer experiences agency and freedom, regardless of the imaginative problem involved. There may indeed be some dances that inhibit feelings of freedom because of concept, as I experienced myself in doing a dance based on Mary Wigman's descriptions of her *Dreh Monotonie*. In this dance, I turned steadily in a circle for five minutes; thus, I had to cope with feelings of nausea, not freedom. But gradually I became accustomed to the continuous turning until I overcame the nausea and achieved the meditative free presence I sought. Josephine Endicott, who described to me her feelings of performing Pina Bausch's *Rites of Spring* in ecstatic terms, also told me that she felt burned out after 12 years of performing Bausch's emotionally charged Tanztheater works, not to mention the pain of dancing in high heel spike shoes much of the time.

There is obviously a limit to the extent of cases wherein the performer can realize the ideal of freedom in dance. In terms of performance, the subject is fraught with complexity. When I discussed these ideas with Butoh artist Natsu Nakajima, she spoke of freedom not only in terms of moving freely but also as a release of unconscious energies. In terms of working with restrictive movement or even brutal imagery, she said: "Often we come to freedom from the opposite side."

The metaphysical ideal of freedom is the rule and not the exception of dance. It defines dancing moments, even in the face of contrary examples and performance situations. Professional dancers are sometimes cognizant of this ideal. As Trisha Brown has put it: "Participation is rapturous for me"

(1988). It is easy to observe in the playful dances of children and even in the simplest of folk dances. But in theater dance, creative incorporation of the imagination lends the ideal of freedom a fortunate complication, for the dancer deals not just with the movement but with the motivational source, idea, or metaphor behind the movement, that which the movement will bring to mind and cause us (perhaps) to reflect upon. Thus the dancer has the opportunity to develop her expressive capacities, to communicate to others the meaning of the movement as she interprets it, a meaning that will be embodied in her movement and also interpreted by the viewer. In the interpretive process, the dancer's own imagination is extended and developed. The metaphysic of movement contains the metaphoric, as the dancer realizes and can communicate it, be it symbolic or abstract.

In this, there is also a freedom, a pure presence, because each dance (with its self-contained meaning) is a free essence. I describe this "pure presence" or "free essence" in view of space–time (because dance is a space–time movement image art):

As a dancer, I experience space–time as a continuum of my own motion when my consciousness is centered through realization of intent. As I move up, down, or in a turn, I feel the purity of these directions. The upward reaching arm continues beyond itself, and the turn opens and expands my volume. My motion is not restricted to time and place, thus it exhibits a "pure presence." My dance could be done anywhere, and its unique configuration would not change. I can depend on the fast parts being fast, no matter when or where I perform it. The up will always oppose the down of it, and the turn will always be round. If the dance is slow (infinitely slow like Japanese Nō or the patience of contemporary Butoh), I will stretch my lived experience of time to its limits, eking out every tiny gesture, magnifying the gesture nonetheless.

I experience time as a pure entity when I dance, because I create and control the time of my dance in my performance. The time of the dance, as the time present in any artwork, is a free essence. Arturo Fallico, in *Art and Existentialism,* has represented the pure or free essence of art as one of self-containment (1962, pp. 18–25). The artwork contains an inner structure of its own, however related or unrelated to the world from which it sprang. The time of the dance has its own inner coherence, free from the erosions of clock time. In other words, the dancer can bring back the time of the dance again and again (with slight variations depending on interpretation). But she cannot bring back yesterday or last year. They go the way of calendar or clock time.

The same holds true for space, as the dancer relates to it imagistically and orients her movement purely in terms of shape and direction. As a dancer, I experience space as a free essence and embody it imagistically:

I can touch the mystical four cardinal points. I can explore the further extent of my own bodily powers in every direction for the sake of extending my lived space alone. That is: There is no other purpose in my movement but the destination and purpose of the dance, because I am going nowhere outside of the dance and doing nothing in any functional, utilitarian sense. The movement of the dance will accomplish nothing beyond itself and its meaningful substance. The space of my dance may be as large or as small as I can conceive it to be. I can leap across continents, or fit into a tiny crevice. If I sway from side to side, back and forth, I may feel the foreverness of time and space alternating and repeating itself. My reach into space is not limited to the outer reaches of my own kinesphere. I can pluck the moon from the sky, recline with heavy restraint, giving slowly into the earth, like a sleepy lion, or become invisible, like a city when the lights go out. My state of being is limited only to my imagination, and the movement I create and experience imagistically, bodily, as an extension of my own free will and good intentions.

REFERENCES

Armelagos, A., & Sirridge, M. (1977, Fall). The ins and outs of dance: Expression as an aspect of style. *Journal of Aesthetics and Art Criticism, 36,* 13–24.

Bergson, H. (1910). *Time and free will* (F. L. Pogson, Trans.). London: Allen & Unwin.

Brown, T. (1988, April). Public address at SUNY Dance Festival, State University of New York, Brockport.

Cohen, S. J. (1982). *Next week Swan Lake: Reflections on dance and dancers.* Middletown, Wesleyan University Press.

Csikszentmihaly, M. (1988). *Beyond boredom and anxiety.* San Francisco: Jossey-Bass.

Fallico, A. (1962). *Art and existentialism.* Englewood Cliffs, NJ: Prentice Hall.

Fraleigh, S. H. (1987). *Dance and the lived body.* Pittsburgh: University of Pittsburgh Press.

Hoff, F. (1985, Spring). Killing the self: How the narrator acts. *Asian Theatre Journal, 2* (1), 1–25.

Johnson, M. (1987). *The body in the mind.* Chicago: University of Chicago Press.

Kleist, H., von. (1983). *Uber das Marionetten Theater.* In Marshall Cohen & Roger Copeland (Eds.), *What is dance?* (pp. 178–184). Oxford University Press.

Masson-Sekine, N., & Viala, J. (1988). *Butoh: Shades of darkness.* Tokyo: Shufunotomo.

Nakajima, N. (1988, July). *Butoh workshop: The primal body.* Paper presented at Dance and culture, conference of the Congress on Research in Dance, Toronto.

Neisser, U. (1988). Five kinds of self-knowledge. *Philosophical Psychology, 1,* 35–59.

Ricoeur, P. (1966). *Freedom and nature: The voluntary and the involuntary.* (Erazim V. Kohak, Trans.). Chicago: Northwestern University Press.

Ryle, G. (1963). *The concept of mind.* London: Hutchinson.

Salem, L. A. (1988). The Dancing Moment. Certification project, Laban Institute for Movement Studies, New York.

7

The primacy of the ecological self

MARJORIE GRENE

The starting point for these reflections is Ulric Neisser's essay "Five Kinds of Self-Knowledge" (1988), which I wish to challenge or, at any rate, to read with an emphasis differing from its author's.

During the semester preceding the conference for which this essay was prepared, E. J. Gibson conducted a seminar on the ontogenesis of the perceived self. At the head of her outline for the seminar, she placed a statement from J. J. Gibson: "To perceive the world is to coperceive oneself" (1979, p. 141). Accepting this maxim, I want also to reverse it: To perceive oneself is, except in very peculiar circumstances, to coperceive the world. As J. J. Gibson put it some pages earlier than the statement just cited, "We were created by the world we live in." Thus, to be aware of ourselves, I would say, is to be aware not only of a product of that world but also of aspects of the world that bear on its production.

Self-knowledge is fundamentally and inalienably ecological, and so is the object of such knowledge. Of course, as Neisser argues, there are a number of paths to self-knowledge: If I want to know who I am, I can consult my children, my colleagues, my tax accountant, my bathroom scale, my birth certificate, even, to a degree, my memory images or my aches and pains, and so on. Yet I doubt if it is different *selves* I thus (or any way) have access to but simply *my*self under different aspects. Basically, I am a precipitate, so to speak, of a flow of events that both locate and define me and that, reciprocally, I have helped to shape through my own activity. In the following discussion, I want to make several separable points about this kind of eco-logical self-definition.

First, who one is is also and very basically *where* one is. Eleanor Gibson has given psychological content to this statement in terms of the self as a place. Not only literally, however, but metaphorically, the self is *placed* at various, sometimes coordinated, sometimes conflicting areas in a culture. It is now more common to speak of social roles than of "one's place"; that phrase has Victorian overtones we would like to reject. But roles need a stage to be played on. They demand a place, or, where there are several roles, a number of places. The philosophical, and indeed psychological, tradition of what Neisser calls the "private self" has attempted, ever since the *cogito*, to deny this insight. It is time we in turn denied that denial.

Naturally, I cannot feel your toothache, and I cannot see the traffic light

112

precisely as you do if you are color-blind. Unless one is constantly racked by intense pain, however, such subjectivities form a relatively trivial aspect of oneself. Even Proust recalled the madeleine not only as a pure sensation but as a sensation with a meaning: Its recollection afforded him a moment of past time in all its reverberations. Perhaps I might even venture to suggest that for self-knowledge, or more generally for knowledge, sensation is so vastly uninteresting because, taken in itself, it undercuts affordances: It cancels out the relations, the potentialities, that make things and events of interest to us.

Second, if who we are is where we are, where we are includes not only being in a world of inanimate sights and sounds but being with our conspecifics in a shared (in our case) human environment. J. J. Gibson remarks at the very start of *Ecological Approach*:

> The surroundings of *any* animal include other animals as well as the plants and the nonliving things. The former are just as much parts of its environment as the inanimate parts. For any animal needs to distinguish not only the substances and objects of its material environment but also the other animals and the differences between them. It cannot afford to confuse prey with predator, own-species with another species, or male with female. (1979, p. 7; italics in original)

Such matters are dealt with, presumably, in the study of what Neisser has called the "interpersonal self." But, again, I want to ask: Is this *another*, other than ecological, self? Surely not. Other persons are parts of each person's environment; being with others is one aspect of being in a world. What's more, the *in* is crucially significant: It is not only a question of the relations of *A* to *B* and *C* but also of the social world that *A* and *B* and *C* together inhabit. To study interpersonal relations as causal links between isolated entities would be to risk losing that ecological aspect of social life.

Edward Reed, in his study on James Gibson (1988), quotes two notes of Gibson's, one from 1932 and one from 1960, that emphasize the being-in character of human sociality and of the human self as social. "Only in a group," Gibson wrote in 1932, "can a person *become* highly individualized"; and in 1960 he denied that the self is "inner" and "secret," remarking that it arises "in connection with group life," and that it is, moreover, "one of the most public aspects of personality" (p. 59). That is not to say, with Mead, that the self is a "social contrast effect" – that would be too atomistic and mechanical a view – but, rather, the groups in and through which a self comes to itself make it the self it is, as it in turn helps to constitute the groups.

Third, still with respect to the interpersonal self, even at the physical level – of surfaces, occluding edges, horizons, and so on – to which Neisser seems to be restricting his ecological self, consider how many of the structures and events involved are human, and therefore social, constructs. Recall the diagrams illustrating the optical information for self-perception in chapter

7 of Gibson's *Ecological Approach*: ego's (clothed) legs and left arm, feet resting on a footstool, placed in a room facing a window with various smaller artifacts visible, depending on how ego's head is turned: a plant, a lamp, a sofa, a television set, a bookcase, and so on. We have here not so much a species-specific as a culture-specific environment. Again, we are, both literally and metaphorically, where we are. Michael Polanyi used the term *indwelling* for this relation, extending the concept, appropriately in my view, to intellectual as well as strictly perceptual circumstances (Polanyi, 1969, pp. 134, 148–149, 220–221).

I shall return to "thought" and "perception" in a moment. Meantime, I would suggest (in summary of my second and third points) that if one wants to distinguish selves (as I, for one, do not), one should be speaking here of a social rather than an interpersonal self: Social structures are the essential framework for the relations between persons in societies.

Further – and this will take me to my fourth point – the ecological–social self *can* be studied, as the very existence of experimental psychology attests, at a cross section of the self's life history. But selves also endure over a period, usually, of some decades. Neisser distinguishes a self of longer duration than the space of one experiment as the "extended self," and for him, given his preeminence in that field of study, this self is primarily the remembered self. As my life history, however, I should think, "myself" will be constituted not just by the rather disorganized memories that now flit before me but by the pattern of my lived life from birth to death. Thus I would prefer to speak here, if I must distinguish selves, of the historical self. (It may be, by the way, that even memories occur because of some significant relation to the historical self. Eleanor Gibson has made this suggestion to me, though not in those words [E. J. Gibson, personal communication].)

On the other hand, it should be remembered that Neisser is in fact asking not so much about selves as about self-*knowledge*: and I suppose that for knowledge of myself through time, memory is a kind of preserver or recoverer of lost passages. But if I really want to know who I am, durationally as well as today, memory seems too close to the "private" self to serve as the sole, or even privileged, source of knowledge. I know my life history, or myself as a history, less through a collection of flashbacks than through a kind of moving picture in which I am still playing the lead. But that picture in turn is but a surface sketch, so to speak, of the four-dimensional flow through ecological–social space that constitutes me as this human, female, American, bad-tempered, aged, intellectual, short, fat, lazy animal. You may add your own adjectives; even – or perhaps better, especially – in a diachronic view, there is no privileged access!

Also, what Neisser calls the extended self does not seem, itself, to consist simply of memory images from here or there. He distinguishes between knowing how – remembered skills – and knowing that – more explicit, and less directly action-related, memory, I suppose. But even his knowing thats, in the examples he cites, are related, at one remove, to the learning of skills, and they are certainly social: how mommy bakes cookies, for example, or how daddy (bless his modern, well-trained heart) goes to buy diapers. These seem to be examples of a small person locating him – or herself in his-her environment, both social-personal and local-ecological. And it is through just such processes of orientation that the historical self is achieved.

A fifth point, however, in connection with my suggestion about the historical self: Of the adjectives I suggested for its characterization in my case, Neisser might object that most of them belong not to the extended self as he understands it but to what he calls the "conceptual" self, in the sense of my "self-conception." This is not, we should notice, the conceptual self in the sense of my concept *of* the self, which, of course, I must be able to apply to male, non-American, good-tempered, young, nonintellectual, tall, slender, energetic human animals, as well as to myself. Indeed, I find in Neisser's account some confusion about the distinction between these two notions: that is, the concept of a self as such versus one person's conception of his-or herself. But let me take self-conception, not concept of the self, as what is at issue here. Now, although I have to acknowledge that the self as reflected on is not identical with the self as lived, neither are there here two selves to be existentially distinguished. The self I recall, the self I know of as actor through time, is, yet once more, the ecological–social self, which, from very early in its explorations of its world, has come to include cogitative, that is, perhaps (I don't really know how to put this) more sophisticatedly cerebral and less purely perceptual, episodes. And these cannot be neatly separated.

J. J. Gibson distinguished between perception as tacit knowledge and knowledge mediated by language as explicit. But at the same time he insisted that the theory of information pickup had closed "the supposed gap between perception and knowledge." "To perceive the environment and to conceive it," he said, "are different in degree but not in kind. One is continuous with the other" (1979, p. 258). What they have in common, the same paragraph tells us, is "the extracting and abstracting of invariants." All knowing, perceiving as well as the most sophisticated scientific knowledge, in other words, consists in "an awareness of persisting structure" (p. 258). Awareness of persisting structure describes equally the child's recognition of a kitten and the physicist's recognition of a muon or a pion; the extracting and abstracting of invariants are equally characteristic of both cases.

Yet if knowledge is in fact continuous with perception, why do we persist in making a distinction of kind between "perception" and "thought"? "Our reasons for supposing that seeing something is quite unlike knowing something," Gibson explains, "come from the old doctrine that seeing is having temporary sensations one after another at the passing moment of present time, whereas knowing is having permanent concepts stored in memory" (p. 258).

Once we have shed this albatross, we can acknowledge that, again in Gibson's words, "knowing is an *extension* of perceiving." No one, so far as I know, has yet articulated adequately the philosophical implications of that acknowledgment. To do so would be to present a fully elaborated ecological epistemology. Perhaps Merleau-Ponty on the Continent and Polanyi in Britain came as close to such a view as any one could whose work antedated Gibson's (Merleau-Ponty, 1945; Polanyi, 1958, 1969). However, no one has yet assimilated Gibson's theory into a theory of knowledge as it needs to be assimilated if the triviality of most epistemological discourse and the fatuity of the so-called evolutionary alternative are to be overcome.

All I can do here, therefore, is to continue quoting from the *locus classicus* and to append a small example of my own. Gibson writes:

> The child becomes aware of the world by looking around and looking at, by listening, feeling, smelling, and tasting, but then she begins to be *made* aware of the world as well. She is shown things, and told things, and given models and pictures of things, and then insruments and tools and books, and finally rules and short cuts for finding out more things. Toys, pictures, and words are aids to perceiving, provided by parents and teachers. They transmit to the next generation the tricks of the human trade. The labors of the first perceivers are spared their descendants. The extracting and abstracting of the invariants that specify the environment are made vastly easier with these aids to comprehension. But they are not in themselves knowledge, as we are tempted to think. All they can do is facilitate knowing by the young.
>
> These extended or aided modes of apprehension are all cases of information pickup from a stimulus flux. The learner has to hear the speech in order to pick up the message; to see the model, the picture, or the writing; to manipulate the instrument in order to extract the information. But the information itself is largely independent of the stimulus flux. (1979, p. 258)

That is how all knowledge, perceptual as well as less obviously perceptual, arises and is structured. Thus any more abrupt distinction between "thought" and "perception" becomes inadmissible, nor is there a distinction of kind between tacit and explicit knowledge. Let me try to illustrate the latter thesis with an example from my own experience. I say I am American, and I know what that means. This is not an example, strictly, from perceptual experience, though of course it is related to it and presumably rooted in it. As a small child one learns to recognize the flag, one learns about maps and hears about other places people come from or go to, and throughout one's life one relies on the physiognomy of one's home landscapes and cityscapes to tell one where one is and where one belongs.

But there are also, as people keep telling us, if often in terms we dislike, attitudes (or beliefs?) inherent in being an American, and some of these, I, for one, discovered only when I lived abroad. These were aspects of myself that helped to constitute me, but I had not conceptualized them until I met their contradiction in the attitudes and beliefs of others in other societies. (I know I am cheating by bracketing "attitudes" and "beliefs" without asking what I mean by either or how they are related to one another; but I cannot begin to raise here all the philosophical problems implicit in this complex subject matter. So be it: attitudes or beliefs of others in other societies.) This knowledge of mine was indeed verbalizable, once I became aware of it, but it been a submerged and tacit aspect of my historical self before circumstances shocked me into formulating it. It had been, all along, tacit knowledge.

Thus the self-knowledge that one is American seems to be built of layers of perceptual–conceptual awareness, some, but not all of which, can be made explicit. Just as perceiving and conceiving the environment are different in degree but not in kind, so are perceiving and conceiving oneself. The conceptual self, in other words, like the social or historical self, is an extension or amplification of what is in the last analysis an ecological process with a structure that is best understood from an ecological point of view.

REFERENCES

Gibson, J. J. (1979). *The ecological approach to visual perception.* Boston: Houghton Mifflin.
Merleau-Ponty, M. (1945). *La phénoménologie de la perception.* Paris: Gallimard.
Neisser, U. (1988). Five kinds of self-knowledge. *Philosophical Psychology, 1,* 35–59.
Polanyi, M. (1958). *Personal knowledge.* Chicago: University of Chicago Press.
Polanyi, M. (1969). *Knowing and being.* Chicago: University of Chicago Press.
Reed, E. S. (1988). *James J. Gibson and the psychology of perception.* New Haven, CT: Yale University Press.

Part III

The interpersonal self and its implications

8

The self born in intersubjectivity: The psychology of an infant communicating

COLWYN TREVARTHEN

Introduction

The theory of interpersonal communication and its motives

In this chapter I shall analyze the condition of a human self around the time of birth, as seen when a baby is in communication with an other. Then I shall trace some important changes that have been recorded in the life of the communicating self through infancy.

Communication with persons is possible from birth, and we should not be surprised at this. It is in the nature of human consciousness to experience being experienced: to be an actor who can act in relation to other conscious sources of agency, and to be a source of emotions while accepting emotional qualities of vitality and feeling from other persons by instantaneous empathy. This interpersonal self, this person who breaks the private integrity of the ecological self, splitting its egocenter and reconstituting it as a part of a communication dipole or multipole, is fundamental to the human condition.

Nevertheless, our psychological tradition, observing the limited cognitive powers of the newborn and giving great value to the cultivated intelligence of an educated person, has assumed that the mind of an infant is incoherent, with undefined perceptions and incapable of contributing to communication, except to solicit help reflexively for biological functions. On the evidence from development, however, and from other everyday evidence, it would seem that the communicating interpersonal self is the very foundation for the cognitive or thinking self who will grow up to solve problems "in the head." The core of every human consciousness appears to be an immediate, unrational, unverbalized, conceptless, totally atheoretical potential for rapport of the self with another's mind.

In our research we have found in the primitive state of mind of a baby a readiness to be aware of a human presence and to follow and communicate with human mental states. We believe that it is from this activity of mind that the inspiration comes for the child's subsequent learning of socially constructed meaning (Trevarthen, 1987, 1992a; Trevarthen & Logotheti, 1987). The meaningful world is a consciousness of reality and its affordances that each of us shares with a community and a culture. Shared meanings are part of a long tradition of knowledge, as well as of common everyday sense. Each child is eager to learn this story of cultural life. But first the child has to be able to communicate mind work with those who already know and believe the story.

Even if the mind of a linguistically sophisticated adult may have an autonomous expertise in the mental re-creation of meaningful propositions "in one head," as many philosophers have assumed, this is evidently not the primary condition of our consciousness and thinking. A delicate and immediate with-the-other awareness comes first. Human self-awareness is thus one manifestation of mind in a person who is capable of being a companion and confidant to the responses of the other, at an emotional level, from birth. Infants communicate and think emotionally.

I shall review the evidence that an infant possesses motives and cognitive propensities that are specifically adapted to perceive, respond to, and influence how other persons feel and what they perceive and do. The newborn can seek perceptual information about other persons' motives; he or she will need this intersubjective information to regulate and develop his or her own communicative actions with a known other's assistance. Learning to know the mother's motives by listening to her vocal expressions, and to receive "instruction" from her motives, can actually begin in utero, even though the intersubjective contact must be extremely tenuous and virtually one-sided at this rudimentary stage (De Casper & Fifer, 1980; De Casper & Spence, 1986).

Motives to know persons

How do human beings *know* each other? For an empiricist, this is a question about how we take up, remember, and make sense of experience – how we get physical (nonmental) information about what other persons are and what they do. In order to answer this question, however, we must also consider the processes that make a person want to know other persons. What motivates communication? What are the active communication-seeking functions that give each one of us personal qualities that others seek to perceive? We have to entertain the idea that such other-seeking and other-satisfying properties of the mind could be innate, anticipating experience of others and promoting further communication with them.

The mental activity that seeks experience is accessible. Its motives can be observed. Anticipatory urges and feelings generated within each mind, in the form of attentions, intentions, and emotions, are projected outward in observable behavior. It is simply untrue that human mental states are unobservable, to humans. We can detect the mind states of other people instantly from their expressions, with no training. When we seek human company, the signals from our motives are offered in accentuated form, controlled by others' attention to us – and our interest is in meeting and mixing with the mind or person states that lie behind the signals that they make to us. Those expressions include the features we select to describe that general aspect of another person's consciousness called "personality." We detect evidence from their behavior for the *pro*-formation of their communication, their propensities for communicating. We know, or feel we know, what the other person is seeking from us and what that person is trying to offer us. At the same time, our own consciousness sets up essential conditions for the pickup of the necessary interpersonal *in*-formation about the person's motives and what they want to express.[1]

Ulric Neisser, making use of Gibson's (1966, 1979) theory, argued that perceiving must not be conceived divorced from action. He connected perception of objects with exploratory action by means of a "cognitive schema" (Neisser, 1976). But, though perception coupled to action happens over time, the word *schema* suggests a static pattern or plan that can keep a record in its shape. It has no efficiency of its own. It brings to mind something seen from outside and described, or "schematized." We need a term to designate an active process or system more closely identified with the life of the subject. *Program* is the term used in cognitive science and artificial intelligence, but this is a set of logical or mathematical instructions that determines how information is processed through the system, defining its input–output relations. Again we have a word that does not convey the inner generative and developmental aspect of psychological activities. A program, even one called generative, has to be written and then put into effect by some agency that delivers the right input language of energy and information to the programmable system. It is a rational, symbolic insertion.

Psychological activities, with other life activities, have their own agency: They are autopoetic, or self-creating, like a growing organism, and they generate both awareness and the action in it. The word *motive*[2] seems more appropriate to describe psychological functions that develop in the subject's mind in readiness for perceiving the information needed for acting. The innate releasing mechanism of von Uexküll (1957) and Lorenz (Eibl-Eibesfeldt, 1970; Tinbergen, 1951) is a motive, but it is defined as triggered or released by a "sign stimulus." We need a term that indicates, more directly, the psychological function that explores and that orients toward the consummatory response or goal.

"Motive," in the sense used here, designates a mental function that is a cause and director of movement and, at the same time, a seeker of information to direct and confirm movement – to make it work for a purpose (Trevarthen, 1978, 1982, 1984a). A motive causes a subject to be curious and exploratory, as well as purposeful and effective, to be prepared to react selectively to the information that will be taken up in perception and to seek immediate influences that are appropriate for direct, ongoing control of acts and their effects. The motive regulates what will be chosen for uptake in perception and for retention in memory. Motives originate in largely inaccessible cerebral activity, but because they generate a wealth of movements for aiming and focusing perception as well as for acting on the world (Figure 8.2), they are as real and readily observable as any regulatory principle in behavior. The central energy and self-regulating quality of motives are expressed in emotions.

Motives need perceptual information in their ontogeny, and minds choose experiences to learn and develop. They do not just passively change under the influence of stimuli to the senses, recording experiences indiscriminately. Furthermore, there is an inherent specialization, or modularity, in perception that originates in distinct systems of motives already adapted, through evolution, to generate and guide differing strategies of action and growth (Trevarthen, 1978). This modularity of motivation forms the basis for development of the differing cognitive abilities that have received much attention from psychologists recently (Fodor, 1983; Gardner, 1983). In general, however, these psychologists have sought to understand differences in the information processing function of various cognitions. They have not considered the underlying motives on which modules of perception, memory, and the like are built and integrated in the coherent consciousness and purposefulness of the self. In particular, motives for communication, that determine "intersubjective cognition," have many special aims, requirements, and emotional qualities.

Complementarity and equivalence of behaviors as evidence for coherent psychological motivation

Between the simple reflex movement to capture or cut off stimulation that seems a slave to the stimulus, and the unconscious twitch of a sleeper's muscle that seems completely free of sensory guidance or control, is a world of patterns of activity aimed into a future of sensory information. The causes of these behaviors are (1) within the prescient, information-seeking nervous system of the animal subject, (2) in the assimilable information that comes to perception out of the environment, and (3) in the flow of force and displacement through the muscles of the body that makes the perceptions necessary and effective as information about how to do what the mind is determined to do, or what had better be done.

Intelligent behavior is characterized by an enormous flexibility of goals and expression, yet it is coordinated or cohesive in each individual. The subject moves to execute integrated purposes or plans. These are determined by integrative functions of the brain working through efferent nerve activity and muscle action to organize and complement input factors of body mechanics and mechano-proprioception, in collaboration with the flow of supporting and guiding information from environmental stimuli (Anokhin, 1974). All the extracerebral sources of coordination from the body and from the world can contribute only if they are assimilated in appropriate form, timing, and strength to the motives that instigate behavioral action in a coordinated form (Bernstein, 1967).

Acts with the same effect can be performed by different parts or postures of the body. This "motor equivalence" has been demonstrated and considered theoretically, notably by Lashley (1951), Sperry (1952), Anokhin (1974), and Bernstein (1967). One can draw a shape in the sand with finger, toe, or nose. One can, somewhat gracelessly, sign one's name with a pencil in the mouth, or play a tune on the piano with one's nose. A conceived form of activity (motor image, or, better, motor scheme) is put into effect in the outside world by selection of a sequence of movements that may be one of a vast number of potentially effective ones. Motor equivalence and the coordination it manifests are not dependent on culture-sensitive symbolic mentation, and they are evident, in some degree, in many simple animals (Horridge, 1968).

There is a corresponding "perceptual equivalence" or transmodal awareness of phenomena. The same effect (the event–configuration in one time–space, referred to the same self at a single observation point) can be perceived through different modalities, as well as from different aspects in one modality (perceptual constancy). One can see a letter drawn in the sand and feel it with one's hand. The modalities are not equally competent for detecting a given event. The making of the letter might be heard if the sand were "squeaking" and one listened very carefully while the shape was being built – the steps of the act might be heard, although the persisting, motionless result is quite inaudible. But such differences in awareness of the effects of movement through different modalities are only biases, not absolute distinctions. The senses do not give incompatible perspectives on reality and they often supplement one another. Experience is generally coherent about one self, many invariant features being picked up by several modalities at once.

The coincident physical invariants of perception, such as the rhythm or intensity of all experiences generated by moving, inform several modalities in parallel about the actions of the single body acting from a single locus in time and space (Gibson, 1966). But, in addition, the central coordination or integration of behavior and experience also depends on the mapping of the body in one individuated neural system, a mapping that is fundamentally of embryogenic origin. (Trevarthen, 1978, 1985a), giving the active self a primitive coherence or unity. The excitatory output to the muscles is regulated by one neural conductor, or ecphorator (Bernstein, 1967), with a single time base coupling a coordinated set of motor impulse generators or oscillators (Von Holst, 1936, in Gallistel, 1980).

In short, there is an anatomical-physiological basis in the brain for the endogenous coordination that holds together all of a subject's behaviors and perceptions at any given moment. This determines how behavior and experience will evolve in time, with confirmation and guidance from exogenous perception of the environment. Prospective control is set up by this central motivation of the brain, and it carries the *organized generative parameters* of this motivation. The basic integrity and form of motives is created in the developing central nervous system before it becomes the receiver of input from the body and outside environment. It does not have to be constructed in the infant after birth by "mutual assimilation" or conditioning of reflex systems generated separately, as Piaget (1953) believed – though such processes of accretion and selection play an essential part in further differentiation and development (Fogel & Thelen, 1987; Thelen, 1985).

The coordinated motivation of a subject varies from moment to moment: (1) in the rate in time at which it is generated, (2) in its *energy or power,* and (3) in its spatial distribution or form over the body or in the modality of sensory information it is aimed to excite. Thus the coherence of motivation is expressed in regular *kinematic, energetic,* and *physiognomic* parameters of movement that are generated in the brain (Trevarthen, 1986a).

Symptoms of mental activity in communication: Emotions

Interpersonal selves possess motives that detect complementary motives in others and that require the responses of others. Our task is to define the motives for communication in preparation for tracing their condition at birth and how they develop in infancy.

For a partner mind seeking communication, the features of a subject's motivation become symptoms of the inner psychological activity of the individual who is generating and coordinating them (Trevarthen, 1986a). It is these core, transmodal features of motivation, coded as emotions and transferred from subject to subject in this form, that permit the inter-coordination of psychological states between subjects. Corresponding generative parameters in the two subjects enable them to resonate with or reflect one another as minds in expressive bodies. Their action patterns can become "entrained," and their experiences can be brought into register and imitated. These are the features that make possible the kind of affectionate empathic communication that occurs, for instance, between young infants and their mothers (Trevarthen, 1984a, 1992a).

Core motivating processes determine temporo-spatial patterns of exploration of enviromental affordances and the selective pickup of information to guide actions, thereby determining what will be learned and what can be remembered for later use. Communication of core motives by way of emotions can, therefore, enable one subject to influence not only the immediate perceptions and actions but also the learning, knowledge, and remembering of a partner. The appearance of efficient communication of motives in the first phase of an infant's postnatal life suggests that human learning is founded on a particular kind of curiosity, one that is designed to be regulated intersubjectively, between minds.

The ecological theory of person perception and intersubjective action

The psychological "self as agent" (Macmurray, 1961) perceives and acts in ways that are fitted to the real world's layouts, events, and objects (Brunswik, 1956; Gibson, 1966), discriminating their different and changing "affordances" (Gibson, 1979). As David Lee explains (see this volume), the acting self has to assume *prospective control* as it gears its movements to the environmental arena. On the basis of this prospective control, the active subject learns new cognitive interpretations and concepts of what can be in the world, what can happen, and what can be done. But note: The perceiving self alone in an inanimate world would not have to allow for any prospective psychological control outside its own, because no such control is generated in the geophysical world among its objects. Even physical processes that unfold, releasing or attracting energy in a self-regulating way – fires, avalanches, the weather, waterfalls, a drifting boat, alarm clocks – do not act prospectively. They may seem animate, making "behavior"; but, lacking minds, they do not conceive their futures. Such things have no motives, no cognition, and no power of complementary, evasive, or deceptive action. The physical world and inanimate objects do not act with a self's awareness and foreknowledge. Robotic machines are only partly exceptions.

Intersubjective encounters are quite different. They become psychological *intera*ctions, *between* selves, in which part of each subject's prospective control is estimating what the other subject is knowing and intending (Hamlyn, 1974). Here we are concerned with the special requirements of knowing and perceiving for intersubjective, *dual-prospective motor control* (Trevarthen, 1986a). The kind of perception needed is not proprioceptive or exteroceptive or exproprioceptive; it is *alteroceptive*. It seeks awareness of, and a potentiality for interaction with, another psychological being. It determines the experience of an interpersonal self.

Appropriate psychophysical experiments have demonstrated that human perceivers have remarkable sensitivity to animacy and intentionality, and that they can readily detect parameters of motivation in behavior, such as the "emotion" of an action or its "effort" and "vitality" (Johanssen, 1975; Michotte, 1962; Runeson, 1977). Similar perceptual powers exist in young infants, though they appear to be poorly understood by the contemporary "single-head" psychology of perception and cognition (Legerstee, 1992). But this ability to detect and observe qualitative differences in actions of others, and thereby to perceive their motives, is but a small part of the capacity for imitative identification, emotional empathy, and reciprocal communication that all humans possess. Most importantly, a communicating subject is trying to make an effective complementary reply; to enter into and jointly regulate a dyad of expressive, "conversational" exchange with the other. A motive transfer, and cooperative use of motives, are being sought.

Unique features of human communication

Intersubjective control (social intelligence) is, of course, not unique to humans. It originates well back in animal evolution and is adapted to serve communication and cooperative action, both within and between species. (The latter occurs, for example, in behavioral and emotional adaptations that regulate the balance of killing and escape between lions, and their ungulate prey in the Serengeti Plain.) Intersubjective communication clearly has been a boon to the evolutionary success and diversification of the species that possess it. It emerges as the principal factor in the phenomenal acceleration of the rate of evolution of bodies and brains in the last few million years, a process that has culminated in the explosive emergence of humans as the dominant life form (Wilson, 1985).

Human intersubjectivity should be contrasted with a social motivating capacity that is restricted to the mutual behavioral adjustment of self-serving acts, or acts that immediately serve group survival (Hurford, 1989; Lotman, 1979). Most animals exchange signals to cooperate in the performance of acts that are also, at the same time, changing each communicating subject's own physiological state or relations with things of the inanimate world. They communicate *coactively*, to coordinate what they are doing for themselves with partners that are prepared to act in a complementary or opposing way in a group – they are together locomoting, feeding, mating, caring for young, defending a territory, trying to catch and eat prey or to avoid being eaten. This is the level of behavioral coordination that Piagetian ethologists call "sensorimotor" (Chevalier-Skolnikoff, 1989). Species with a higher level of social intelligence have additional powers of estimating in more detail what other animals are conscious of or intending to do, and their societies have a sort of political organization or hierarchy of decision making and alliance formation (Byrne & Whiten, 1988; De Waal, 1982; Whiten, 1990). Some can even use signals to communicate some useful information about nonpresent items of interest, quasi-symbolically (Cheney & Seyfarth, 1992; Gouzoules, & Marler, 1985).

Human beings have an even more elaborate capacity for direct interaction with one another's motives, emotions, and perceptual processes, and this serves in effective and sustained *cooperative action*. Human powers for specifying, learning, and recording cultural (social, environmental, technical, and scientific) knowledge about nonpresent objects and events are unique, and human intersubjectivity has certain extra specializations for intense mutual regulation of motive states and joint action in the shared world. It has, moreover, an exceptional referential and narrative productivity, for being "about" something. At the same time, it is dependent on an intricate, direct interaction of the motives of actors who demonstrate personalities, obligations, roles, reputations, authority, expertise, and so on. It speaks in many sociocultural "voices" (Wertsch, 1991). Human communication is often closest between participants who are intensely interested in maintaining the interpersonal state of mind and in transferring ideas about nonpresent things.

It has recently been realized that the necessary communicative motives of a peculiarly human kind emerge very early in an infant's development, much earlier than developmental psychologists had assumed. As we shall see, "dialogic" motives (Bråten, 1988) take charge of cognitive growth before the child has control of action on objects or locomotion in the world, and they play a crucial role thereafter in the building of a child's thinking for him- or herself (Rogoff, 1990; Vygotsky, 1962). Even a young child just beginning to speak is expected to be able to understand that the people he or she lives with are sharing meanings – that is, quite arbitrary understandings about things, including concepts specific to items, persons, and events that are not immediately present. Such understanding is a prerequisite for learning language. If a child of age 3 is not speaking intelligibly and understanding what other people say, this is felt to be an unnatural tragedy, almost as frightening to the parents as if the child had contracted a fatal illness.

How infants, and their partners, behave in communication

The discovery of protoconversation

Communication between a mother and a young infant was first called *proto-conversation* by Mary Catherine Bateson (1975, 1979). Using films made by Margaret Bullowa (1979), she described 7- to 15-week-old infants focusing on the mother's face and voice and reacting with smiles and coos in a give-and-take, address-and-reply manner. Earlier, psychologists who looked at how young infants communicate had examined only parts of the behavior, observing the infant for reactions to stimuli, not the communication in the interactions (Spitz & Wolf, 1946; Ahrens, 1954; Fantz, 1963; Haith, 1966; Haith, Bergman, & Moore, 1977; Haith & Campos, 1977). Even when observing natural play, they were recording eye aim, and/or smiles, and/or vocalization, and/or sucking. Observations were made in artificial experimental or clinical situations where the infant was given limited opportunity to negotiate exchanges (Carpenter, Tecce, Stechler, & Freedman 1970; Papousek, 1967; Watson, 1972; Wolff, 1963). The impression was conveyed that the awareness of such a young human could be caught only with difficulty, and then a fragment of a reply would occur as a reflex response of part of the body. The psychoanalysts, some of whom were much more sensitive to the emotions in mother-infant communication (e.g., Fairbairn, 1954; Klein, Heinmann, Isaacs, & Riviere, 1952; Winnicott, 1960), described the mother's holding and identification, without seeing what the very young infant could do when it was fully playful and expressive.

Bateson's claim that the infant was doing something more mutual and cooperative (and potentially constructive for the learning of language and other cultural skills) received support as soon as further accurate descriptions were made of films of mother and infant at play. About the time of Bateson's first report there was good evidence that 2- or 3-month-olds were highly competent at a kind of miming of conversation, expressing not merely unitary emotional reactions to the mother's presence but entering an interaction, regulating the mother's behavior, and now and then attempting a complex of expressive movements something like an utterance (Bullowa, 1979; Stern, 1974; Trevarthen, 1974a, 1977).

The protoconversational cycle and its microanalysis

A protoconversation in full swing between mother and a 6- to 10-week-old has both a developing program of phases of excitement, building in intensity and complexity and then subsiding, and a refined micro-structure in which mother and infant exchange similar or matching contributions (Figure 8.1). It goes something like this:

The mother puts herself in a face-to-face situation, gently taking up the baby and placing it where it is well supported so that the baby's face is lined up with her own. She is, as Winnicott (1960) taught us, "maternally preoccupied", readily "in tune with" the infant's state of awakeness and orientation. She acts particularly quiet and soft if the baby is sleeping, calming if the baby acts distressed, friendly and inviting if the baby is attentive. Although many of her actions seem to be directed to obtaining close eye-to-eye contact, she leads with touch and voice, and she may use the "feel" of the infant's body, especially the hands, to sense awakening and readiness to be active. Her approach will almost always be vocal from the start, calling the infant's attention, but some mothers favor touching more.

The start of communication is marked by orienting of the baby. Babies 6 weeks or older focus on the mother's face and express concentrated interest by stilling of movement and a momentary pause in breathing. The infant's interest as a whole conscious being is indicated by the coordination and directedness of this behavior, which aims all modalities to gain information about the mother's presence and expressions. Hands and feet move and clasp the mother's body or her supporting hand, the head turns to face her, eyes fix on her, eyes or mouth, and ears hold and track her voice.

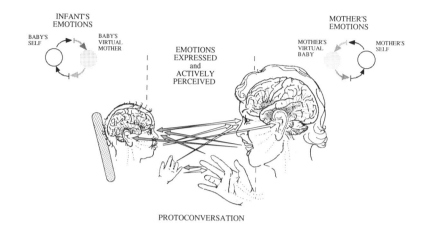

Figure 8.1. Channels of face-to-face communication in protoconversation, and three phases in the cycles of expression between mother and baby. Protoconversation is mediated by eye-to-eye orientations, vocalizations, hand gestures, and movements of the arms and head, all acting in coordination to express interpersonal awareness and emotions. Films for microanalysis of behaviors are made with the infant in a special chair and a front-surface mirror is used to observe the mother. Alternatively, two TV cameras are used. Infants perform a sequence of utterances separated by periods of watching the mother (cf. Figures 8.3 and 8.4).

The next, and crucial, phase is signaled by the infant's making a "statement of feeling" in the form of a movement of the body, a change in hand gesture away from clasping the mother, a smile or a pout, a pleasure sound or a fretful cry. The mother, if she is alert and attentive, reacts in a complementary way. A positive, happy expression of smiling and cooing causes her to make a happy imitation, often complementing or praising the baby in a laughing way, and then the two of them join in a synchronized display that leads the infant to perform a more serious utterance that has a remarkably precocious form.

This infant utterance is the behavior, in that context of interpersonal coordination and sharing of feelings, which justifies the term *protoconversation*. It looks and sounds as though the infant, in replying to the mother, is offering a message or statement about something it knows and wants to tell. Mothers respond and speak to these bursts of expression as if the infant were really saying something intelligible and propositional that merits a spoken acknowledgment. Typical utterances are: "Really?"; "Oh, yes!"; "That's right"; "Tell me a story"; "Oh, what a lot you have to say"; or, if the infant is just watching, "Aren't you going to talk to me?"; "Come on then." The infant appears to be led and supported by the mother's interest and sympathetic emotional response and by her short, periodic utterances of that unique register of speech now known as "intuitive motherese" (Fernald, 1985; Fernald & Kuhl, 1987; Papousek, Papousek, & Bornstein, 1985; Stern, Spieker, & MacKain, 1982).

I am here describing protoconversations that have been staged in a research laboratory with infants 6 to 12 weeks of age (see Figures 8.1 and 8.3). (Before or after this period the infants' playfulness and social sensitivity are different.) The mother is inviting the infant to perform, and she knows that the behavior is being recorded. Nevertheless, the circumstances are such that the experience is natural and pleasurable for her. It does not look like an acquired or rational performance. We do not know how often this kind of play occurs in the home with a 2-month-old, although some very good recordings of protoconversations have been made in homes. Charles Darwin noted important characteristics of a 45-day-old infant smiling socially (1872, p. 211). The mothers in the recordings we have analyzed are left alone with their infants in a quiet and pleasantly furnished studio. They act spontaneously, and they say they enjoy it.

The behaviors of African and European mothers with very different culture, language, education, and literacy, and the behaviors of their infants, support the conclusion that we are describing universal phenomena (Trevarthen, 1988). Claims by anthropologists that protoconversations are an artificial cultural form of play peculiar to middle-class Americans or Europeans who consciously train their infants to be talkers are not supported by adequate observations. It has been suggested that in some cultures infants are never spoken to in a protoconversational way (Ochs, 1983), but insufficient evidence is provided that when those observations were made the situation (for example the privacy or intimacy of the occasion), or the age of the infants, was appropriate for the behavior.[3] Practice of protoconversation may not be essential to the normal development of language. However, the motives revealed in protoconversations are probably essential in subsequent development of communication and thinking, as Bateson (1979) proposed. They certainly require appropriate support from others' communication.

A continuous microanalysis of the behaviors of protoconversation recorded on video, backed up by photographs, brings out what mother and infant are each seeking to perceive through different modalities and confirms their mutual coordination in time (Beebe, Jaffe, Feldstein, Mays, & Alson, 1985; Beebe, Stern, & Jaffe, 1979; Fogel, 1977; Mayer & Tronick, 1985; Trevarthen, 1977, 1979, 1985b). We can plot the searching and interlocking

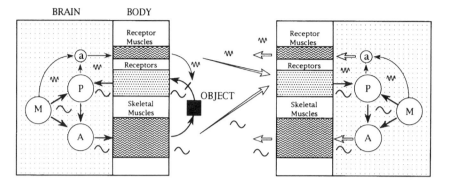

EXPRESSIVE
ACTOR/PERCEIVER   OBSERVER/IMITATOR

Figure 8.2. Motives and motor "gating" of perceptual information and the signals that pass between two subjects, an actor and an observer. Motives (*M*) direct acts (*A*) and motor adjustments of the receptors (*a*), and, at the same time, set perceptual systems (*p*) for uptake of information from receptors. Large acts of the body (*A*), including walking and reaching and grasping objects, have lower periodicities than anticipatory adjustments of receptors (a), such as saccadic eye movements or finger movements to feel objects. All movements can give information to an observer about the motives in an actor (Trevarthen, 1978, 1984c).

of two integrated perceptual-expressive systems, one of a person so young and untutored that we can be confident of picking up from that side a largely innate repertoire of expressions and sensitivities. The adult other appears to move to complement the set requirements of the infant's self. The observed patterns reveal the dynamic expressive motive impulse and the cycles of alerting and focalizing in receptivity that are innate in human communication.

The infant's orientations and attention to the mother

The moments of attention and directions of orientation of the infant's mind are marked by a great variety of organized movements, by which an infant in a quiet-alert state "gates" and aims uptake of perceptual information (cf. Figure 8.2). These include changes in posture of the body and limbs, which positions the chest and belly, head, face, and hands and feet of the baby in comfortable contact with the mother; the opening, orienting, and focusing of the eyes; movements of the muscles of the brows and lids around the eyes linked to stabilization and focusing of the visual image and to protection of the eyes, and opening and exploring movements of the nostrils, lips, tongue, and jaw; breathing; and the extension of the arms and opening out and grasping of the hands. These are the kinds of movements that Charles

Darwin explored so assiduously in his attempt to explain the evolution of expressions for communicating "states of mind." He thought the expressions came from "serviceable associated habits" that were originally voluntary and then became instinctive through repeated practice (Darwin, 1872).

Preferential orientation tests (mentioned below) have shown that even a newborn baby can detect approach of the mother and identify her as a particular individual, from her touch, odor, voice, or appearance. Having recognized her, the 2-month-old stills, stops fretting or crying, arrests or reduces breathing, or may start to breathe quickly, turns toward her, seeks to look at her face, focuses gaze on her eyes or mouth with the attentive expression called "knit-brow with jaw-drop" (Oster, 1978), touches or grasps with hands or feet, or orients the head toward her sounds. Some of these orientations and focusing movements are clearly visible and can serve as communicative signals; others, like pupil or lens movements in the eye, are harder to see. All act to favor improved visual, auditory, tactile, olfactory, and oral perception of the mother, within limits set by the immaturity of the perceptual apparatus of the baby. The infant is apparently capable of monitoring all the modalities mentioned, separately or combined.

If instead of seeking playful communication the baby is tired or distressed, and signaling need for attention to some internal physiological need or for comfort, then movements in the converse direction are made, to close and turn away the receptors of all stimuli but those associated with caretaking, warming, and caressing to calm. The distressed baby pulls away, threshes about, closes eyes firmly, and cries with rejecting (disgusted) movements of the mouth. The hungry baby avoids eye contact and roots for the nipple. The sleepy baby seeks support and a comfortable contact with the mother and closes mouth, hands, and eyes.

All these complex, organized movements can be related to exploratory, perception-seeking, or perception-avoiding, processes in the infant. Related movements, such as smiles, coos, and hand gestures, are manifest signals for the partner to perceive. The vocal apparatus of a young infant is relatively undeveloped, but it is capable of signaling subtle changes in interest and emotional state (Lester, 1984), including positive need for vocal-facial-manual interaction with the mother (Wolff, 1963). Newborns perceive the vocalizations of other babies as different from their own, and when they imitate crying, which Piaget (1962) assumed must be reflex "contagion," they in fact do so as if to join in communication with the other infant (Martin & Clark, 1982; Sagi & Hoffman, 1976). Some movements of the hands to touch the mother, or projected in complex turns, with finely individuated finger movements different from those made in "pre-reaching" directed toward objects (Trevarthen, 1974a, 1984c), and the accompanying kicks and pulling up of the legs with opening and contraction of the toes, also appear to have the potential to be communicative expressions. The facial expressions of infants, whatever their evolutionary origins, are obviously adapted from birth to indicate subtle shifts in emotion and need (Oster, 1978; Trevarthen, 1985b, 1992a).

Mothers (like researchers) give mutual visual contact high importance, but other responses, too, are dependable signs of a readiness for perceiving the mother and her expressions. A totally blind baby·can orient face and eyes toward a mother's voice, centering on her so well that the blindness can go undetected. Selma Fraiberg (1974) documented that mothers of blind babies can be misled by the baby turning to aim one ear toward her, to better locate her voice, the mother thinking her infant is looking away. They may also fail to respond to the expressive movements of the baby's hands. Mothers can use the tenseness and movements of the arm and hand to monitor the infant's state of alertness or emotion. I have noticed that in protoconversation most mothers unconsciously favor their infant's right hand when seeking contact (Trevarthen, 1986b). In short, orientations of any of the special receptors that are important either in exploration of objects or in communication (i.e., eyes, ears, mouth, or hands) offer a mother critical evidence about the pace and direction of information seeking by the baby, and they also transmit some positive signals for communication.

The mother's orientations and supportive behaviors

The behaviors of a mother seeking contact with her baby match, complement, and confirm the information-seeking or communication-seeking efforts of the baby (Trevarthen & Marwick, 1986). She looks intently at her infant's face, fixating the eyes for many seconds at a time, and she feels the baby's hands or body while alert for any vocalization. Her expressive behavior has special characteristics that are clearly adapted to or ready to mesh with the multimodal perceptual readiness of the baby. These movements of the mother, which will simultaneously excite her own self-awareness, include general dynamic features detectable simultaneously by most sensory modalities; the fundamental beat of repeating movement, short bursts of expression, repetition of rhythmic groups of movement, exaggerated dynamic expressive "sentic" forms (Clynes, 1980), and precise modulation of the intensity or force of expression in a moderate to weak range. These paralinguistic or poetic aspects are described by such terms as "animacy," "vitality," or "energy," and they transmit emotion to confirm infant expressivity by "affect attunement" (Stern, Hofer, Haft, & Dore, 1985).

The cyclic, repeating rhythms of mothers' movements with a very regular pulse appear to tap into a fundamental level of motivation for human contact. Research by Burford (1988) has shown that body contact behaviors very similar to those used intuitively by mothers with young infants are also the most effective means caregivers have of communicating with profoundly

mentally handicapped adolescents. The motive forms of this level of communication are evidently very basic, robust, and resistant to destruction by
damage or degeneration of the brain. They appear not to undergo elabo-
ration in development as other functions do.

When she speaks to her baby, a happy mother's facial expressions are
exaggerated and friendly, playful and affectionate. Her voice assumes a
gentle, relaxed, breathy quality, with a singing pitch set high, about 300 Hz.
She makes short utterances with spiked, undulating or gliding pitch contours (see Figure 8.3). These are the defining characteristics of "intuitive
motherese," which has been shown to be the same when mothers are
speaking very different languages. That is, the prosodic, tonal, and syllabic
features peculiar to the language of the mother's culture are modified, so
the mothers come to speak in the same universal temporal and intonational
patterns (Fernald et al., 1989; Grieser & Kuhl, 1988; Papousek et al., 1985;
Papousek & Papousek, 1989). The comparison of mothers' utterances when
they are talking to their young infants in Mandarin Chinese (a tonal language) and English (which uses few tonal inflections to vary meaning) is
conclusive, because their motherese is virtually the same.

The hand movements the mother makes as she pats or strokes the baby
are gentle, periodic, and with repeating rhythms superimposed. The frequency of these touchings gives a clear message of her emotion and sensitivity.
Face and head movements, vocalizations, and hand movements are coordinated or synchronized; clearly, they are regulated by one mechanism
in the mother that conveys the dynamic motive states of her integrated self
as she seeks to have the best communication with her infant.

Joint generation of the utterance

When they have greeted one another and shown recognition, the further
communication between a mother and her infant shows how each has
become open to motivation from the other. The excitement builds between
them by a traffic of signals that have instant emotional effect. At first the
mother calls in an inviting questioning tone, watching closely for the response and imitating or shadowing the baby's movements. Distress is comforted with different downfalling intonation and slower insistent rhythms
(Papousek et al., 1985). Expressive reactions are imitated, and as soon as
the baby gives a clear, positive reaction, the mother smiles and signals her
pleasure and excitement with undulating cries.

After watching her invitations closely, the infant smiles and then becomes
animated in that expressive complex that resembles effort at an utterance.
There is a momentary relaxing of the interpersonal emotion (the baby often
stops smiling and seems to get "seriously" involved). Coo vocalizations, or
"prespeech" movements of jaws, lips, and tongue (Trevarthen, 1974a, 1977),

are made in synchrony with gesturelike hand and finger movements, most often with the right hand raised higher than the left (Trevarthen, 1986b). Coos (in French, "*les a-geu*") comprise a lax vowel [u], [a], or [ə] and may be articulated with a glottal stop [k] or [g], as in [ku] or [a gu]; that is, they are already formed as rudimentary speech units (Oller, 1986). The hand movements made in communication are also distinct from those made when the infant's attention is fixed on an object and "pre-reaching" is elicited (Von Hofsten, 1983; Von Hofsten & Rønqvist, 1991). Commonly, the infant breaks eye contact with the mother at the moment of the utterance and turns away to the right (MacKain, Studdert-Kennedy, Spieker, & Stern, 1983; Trevarthen, 1990a).

The timing of these cycles of behavior is regular and predictable. The two subjects become entrained on one beat, so the pattern of engagement draws them along in a duet of synchronized or alternating parts (Figure 8.3), to the regulation of which both contribute (Beebe et al., 1985). The mother is helping the infant to regulate the exchange, and she gives animation and support to the baby's expressions, but the basic rate and duration of their joint performance are paced by what draws out the infant best, and the infant is actively contributing. Protoconversations are generally organized about a relatively slow adagio pulse or beat (approximately 1/700–800 ms, or 90/min). The infant tends toward utterance cycles of 3–5 s, and does not usually sustain a lively communication for more than a minute or two (Figure 8.4).

The infant's motivation for an interaction that progresses through these phases has been shown to take essentially the same form in very different cultures. Whatever proscriptions, recommendations, or other rules of baby care mothers may operate on in different social classes and different cultures or ethnic groups, protoconversation appears to be universally available when the interaction is spontaneous and close, provided that neither infant nor mother is distracted by some self-conscious reserve, distress, or fear. Note that young infants do not tend to be "conversational" unless the appropriate receptive invitations are given by the partner, and that the frequency of invitations may differ considerably in different families and cultural groups. Moreover, infants under 1 month of age may be incapable of becoming engaged in reciprocal communication as quickly as older infants; they appear to take several seconds of observation of the partner before becoming sufficiently animated to respond (Holmlund, 1990).

The analogy of a musical duet

Perhaps the most familiar analogy for a conversation of motives for communication (and, indeed, a principal form of human dyadic communication that is cultivated in a great variety of traditions) is a musical duet, in

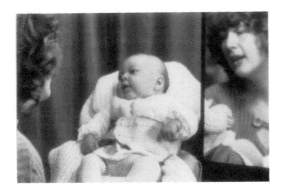

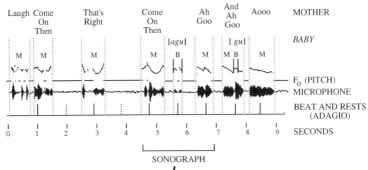

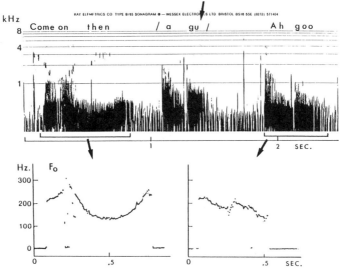

which two performers (singers or instrumentalists) seek harmony and counterpoint on one beat to create together a melody that becomes a coherent and satisfying narrative of feelings in a time structure that they share completely. In a good performance by two or more musicians each partakes of, or identifies with, the expression of the whole piece, the ensemble. Each gains musical understanding or satisfaction from the actions of the other(s), as well as separately from within themselves. The improvisation of a performance on two instruments can be used by a trained music therapist to explore and transform the emotions of patients with mental illness (Pavlicevic & Trevarthen, 1989). This is the kind of coherence or confluence of narratives of feeling between subjects that one also observes in protoconversation.

The role of imitation and attachment

Two-month-olds can imitate their mother's expressions, and they often mirror her changes of mood immediately, but they are more reluctant to imitate some isolated expressions than newborns are (described in the next section). Most imitations in protoconversation with a 2-month-old are by the mother (Trevarthen, 1977, 1979). Usually, the communication is sympathetic in tone or feeling rather than imitative in form, and most responses are complementary translations of the partner's expressions, creating a negotiation of feelings by a sequence of differing signals. However, the imitations that occur spontaneously in ordinary protoconversational play with a young baby may have a function in teaching speech and language, as Bateson (1979) proposed for the whole behavior. Kugiumutzakis (1992) has found that mothers of young infants imitate sounds that are related to speech, and the infants are also selective in their imitating (Figure 8.5). Both of them are more likely to match language-related communicative expressions, not accidental or self-regulatory expressions, such as sneezes.

Tests show that infants have preference for all the features of the mother's behavior that have been discussed here and for their synchronous use to show the mother's feelings. Recognition of the mother from her voice and attachment to her as a person who is a different, especially valuable, individual from others is an important factor from the beginning (De Casper & Fifer, 1980; De Casper & Spence, 1986). In addition, there appear to be

Figure 8.3. (*opposite*) A recording of vocal interaction between a 6-week-old infant and her mother, the same pair as shown in Figure 8.1. Mothers communicating with 2-month-old infants express themselves in short, evenly spaced, musical utterances of "intuitive motherese" that have controlled pitch and loudness contours signaling different interpersonal feelings. Infants interact precisely with this speech, alternating or synchronizing with the mothers' vocalizations and other expressions, and inserting coos on the same adagio beat. The sonogram charts the change in the mother's intonation either side of a bisyllabic [a-gu] utterance by the infant.

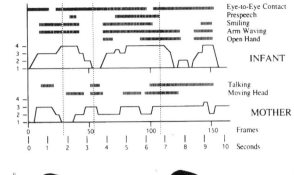

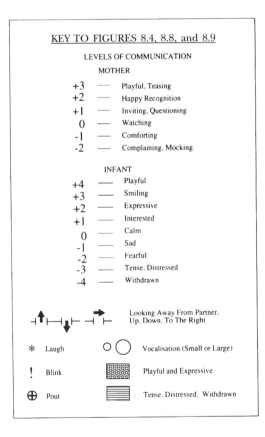

KEY TO FIGURES 8.4, 8.8, and 8.9

LEVELS OF COMMUNICATION

MOTHER

+3	—	Playful, Teasing
+2	—	Happy Recognition
+1	—	Inviting, Questioning
0	—	Watching
-1	—	Comforting
-2	—	Complaining, Mocking

INFANT

+4	—	Playful
+3	—	Smiling
+2	—	Expressive
+1	—	Interested
0	—	Calm
-1	—	Sad
-2	—	Fearful
-3	—	Tense, Distressed
-4	—	Withdrawn

Looking Away From Partner.
Up, Down, To The Right

*	Laugh	○ ◯	Vocalisation (Small or Large)
!	Blink	�(dotted)	Playful and Expressive
⊕	Pout	▤	Tense, Distressed, Withdrawn

Figure 8.4. (*above*) (Trevarthen, 1979): Utterance cycles observed in an analysis of a film with a 9-week-old boy. At 29 frames the baby is vocalizing and gesturing excitedly and the mother is watching. At 53 frames the baby is watching while the mother speaks. Both are vocalizing at 109 frames, the mother imitating the infant. (*opposite*) (Trevarthen, 1985b): A double TV interaction between an 8-week-old-infant and her mother in the apparatus shown at the bottom of Figure 8.9. The baby makes utterances (*U*) each of 2 to 3 s duration and 5 or 6 s apart, and the mother paces her expressions to match the infant. They take turns or synchronize their expressions (cf. figures 8.3 and 8.8).

Live Double TV Communication

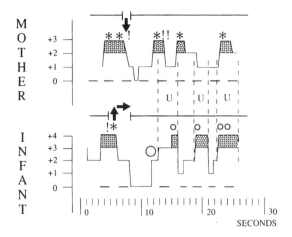

general criteria for perception of any other person's affection and willingness to communicate. Infants prefer intuitive motherese in the female voice (Fernald, 1985). Langlois (Langlois, Roggman, & Rieser-Danner, 1990) has found that they can discriminate and prefer photographs of young females who have configurations or expressions that adults, too, judge to be more beautiful. Computer blends of photographs of young female faces become more attractive as more individuals are added to the blend (Langlois & Roggman, 1990). The basis for this preference, and the sense of personal beauty, are not known, but it is likely to be related to a harmonious and slightly animated expression of the face that signals an affectionate readiness for gentle play. Beauty of the person is not only "in the eye of the beholder," though it must appeal there; it is also a quality of interpersonal relating, like the joy of a smile (see Darwin, 1872, for discussion of the function of smiling).

Neonates

Motives for communication at or before birth

By the end of the 1970s, evidence was presented that newborns, even prematurely born ones, might have the innate ability to enter into proto-conversation. Medical management of birth and neonatal assessment and care of prematurely born or sick infants have been changed by recognition that a degree of sensitivity to human care and communication is elaborated in the infant before term (Brazelton, 1973, 1979). Adjustment of care and assessment of the physiological-state regulation and supposed reflex responses of newborns have gradually been supplemented by examination of

(a)

Figure 8.5. (a) An infant less than 30 min after birth imitates her mother's tongue protrusion and mouth opening in a hospital in Hyderabad, India. (Photographs by Kevin Bundell.) (b) (*opposite*) Data from Kugiumutzakis (1985, 1992) show how different imitations are performed by infants of different ages. Vocalizations are imitated much more readily by infants between 2 and 4 months of age, but neonates imitate mouth movements. Changing communicative motives affect the infant's identification with the partner's expressions. The graphs summarize findings from a longitudinal study of seven infants filmed in Greece.

coordinated adaptations for interaction and communication with affectionate mothering (Als, 1987; Brazelton, 1982; Wolke, 1987). More recently the observation of fetal movements in utero by ultrasound has caused a revolution in concepts of the coordinative abilities of the preterm brain, and acceptance that postnatal movements are continuous with the rhythmic and smoothly integrated spontaneous patterns observed before birth in a healthy fetus (Cioni & Castellaci, 1990; Prechtl, 1984).

Neonates, including prematurely born ones, attend to expressions of persons and can be led by them into rudimentary communication (Figures 8.5 and 8.6). The sequences of expression do not have the coherence and regularity of protoconversation with a 2-month-old, and the infant's orientation is insufficiently definite and reactive to encourage the most lively expressions from a partner, but newborns do respond selectively to people

(b)

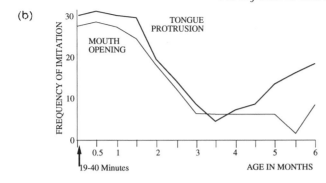

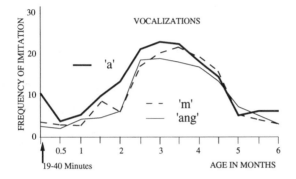

and they will look hard at faces and listen to voices. Oster and Ekman (1978) made a meticulous study of the facial motor actions of neonates, demonstrating many discrete configurations of expression. Alegria and Noirot (1978) demonstrated sensitive orientation and searching in response to the mother's voice within hours after birth.

Neonatal imitation

When model expressions, such as tongue protrusion, mouth opening, vocalizations, and exaggerated facial expressions of emotion, are presented to them with periodic insistence, followed by waiting, some newborns are very attentive and may make a matching expression (Field, 1985; Field, Woodson, Greenberg, & Cohen, 1982; Kugiumutzakis, 1985; Maratos, 1982; Meltzoff, 1985; Meltzoff & Moore, 1983). It is important to note that the imitations are usually not produced by matching of a reflex kind. Newborn infants often observe or watch for many seconds; when they do imitate, they do so with evident effort and progressive approximation to the model. Furthermore, imitations require that the newborn be in an optimal state of calm alertness, and the modeling must be carefully adjusted to their signs of readiness or interest. Some subjects do not imitate the most careful and

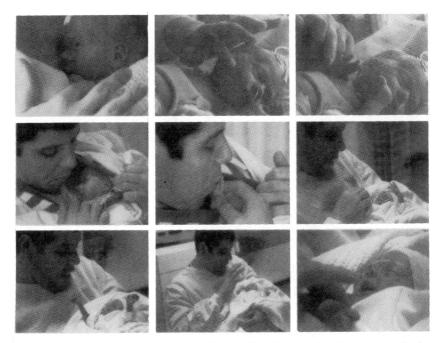

Figure 8.6. Premature infants of about 30 weeks' gestational age communicating. Stills from a documentary video of parents gently touching and speaking to their newborns in an intensive care unit in Amsterdam. A mother strokes her sleeping 28-week gestational age child before leaving the ward. A father who took over care of his premature daughter while the mother was isolated from her infant to have an operation, speaking rhythmic "motherese," imitating hand movements and stimulating the infant to look at his face and listen to his voice. This pair vocalized in alternation on an adagio beat when the infant was at 32 weeks' gestational age. (From a video made in a hospital in Amsterdam by Saskia van Rees; van Rees and de Leeuw, 1987).

persistent modeling (Kugiumutzakis, 1985, 1992). Evidently there are considerable individual "temperamental" differences in readiness to imitate (Field, 1985).

Interpretation of neonatal imitation is difficult. Imitation has been a controversial topic in philosophy for more than 2,000 years (Kugiumutzakis, personal communication). Most psychologists have held the view that newborn cognitive process are too uncoordinated to permit intermodal matching, and yet such matching is assumed to be necessary if a visible protruding tongue is to be imitated by the infant's own unseen tongue. Therefore, the recent discovery of such imitation has been seen as a paradox (Meltzoff, 1985). It has been assumed by behaviorists and cognitive theorists alike that a young infant could not possibly "represent" another person's face, and many ways of explaining away the behavior as not true imitation have been proposed (see Kugiumutzakis, 1985).

Communicative responses of a nonimitative kind indicate that infants are capable at birth of complementing a partner's expressions with an emotionally appropriate response. For example, a prematurely born infant at 30 weeks' gestational age can smile to an affectionate vocal greeting (see Figure 8.6). To perceive another person and respond appropriately, the neonate must be capable of integrating an awareness of the emotion itself from perception of the other's face movements, vocalizations, and touching. A detection of emotion-defining invariants in the expressions must occur. This requires some specific readiness for the other's behavior, one that can discriminate and respond differentially to the different expressions. Thus both imitation and communication require the infant to be ready to interact with the other in a matching and self-coordinated way. In this sense the neonate's mind does represent qualities or states of the other.

To explain imitation, one must turn away from an exclusive preoccupation with sensory information processing, perceptual equivalence, and symbolic representation to consider the motives and motor coordinations that are required for the reproduction of these forms of movement, and also for the kind of developing exchanges of expression that make protoconversation possible (Trevarthen, 1986a, pp. 236–241). Neonatal imitation, like neonatal "pre-reaching" is the result of activity of a purposeful or exploratory motive system that is seeking an aspect of reality (an object) that will complete or satisfy it.

Neonates imitate movements that are close to their own spontaneous repertoire of expressions, which in turn are highly sensitive to others' expressions. As Baldwin (1894) showed, learning motor coordinations requires repeated practice that he called "self-imitation." This was subsequently incorporated into Piaget's (1953) theory of "circular reactions." Imitations of other persons' actions are also self-related, and they provide the other who gave the model with a reflection of that act. In an interesting sense, imitations are metacommunicative; they become a classic form of joke in communication among older children. The fact that neonates imitate shows that they are ready to begin exploring with communication about communication. In a human newborn, this ability may be an essential preparation for the development of referential or linguistic communication. As already noted, Kugiumutzakis (1992) has found that spontaneous imitations between mothers and young infants – both mothers imitating infants and infants imitating mothers – are selective of behaviors that constitute, or are preparatory to, speech and gesture.

Fetal responses to maternal vocalization

De Casper's discovery of a fetal learning that prefers certain patterns of the maternal voice strongly confirms that newborns are ready for communication, especially with the mother. The auditory awareness of a newborn is already oriented to human vocal communication. Alert newborns are capable of coordinating their behavior in relation to events in the outside world, and this is helped when their heads are supported in upright position (Amiel-Tison, 1985). De Casper has shown that they can quickly learn to discriminate events that are contingent on their own activity, and that they rapidly develop preferences for effects that they have brought under the control of their own actions (De Casper & Carstens, 1981; De Casper & Prescott, 1984). He considers this to be evidence of a self-awareness that distinguishes the "self-produced" from the "external." Neonates' bias toward learning how to interact predictively with human expressions would seem to be evidence for an "interpersonal self-awareness."

Pregnant mothers talk to their fetuses, and what they say reveals that they are developing a strong readiness for a partner in feelings and communication. This is what Winnicott (1960) called "primary maternal preoccupation." The emotional readiness of the mother for her infant and her subsequent readiness to develop new forms of communication and cooperation as the infant's motives grow after birth have a strong relation to the eventual success of her mothering and the baby's development (Trad, 1990; Murray, 1992; Stern, 1985). It is increasingly clear that the natural mother-infant system is sustained by elaborate and specialized forms of interpersonal consciousness on both sides. Thus one can learn much about the infant's requirements from the behavior of a mother who is emotionally prepared for her baby.

A mother's containment and management of the infant's feelings and activity, dependent on her feelings leading to an adequate "previewing" (Trad, 1990), can be contrasted with the ministrations of a trained, experienced nurse in an intensive care unit (Van Rees & Leeuw, 1987). In the latter situation the infant is not being treated as a person, with a right to exchange feelings with the intruder on an equal plane, but only as a sensitive and reactive body that may even be presumed, in that situation, to have little or no sense of pain. The reflex infant is one that has been "taken in hand" and has not been granted the right to a dialogue or voluntary exploration of feeling with the other. The approach of a doctor or nurse to an infant, intending to minister to overriding physiological needs – often a matter of life and death in the caregiver's mind – causes the infant to withdraw into passive acceptance of intervention. Adults, too, are "patients" in medical care, but the passivity of infants in such a situation is apparently greater, which may be regarded as an adaptive response. A kitten goes limp and silent when picked up by the scruff of the neck, an important reflex when the mother is stealthily carrying it away from a predator.

A different, more affectionate and communicative approach is needed to bring out the newborn's full potentialities for expressive action as Wolff (1963), Sander (1964), and Brazelton (1973) have demonstrated. Recent changes in birth management and postnatal care have further demonstrated that the health of infants (and mothers) benefits from some relaxation of the standard medical practice, to admit conditions that encourage the infant's communicative motives to "open out" and seek contact. The same applies to prematurely born infants, it now being clear that coordinated behaviors and cognitive capacities in the last months of gestation are continuous with the psychological abilities evident after birth (Prechtl, 1984; Van Rees & Leeuw, 1987).

Emotions in mother–infant communication

We concluded from our analysis of protoconversations that a 2-month-old has expressions that can be shared with an adult, as well as physiognomic or body-matching equivalents for the expressions of the adult's face, voice, and hands (as is demonstrated in imitation). Emotional states that coordinate the rates and forms of expression must be equivalent in mother and infant, too (Trevarthen, 1992a). The organization of infant emotions in a functional system is clearly demonstrated when one observes the effects of interrupting the normal flow of interest and pleasure between mother and baby (Figures 8.7 and 8.8). Such a breakdown causes the infant to show confusion, withdrawal, and anger or distress.

Happy protoconversation is sustained by an active mutual engagement of highly specific intersubjective motives or programs of communicative expression in mother and baby. Very different behaviors occur if either mother or infant does not act in the appropriate way. If the mother does not approach her baby with attentive and responsive concern and happy affection, and does not adapt her style of expression to the baby's needs, the baby does not engage with her (Papousek & Papousek, 1977; Tronick, Als, Adamson, Wise, & Brazelton, 1978). If her responses are of the correct, positive form but inappropriately timed, the baby will look puzzled, then protest and withdraw (see Figure 8.8; Murray, 1980; Murray & Trevarthen, 1985; Trevarthen, 1974b; Trevarthen, 1985b; Trevarthen, Murray, & Hubley, 1981).

Failure of the infant to engage is signaled by organized patterns of expression that signify anger or distress, or a condition of withdrawal with motivational and emotional "freezing" (Murray & Trevarthen, 1985; Trevarthen, 1985b). At all times the infant has control of the contact, to the exent that the mother cannot continue to speak and move as if with a conversational partner if the infant does not smile, and withdraws gaze from her eyes. If the baby's behavior is artificially detached from the mother, as is done by replaying to her a video record of the baby communicating (without her knowledge that it is a replay), the mother feels that something is wrong. She may exhibit any of a variety of expressions of concern, unease, or distress, projecting the "problem" to the baby or blaming herself (Murray & Trevarthen, 1986).

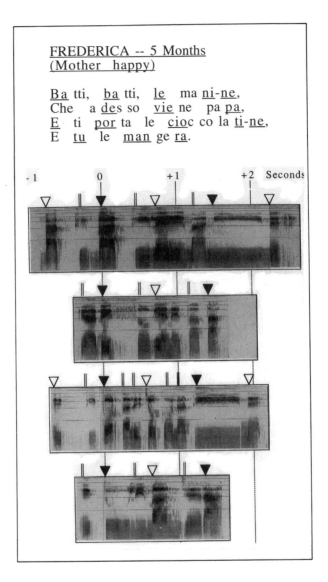

Figure 8.7. Sonographs of two Italian mothers singing the same baby song to their 6-month-old infants. The mother on the left is happy and sings her song with lively change in pitch and expression and on an allegro beat. Her infant joined in joyfully on the beat with prolonged coos. The mother on the right, who has postnatal depression, sings a monotonous, low pitched, largo. The infant in the latter case protested and avoided the song (Trevarthen, 1986a; songs recorded in Calabria by Maria Luisa Genta). The beat or pulse is marked by inverted triangles, black indicating a stressed beat. Double vertical lines indicate the "pre-beat" which creates a lilting rhythm. Horizontal lines, from 1kHz (the lowest) to 7 kHz (the highest) mark frequency levels of sound.

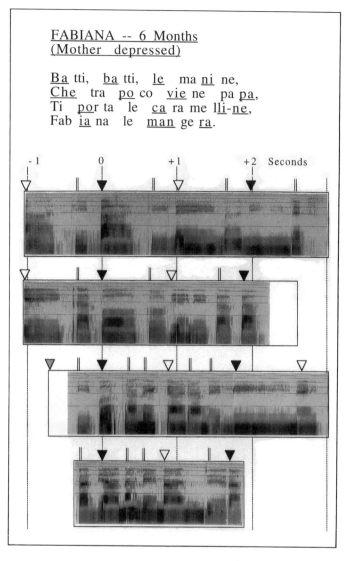

FABIANA -- 6 Months
(Mother depressed)

Ba tti, ba tti, le ma ni ne,
Che tra po co vie ne pa pa,
Ti por ta le ca ra me lli-ne,
Fab ia na le man ge ra.

The expectation of the infant for affectionate, happy, and playful responses from the mother is also shown dramatically when the mother has
a clinical depression that is focused on the infant (see Figure 8.7; Murray,
1988). Even simulated maternal depression causes a severe disruption of
protoconversation, the infant becoming withdrawn and distressed (Cohn
& Tronick, 1983). Murray (1992) has found that depression focused on the
baby can have a severe, immediate effect on the baby's cognitive and social
development over the first year.

LIVE   REPLAY

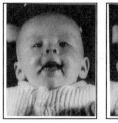

Figure 8.8. When the record of the mother's happy contribution from the double TV communication (LIVE) is replayed to the 8-week-old infant (REPLAY), the infant becomes withdrawn and depressed. The photogaphs show corresponding moments in the two sessions (Murray & Trevarthen, 1985; Trevarthen, 1985b). (See diagram of apparatus in Figure 8.9.)

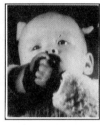

Double TV Communication

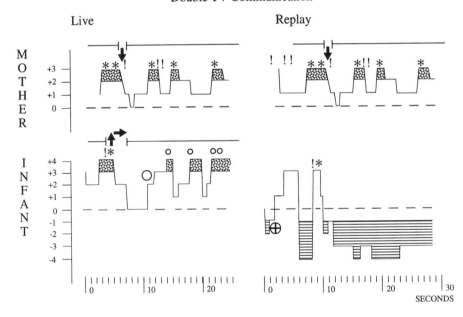

The functions of emotional dynamics in direct communication

Perceptual uptake of information for interpersonal knowing cannot be divorced from the generation of expressive forms of acting because the communicative signals are made by highly specific forms of movement that are adapted to fit a perceiver's sensitivities. The peculiar character of intersubjective control is that the feelings perceived directly identify with differentiated forms of expressive movement and the flow of expression: A smile *is* happy, as is walking with a fast, tripping step; tears *are* sad, as is a slow dragging way of walking and a downcast look; and emotions expressed by one person can lead to instantaneous sympathetic mimicry in another. Expressions of the self "invade" the mind of the other, making the moving body of the self resonant with impulses that can move the other's body too. The close following of emotions between persons in direct and intimate communication permits transfer and imitation of internal motives by which each is regulating the dynamics of consciousness and purpose. Mental processes are communicated in chains of transient emotional shifts, or *emotional transients* (Figure 8.9).

Details in the intrinsic organization of the human motivation system that are adapted to fine and rapid transfer of mental dynamics between subjects may be observed in the various glides and leaps of pitch or volume of voice, eyebrow flashes, prebeat syllables, suffix morphemes, rhythmic details and embellishments, rapid hand gestures, quick head moves, shifts of gaze, and so on, that appear in abundance in all spontaneous "conversational" communication (Buck, 1984; Duncan & Fiske, 1977; Eibl-Eibesfeldt, 1989; Kendon, 1980). As "vitality affects" (Stern, 1985), these are the fundamental carriers of information about motivation changes in the short term. These behavioral particles are organized in a stream of emotional signals, which can have the equivalent of syntactic organization or narrative structure – they may be described as forming an *emotional narrative*. Organization at both levels, morphemic and syntactic, is adapted to intersubjective functions – that is, the coordination of cognitive dynamics, attention shifts, impulse of purpose, changes in motive force, and so on, in each self and between selves.

McNeill (1992) has shown, by a cross-cultural and developmental TV study of how people convey thinking in gestures and speech when they are telling a dramatic story, that there is an unconscious unity of expression that unfolds with regulated timing. People, including toddlers just beginning to master sentences, "think aloud" in an integrated mixture of hand gestures and speech that must come from one stream of "inner speech." The coupling of hand gestures with coos and prespeech in young infants (Trevarthen, 1986b) indicates that this expressive system has an inherent unity, presumably adapted to transmission of mental dynamics that precede language and become incorporated in it later in development.

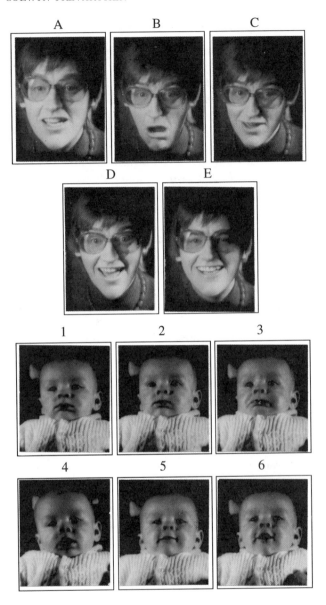

Figure 8.9. Emotional transients. When the 8-week-old infant in the Double TV setup was startled by a loud noise, she showed rapid changes in expression and nearly cried, but within 10 s became cheerful after establishing eye-to-eye contact with her mother. In 30 s both mother and infant showed many different emotions (Trevarthen, 1985b). (*opposite, bottom*): The Double TV apparatus (Murray & Trevarthen, 1985; Trevarthen, 1985b).

Live Double TV Communication

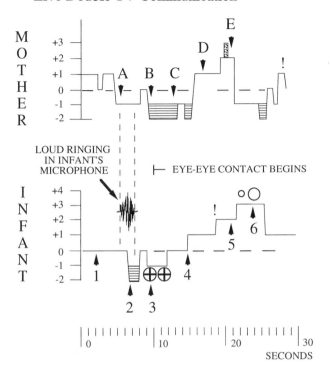

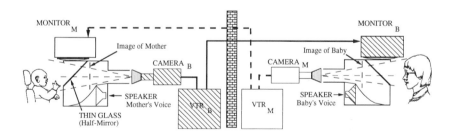

The field of emotions

The total range of emotional shifts seen in spontaneous communications shows the organization and dynamic availability of the emotion field (Figure 8.10). People can describe this field, naming the emotions in their felt relationships (Kellerman, 1980; Plutchik, 1980). Although it is difficult to

(a)

ERGIC
AXIS
STRONG

TROPHIC
AXIS

A C C E P T I N G

R E J E C T I N G

ANGRY
SURPRISED
CURIOUS
EAGER
JOYFUL
DISGUSTED
PLAYFUL
AFRAID
CONFUSED
ACCEPTING
RECEPTIVE
UNHAPPY
CAUTIOUS
SHY
SAD

WEAK

(b)

STRONG

IZARD'S
10 PRIMARY
EMOTIONS

P O S I T I V E

N E G A T I V E

SURPRISE
ANGER
CONTEMPT
DISGUST
INTEREST
JOY
ACCEPTANCE
FEAR
SADNESS
SHAME
SHYNESS
GUILT?

WEAK

DEVELOPMENTAL
STAGES

▓ Sensory
░ Perceptual
☐ Cognitive

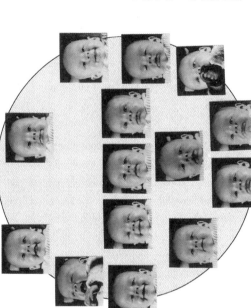

(c)

Figure 8.10. (a) The field of emotions and axes of emotional regulation – *ergic* (force in action) against *tropic* (assimilating; or approach/avoidance). Feelings are organized in a field that can be plotted by semantic analysis of emotion words (Plutchik, 1980). They relate to interpersonal or social "accessibility" (Kellerman, 1983). (b) Izard (1980) interpreted 10 basic emotions as developing in infants with attainment of perceptual and cognitive levels of processing. This concept is shown on the field generated by Plutchik (1980). ((a) and (b) from Trevarthen, 1990b, 1992). (c) The range of emotions shown by a 2-month-old girl in communication with her mother by way of the Double TV system and in the replay test (Trevarthen, 1985b), plotted on the same field as in part (a). The field may not reflect the natural relations between emotions, but illustrates the variety of expressions in a young infant.

obtain agreement about the meanings of emotion words, and different cultures map the emotions into their languages differently, the relations between the forms, oppositions, and affinities or tensions between the emotions appear to be the same, and there is agreement about the positive or negative valence of feelings and their relative power or weakness. Emotional reactions to experiences are shared by universal signals of interest, surprise, puzzlement, disgust, and so on. There is evidently a universal field of emotions that is also reflected in the ways we categorize personalities, emotional illnesses, and dramatic performances (Darwin, 1872; Kellerman, 1983). A good analogy is the field of color vision. Cultures vary in their discrimination of colors and the ways they codify color in language, but the relationships and mixing rules between colors and the principal color categories are universal and innate (Bornstein, 1985; Thompson, Palacios, & Varela, 1992).

In the theory of innate intersubjectivity, the emotion field is held to be set out in utero (Trevarthen, 1990b). The frequency and variety of transient emotional shifts indicates the "mobility" of the emotions over the whole field. The field is restricted when the subject is in a pathological state (Kellerman, 1980), as in infantile autism (Hobson, this volume; Kanner, 1943), or when the human environment is not responsive and supportive, as in an infant whose mother has postnatal depression (Murray, 1992).

Emotional narratives are organized in "healthy" communication by motivating processes that transform and sequence emotions in the field. To understand the organization of these narratives, their motivational understructure, we need to consider both the temporal base for emotional dynamics and the qualitative distinctions that are laid out in the emotion field. The emotions constitute a time–space field of intrinsic brain states of mental and behavioral vitality that are signaled for communication to other subjects and that are open to immediate influence from the signals of these others (Buck, 1984, this volume; Tucker, 1991).

In young human infants, the use of emotional signaling is primarily developed for direct engagement with a loving and playful partner, as well as for soliciting acts of care and maintenance. Other "biobehavioral" functions of emotions (Plutchik, 1980), that are in strong evidence between adults and in the societies of animals, have no function at this stage of human development because the infant has none of the associated life-sustaining responsibilities. It does not help us understand the interpersonal functions of infant emotions to go into the theory of how lower animals with less intersubjectivity evolved emotions to regulate group behavior, or the vital integrity of the individual.

156   *COLWYN TREVARTHEN*

Development of communication about a topic: The self-consciousness of the message giver

Memory and motive dynamics: Adaptations of the mother–infant system to aid infant learning

It is probable that cognitive dynamics and the chronometrics of awareness and thinking in active behavioral engagement with the environment are coincident with motive dynamics – that is, behaving and perceiving are generated in the same core motivating system of the brain. If motive dynamics fixed by innate autopoetic rules can be coupled efficiently between subjects, this would, under optimal conditions of intersubjectivity, result in near complete confluence or harmonization of their internal thinking, learning, and remembering. If the directions and targets of interest in the environment they share were also specified in this communication, to express orientation to designated events and objects, then they would tend to perceive the same world.

Emotions generated and perceived intersubjectively appear to have a unique function in regulating learning and memory in human society. Emotional processes carry the "cognitive prospectuses" of the individual and the society, which construct the memory records of what a child has needed and will need to become proficient in cooperative communication. Emotions mediate cognitive transfer of meanings or knowledge in teaching or learning. In other words, the emotions regulate the development of the socioecological self or cooperative self, the self that is cognitively cooperative, interpreting and using the world according to agreed-upon meanings conferred on acts and objects (Trevarthen, 1992b).

If optimal mother–infant (and, later, mother–child) communication achieves the same kind of confluence of emotions as one observes in conversation between adults, analysis of that communication will bring out detailed indication of the components of motivation that are active in the child's mind at each age. It will, furthermore, reveal how the mother is able to direct and reinforce the child's cognitive exploration and learning through play. Darwin (1872) concluded that teaching of the young was a main function of human emotions.

Indeed, developments in the dynamic regulation of play beyond the stage of protoconversations show that, in the course of the first year, the motives of infants are undergoing rapid change in a direction that leads to just this kind of communication-guided, or "guided participation," learning (Rogoff, 1990). This places the interpersonal communications of the early months in a new practical context, giving them a developmental function. The infant's interpersonal self is transforming step by step into cooperative self, capable of sharing experiences and purposes that refer to a common consciousness of reality and its affordances – that is, to "meaning."

Emotional dynamics and metacommunication in baby games and baby songs

The complex communications of teasing games and rituals in play (including baby songs) that appear in the middle of the first year represent negotiations of will between the infant and a sympathetic, affectionate partner. Such negotiation appears to be necessary to establish new, more efficient and more intricate intersubjective cooperation. The games bring out the tendencies of both subjects to project the interaction "dialogically," in Bråten's (1988) sense, and to negotiate agreements of purpose or rivalry. They also confer on the infant a new kind of self-awareness that is capable of studying and adjusting to the other person's reactions. Soon, the baby is experimenting with a wide range of self-presentations.

In the "period of games" (3 to 9 months), the infant's technique of self-presentation grows conspicuously (Trevarthen, 1990c). He or she is becoming markedly more complex and sensitive to the "audience-spectator." One can discern a growing self-consciousness, too; that is, the other's attention and feelings increasingly become the main part of the control of the communication. The infant's behavior aims the interaction so that the other's attention is drawn back to the infant, not absorbed in the direct exchange of feelings and not directed sideways to some third person or object. It becomes communication about communication – metacommunication, to use Gregory Bateson's (1956) term. This is the first step to defining a social self, a "Me," with the potentiality for a superego, self-regulated by others' attitudes. It is characteristically manifested in "teasing, joking, showing off and mucking about" (Reddy, 1990). It ebulliently, and sometimes outrageously, has fun. There is even a conspiratorial quality to the way infants in the second half of the first year share feelings about events and other persons with identified trusted familiars, as if they are starting to feel glimmerings of the pleasure of gossip (Levi, 1986).

Increased social awareness brings increased attachment to familiar, trusted companions and heightened fear of strangers. The interactions of infants about 6 to 12 months old with strangers are very interesting. They include timidity, coyness, showing off, and angry dislike. The opponent is watched intently, as the baby probes the feelings of a person who is assumed to be a threat until proven innocent.

This is also the time when infants make deliberate orientations to their familiar caretakers for help and for emotional information about unfamiliar objects or situations, a behavior known as "emotional referencing" (Klinnert, Campos, Sorce, Ende, & Svejda, 1983). All this increased social discrimination finds application in the next year when the infant begins to be an imitator and pupil, seeking conventional knowledge about the world and what one should or should not do in it. Establishment of efficient and creative cooperation is favored by feelings of affection on recognition of a familiar and trusted partner. Attachment relations, and their converse, the suspicious watchfulness or fear given to strangers, regulate contact and the sharing of meaning. Felt security is a prerequisite for the efficient transfer of motives that cooperation requires.

Practical and communicative motives prior to language

Integration between the infant's motives for object tracking and haptic exploration, which develop after 4 months, and motives for communication in protoconversation that were already established in the first 3 months, continues in games. Gradually the infant is enticed to play with objects that other people are presenting in a game. "Person–person" games give way to "person–person–object" games (Trevarthen & Hubley, 1978).

A mother's play with her infant is transformed as the baby gains more vigorous ways of moving the body and experiencing its feel. Then the infant has to learn how to control and subordinate body action to achieve a stable base for precise inspection of, and action on, objects in manipulation. This leads the infant often to refuse play, to push a would-be playmate aside, so the task in hand can be achieved. Further changes in agency are experienced with development of independent locomotion and standing. Expansion of the memorable field of experience is a prerequisite for learning to share knowledge about the family world of day-to-day activity. In time, foci of routine activity are recognized and named, and this needs a space–time context in the learner's mind.

Observations of how infants communicate about the end of the first year show how, in the small community of the family in its familiar social and cultural context, a shared worldview and shared purposes are built up, with the option for each participating subject (infant or adult), to innovate and instruct. Messages of meaning give news and affirm knowledge and belief. Negotiations of meaning match, contrast, revise, displace, and give and take ideas and plans. Assertive differencing (in the form of refusals, antagonistic repulsions, withdrawals, etc.) is as necessary as compliant or encouraging agreement. As a result of genuine negotiations, reasonable (meaning "fair" and not necessarily rational or calculated) agreement is obtained without threat to relationships or to the security of interpersonal selves. Passionate, unreasonable insistence on agreement and violent disagreement both threaten relationships, not only the cooperation within relationships. Willing cooperation strengthens relationships.

All this implies that the infant beyond 1 year of age is moving into an increasingly clear moral as well as cooperative set of relationships, where such feelings as loyalty, jealousy, shame, and guilt can be differentiated. We have much to do in the exploration of the motives that define these more complex interpersonal states.

Conclusions: Why early communication was not studied, and why it is difficult to understand

> *Basic human communication is direct and intuitive; its*
> *intersubjectivity is innate*

Conversation, the main traffic of human social understanding and meaningful cooperative work, is full of an immediate interpersonal vitality that goes beyond, or beneath, the words. Formal, rule-bound, rational, or decontextualized discussion, as well as texts and their reading, are special, cultivated forms derived (in individual learning as in history of culture) from the more informal, spontaneous kinds of communication. Everyday conversational discourse is not held together by cognitively tidy grammatical rules or abstract theoretical explanations but by empathic cooperation of an immediately persuasive, "phatic" kind. Interpersonal relationships in the family and in society are certainly supported on this level of direct, intuitive, and emotional communication.

Given this universal immediacy of human interpersonal understanding in communication, why should we be surprised that a young infant can experience others and their psychological activities with a well-formed readiness that requires little practice to be functional? We need not suppose that awareness of the human self in relation to the human other is *constructed* by reason from accumulating social experience, or built from verbally encoded concepts or theories about other persons' minds, personalities, intentions, consciousness, or beliefs. Mead's (1934) social Me, for example, reflecting on itself with the aid of learned social judgments, standards, and codes, is built around an intuitively communicative I who does not need to learn how to gain responses from the other in an I–Thou relation (Buber, 1958; Macmurray, 1961). Humans do not need to be instructed by mothers acting as if babies knew and training them in the skills of turn taking and emotional response, as has been assumed by some developmental psychologists influenced by Mead's social behaviorism (e.g., Kaye, 1982; Lock, 1980). Nor is it possible to explain the development of their communication entirely from the effects that emerge by co-construction in the dynamic interactions between the systems of sensorimotor coordination in the mother and infant (Fogel & Thelen, 1987). Infants have the ability for communication in them, and this grows from within as well as by entering into dialogues with others.

The way a young infant behaves when face to face with the right kind of available person supports a theory of innate intersubjectivity, a theory that I proposed on the evidence of descriptions of mother–infant interactions (Trevarthen, 1974b, 1977, 1979). A newborn infant does not know much – at least not of the tried and tested, conscious and reasoned experience of the world we adults are expected to have. Yet a baby a few weeks' old does respond sensitively, actively, and appropriately to signs of mental activity in the mother, and most of all to her emotions. This responsiveness appears without training, and – when the infant is properly approached – with little searching or constructive thought. At times, the infant's expressions seem to enter quickly into *direct and immediate contact* with the motives and emotions of the other person.

Infants are so proficient at communication, a very short time after birth, that we are led to reconsider everyday adult knowing of the human other. Is it, too, driven by these basic innate motives, and similarly direct and immediate? As intellectuals, we may be in the habit of exaggerating the cognitive and rational (or, if we are psychoanalysts, symbolic) aspect of our own responses to others, whether they be adults or children.

The problem of reason in relating

We wade in much tramped-about, muddied waters, full of semantic eddies, when we enter a debate on the rationality of interpersonal life for any stage of development. Use of the widely accepted terms for cognition, chosen as they are to describe the thoughts in a unitary, isolated Cartesian thinker solving problems, generates profound misapprehensions of human relating and its emotional regulation. Communication of what Wittgenstein (1972) came to recognize as "forms of life" cannot be explained rationally.

The progress of our inquiry is constrained by the conventions of our discipline. Contemporary psychology, especially its cognitive arm, has preferred explanations in terms of rational or computational processes. Emotions are generally treated as by-products of cognition. Behaviorists assumed that processes of perceiving, thinking, and willing are entirely built up from atoms of experience by learning. Cognitivists now conceive those processes as innate modules for processing different forms of information. The conservative mainstream of cognitive psychology is as reluctant as was behavioristic psychology to allow innate or prefabricated motives that would be capable of directing awareness of a coherent self – especially the specialized motives that are required to detect another human subject and to interact immediately, intimately and productively. Yet, there are notable exceptions, and we can sense movement in a new direction.

The objective reality of subjective states in communication

A major philosophical obstacle to understanding human communication (and therefore a distortion of our understanding of human consciousness) lies in the idea that mental processes are inaccessible except within the self, that they are inevitably obscure in others, and that they are essentially immiscible with facts of "objective" reality. The theories I am referring to are those called dualistic, positivistic, and rationalistic. They are the product of a tradition of artificial scholarly discussion and introspection, distanced from everyday human communication and the ordinary, practical, conscious use of a reality that communication has made meaningful. Such concepts have gained influence because they are appropriate to the logical analysis of propositions about elements in verbal texts, theories, systems of description, and belief. There is, however, much in human consciousness that they do not comprehend.

The effect on the natural science of psychology of this text-bound epistemological tradition has been to give primary authority to research findings on the perceptual and cognitive achievements of single minds, their individual perceptual discriminations and judgments, concepts, reasonings, and so forth. Explanations of higher mental phenomena, including communication, have been sought either in associative learning and conditioning or, more recently, in the cognitive work of problem solving and computation. Paradoxically, modern psychology assumes both that the mental phenomena of thinking and reasoning are subjective and hidden and that they are learned from experience of objective reality or solving problems in mastery of reality.

The facts of infant communication, above all its efficiency and organizing potency over the infant's experience – as well as that of other persons who are in communication with the infant – support a totally different conception of human consciousness, more easily reconciled with common sense. (It is also more compatible with what we know of how the human brain grows, but that problem will not be dealt with here; see Trevarthen, 1989a, 1990a.)

Primary to secondary intersubjectivity: From direct conversational consciousness to negotiation of conventional knowledge and common purposes communicated in symbols

We have shown that from birth infants have no trouble in detecting and interacting discriminately and optionally with the mental states of other persons. Very soon after birth, they can enter into a dynamic exchange of mental states that has a conversational, potentially intention-and-knowledge-sharing organization and motivation. The emotional and purposeful quality of these interchanges of motives undergoes rapid differentiation in the games of ensuing months. It becomes more elaborate, more quickly reactive, and more directive in relation to the responses of the other and is protracted into longer narratives of feeling. We say the infant is developing a more assertive, more conscious self, but we mean that the infant's experience of being a performer in the eyes of the other is gaining in power, presence, and pleasure. This self is essentially one in relation to the other's (or several others') consciousness – ready to enter into "dialogic closure" with their motives and thoughts (Bråten, 1988). The intersubjectivity of the communication, which was there from the first opportunity for its use, is developing a new alertness and richness of emotions, as well as an increased autonomy within the affectionate attentions and companionship of caretakers which is its natural context. There is already an element of metacommunicative pretension, of showing off and making special, which I have called *protosymbolic* (Trevarthen, 1990c). It is also relevant that many of the infant's acting-up or demonstrative behaviors are recollected from previously marked occasions; they are favorite and customary and ritualized tricks for celebratory exchange.

We have examined the crucial further development in communication and cooperative self-expression that makes it possible for the infant, at about 1 year after birth, to begin sharing and comparing experiences of reality. The infant now begins to play a part in the execution of tasks the aim of which is to transform that shared reality, to bring it under the organizing influence of the consciousnesses and intentions of infant and partner together. From this point we can talk of jointly constructed meaning, of symbolic expressions that refer to items of negotiated knowledge and to ideas that have been given social significance in a community.

The infant demonstrates the essential cooperative motives before speaking, so the crucial awareness of the other's feelings and purposes with application to objects in the shared world comes without the intervention of words and language. It leads to the formation of concepts situated in a matrix of knowledge that has been built up arbitrarily in the history of the society.

The communicative understanding of a 1-year-old contains primitive concepts that have been given value and distinctness through emotional referencing and joint attention, in communication games where the child is invited to be an active initiator. Research has demonstrated that no amount of instruction, demonstration, affective attunement, or embellishment by the mother will lead the infant under about 35 weeks to observe and learn common, arbitrary ideas. The infant has to be *ready* to look for, imitate, and complement what the mother is doing. The crucial change takes place when the infant is between 35 and 40 weeks of age (Hubley & Trevarthen, 1979; Trevarthen & Hubley, 1978). By 60 weeks, infants generally are active in the production of vocalizations and gestures, in the "acts of meaning" of protolanguage by which other persons' actions and interests are manipulated (Halliday, 1975; Trevarthen, 1987, 1990c).

Subsequent development of concepts of other people, of their interests, purposes, beliefs, and feelings, depends on discussion. That development gains from the capacity of language to specify ideas about non-present things, events, and places and people's actions and feelings. It is built up by learning stories that people tell about themselves, each other, and the world, that is, from characterful and dramatic narratives. The value terms and dynamic processes recorded in such narratives are not new for the 1-year-old, even though an entirely new vocabulary is being learned. The narrative dynamics are built on the intuitive empathic understandings of persons' awareness of each other that have been in evidence since the early months. What is new is use of language to strengthen and extend the remembered, imagined, and referred-to things – the facts. In time the actions of play themselves become part of the discussion, as does the described and retained verbal description of the child's self and the selves of the known, and named, playmates. Eventually speaking and language forms become topics for play. The talk becomes habitual, second nature, and it can increasingly assume the private form of an internal conversation, or thinking (Vygotsky, 1962).

Logic, propositional argument, arises out of the need for a verbally described consciousness to justify what it thinks to itself against what it says in conversation to others. The internal dyad and the external one have to be reconciled or made consistent in their stories. We are inclined to grant a responsible "self" and a reliable and sensible consciousness to any person who can make a reasonably confident defense of his or her thought on some matter of common concern. Quickness of such thought is called intelligence. But the whole existence of such a self and its consciousness depends on the prior activity of a self capable of being in immediate mutually responsive communication with an other at the level of motives and emotions, regardless of words and what facts words are "about." That is what the interpersonal self, with its inherently dyadic conversational mind, can do. Analysis of protoconversation between a mother and her infant gives us detailed information about the organization of the basic mental processes that make the communicative life of the interpersonal self possible.

NOTES

1 In Charles Darwin's famous treatise on emotions in humans and animals (1872), he proposed that emotional expressions have evolved from voluntary acts of exploration or performance and that, through repeated activation of the nerve pathways, these behaviors became instinctive. Thus he placed motivated actions, aimed to regulate experience and the effects of motor transactions with the environment, at the evolutionary source of the intuitive expressions of emotion that come to serve exclusively in communication.
2 Motive is "that which moves or induces a person to act a certain way; a desire, fear, reason, etc., which influences a person's volition" (*Shorter Oxford English Dictionary*, 3rd ed., 1944).
3 Observations on the ways mothers and other caregivers attend to and communicate with infants in different cultures (Goshen-Gottstein, 1980; Weintraub & Shapiro, 1968), as well as analyses about what caregivers say when they are interrogated about their ideas of infancy (Ninio, 1988; Goodnow, 1984; Tulkin & Cohler, 1973), have led to claims that perception of these behaviors is either profoundly influ-

enced or entirely determined by cultural rules and beliefs (Bradley, 1991). Some groups are said to discourage verbal communication with infants because they think infants can make no sense of language (e.g., Tulkin & Kagan, 1972). They simply care and comfort them with touch and movement and through breast-feeding.

Traditional cultures (and lower socioeconomic groups in technologically advanced cultures) are said to have differing ideas from the much studied urban Western middle-class on the rate at which infants develop their own minds with intentions and perception (Schiefflin, 1979). Traditional cultures apparently, believe that children mature rapidly in moral skills of relating but slowly in cognition; Western cultures are impressed with how fast infants develop cognitively, but they do not find emotions and moral abilities to be part of early endowment (LeVine & White, 1986).

While acknowledging such differences, I do not believe that they are incompatible with the concept of an innate intersubjectivity and a capacity in all infants for protoconversational communication with caregivers soon after birth. Different cultural ideas and practices can influence development, and indigenous practices may be very important in adapting motives, feelings, skills, and perceptions to the particular psychosocial ecology of the family and community (Hundeide, 1991; Whiting & Whiting, 1975). However, this adaptability is negotiated by universal communicative processes and emotions. Furthermore, a culture's ideas or theories about infancy and childhood are often not in line with actual intuitive practices in spontaneous communication with children.

REFERENCES

Ahrens, R. (1954). Beitrag zur Entwicklung des Physiognomie und Mimikerkennens. *Zeitschrift fur Experimentelle und Angewandte Psychologie, 2,* 412–454.

Alegria, J., & Noirot, E. (1978). Neonate orientation behavior towards the human voice. *Early Human Development, 1*: 291–312.

Als, H. (1987). In C. von Euler, H. Forssberg, & H. Lagercrantz (Eds.), *Neurobiology of early infant behaviour.* Wenner-Gren Center International Symposium Series, Vol. 55. Basingstoke, Hants.: Macmillan; New York: Stockton.

Amiel-Tison, C. (1985). Pediatric contribution to the present knowledge on neurobehavioral status of infants at birth. In J. Mehler & R. Fox (Eds.), *Neonatal cognition: Beyond the blooming, buzzing confusion.* Hillsdale, NJ: Erlbaum.

Anokhin, P. K. (1974). *Biology and neurophysiology of the conditioned reflex and its role in adaptive behavior* (S. A. Carson, Sci. and Trans. Ed., Oxford: Pergamon.

Baldwin, J. M. (1894). *Mental development in the child and the race.* New York: Macmillan.

Bateson, G. (1956). The message "this is play." In B. Schaffer (Ed.), *Group processes.* New York: Josiah Macy Foundation.

Bateson, M. C. (1975). Mother-infant exchanges: The epigenesis of conversational interaction. In D. Aronson & R. W. Rieber (Eds.), *Developmental psycholinguistics and communication disorders. Annals of the New York Academy of Sciences* (Vol. 263). New York: New York Academy of Sciences

Bateson, M. C. (1979). "The epigenesis of conversational interaction": A personal account of research development. In M. Bullowa (Ed.), *Before speech: The beginning of human communication* (pp. 63–77). Cambridge University Press.

Beebe, B., Jaffe, J., Feldstein, S., Mays, K., & Alson, D. (1985). Interpersonal timing: The application of an adult dialogue model to mother–infant vocal and kinesic interactions. In F. M. Field & N. Fox (Eds.), *Social perception in infants.* Norwood, NJ: Ablex.

Beebe, B., Stern, D., & Jaffe, J. (1979). The kinesic rhythm of mother–infant interactions. In A. W. Siegman & S. Feldstein (Eds.), *Of speech and time: Temporal speech patterns in interpersonal contexts.* Hillsdale, NJ: Erlbaum.

Bernstein, N. (1967). *Coordination and regulation of movements.* New York: Pergamon.

Bornstein, M. H. (1985). Infant into adult: Unity into diversity with the development of visual categorization. In J. Mehler & R. Fox (Eds.), *Neonatal cognition: Beyond the blooming, buzzing confusion.* Hillsdale, NJ: Erlbaum.

Bradley, B. S. (1991). Infancy as paradise. *Human Development, 34,* 35–54.

Brazelton, T. B. (1973). *Neonatal Behavioural Assessment Scale.* Clinics in Developmental Medicine, 50. Spastics International Medical Publications. London: Heinemann.

Brazelton, T. B. (1979). Evidence of communication during neonatal assessment. In M. Bullowa (Ed.), *Before speech: The beginning of human communication* (pp. 79–88). Cambridge University Press.

Brazelton, T. B. (1982). Joint regulation of neonate–parent behavior. In E. Z. Tronick (Ed.), *Social interchange in infancy: Affect, cognition and communication.* Baltimore: University Park Press.

Brazelton, T. B., Koslowski, B., & Main, M. (1974). The origins of reciprocity: The early mother-infant interaction. In M. Lewis & L. A. Rosenblum (Eds.), *The effect of the infant on its caregiver* (pp. 49–76). New York: Wiley.

Brazelton, T. B., Tronick, E., Adamson, L., Als, H., & Wise, S. (1975). Early mother–infant reciprocity. *Ciba Foundation Symposium, 33.* Amsterdam: Elsevier.

Brunswik, E. (1956). *Perception and representative design of psychological experiments.* Berkeley: University of California Press.

Bråten, S. (1988). Dialogic mind: The infant and adult in protoconversation. In M. Cavello (Ed.), *Nature, cognition and system.* Dordrecht: Klewer.

Buber, M. (1958). *I and Thou* (2nd ed.). Edinburgh: Clark.

Buck, R. (1984). *The communication of emotion.* New York: Guilford.

Bullowa, M. (Ed.). (1979). *Before speech: The beginning of human communication.* Cambridge University Press.

Burford, B. (1988). Action cycles: Rhythmic actions for engagement with children and young adults with profound mental handicap. *European Journal of Special Needs Education, 3,* 189–208.

Byrne, R. W., & Whiten, A. (1988). *Machiavellian intelligence: Social expertise and the evolution of intellect in monkeys, apes and humans.* Oxford: Oxford University Press.

Carpenter, G. C., Tecce, J. S., Stechler, G., & Friedman, S. (1970). Differential visual behavior to human and humanoid faces in early infancy. *Merrill-Palmer Quarterly, 16,* 91–108.

Cheney, D. L., & Seyfarth, R. M. (1992). Precis of "How monkeys see the world." *Behavioral and Brain Sciences, 15,* 135–182.

Chevalier-Skolnikoff, S. (1989). Spontaneous tool use and sensorimotor intelligence in *Cebus* compared with other monkeys and apes. *Behavioral and Brain Science, 12* (3), 561–627.

Cicchetti, D., & Hesse, P. (1983). Affect and intellect: Piaget's contributions to the study of infant emotional development. In R. Plutchik & H. Kellerman (Eds.), *Emotion, theory, research and experience: Vol. 2. Emotions in early development.* New York: Academic Press.

Cioni, G., & Castellaci, A. M. (1990). Development of fetal and neonatal motor activity: Implications for neurology. In H. Block & B. Bertenthal (Eds.), *Sensory-motor organization and development in infancy and early childhood*. Dordrecht: Kluwer.

Clynes, M. (1980). The communication of emotion: Theory of sentics. In R. Plutchik & H. Kellerman (Eds.); *Emotion: Theory, research and experience: Vol. 1. Theories of emotion*. New York: Academic Press.

Cohn, J. F., & Tronick, E. Z. (1983). Three-month-old infants' reaction to simulated maternal depression. *Child Development, 54*, 185–193.

Darwin C. (1872). *The expression of emotion in man and animals*. London: Methuen.

De Casper, A. J., & Carstens, A. A. (1981). Contingencies of stimulation: Effects on learning and emotion in neonates. *Infant Behavior and Development, 4*, 19–35.

De Casper, A. J., & Fifer, W. P. (1980). Of human bonding: Newborns prefer their mothers' voices. *Science, 208*, 1174–1176.

De Casper, A. J., & Prescott, P. (1984). Human newborns' perception of male voices: Preference, discrimination and reinforcing value. *Developmental Psychobiology, 17*, 481–491.

De Casper, A. J., & Spence, M. J. (1986). Prenatal maternal speech influences newborns' perception of speech sounds. *Infant Behavior and Development, 9*, 133–150.

De Waal, F. (1982). *Chimpanzee politics*. New York: Harper & Row.

Duncan, S., & Fiske, D. W. (1977). *Face-to-face interaction*. Hillsdale, NJ: Erlbaum.

Eibl-Eibesfeldt, I. (1970). *Ethology: The biology of behavior*. New York: Holt, Rinehart & Winston.

Eibl-Eibesfeldt, I. (1989). *Human ethology*. New York: Aldine de Gruyter.

Fairbairn, W. R. D. (1954). *An object relations theory of the personality*. New York: Basic Books.

Fantz, R. L. (1963). Pattern vision in newborn infants. *Science, 140*, 296–297.

Fernald, A. (1985). Four-month-old infants prefer to listen to motherese. *Infant Behavior and Development, 8*, 181–195.

Fernald, A., & Kuhl, P. K. (1987). Acoustic determinants of infant preference for motherese speech. *Infant Behavior and Development, 10*, 279–293.

Fernald, A., Taeschner, T., Dunn, J., Papousek, M., Boysson-Bardies, B. de, & Fukui, I. (1989). A cross-language study of prosodic modifications in mothers' and fathers' speech to preverbal infants. *Journal of Child Language, 16*, 477–501.

Field, T. N. (1985). Neonatal perception of people: Maturational and individual differences. In T. N. Field & N. Fox (Eds.), *Social perception in infants* (pp. 177–197). Norwood, NJ: Ablex.

Field, T. N., Woodson, R., Greenberg, R., & Cohen, D. (1982). Discrimination and imitation of facial expressions by neonates. *Science, 218*, 179–181.

Fodor, J. (1983). *The modularity of mind*. Montgomery, VT: Bradford.

Fogel, A. (1977). Temporal organization in mother–infant face-to-face interaction. In H. R. Schaffer (Ed.), *Studies in mother-infant interaction. The Loch Lomond Symposium*. London: Academic Press.

Fogel, A. (1985). Sensorimotor factors in communicative development. In H. Bloch & B. I. Bertenthal (Eds.), *Sensory-motor organizations and development in infancy and early childhood*. Amsterdam: Kluwer.

Fogel, A., & Thelen, E. (1987). Development of early expressive action from a dynamic systems approach. *Developmental Psychology, 23*, 747–761.

Fraiberg, S. (1974). Blind infants and their mothers: An examination of the sign system. In M. Lewis & L. A. Rosenblum (Eds.), *The effect of the infant on its caregiver*. New York: Wiley.

Fraiberg, S. (1979). Blind infants and their mothers: An examination of the sign system. In M. Bullowa (Ed.), *Before speech: The beginning of interpersonal communication* (pp. 321–347). Cambridge University Press.

Gallistel, C. R. (1980). *The organization of action: A new synthesis.* Hillsdale, NJ: Erlbaum.

Gardner, H. (1983). *Frames of mind: The theory of multiple intelligences.* New York: Basic Books.

Gibson, J. J. (1966). *The senses considered as perceptual systems.* Boston: Houghton Mifflin.

Gibson, J. J. (1979). *The ecological approach to visual perception.* Boston: Houghton Mifflin.

Goodnow, J. (1984). Parents' ideas about parenting and development: A review of issues and recent work. In M. E. Lamb, A. L. Brown, & B. Rogoff (Eds.), *Advances in developmental psychology* (Vol. 3). Hillsdale, NJ: Erlbaum.

Goshen-Gottstein, E. R. (1980). Treatment of young children among nonwestern Jewish mothers in Israel: Sociocultural variables. *American Journal of Orthopsychiatry, 50,* 323–340.

Gouzoules, H., Gouzoules, S., & Marler, P. (1985). External reference and affective signaling in mammalian vocal communication. In G. Zivin (Ed.), *The development of expressive behavior: Biology–environment interactions.* Orlando, FL: Academic Press.

Grieser, D. L., & Kuhl, P. K. (1988). Maternal speech to infants in a tonal language: Support for universal prosodic features in motherese. *Developmental Psychology, 24,* 14–20.

Haith, M. M. (1966). Response of the human newborn to visual movement. *Journal of Experimental Child Psychology, 3,* 235–243.

Haith, M. M., Bergman, T., & Moore, M. J. (1977). Eye contact and face scanning in early infancy. *Science, 198,* 853–855.

Haith, M., & Campos, J. J. (1977). Human infancy. *Annual Review of Psychology, 28,* 251–293.

Halliday, M. A. K. (1975). *Learning how to mean.* London: Arnold.

Hamlyn, D. W. (1974). Person-perception and our understanding of others. In T. Mischel (Ed.), *Understanding of other persons.* Oxford: Blackwell.

Holmlund, C. (1990). *Development of turntaking as a sensorimotor process in the first 3 months: A sequential analysis.* Paper presented at the 5th International Congress of Child Language, Budapest.

Horridge, G. A. (1968). *Interneurons: Their origin, action, specificity, growth and plasticity.* San Francisco: Freeman.

Hubley, P., & Trevarthen C. (1979). Sharing a task in infancy. In I. Uzgiris (Ed.), *Social interaction during infancy: New directions for child development* (Vol. 4, pp. 57–80). San Francisco: Jossey-Bass.

Hundeide, K. (1991). *Helping disadvantaged children: Psychosocial intervention and aid to disadvantaged children in third world countries.* London: Jessica Kingsley.

Hurford, J. R. (1989). Biological evolution of the Saussurean sign as a component of the language acquisition device. *Lingua 77,* 187–222.

Izard, C. E. (1980). The emergence of emotions and the development of consciousness in infancy. In J. M. Davidson & R. Davidson (Eds.), *The psychobiology of consciousness.* New York: Plenum.

Jaffe, J., Stern, D. N., & Peery, J. C. (1973). Conversational coupling of gaze behavior in prelinguistic human development. *Journal of Psycholinguistic Research, 2,* 321–330.

Johanssen, G. (1975). Visual motion perception. *Scientific American, 232* (6), 76–88.

Kanner, L. (1943). Autistic disturbances of affective contact. *Nervous Child, 2,* 217–250.

Kaye, K. (1982). *The mental and social life of babies.* Chicago: University of Chicago Press.

Kellerman H. (1980). A structural model of emotion and personality. In R. Plutchik & H. Kellerman (Eds.), *Emotion: Theory, research and experience: Vol. 1. Theories of emotion.* New York: Academic Press.

Kellerman, H. (1983). An epigenetic theory of emotions in early development. In

R. Plutchik & H. Kellerman (Eds.), *Emotion: Theory, research and experience: Vol. 2. Emotions in early development.* New York: Academic Press.

Kendon, A. (1980). Gesticulation and speech: Two aspects of the process of utterance. In M. R. Key (Ed.), *The relationship of verbal and nonverbal communication.* New York: Mouton.

Klein, M., Heinmann, P., Isaacs, S., & Riviere, J. (1952). *Developments in psychoanalysis.* London: Hogarth.

Klinnert, M. D., Campos, J. J., Sorce, J. F., Ende, R. N., & Svejda, M. (1983). Emotions as behavior regulators: Social referencing in infancy. In R. Plutchik & H. Kellerman (Eds.), *Emotion: Theory, research and experience: Vol. 2. Emotions in early development.* New York: Academic Press.

Kugiumutzakis, G. (1985). The origins, development and function of early infant imitation (PhD thesis, Uppsala University), *Acta Universitatis Uppsaliensis, 35.*

Kugiumutzakis, g. (1992). Intersubjective vocal imitation in early mother–infant interaction. In J. Nadel & L. Camaioni (Eds.), *New perspectives in early communicative development.* London: Routledge.

Langlois, J. H., & Roggman, L. A. (1990). Attractive faces are only average. *Psychological Science, 1*(2), 115–121.

Langlois, J. H., Roggman, L. A., & Rieser-Danner, L. A. (1990). Infants' differential social responses to attractive and unattractive faces. *Developmental Psychology, 26,* 153–159.

Lashley, K. S. (1951). The problems of serial order in behavior. In L. A. Jeffress (Ed.), *Cerebral mechanisms in behavior.* New York: Wiley.

Legerstee, M. (1992). A review of the animate-inanimate distinction in infancy: Implications for models of social and cognitive knowing. *Early Development and Parenting, 1,* 59–67.

Lester, B. (1984). A biosocial model of infant crying. In L. P. Lipsett & C. Rovee-Collier (Eds.), *Advances in infancy research* (Vol. 3). Hillsdale, NJ: Ablex.

Le Vine, R. A., & White, M. I. (1986). *Human conditions.* London: Routledge & Kegan Paul.

Lock, A. (1980). *The guided reinvention of language.* London: Academic Press.

Lotman, Y. (1979). Culture as collective intellect and problems of artificial intelligence. In L. M. O'Toole & A. Shukman (Eds.), *Dramatic structure: Poetic and cognitive semantics/Russian poetics in translation, 6,* 84–96.

MacKain, K. S., Studdert-Kennedy, M., Spieker, S., & Stern, D. N. (1983). Infant intermodal speech perception is a left hemisphere function. *Science, 219,* 1347–1349.

Macmurray, J. (1961). *Persons in relation.* London: Faber & Faber.

McNeill, D. (1992). *Hand and mind: What gestures reveal about thought.* Chicago: University of Chicago Press.

Malatesta, C. Z. (1985). Developmental course of emotion expression in the human infant. In G. Zivin (Ed.), *The development of expressive behavior: Biology-environment interactions.* Orlando, FL: Academic Press.

Maratos, O. (1982). Trends in development of imitation in early infancy. In T. G. Bever (Ed.), *Regressions in mental development: Basis phenomena and theories* (pp. 81–101). Hillsdale, NJ: Erlbaum

Martin, G. B., & Clark, R. D. (1982). Distress crying in neonates: Species and peer specificity. *Developmental Psychology, 18,* 1, 3–9.

Levi, P. (1986). About gossip. *La Stampa,* June 24, 1986. (Reprinted in *The mirror maker: Stories and essays by Primo Levi,* trans. Raymond Rosenthal). New York: Schocken Books.

Mayer, N. K., & Tronick, E. Z. (1985). Mothers' turn-giving signals and infant turn-taking in mother–infant interaction. In T. M. Field & N. A. Fox (Eds.), *Social perception in infants.* Norwood, NJ: Ablex.

Mead, G. H. (1934). *Mind, self and society.* Chicago: University of Chicago Press.

Mehler, J. (1985). Language related dispositions in early infancy. In J. Mehler & R. Fox (Eds.), *Neonate cognition: Beyond the blooming, buzzing confusion.* Hillsdale, NJ: Erlbaum.

Meltzoff, A. N. (1985). The roots of social and cognitive development: Models of man's original nature. In T. M. Field & N. A. Fox (Eds.), *Social perception in infants.* Norwood, NJ: Ablex.

Meltzoff, A. N., & Moore, M. H. (1983). Newborn infants imitate adult facial gestures. *Child Development, 54,* 702–709.

Michotte, A. (1962). *Causalité, permanence et réalité phénomenales.* Louvain: Publications Universitaires.

Montgomery, W. (1985). Charles Darwin's thought on expressive mechanisms in evolution. In G. Zivin (Ed.), *The development of expressive behavior: Biology–environment interactions.* Orlando, FL: Academic Press.

Murray, L. (1980). *The sensitivities and expressive capacities of young infants in communication with others.* Ph.D. Thesis, University of Edinburgh.

Murray, L. (1988). Effects of postnatal depression on infant development: Direct studies of early mother–infant interactions. In I. Brockington & R. Kumar (Eds.), *Motherhood and mental illness* (Vol, 2). Bristol: John Wright.

Murray, L. (1992). The impact of postnatal depression on infant development. *Journal of Child Psychology and Psychiatry, 33*(3): 543–561.

Murray, L., & Trevarthen, C. (1985). Emotional regulation of interactions between two-month-olds and their mothers. In T. Field & N. Fox (Eds.), *Social perception in infants.* Norwood, NJ: Ablex.

Murray, L., & Trevarthen, C. (1986). The infants in mother–infant communication. *Journal of Child Language, 13,* 15–29.

Neisser, U. (1976). *Cognition and reality: Principles and implications of cognitive psychology.* San Francisco: Freeman.

Ninio, A. (1988). The effects of cultural background, sex and parenthood on beliefs about the timetable of cognitive development in infancy. *Merrill-Palmer Quarterly, 34,* 369–388.

Ochs, E. (1983). Cultural dimensions of language acquisition. In E. Ochs & B. B. Schiefflin (Eds.), *Acquiring conversational competence.* New York: Routledge & Kegan Paul.

Oller, D. K. (1986). Metaphonology and infant vocalizations. In B. Lindblom & R. Zetterstrom (Eds.), *Precursors of early speech.* Basingstoke: Macmillan.

Oster, H. (1978). Facial expression and affect development. In M. Lewis & L. A. Rosenblum (Eds.), *The development of affect* (pp. 43–75). New York: Plenum.

Oster, H., & Ekman, P. (1978). Facial behavior in child development. In A. Collins (Ed.), *Minnesota symposia on child psychology* (Vol. 11). New York: Crowell.

Papousek, H. (1967). Experimental studies of appetitional behavior in human newborns and infants. In H. W. Stevenson, E. H. Hess, & H. L. Rheingold (Eds.), *Early behavior: Comparative and developmental approaches.* New York: Wiley.

Papousek, H., & Papousek, M. (1977). Mothering and cognitive head start: Psychobiological considerations. In H. R. Schaffer (Ed.), *Studies in mother–infant interaction: The Loch Lomond Symposium.* London: Academic Press.

Papousek, M., & Papousek, H. (1989). Forms and functions of vocal matching in interactions between mothers and their precanonical infants. *First language, 9,* 137–158.

Papousek, M., Papousek, H., & Bornstein, M. H., (1985). The naturalistic vocal environment of young infants: On the significance of homogeneity and variability in parental speech. In. T. M. Field & N. Fox (Eds.), *Social perception in infants*. Norwood, NJ: Ablex.

Pavlicevic, M., & Trevarthen, C. (1989). A musical assessment of psychiatric states in adults, *Psychopathology, 22*, 325–334.

Piaget, J. (1953). *The origins of intelligence in children*. London: Routledge & Kegan Paul.

Piaget, J. (1962). *Play, dreams and imitation in childhood*. London: Routledge & Kegan Paul.

Plutchik, R (1980). A general psychoevolutionary theory of emotion. In R. Plutchik & H. Kellerman (Eds.), *Emotion: Theory, research and experience: Vol. 1: Theories of emotion*. New York: Academic Press.

Prechtl, H. F. R. (1984). Continuity and change in early human development. In H. F. R. Prechtl (Ed.), *Continuity of neural functions from prenatal to postnatal life*. Oxford: Blackwell.

Reddy, V. (1990). Playing with others' expectations: Teasing and mucking about in the first year. In A. Whiten (Ed.), *Natural theories of mind: Evolution, development and simulation of everyday mindreading* (pp. 143–158). Oxford: Blackwell.

Rogoff, B. (1990). *Apprenticeship in thinking: Cognitive development in social context*. New York: Oxford University Press.

Runeson, S. (1977). On the possibility of "smart" perceptual mechanisms. *Scandanavian Journal of Psychology, 18*, 172–179.

Sagi, A., & Hoffman, M. L. (1976). Empathic distress in the newborn. *Development Psychology, 12*, 175–176.

Sander, L. (1964). Adaptive relationships in early mother–child interaction. *Journal of the American Academy of Child Psychiatry, 3*, 231–264.

Schiefflin, B. B. (1979). Getting it together: An ethnographical approach to the study of the development of communicative competence. In E. Ochs & B. B. Schiefflin (Eds.), *Developmental pragmatics*. New York: Academic Press.

Sperry, R. W. (1952). Neurology and the mind-brain problem. *American Scientist, 40*, 291–312.

Spitz, R. A., & Wolf, K. M. (1946). The smiling response: A contribution to the orthogenesis of social relations. *Genetic Psychology Monographs, 34*, 57–125.

Stern, D. N. (1974). Mother and infant at play: The dyadic interaction involving facial, vocal and gaze behaviors. In M. Lewis & L. Rosenblum (Eds.), *The effect of the infant on its caregiver*. New York: Wiley.

Stern, D. N. (1985). *The interpersonal world of the infant: View from psychoanalysis and development psychology*. New York: Basic Books.

Stern, D. N., Hofer, L., Haft, W., & Dore, J. (1985). Affect attunement: The sharing of feeling states between mother and infant by means of intermodal fluency. In T. N. Field & N. Fox (Eds.), *Social perception in infants*. Norwood, NJ: Ablex.

Stern, D. N., Spieker, S., & MacKain, K, (1982). Intonation contours as signals in maternal speech to prelinguistic infants. *Developmental Psychology, 18*, 727–735.

Thelen, E. (1985). Expression as action. In G. Zivin (Ed.), *The development of expressive behavior: Biology–environment interactions*. Orlando, FL: Academic Press.

Thompson, E., Palacios, A., & Varela, F. J. (1992). Ways of coloring: Comparative color vision as a case study for cognitive science. *Behavioral and Brain Sciences, 15*, 1–74.

Tinbergen, N. (1951). *The study of instinct*. Oxford: Clarendon Press.

Trad, P. V. (1990). *Infant previewing: Predicting and sharing interpersonal outcome*. New York: Springer.

Trevarthen, C. (1974a). The psychobiology of speech development. In E. H.

Lenneberg (Ed.), *Language and brain: Developmental aspects. Neurosciences Research Program Bulletin, 12,* 570–585.

Trevarthen, C. (1974b, May). Conversations with a two-month-old. *New Scientist, 2,* 230–235.

Trevarthen, C. (1977). Descriptive analyses of infant communication behavior. In H. R. Schaffer (Ed.), *Studies in mother–infant interaction: The Loch Lomond Symposium* (pp. 227–270). London: Academic Press.

Trevarthen, C. (1978). Modes of perceiving and modes of acting. In J. H. Pick (Ed.), *Psychological modes of perceiving and processing information* (pp. 99–136). Hillsdale, NJ: Erlbaum.

Trevarthen, C. (1979). Communication and cooperation in early infancy. A description of primary intersubjectivity. In M. Bullowa (Ed.), *Before speech: The beginning of human communication* (pp. 321–347). Cambridge University Press.

Trevarthen, C. (1982). The primary motives for cooperative understanding. In G. Butterworth & P. Light (Eds.), *Social cognition: Studies of the development of understanding* (pp. 77–109). Brighton: Harvester.

Trevarthen, C. (1984a). Biodynamic structures, cognitive correlates of motive sets and development of motives in infants. In W. Prinz & A. F. Saunders (Eds.), *Cognition and motor processes* (pp. 327–350). New York: Springer. Verlag.

Trevarthen, C. (1984b). Emotions in infancy: Regulators of contacts and relationships with persons. In K. Scherer & P. Ekman (Eds.), *Approaches to emotion* (pp. 129–157). Hillsdale, NJ: Erlbaum.

Trevarthen, C. (1984c). How control of movements develops. In H. T. A. Whiting (Ed.), *Human motor actions: Bernstein reassessed* (pp. 223–261). Amsterdam: Elsevier (North Holland).

Trevarthen, C. (1985a). Neuroembryology and the development of perceptual mechanisms. In F. Falkner & J. M. Tanner (Eds.), *Human growth* (2nd ed., pp. 301–383). New York: Plenum.

Trevarthen, C. (1985b). Facial expressions of emotion in mother–infant interaction. *Human Neurobiology, 4,* 21–32.

Trevarthen, C. (1986a). Development of intersubjective motor control in infants. In M. G. Wade & H. T. A. Whiting (Eds.), *Motor development in children: Aspects of coordination and control* (pp. 209–261). Dordrecht: Martinus Nijhof.

Trevarthen, C. (1986b). Form, significance and psychological potential of hand gestures of infants. In J.-L. Nespoulous, P. Perron, & A. R. Lecours (Eds.), *The biological foundation of gestures: Motor and semiotic aspects* (pp. 149–202). Hillsdale, NJ: Erlbaum.

Trevarthen, C. (1987). Sharing makes sense: Intersubjectivity and the making of an infant's meaning. In R. Steele & T. Threadgold (Eds.), *Language topics: Essays in honour of Michael Halliday.* Philadelphia: John Benjamins.

Trevarthen, C. (1988). Universal cooperative motives: How infants begin to know the language and skills of the culture of their parents. In G. Jahoda & I. M. Lewis (Eds.), *Acquiring culture: Cross-cultural studies in child development.* Beckenham, Kent: Croom Helm.

Trevarthen, C. (1989a). Development of early social interactions and the affective regulation of brain growth. In C. von Euler, H. Forssberg, & H. Lagercrantz (Eds.), *Neurobiology of early infant behaviour.* Wenner-Gren Center International Symposium Series, Vol. 55. Basingstoke, Hants.: Macmillan; New York: Stockton.

Trevarthen, C. (1989b). Les relations entre autisme et développement socio-culturel normal: Arguments en faveur d'un trouble primaire de la régulation du développement cognitif par les émotions. In G. Lelord, J. P. Muh, M. Petit, &

D. Sauvage (Eds.), *Autisme et troubles du développement global de l'enfant* (pp. 56–80). Paris: L'Expansion Scientifique Française.

Trevarthen, C. (1990a). Growth and education of the hemispheres. In C. Trevarthen (Ed.), *Brain circuits and functions of the mind: Essays in honour of Roger W. Sperry.* Cambridge University Press.

Trevarthen, C. (1990b). Intuitive emotions: Their changing role in communication between mother and infant. [Le emozioni intuitive: L'evoluzione del loro ruollo nella comunicazione tra madre e bambino.] In M. Ammaniti & N. Dazzi (Eds.), *Affetti: Natura e Sviluppo delle Relazione Interpersonali* (pp. 97–139). Rome: Laterza.

Trevarthen, C. (1990c). Signs before speech. In T. A. Sebeok & J. Umiker-Sebeok (Eds.), *The semiotic web, 1989* (pp. 689–755). Amsterdam: Mouton de Gruyter.

Trevarthen, C. (1992a). The function of emotions in early infant communication and development. In J. Nadel & L. Camaioni (Eds.), *New perspectives in early communicative development.* London: Routledge.

Trevarthen, C. (1992b). An infant's motives for speaking and thinking in the culture. In A. H. Wold (Ed.), *The dialogical alternative.* Festschrift for Ragnar Rommetveit. Oslo: Scandanavian University Press; Oxford: Oxford University Press.

Trevarthen C., & Hubley, P. (1978). Secondary intersubjectivity: Confidence confiding and acts of meaning in the first year. In A. Lock (Ed.), *Action: Gesture and symbol: The emergence of language* (pp. 183–229). London: Academic Press.

Trevarthen, C., & Logotheti, K. (1987). First symbols and the nature of human knowledge. In J. Montangero, A. Tryphon, & S. Dionnet (Eds.), *Symbolisme et connaissance/Symbolism and knowledge* (pp. 65–92). Cahier No. 8. Geneva: Jean Piaget Archives Foundation.

Trevarthen, C., & Marwick H. (1986). Signs of motivation for speech in infants, and the nature of a mother's support for development of language. In B. Lindblom & R. Zetterstrom (Eds.), *Precursors of early speech* (pp. 279–308). Basingstoke: Macmillan.

Trevarthen, C., Murray, L., & Hubley, P. (1981). Psychology of infants. In J. Davis & J. Dobbing (Eds.), *Scientific foundations of clinical paediatrics* (2nd ed.). London: Heinemann.

Tronick, E., Als, H., Adamson, L., Wise, S., & Brazelton, T. B. (1978). The infant's response to entrapment between contradictory messages in face-to-face interaction. *Journal of the American Academy of Child Psychiatry, 17,* 1–13.

Tucker, D. M. (1991). Developing emotions and cortical networks. In M. Gunnar & C. Nelson (Eds.), *Minnesota symposium on child psychology: Vol. 24. Developmental behavioral neuroscience.* Hillsdale, NJ: Erlbaum.

Tulkin, S. R., & Cohler, B. J. (1973). Child-rearing attitudes and mother–child interaction in the first year of life. *Merrill-Palmer Quarterly, 19,* 95–106.

Tulkin, S. R., & Kagan, J. (1972). Mother–child interaction in the first year of life. *Child Development, 43,* 31–41.

Van Rees, S., & de Leeuw, R. (1987). *Born too early: The kangaroo method with premature babies* [Video]. Stichting Lichaamstaal, Scheyvenhofweg 12, 6092 NK, Leveroy, Netherlands.

Von Hofsten, C. (1983). Developmental changes in the organization of prereaching movements. *Developmental Psychology, 20,* 378–388.

Von Hofsten, C., & Rønqvist, L. (1988). Preparation for grasping an object: A developmental study. *Journal of Experimental Psychology: Human Perception and Performance, 14,* 610–621.

Von Holst, E. (1936). Versuche zur Theorie der relativen Koordination. *Archives für Gesamte Physiologie, 236,* 93–121.

Von Uexküll, J. (1957). A stroll through the worlds of animals and men. In C. H. Schiller (Ed.), *Instinctive behavior.* New York: International Universities Press.

Vygotsky, L. S. (1962). *Thought and language.* Cambridge, MA: MIT Press.

Watson, J. S. (1972). Smiling, cooing and the game. *Merrill-Palmer Quarterly, 18,* 323–339.

Weintraub, D., & Shapiro, M. (1968). The traditional family in Israel in the process of change: Crisis and continuity. *British Journal of Sociology, 19,* 284–299.

Wertsch, J. V. (1991). *Voices of the mind: A sociocultural approach to mediated action.* Cambridge, MA: Harvard University Press.

Whiten, A. (1990). *Natural theories of mind: Evolution, development and simulation of everyday mindreading.* Oxford: Blackwell.

Whiting, B., & Whiting, J. (1975). *Children of six cultures: A psychocultural analysis.* Cambridge, MA: Harvard University Press.

Wilson, A. C. (1985). The molecular basis of evolution. *Scientific American, 253* (4), 164–173.

Winnicott, D. W. (1960). The theory of the parent–infant relationship. *International Journal of Psychoanalysis, 41,* 585–595. Republished in D. W. Winnicott, *The maturational process and the facilitating environment* (London: Institute of Psychoanalysis/Karnak Books, 1990).

Wittgenstein, L. (1972). *Philosophical investigations* (G. E. M. Anscombe, Trans.). Oxford: Blackwell and Mott.

Wolff, P. H. (1963). Observations on the early development of smiling. In B. M. Foss (Ed.), *The determinants of infant behavior* (Vol. 2, pp. 113–138). London: Methuen.

Wolke, D. (1987). Environmental and developmental neonatology. *Journal of Reproductive and Infant Psychology, 5,* 17–42.

9

On the interpersonal origins of self-concept

MICHAEL TOMASELLO

Neisser (1988; see also this volume) has done a great service by attempting to specify the different kinds of knowledge that human beings may have of themselves. My concern is with both interpersonal and conceptual knowledge of the self, as I believe that these are intimately related. I am interested in how human beings form a concept of themselves – the "me" of Mead and James – and I believe, as they did, that this can be done only by organisms that are social or interpersonal in a very special way. This chapter is an attempt to specify the nature of this special form of sociality by focusing on recent research and theory in developmental psychology.

The 9-month miracle

Human infants are social creatures from the beginning. They show an interest in people's faces and behavior from as early as we care to measure it (Stern, 1985; see also this volume). They engage in rhythmic interactions with their caregivers (Trevarthen, 1979; see also this volume) and match their behaviors to those of their caregivers within minutes after birth (Meltzoff & Moore, 1989). This face-to-face interaction dubbed *primary intersubjectivity* by Trevarthen and others (see especially Murray & Trevarthen, 1985), is a primary focus of this volume. However, though primary intersubjectivity does involve a kind of self-perception or awareness (that is what is meant by the "interpersonal self"), it does not yet produce anything like a self-*concept*.

The important step, in my view, is secondary intersubjectivity (Trevarthen & Hubley, 1978). At about 9 months of age, infants begin to behave in a number of ways that demonstrate their growing awareness of how other persons work as psychological beings. They look where adults are looking (joint attention), they look to see how adults are feeling toward a novel person or object (social referencing), and they do what adults are doing with a novel object (imitation learning). Furthermore, they do not direct any of these behaviors to inanimate objects. Infants also at this time first direct intentional communicative gestures to adults, indicating an expectation that adults are causal agents who can make things happen. All of these behaviors indicate a kind of social–cognitive revolution: At 9 months of age infants begin to understand that other people perceive the world and have

174

intentions and feelings toward it; they begin to understand them as intentional agents.

Tomasello, Kruger, and Ratner (in press) argue that it is at this point, and only at this miraculous point, that human infants can begin to engage in cultural learning – which, in the current account, forms the basis for the ontogeny of self-concept. Whereas many animals learn from one another socially – by attending to the place where another is interacting or to the results that another has produced – only humans learn from one another culturally (Tomasello, 1990). In cultural learning, learners do not just direct their attention to an individual and its behavior, they actually attempt to see the world the way the other individual sees it – from inside the other's perspective, as it were. Learning in this case is social in a way that individual learning enabled or supported by the social environment is not. It is learning in which the learner is attempting to learn not *from* another but *through* another. This qualitative difference is possible because human beings, from the age of 9 months on, are able to, depending on one's choice of theory and terminology: take the role of the other (Mead, 1934), take the perspective of the other (Piaget, 1932), attribute mental states to the other (Premack, 1988), simulate the mental states of the other (Harris, 1991), engage in joint attention with the other (Bruner, 1983), engage in mindreading of the other (Whiten, 1991), or participate with the other intersubjectively (Trevarthen, 1979).

The process of cultural learning may be seen most clearly in children's early language acquisition. Various researchers have shown that children learn their first words when they are in some type of intersubjective, or joint attentional, interaction with a mature speaker (e.g., Bruner, 1983). In fact, the stronger point is that because linguistic symbols are connected to their referents arbitrarily, infants can learn the appropriate use of a new word *only* if they understand what the mature speaker is focused on (Tomasello & Farrar, 1986; Tomasello, 1988). This point is normally made with reference to the child's learning of object labels in states of joint visual attention with an adult on a concrete object. It can be even more clearly illustrated, however, in the case of words for actions (usually verbs). This is because infants in their second year of life hear most of their early verbs at moments when no action is actually occurring – mostly when an adult is checking the infant's intentions ("Do you want to go?"), anticipating an impending action ("Are you going to eat it?"), or requesting a behavior ("Kick it"). In none of these cases is joint visual attention possible at the time the verb is uttered. Yet, what is most surprising, young children learn verbs better in these "impending action" contexts than they do in ostensive action-naming contexts (Tomasello & Kruger, 1992). To learn verbs in impending action contexts, infants clearly must be able to tune in to the adult's perspective on the situation in a way that does not depend on visual gaze alone.

Joint attention is not just shared visual gaze but a true perspective taking, intersubjectivity, mind reading, simulation – or whatever one chooses to call it – of another's mental state.

What all of this means for self-concept is this: After the 9-month milestone – after the infant can take the perspective of others and learn from it – the adult's face-to-face engagement with the child takes on a new meaning. Whereas before 9 months face-to-face interactions involve only spontaneous communication processes (cf. Buck, this volume), after this period they have the potential to include something new. If the infant can see from the adult's point of view, or at least make efforts in this direction, then face-to-face interactions may also include an element of cultural learning. Just as the infant can learn about external situations from the point of view of the adult, in face-to-face interactions the infant can now learn about the adult's perception of and intentions toward her, the infant, when the adult's attention is on her. Face-to-face interactions are now truly intersubjective, if what is meant by that is that each participant is not only interacting with the other but is also aware of the other's intentional participation.

It is important that in cultural learning the organism employ all of the basic perceptual and categorization processes that it uses in learning about the world directly. Infants' abilities to categorize the world are in a process of rapid development at 9 months of age (Reznik, 1989) and, as argued, allow them to begin to form a concept of person as intentional agent (possessing perceptions and intentions). For the infant to assimilate herself to this category, she must be able to see herself in the same way – from the same vantage point – that she sees others. She does this by simulating others looking at her and then using those simulations as raw material in the categorization process. My claim is that the interactions prior to 9 months are not the appropriate raw material for constructing a self-concept; all the infant has at that time are her own perceptions of her direct, primary, spontaneous interactions with others and a perception of herself from the inside (the interpersonal self). After 9 months of age, the raw material for categorization is her perception of the adult's view of her from the outside, along with her own view of other persons from the outside, which allows for the sorting out of similarities and differences all from the same outside perspective.

The process is summarized in Figure 9.1. Before 9 months of age the infant may interact with a person or with an object, but never does she coordinate the two (Bakeman & Adamson, 1982). Thus, at this early age, even when an adult is looking at the same object that the infant is looking at (Figure 9.1a), the infant is not aware of this, and so there is no state of joint attention; from the child's point of view there is only the object. The child may also look at the person with no regard to any objects in the immediate surroundings (Figure 9.1b); in this state as well the infant has no awareness of the

Before 9 Months of Age

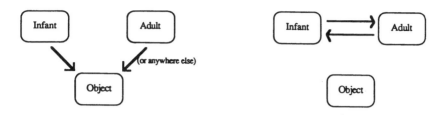

(a) Infant engagement with object prior
    to 9 months (adult passive onlooking).

(b) Infant engagement with person prior to
    9 months (object not part of interaction).

After 9 Months of Age

(c) Joint attention after 9 months.

(d) Self-perception after 9 months.

Figure 9.1.   Object and person engagement before and after 9 months of age. Solid arrows indicate perception; dotted arrows, simulation of other's perspective (pretense).

other person's focus of attention, even though it happens to be on the infant herself. After 9 months of age the situation changes dramatically. Joint attention to an object now means that the infant is not only aware of the object but simultaneously aware of the person's attention to the object (and the adult is engaged in the same process, of course); this is true joint attention (Figure 9.1c). When the object of the adult's attention is the child herself at this same age (as in Figure 9.1d), the child's awareness of adult attention is still operative, and thus the object of their joint attention is the child herself. When the child is simulating and culturally learning from the adult's attention to herself, she may then use her developing abilities of categorization to begin forming a true self-*concept*.

Later development

Once the category of intentional agent is formed and the infant places himself in that category, beginning at about 9 months of age, the groundwork for a human concept of self has been laid. What changes in ontogeny is what kinds of other categories the child places himself in and the social–cognitive concept of person on which these new categories depend. Thus, based only on their concepts of intentional agents, children during toddlerhood and early preschool are placing themselves in concrete categories such as child, male, good at tree climbing, bad at bike riding, and so forth. Which particular categories these are for a particular child is a function of how each child perceives others' views of himself (Harter, 1983). And children during this period are also concerned with their unique characteristics, the unique combination of categories that defines them as individuals (in Western culture, at least).

This process of self-categorization based on how others treat the self continues throughout the lifespan. What changes is the concept of "person" on which this process depends. Thus, at about 4 years of age, children become able to conceive of the mental states of other persons in terms of *beliefs*: mental states that may be right or wrong and may differ from the child's (Harris, 1991). When the child's concept of person was only as an intentional agent with perceptions and intentions, before 4 years of age, beliefs were not a part of his simulation of their psychological states and there was thus no awareness that they were fallible or changeable. From 4 years of age, however, the child's simulations are based on the concept of a mental agent. This concept allows for the first time the child's active manipulation of others' beliefs, including beliefs about himself, and thus it is only at this time that children actively engage in deception and the impression management techniques that are at the core of adult social interaction and self-concept (Goffman, 1959). The result of such learning is the child's ability to engage in a Vygotskian dialogue with himself, and thus self-concept at this age undergoes an important further process of objectification: My self is not just something I can look at from the outside and categorize as I do other things. It is something I can actively control and self-regulate. It is thus during the later preschool period that we first see evidence supporting Mead's (1934) conception of the two-part of self composed of the "I" – the experiencer always inhabiting the temporal present and thus never able to catch itself – and the "me" – that part of myself that has passed and thus can be caught in the conceptual web and controlled as needed.

At about 6 years of age, children's concept of person changes again, and so does their concept of self. They are now able to conceive of such situations as "Mary's thinking that I'm thinking that . . . ," and thus they now perceive that just as they are managing the impression they are creating with others,

others are doing the same thing to them (Perner, 1988). The intersubjectivity characteristic of children of this age, and therefore their self-concept, are immediately reflective and recursive. Self-concept at this point is based on a concept of person as reflective agent and is thus very much adultlike, although in adolescence the agent whose perspective the child takes becomes in some cases the society as a whole (Mead's "generalized other"), or perhaps some abstract philosophical system or political group.

It is legitimate to ask in this context if perhaps I have the whole thing backward. Perhaps children learn first about themselves, construct a concept of person based on this learning, and only then project this concept onto other people. Although I know of no data to answer this question directly – and I am not even sure what such data would look like if they did exist – my inclination is to follow Vygotsky's (1978) lead in positing the primacy of the interpersonal over the intrapersonal. Basically I do not see how the major changes in the concept of person and self could be determined by a child observing his own thoughts and behavior Cartesian style; I see no mechanism for development there, no reason for the child's concept to change over time. On the other hand, people are always doing things that confound young children, and it thus seems reasonable to suppose that intentional agents with perceptions and intentions, mental agents with thoughts and beliefs, and reflective agents with reflective thoughts and beliefs are concepts constructed by children *to explain the behavior of others.* Only after the child has constructed one of these concepts of person does his simulation of the point of view of others allow him to assimilate himself to that concept. This is not to deny that after this has been done the child can in a concrete situation apply knowledge of himself to others by imagining "what I would do if I were in that situation" (Gordon, 1986); it is only to claim that the major developmental changes in the concept of self are all instigated by changes in the concept of the other.

Autistic children

Autistic children do not engage in this same process of self-concept formation. The chapters in this volume by Hobson and by Loveland demonstrate this quite clearly, and they further demonstrate that social-interactional deficits and self-concept deficits are intimately related. It is difficult to be specific about autistic children because they are such a diverse lot, some seeming almost normal and some seeming almost not human, using no language at all, for example. And there are any number of theories to explain the nature of the autistic deficit, from affective problems to social and joint attention problems to problems in the child's "theory of mind" (see Baron-Cohen, 1988, for a review). For our purposes here, however, all autistic children may be seen on a continuum involving their abilities to simulate the psychological states of others. Normal children are tuned into adults during early infancy via affect, toddlers via joint attention with intentional agents, and preschool and school-age youngsters via mutual knowledge with mental and reflective agents. The vastly different capabilities displayed by different autistic children – and perhaps even the different theories of autism – may thus be a function of the different developmental period at which the insult occurs.

The implications of this view for the self-concept of autistic children are straightforward. In the current approach the self-concept of autistic children should be directly tied to the social–cognitive concepts underlying cultural learning. Thus, it should be the case that autistic children who show deficits in conceiving of others as intentional agents should have deficits in their understanding of themselves as intentional agents – and this will be evidenced by their inability to imitatively learn from others (which is usually severely retarded in these children). Autistic children who show an inability to conceive of others as mental agents should have problems treating themselves as mental agents, and thus should show impaired abilities in impression management (including deceit) and in having Vygotskian (self-regulating) dialogues with themselves. And those who show an inability to conceive of others as reflective agents should have a self-concept lacking reflective qualities as well. The general point is that autistic children should have self-concept deficits to the extent that they have deficits in their concept of person or – and this may be the same thing – deficits in their ability to simulate the psychological states of others. Some hints at such a connection are presented by Hobson (1989; see also this volume), whose views on self-concept formation are very similar to those presented here.

A note about phylogeny

Although constructing evolutionary fairy tales is far beyond the scope of my comments here, I would like to make one point about the phylogeny of self-concept that parallels the previous point made about ontogenetic process. As I see it, self-concept is not something that was directly selected for in human evolution. The phylogenetic context in which cultural learning evolved was taking the perspective of and learning about *others*. For example, perspective taking and joint attentional ability evolved to allow or facilitate processes of communication, competition, deception, social learning, and cooperation – that is, all types of social interaction toward all types of pragmatic ends. Research with a variety of primate species and a comparison of these to other animal species demonstrate that nascent forms of these kinds of social interactions are indeed a distinguishing characteristic of primate intelligence and that humans have evolved their own special variants of them (Tomasello, 1990). The important point for our current discussion is that interactions of this sort have obvious evolutionary consequences for surviving and passing on genes, making them excellent candidates for natural selections. The formation of a self-concept, on the other hand, would seem to have, by itself, few directly relevant evolutionary implications for survival and procreation. It is an accident of evolution that when I am taking the perspective of the other – which is useful in many social contexts for many social ends – the other is sometimes focused on me.

Thus it is my contention when looking across the animal kingdom that to the extent that an organism engages in perspective taking and cultural learning, to that extent will they have a concept of themselves as an object in the world. If this is true it is a useful fact because we have very few reliable or valid ways of assessing the self-concept of nonverbal creatures with anything other than mirror self-recognition tasks, whose interpretation is far from straightforward (Neisser, this volume). I will say that based on current research in primate social cognition and social learning, it is my belief that only humans and perhaps to some degree chimpanzees – especially those whose attention has been socialized by human beings early in their development – are capable of simulating others looking at themselves (and chimpanzees clearly are not capable of reflective simulations and probably not mental simulations). Other animals may have interpersonal awareness of some sort, perhaps as in the direct perception of an interpersonal self or perhaps of a type we cannot envision, but self-*concept*, James's concept of *me* characteristic of human children after their first 9 months of life, may turn out to be the exclusive province of human beings.

Conclusion

My overall conclusion is that the ontogenetic construction of a conception of self having the same epistemological status as other persons in the world has two aspects: the simulation of the point of view of others while they are interacting with me and the categorization of the self based on these simulations into various categories all depending on the basic category of person, which is constructed to explain the behavior of others and which changes during ontogeny.

I would like to conclude with some speculation based on this overall perspective. I have argued here that the turning of perspective taking and cultural learning onto the self results in the formation of a self-concept. But cultural learning may be turned on the self in another way with a different result. Whereas the present account concerns those situations in which I take the perspective of another person on myself, when coupled with human abilities of representation and pretense, such perspective taking leads inevitably to a different application of the process: I may in some cases observe, without any other persons present, my own just performed intentional behavior, that is, I may act *as if* I were another person looking at my behavior.

Once again, in this observation of self as object – in this case the behavior produced by self (and the knowledge it embodies) – the individual uses all of the powers of cognition and categorization that he or she uses in understanding the outside world. This self-observation, or self-reflection, may then lead to the formation of many of the abstract systems of thought characteristic of human cognition. Piaget (1985), for example, has argued that basic mathematical concepts are based on subjects' reflections on their own actions on objects, such things as placing objects in groups, dividing them into subgroups based on perceptual or functional characteristics, ordering them in terms of some physical characteristic, or mapping objects onto culturally provided counting systems. Karmiloff-Smith (1986) and Tomasello (1992) have argued that, likewise, the grammar of human languages is constructed by young children as they reflect on their productive use of individual linguistic symbols, especially those with inherently relational content such as verbs. These relational symbols then serve as raw material for the construction of grammatical categories such as agent, patient, and instrument, which are a major source of the productivity of language as a communicative system. It may even be that this process of self-observation has something to do with the recursively self-reflective processes we experience as human consciousness (Humphrey, 1983).

These speculations simply serve to underscore the major point now emerging from the study of both primate intelligence and human social cognition and cultural learning: Human cognition, including cognition of the self, is in large measure a social enterprise. This perspective was first championed decades ago by such thinkers as Baldwin, James, Mead, Dewey, and Vygotsky, but it is only recently, as our research on human and animal cognition has progressed, that we are able to fill in many important details about how this actually plays itself out in human ontogeny and phylogeny. Accounts that ignore the social dimension of human cognition and focus only on information processing will not only distort many facts about human cognition but also will be incapable of explaining even the most rudimentary phenomena of human self-understanding.

ACKNOWLEDGMENT

My thanks to Ulric Neisser and Ann Kruger for helpful comments on an earlier version of this essay.

REFERENCES

Bakeman, R., & Adamson, L. (1982). Coordinating attention to people and objects in mother–infant and peer–infant interactions. *Child Development, 55,* 1278–1289.

Baron-Cohen, S. (1988). Social and pragmatic deficits in autism: Cognitive or affective? *Journal of Autism and Developmental Disorders, 18,* 379–401.

Bruner, J. (1983). *Child talk.* New York: Norton.

Goffman, E. (1959). *The presentation of self in everyday life.* New York: Anchor.

Gordon, R. (1986). Folk psychology as simulation. *Mind and language, 1/2,* 158–171.

Harris, P. (1991). The work of the imagination. In A. Whiten (Ed.), *Natural theories of mind.* Oxford: Oxford University Press.

Harter, S. (1983). Developmental perspectives on the self system. In P. Mussen (Ed.), *Carmichael's manual of child psychology* (Vol. 4). New York: Wiley.

Hobson, P. (1989). Beyond cognition: A theory of autism. In G. Dawson (Ed.), *Autism: Nature, diagnosis, and treatment.* New York: Guilford.

Humphrey, N. (1983). *Consciousness regained: Chapters in the development of mind.* Oxford: Oxford University Press.

Karmiloff-Smith, A. (1986). From meta-process to conscious access: Evidence from children's metalinguistic and repair data. *Cognition, 23,* 95–147.

Mead, G. (1934). *Mind, self, and society.* Chicago: University of Chicago Press.

Meltzoff, A., & Moore, K. (1989). Imitation in newborn infants: Exploring the range of gestures imitated and the underlying mechanisms. *Developmental Psychology, 25,* 954–962.

Murray, L., & Trevarthen, C. (1985). Emotional regulations of interactions between two month olds and their mothers. In T. Field & N. Fox (Eds.), *Social perception in infants.* Norwood, NJ: Ablex.

Neisser, U. (1988). Five kinds of self-knowledge. *Philosophical Psychology, 1,* 35–59.

Perner, J. (1988). Higher order beliefs and intentions in children's understanding of social interaction. In J. Astington, P. Harris, & D. Olson (Eds.), *Developing theories of mind.* Cambridge University Press.

Piaget, J. (1932). *The moral development of the child.* New York: Norton.

Piaget, J. (1985). *The equilibration of cognitive structures.* Chicago: University of Chicago Press.

Premack, D. (1988). "Does the chimpanzee have a theory of mind?" revisited. In R. Byrne & A. Whiten (Eds.), *Machiavellian intelligence.* Oxford: Oxford University Press.

Reznik, S. (1989). Research on infant categorization. *Seminars in Perinatology, 13,* 458–466.

Stern, D. (1985). *The interpersonal world of the infant.* New York: Basic Books.

Tomasello, M. (1988). The role of joint attention in early language development. *Language Sciences, 10,* 69–88.

Tomasello, M. (1990). Cultural transmission in the tool use and communicatory signaling of chimpanzees? In S. Parker & K. Gibson (Eds.), *Language and intelligence in monkeys and apes: Comparative developmental perspectives.* Cambridge University Press.

Tomasello, M. (1992). *First verbs: A case study of early grammatical development.* Cambridge University Press.

Tomasello, M., & Farrar, J. (1986). Joint attention and early language. *Child Development, 57,* 1454–1463.

Tomasello, M., & Kruger, A. (1992). Joint attention on actions: Acquiring verbs in ostensive and non-ostensive contexts. *Journal of Child Language, 19,* 311–333.

Tomasello, M., Kruger, A., & Ratner, H. (in press). Cultural learning. *Behavioral and Brain Sciences.*

Trevarthen, C. (1979). Instincts for human understanding and for cultural co-operation: Their development in infancy. In M. von Cranach, K. Foppa, W. Lepenies, & D. Ploog (Eds.), *Human ethology: Claims and limits of a new discipline.* Cambridge University Press.

Trevarthen, C., & Hubley, P. (1978). Secondary intersubjectivity. In A. Lock (Ed.), *Action, gesture, and symbol: The emergence of language.* New York: Academic Press.

Vygotsky, L. (1978). In M. Cole (Ed.), *Mind in society: The development of higher psychological processes.* Cambridge, MA: Harvard University Press.

Whiten, A. (Ed.). (1991). *Natural theories of mind.* Oxford: Oxford University Press.

10

Infants' knowledge of self, other, and relationship

SANDRA PIPP

Infants' sense of self and other has been supposed by both attachment theory (Bretherton, 1987; Harter, 1983; Main, Kaplan, & Cassidy, 1985; Sroufe & Fleeson, 1985) and psychodynamic theory (Emde, 1983; Kernberg, 1976; Kohut, 1984; Mahler, Pine, & Bergman, 1975; Stern, 1985) to be a function of interactions with primary caregivers. Primary emphasis on the influence of interactions on infants' acquisition of self reflects a bias in our theorizing. Winnicott (1965), for example, stated that "there is no such thing as an infant" to underscore the importance of the mother–infant relationship. In nature, of course, there is not only the infant and the mother but also ongoing interactions between infant and mother. Current theories of infants' self-development vary in their emphasis on infants' capacities that reflect normative functioning (e.g., Neisser, 1988, 1991) and those that emphasize individual differences as a function of variability in infants' interactions with their mothers (e.g., Mahler, et al., 1975). Although infants' biological survival depends on caregivers' support, once this support is assumed within an average expectable environment, our thesis is that infants' sense of self and other is related to a number of diverse factors, including species characteristics, the development of infants' capacities, and characteristics of interactions between infants and mothers.

Historically, theory regarding the sense of self has precluded infancy because the self was defined so as to require the capacity for representational or symbolic thought. Perhaps following James (1890), earlier theorists argued that self-concept, the "me," was the appropriate domain of self to be studied, while the "I," representing the self as actor or processor of information, was the domain of all other aspects of psychology. More recently, however, current theorizing has enlarged to include both the "I" and the "me" (e.g., Case, 1991). Unlike earlier theories, which focused primarily on children's representational self-concept, current theories of infants' sense of self have noted the importance of understanding the preverbal self.

The preverbal self is important because a person's self-structure is assumed to inform characteristic ways of coping with and acting on the world, independent of symbolic mediation even in adults (Squire, 1986). Nonsymbolic structures guide important aspects of the therapeutic process (Clyman, 1991). The development of infants' sense of self is hypothesized to be important clinically because it determines certain forms of adult psychopathology (e.g., Kernberg, 1976; Kohut, 1984) and the understanding of severe pathologies such as autism (Hobson, 1990, see also this volume; Rogers & Pennington, 1991). Additionally, actions, expectancies, and feelings that are guided by nonsymbolic structures characterize infants' interactions with others in normative and maltreated samples (Crittenden, 1989; Pipp, 1990). The exponential increase in our understanding of infants' capacities has resulted in an explosion in the number of theories on the infants' sense of self (see Cicchetti & Beeghly, 1990, and Kopp & Brownell, 1991). Brownell and Kopp (1991), for example, summarizing an impressive collection of articles on the development of self in the first 3 years, state that "the core function of self remains invariant: to define, locate, demarcate the world from a consistent perspective by organizing, integrating, and representing experiences from that vantage point" (p. 288). These authors go on to say that the development of a consistent perspective implies the formation of boundaries between self and other.

The aim of this chapter is to explore species characteristics, changing infants' capacities, and characteristics of the relationship that influence infants' developing sense of self, other, and relationship. Based on empirical findings, I will argue that infants' self-knowledge is initially bodily based (Freud, 1958; James, 1890; Neisser, 1988, 1991) and that species characteristics influence how infants know self, other, and relationship. With the onset of symbolic thought, infants' knowledge changes and a different relation between self, other, and relationship is obtained.

Self and other

Our species evolved in the context of the specific physical characteristics of the earth, and the biological capacities formed in this context force certain perspectives on self and other. The biological base of the infant's core sense of self includes biologically mediated self-organizing properties. At the simplest, biological level, healthy neonates breathe for themselves and digest their food. Autonomic nervous system functioning thus provides structure that serves to organize the biological self. Characteristics of our species lead to factors that contribute both to differentiation and confusion between self and other. Differentiation is caused by the fact that self and other reside in different bodies, and so certain perspectives on the self differ from those on others. Confusion is created by the permeability of physiological regulation between infant and mother.

Components of infants' self-regulation are delegated to the mother–infant relationship both in utero and after birth. Newborn infants adapt to new forms of regulation after being part of the biological system of the mother: Whereas fetuses obtain nutrients through the umbilical cord, to take an obvious example, infants must adapt to digesting their own food after birth.

Nevertheless, human infants are connected biologically to the caregiver after birth, although the form may change. Hofer (1987), for example, reported that homeostatic regulation of the mammalian newborn is delegated to the interaction between caregiver and infant. These regulating functions are observed in neurochemical, immunologic, metabolic, cardiovascular, endocrine, and sleep–wake cycles. The relationship between infant and mother allows the mother to regulate the internal homeostasis of her infant, as well as allowing the infant to regulate the maternal functions (Field, 1985; Hofer, 1987; Reite, Short, Seiler, & Pauley, 1981). Thus, initial mother–infant interactions are based on negotiations concerning biological regulation (Sander, 1975; Pipp & Harmon, 1987).

Another avenue of internal regulation of the infant concerns emotional regulation. Evidence for permeability between the self and other's emotions, for example, is observed in affect contagion, or the automatic induction of one's own affect from another's: Infants have been shown to cry more when hearing another's or the self's taped cries (Sagi & Hoffman, 1976; Simner, 1971; Wolff, 1969). Neisser (1988) suggests that the interpersonal self is specified at birth by direct perception of the other's emotions. This accords with Trevarthen's (1988) account of infants' initial capacity "to link their subjective evaluations of experience with those of other persons" (p. 37). From very early on, infants and mothers appear to regulate each other's emotional and turn-taking behavior (Stern, 1985; Trevarthen, 1988).

With development, however, physiological permeability between self and other changes as a function of increased capacities. Biological regulation in intimate relationships is similar throughout development. Physiological changes in adults after bereavement, for example, bear striking resemblance to those observed in infants separated from their mothers (Hofer, 1984). Yet our species' coping abilities and strategies serve to mediate physiologically based connectedness. With the onset of symbolic capacity, infants are capable of knowing self and other differently. To take one example, the physiological upsets felt when 1- and 4-year-old human infants are separated from their mothers for a short time are different. Increased cognitive capacity leads to understanding that the mother will be right back, and this capacity mediates physiological responsiveness. (Pipp, 1990).

Differentiation between self and other is aided by the fact that self and other exist in different bodies and because the architecture of the body specifies certain perspectives on self and other. For the young infant, the bodies of self and other also serve as objects to be acted upon and explored and as an object from which to act. Perceptual systems serve to focus infants' attention to the self in relation to the world. Neisser (1988, 1991) specified two capacities of which newborn infants are capable. The ecological self specifies infants' direct and immediate perception of self "in terms of its ongoing relationship with the local physical environment" (1991, p. 203). The interpersonal self, in contrast, specifies infants' direct and imme-

diate perception of self in relation to the social other, specified by emotional communication and contingencies "between each person's actions on
those of the partner, both temporally (as in turn-taking) and spatially
(as in keeping eye contact)" (1991, p. 204). Neisser thus distinguishes
between the direct perception of the physical and social environments. In
the following sections we shall examine the development of infants' understanding of self and other as physical objects and as members of a social
unit.

Self and other as physical objects

The architecture of the body results in different body maps for self and other.
The 3-month-old infant's exploration of his own hands, for example, gives
the tactile sense both of being touched and touching, whereas touching
another's hands gives only the tactile sense of touching (Sullivan, 1953).
Visual maps of self and other should also differ. Because the eyes turn
outward, a bias should obtain so that infants have visual knowledge of their
mother's face before acquiring visual knowledge of his or her own face. In
order to test whether knowledge of the features of mother develops before
knowledge of the features of self, we administered a number of tasks to
infants in the first 3 years of life. As shown in Table 10.1, these tasks included
those typically used in the literature on featural recognition – for example,
self-recognition, spatial location, knowledge of name, possession, and gender (Amsterdam, 1972; Bertenthal & Fischer, 1978; Lewis & Brooks-Gunn,
1979). We found that knowledge of the mother's and father's visual features
was acquired earlier than the infant's own visual features, with infants passing
the first three tasks earlier for parents than self (Pipp, Easterbrooks, &
Brown, 1993; Pipp, Easterbrooks, & Harmon, 1992; Pipp, Fischer, & Jennings,
1987). Infants younger than 2 years recognized other's visual features before
their own. No difference between recognition of visual features for self and
parent, however, was obtained for infants older than 2 years.

Differences also appear in the age at which infants direct actions toward
self and other. Certain self-directed behaviors, for example, seem to have
precedence over other-directed behaviors. Infants have a predisposition to
put their hands to their own mouth, not the other's. In those studies that
examined self- or other-directed behavior, infants and children were found
to produce labels of actions concerning the self before applying them to
others, whether they be action words (Huttenlocher, Smiley, & Charney,
1983) or emotion words (Bretherton, Fritz, Zahn-Waxler, & Ridgeway, 1986).
In order to test whether the ability to act on self and on mother was the
same, a number of tasks were presented to infants 3 1/2 years and younger
(Pipp et al., 1987; Pipp et al., in press). Less complex tasks included being
able to feed self or mother, and more complex ones reflected an infant's

Table 10.1. *Infant and mother versions of the featural recognition tasks*

Task	Infant version	Mother version
Visual recognition		
1	Sticker-nose: Infant pulls sticker off own nose.	Sticker-nose: Infant pulls sticker off mother's nose.
2	Sticker-hand: Infant pulls sticker off own hand.	Sticker-hand: Infant pulls sticker off mother's hand.
3	Rouge task: Infant touches own nose after detecting rouge in the mirror.	Rouge task: Infant touches mother's nose after detecting rouge in the mirror.
Spatial location		
4	"Where's (child's name)?" Infant responds by pointing to self or by stating "here" or "there."	"Where's Mommy?" Infant responds to mother or by saying "here" or "there."
Verbal label		
5	"Who's that?" When experimenter points to infant, infant responds by stating his or her own proper name or by stating "me."	"Who's that?" When experimenter points to mother, infant responds by stating mother's proper name or "Mommy."
Featural possession		
6	"Whose shoe is that?" When experimenter points to infant's shoe, infant responds by stating his or her own proper name or by stating "mine."	"Whose shoe is that?" When experimenter points to mother's shoe, infant responds by stating mother's proper name or "Mommy."
7	"Who do you belong to? Whose baby are you?" Infant responds by stating a family member.	"Who does your Mommy belong to? Whose Mommy is she?" Infant responds by stating a family member.
Identification of gender		
8	"Are you a boy? Are you a girl?" Infant responds correctly to both questions.	"Is Mommy a boy? Is Mommy a girl?" Infant responds correctly to both questions.

ability to understand baby or mother behavioral roles, as shown in Table 10.3. These tasks were presented within the context of symbolic play (Vygotsky, 1978), as play is an important context for the development of symbolic representation of self as an actor on self and others. Our studies showed that infants younger than 2 years were found to act on self before acting on others; no difference was obtained for infants older than 2 years (Pipp et al., 1987; Pipp, Easterbrooks, Brown, & Harmon, 1992; Pipp et al., in press). (See Table 10.2.)

Taken together, these data show that infants' development of knowledge of self and other occurs at different ages depending on the domain to be known. Action on self occurs before action on others, and visual recognition of other's features occurs before recognition of one's own features. Because individual studies have replicated this finding, Table 10.3 presents

Table 10.2. *Infant and mother versions of the agency tasks*

Task	Infant version	Mother version
Actor		
1 Infant acts on self by eating a Cheerio.	Infant acts on mother by feeding the mother a Cheerio.	
Passive agent		
2 Infant acts as agent by passively pretending to feed self with a spoon or pretending to give self a drink with a cup.	Infant acts as agent by passively pretending to feed the mother with a spoon or pretending to give the mother a drink with a cup.	
Active other agent		
3 Infant pretends to have a doll walk to a toy table and drink with a cup or eat with a spoon.	Infant asks (verbally or by action) the mother to come to the table and drink with a cup or eat with a spoon.	
Baby behavioral role		
4 Infant treats a doll as a baby by calling it a baby, giving it a drink with a baby bottle, giving it a rattle to play with, or having the doll kiss a toy teddy bear. (Two out of four actions are required for a pass.)	Infant treats the mother as a baby by calling her a baby, giving her a drink with a baby bottle, giving her a rattle to play with, or having her kiss a toy teddy bear. (Two out of four actions are required for a pass.)	
Mother behavioral role		
5 Infant pretends that the mother doll gives the baby doll a baby bottle, a rattle to play with, or a teddy bear to kiss, or the infant calls the mother doll a "mother" or the baby doll a "baby." (Two out of the five actions are required for a pass.)	Infant asks (verbally or by action) that the mother give the baby doll a baby bottle, a rattle to play with, or the teddy bear to kiss, or the infant calls the mother a "mother" or the baby doll a "baby." (Two out of the five actions are required for a pass.)	

the aggregate data from three different samples (Pipp et al., 1987; Pipp et al., 1992; Pipp et al., in press). Following James (1890), before 2 years, acquisition of the self as actor, or "I," and the self-concept, or "me," occurs at different times. After 2 years, however, differences between self and mother disappeared altogether when either featural or agency tasks were considered. We hypothesized that the architecture of the body influences how young sensorimotor infants acquire knowledge of self and mother. With the onset of representational skills, infants are able to transcend the limitations of the perspective offered by living in their own body, and so fewer differences are obtained between cognitive knowledge of self and other (Pipp et al., 1987).

Physical and cognitive development should change infants' and toddlers' relation to their own bodies as well as to others' bodies. With development,

Table 10.3. *Number of featural knowledge and agency tasks passed* (N) *as a function of age and version*

	N	Infant	Parent
Featural knowledge tasks			
Younger than 2 years	127	1.78	2.90
Older than 2 years	114	6.29	6.21
Agency tasks			
Younger than 2 years	130	1.73	1.48
Older than 2 years	116	3.23	3.20

Note: These numbers represent data aggregated from the infants who served as subjects in the following studies: Pipp et al., 1987; Pipp et al., 1992; Pipp et al., in press. For each of these studies, younger infants showed significant differences between the infant and parent versions, whereas the older infants did not. The average number of featural knowledge tasks corresponds to those presented in Table 10.1; the average number of agency tasks corresponds to those shown in Table 10.2.

bodies become larger and capable of more complex actions. As Mahler et al. (1975) pointed out, changes in physical abilities change the type of relation one has with important others. The ability to walk, for example, changes the distance one can move from mother. Not surprisingly, greater knowledge of the visual features of the self is also possible, as shown by toddlers' discovery of their backsides in the mirror. Greater complexity of knowledge of the other is also possible as a function of increased symbolic structure. The onset of representation enables the infant to create psychological means by which to transcend the architecture of the body. Body maps of the other include what is not seen as well as what is directly perceived. Preschoolers become able to think about something without actually doing it. They can therefore take either self or other as an object to be mentally manipulated independently of the actions required for acting on either self or other. One can imagine the visual characteristics of one's own face without recourse to the mirror and can imagine the back of the other when gazing at the face.

Infants code different contents for self and other, of course. When learning names for self and other, for example, normal children do not call the self "Mommy" or their mother by their own name (Hart & Damon, 1985). Although the abstract definition of the process of acquiring and coding content regarding self and other may be similar (Baldwin, 1899; Lewis & Brooks-Gunn, 1979; Pipp et al., 1987), the specific content changes as a function of the person to whom it applies.

192   *SANDRA PIPP*

Self and other in interactions

When infants interact with others, two physical bodies interact. The physical
bodies represent both physical objects with particular characteristics and
perspectives on the other and systems with physiological mechanisms that
are semipermeable to regulation from the other. Interactions with others
occur in real time and real space and represent interactive sequences between
self and other. The interactive sequences specify the other in relation to
the self. The sense of the "I" as an actor on the other, thus, is implicated
in the "we" of the interaction. The other is known through the self's perceptual systems and sensorimotor actions, and so enactive representations
of the other are coded in reference to the self. Because of this, it may be
that codings of other are inextricably bound to codings of the self.

For any interaction, the information about the interaction is contained
at the sensorimotor level, for example, perceptual, gestural, and/or verbal
acts that specify the interactional sequence. Infants whose knowledge system
is primarily sensorimotor in nature know self and other only through the
sensorimotor interactive sequences. Sensorimotor information about interactions may be coded in the form of scripts, defined as temporally ordered
sequences of actions or generalized event structures (Fivush, 1987; Nelson
& Gruendel, 1981). Infants may first form interactive scripts, for example,
about the actions of self and mother needed to have breakfast that include
the actions of both needed to get up on the high chair, put the bib on,
have food served, and so on.

With the gradual onset of symbolic representations, toddlers are capable
of storing their knowledge of the interactions in the form of representations
of relationships. One's representations of one's mother may develop to
include generalized "superscripts" of lower-level action sequences of, for
example, being fed, going to sleep, playing, and so on. With the onset of
representational capacities, infants become capable of coding any event at
two levels: the actual sensorimotor level and the level of representations.
The representational infant is coding – or decoding – information about
the ongoing interaction, and is also accessing stored representations of interactions that are similar to the one being enacted. Thus the representational
infant continues to code sensorimotor components of interactions while
accessing, creating, or storing the representational form of the interaction.
Infants become dual processors.

The distinction drawn here between sensorimotor and representational
knowledge structures obviously stems from a Piagetian framework (Piaget,
1962). It is similar, however, to the distinction between procedural and
declarative knowledge that is drawn from cognitive science (see, e.g., Squire,
1986) and has recently been applied to explain the behavior of patients
in therapy or maltreated infants (Crittenden, 1992). Sensorimotor knowledge from a Piagetian framework refers to knowing through sensory or

motor actions on objects, and the emphasis is on how infants construct reality from the coordination of actions around objects or people. In contrast, procedural knowledge is defined as knowledge of procedures of skills that are unconscious. Procedures are flexible and organized around goals, and procedural knowledge would be used to explain the microattunements one automatically carries out when, for example, skiing a new course. In contrast, representational ability refers to symbolic structures that result from coordination between sensorimotor skills and that develop in complexity from preoperational to formal operational thought from a Piagetian framework. Declarative knowledge is similar to representational ability in that it refers to knowledge structures that stand for something else and refers to information that is learned, stored, and later recalled. It differs, however, in that it is not embedded in a developmental framework. These two different theoretical traditions, however, both focus on the importance of distinguishing between knowledge that specifies non-symbolized actions in the world and representations of those actions, thoughts, or feelings.

Both of these traditions (e.g., Piaget, 1962; Squire, 1986) have often been contrasted with the ecological perspective (Gibson, 1966; Neisser, 1988, 1991). Proponents of the ecological perspective have emphasized that perception of the world is direct and is not constructed. The view that I have advanced in this chapter is that, through our species' adaptation to the world in which we have evolved, perception of ourselves and the world is direct and not constructed. Procedural and sensorimotor knowledge bases reflect direct perceptual knowledge. The shift in the structure of knowledge that has been observed at around 18 to 24 months adds another component to direct perception, and this component is constructed knowledge bases. This shift has been noted by a number of authors and has variously been labeled as the onset of representation (Piaget, 1962), declarative knowledge (Squire, 1986), metarepresentation (Leslie, 1987), or second-order representations (Perner, 1991). This viewpoint suggests that our species has adapted to characteristics of the world with (at least) two mechanisms: direct perception of invariant features of the world and a capacity to construct or combine these direct perceptions to provide unique or idiosyncratic meanings of what is directly perceived with development. Proponents of both sides (direct perception versus constructed reality) have engaged in lively debate, suggesting no compromise between the two theoretical approaches. The developmental analysis proposed here postulates initial perception through direct means as hypothesized by Gibson (1950, 1966) and Neisser (1976). With development, a representational system is constructed upon knowledge gained through direct perception. The direct perceptual system, however, maintains its own integrity alongside the development of the representational system, and so maintains its capacity to perceive the structural invariants of the perceptual world throughout development.

In sum, lack of differentiation between self and other results because of the semipermeability of physiological regulation between infant and mother. Additionally, infants code the self in interaction with the other. Differentiation is engendered because of the architecture of the body, which predisposes infants to act on self before acting on others and to recognize the features of self differently than features of others. With development, symbolic structures enable the infant to transcend the architecture of the body. The content of self and other differ (e.g., mother becomes labeled as "Mom" while the self has a proper name), whereas the formal cognitive structure needed to acquire information about self and other results in similarities in how one processes information about self and other. Self and other become increasingly differentiated as higher-order representations of categories of action are formed. The self is constructed by the actions unique to the self, whereas infants' understandings of others are constructed by those unique constellations of actions that characterize each of the others. Thus, infants' acquisition of self and other knowledge is related to species characteristics as well as to the development of infants' increasing cognitive capacities. The structure of the physical world influences the development of infants' ecological self and other (Neisser, 1991). In infancy, individual differences between infants reflect differences in biological capacity (e.g., autism or blindness). Constructed knowledge bases differ because the contents of direct perception differ or because the way in which the construction processes develop differs. Yet infants are also affected by differences in relationships with caregiving others. To this we now turn.

Self, other, and relationship

How do interactive sequences between infants and mothers come together in the infant's mind to form internalized representations of relationships? One represents a relationship with another person by abstracting commonalities between interactions with a particular person. For infants, the interpersonal sense of self should result from stereotypical action sequences, such as tickle games, change-the-diaper routines, and feeding routines. Interactional sequences that share commonalities between one episode and the next will develop into sensorimotor internal working models of relationships. With development, these sensorimotor internal working models will eventually turn into representational internal working models. (See Stern, 1985, for a treatment of this theme). Though not all interactions with others are stereotyped to such a degree that generalities can or should be abstracted, intimate relationships with important caregivers contain both the frequency and emotional importance so that internal working models can be built. Caregiving routines and games between infants and mothers are two common mechanisms by which the "interactional I" derives from the "we" of the relationship. The sense of self as an interpersonal agent is created in the matrix of shared meaning between the caregiver and infant.

One important question is how generalized differences among interactions give rise to differences in types of relationships between infants and mothers. These differences have been shown to be related to more generalized indices of mother–infant relationships. Attachment research, for example, has repeatedly demonstrated the importance of emotional availability, and especially maternal sensitivity, as a primary factor related to attachment security (Ainsworth, Bell, & Stayton, 1971; Ainsworth, Blehar, Waters, & Wall, 1978). Securely attached infants have mothers who are more sensitive to them and are themselves more responsive to their mothers. Mothers who are highly sensitive, for example, follow the child's lead during interactions, respond promptly to distress, and soothe warmly. Maternal behavior appears to be flexible. In contrast, the insensitive mother is inflexible in her approach to interactions with the child, shows inappropriate affect, and does not follow her child's lead. Another theoretically important aspect of mother–infant interactions that may influence infants' attachment classification is synchronous affect exchanges (Osofsky & Eberhart-Wright, 1990; Stern, 1985). Stern (1985) describes the concept of "affect attunement" as shared affect states between infant and mother. Because emotions have been hypothesized as providing a core of continuity (Emde, 1983), affect attunement between mother and infant is one important mechanism by which mothers can support and scaffold infants' core affective sense of self. Individual differences in interpersonal aspects of the self, therefore, may be a function of the quality of intersubjectivity (Trevarthen, 1988) or affect attunement (Stern, 1985) between infant and mother.

Infants' acquisition of knowledge of self and other is related to characteristics of their relationships to their caregivers, according to psycho-dynamic and attachment theories. One of the most articulated theories regarding the relation between infants' developing sense of self and interactions with caregivers has found its voice in attachment theory. Infants' attachment behavior to mother has been hypothesized to reflect the internal working model of the caregiving relationship (Bretherton, 1985, 1988). Internal working models are defined as dynamic internalized representations of relationships, and with development, infants first internalize features of the relationship and then differentiate self and other from the initial internalization (Bretherton, 1985). Although inferences are commonly made about how maternal capacities and mother–infant interactions influence variations in infants' sense of self, the bulk of the empirical work has focused primarily on how these characteristics relate to infants' attachment to mother (Bowlby, 1988; Sroufe, 1989; Sroufe & Fleeson, 1985).

A few studies, however, have targeted the relation between attachment classification and infants' knowledge of self and other. In these studies attachment classification has been defined by infants' responses to separation from mother in the "Strange Situation" (Ainsworth & Wittig, 1969). Infants who are securely attached are able to be comforted by mother during reunions with her, whereas infants who are insecurely attached either seek mother after separation but are unable to be comforted by her or avoid the mother upon reunion. Focus on the infants' cognitive aspects of self-knowledge and concurrent relationships to primary caregivers has shown that a larger percentage of securely attached than insecurely attached infants recognized themselves (Schneider-Rosen & Cicchetti, 1984). Additionally, when complexity of self- and parent-knowledge was assessed by noting the number of tasks passed (see Table, 10.1 and 10.2), securely attached infants had more complex knowledge of self and parent than insecurely attached infants (Pipp et al., 1992; Pipp et al., in press; Pipp & Foltz, 1992). This general finding held true whether infants were assessed with mothers or fathers, suggesting that the relation between complexity of self- and other knowledge and attachment status is a robust one.

The relation is not a simple one, however. Our research has shown that the general relation between attachment status and complexity of self- and other knowledge is a function of both the domain of knowledge under study and the age of the infant. Independent of age, infants who were securely attached to their mothers acted on themselves and their mothers with greater complexity than did infants who were insecurely attached (Pipp et al., in press). That is, the "I," perhaps representing sensorimotor or procedural knowledge, differentiates the two attachment statuses independent of the representational components of the self–other tasks. It may be that mothers whose interactive style is more sensitive to their infant's needs provide an environment that enhances infants' capacity to act on self and other. In contrast, securely attached infants have more complex featural knowledge of self and parent after 18 months but not before (Pipp et al., 1992; Pipp et al., in press). Infants' featural knowledge, the "me," appears to be sensitive to attachment classification as a function of the sensorimotor or representational components of the tasks. Symbolic representation may mediate the linkage between featural knowledge, the "me," and attachment security, whereas infants' actions are related to attachment independent of representational components.

This developmental shift in the relation between attachment status and complexity of knowledge of self and other is also mirrored by an acquisition sequence found regarding the two versions of the tasks. What is the relation between attachment and infants' knowledge of self and other? Attachment has a pervasive influence on acquisition of self- and other knowledge. Because infants simultaneously code both sides of an interaction, differences in the quality of relationships are hypothesized to influence the acquisition of self and other concepts in an equal manner (Sroufe & Fleeson, 1985). An alternative argument focuses on the nature of our current assessment of attachment. The Strange Situation (Ainsworth & Wittig, 1969) is a construct that measures how infants respond to separation from the other. Thus the initial correspondence between attachment and knowledge should be found for infants' knowledge of the other before the self. In fact, data from several studies show a developmental sequence that reflects the progression of the relation between attachment classification and self- and other knowledge. No relation between attachment and self- and parent featural knowledge was reported at 1 year (Pipp et al., 1992; Pipp et al., in press; Pipp & Foltz, 1992). At 20 months, however, the relation between attachment status and the complexity of featural knowledge was found to be greater for the complexity of infants' knowledge of parents than of self (Pipp et al., 1991). Because attachment is a concept that relates to how infants respond to the other, variations in attachment to others is first reflected in complexity of knowledge of the other. The next developmental step was found when infants were tested at 24 months (Pipp et al., in press; Pipp & Foltz, 1992). Securely attached infants were found to have significantly and equally more complex knowledge of self *and* parent, with an even larger difference obtained between infants of the two attachment statuses at 36 months (Pipp et al., in press). With increasing age, therefore, the initial relation between attachment status and featural knowledge of the other generalizes to include self-knowledge. Variations in interpersonal relationships influence infants' representations of other's features before the self.

More often than not, previously published research has compared securely attached infants to those who are insecurely attached. Although theoretically meaningful differences are often predicted between the insecure categories, the small number of subjects in most studies results in a collapse across insecure groups, and the difference found between secure and a collapsed insecure group shows the most predictive validity (Bretherton, 1985). Originally, however, two insecure groups were identified: Insecure-avoidant infants are infants who tend to avoid their mothers upon a reunion, whereas insecure-ambivalent infants approach their mothers but are unable to be soothed by her.

It is an empirical question as to whether infants' sense of self and other is differentiated as a function of the insecure attachment categories. Differentiation of the insecure categories, however, may provide an answer to discrepancies in studies investigating the relation between attachment and infants' sense of self. In contrast to research previously reviewed in this chapter, Lewis, Brooks-Gunn, and Jaskir (1985) and Tajima (1984) reported that more *insecurely* attached infants recognized themselves when compared to infants who were securely attached. Lewis stated that his sample of insecurely attached infants was predominantly of the insecure-avoidant type, and hypothesized that the stress of inadequate parenting may lead to accelerated acquisition of self-recognition even though the relationship may not be more positive. Following Lewis et al., avoidantly attached infants may prematurely develop a differentiated sense of self and other, whereas ambivalently attached infants may be enmeshed in the relationship so that less differentiation between self and other is exhibited. Securely attached infants, in contrast, may demonstrate acquisition of self–other differentiation intermediate between the avoidant and ambivalently attached infants. A third type of insecure attachment has been labeled as insecure–disorganized-disoriented [Main & Solomon, 1986]. It is unclear where the disorganized-disoriented group of insecurely attached infants would fit in this scheme.

It should be noted that Lewis et al. (1985) and Tajima (1984) did not obtain concurrent assessments of attachment and self-recognition but instead measured attachment classification at 1 year, and self-recognition when infants were 18 or 24 months. In contrast, studies in which securely attached infants had more complex self- and other knowledge used concurrent assessments of attachment and self- and other knowledge. This is not a trivial point in that attachment classification has been reported to be unstable during the second year of life (Vaughn, Egeland, Waters, & Sroufe, 1979). We wondered, nevertheless, whether the differences between the findings could be accounted for by different proportions of insecurely attached infants. In order to provide a large enough sample of infants, data from two studies were combined (Pipp et al., in press; Pipp et al., 1992). A 1-year-old group included infants at 12 and 13 months, and the 2-year-old group included infants at 20 and 24 months of age. Attachment classification was obtained by administering the Strange Situation (Ainsworth & Wittig, 1969), and complexity of self- and mother knowledge was obtained by administering the tasks presented in Tables 10.1 and 10.2. Analyses of these data (Pipp, et al., 1992) revealed significant differences between the insecurely attached groups as a function of the domain under question.

Replicating previous findings, featural knowledge of self and mother was not related to attachment classification at 1 year. At 2 years, however, infants who were securely attached and infants who were insecure-avoidantly attached had equally complex knowledge of self and other. Together, these two groups had significantly more complex self- and other knowledge than infants in the two other insecure categories (insecure-ambivalent and insecure–disorganized-disoriented). Main (1987) argued that each of the four attachment categories represents infants' coping reactions to stress. Following Lewis et al. (1985), infants who cope with significant others through avoidant styles acquire featural knowledge of self and other in a manner that is as efficient as infants who are securely attached. The coping styles represented by enmeshment with mother, or by no coping style at all (disorganization), lead to less complex featural knowledge of self and mother.

Infants' capacity to act on self and other as assessed through the agency sequences, however, revealed a different pattern of results. Independent of infants' age, securely attached infants were capable of significantly more complex actions on self and mother than infants who were insecurely attached in either an avoidant or in a disorganized-disoriented manner. In turn, these two groups of insecurely attached infants had significantly more complex actions on self and mother than those infants who were insecurely-ambivalently attached to their mothers. Infants whose style of coping reflects use of the mother as a resource (as a function of her more sensitive caregiving) act on themselves and their mothers in the most complex manner. Interestingly, infants whose coping style reflects either avoidance of mother or no style at all through disorganization appear to have more complex ways of acting on self and mother than those infants whose coping style reflects enmeshment with mother.

Together, these data suggest that securely attached infants have more complex knowledge of self and mother in the domains of both featural knowledge and agency. How the three insecure attachment classifications relate to complexity of self- and other-knowledge, however, differs as a function of the domain under question. Infants who are avoidantly attached to their mothers and infants who are securely attached have equally complex self- and mother featural knowledge, suggesting that an avoidant attachment style serves as an adaptive mechanism in acquiring featural knowledge. This adaptive style, however, breaks down and serves infants less well when acting on self or mother. If one's coping style is to avoid the other, actions are inhibited both when acting on self and other.

Infants who are ambivalently attached to mother have the least complex featural knowledge of and capacity to act on self and mother. Paradoxically, styles of coping and mother–infant interactions that lead infants to stay enmeshed in the relationship appear to be least helpful in enabling infants to create more complex knowledge structures of either self or mother. Finally, little is known about the insecure disorganized-disoriented category, although infants who are from high-risk families and are at risk for maltreatment appear disproportionately often in this category (Carlson, Ciccheti, Barnett, & Braunwald, 1989). The present data suggest that disorganized coping styles are associated with self- and other featural knowledge in a way that is similar to ambivalently attached infants, yet fall between ambivalently and securely attached infants in the domain of actions on self and mother. At the current time, it is unclear why this is so.

Attachment classifications are related both to characteristics of interactions between infants and mothers (Ainsworth et al., 1971; Ainsworth et al., 1978) and to the styles infants use to cope with these interactions (Main, 1987). We suspect that how infants cope with these interactions is related to the complexity of their knowledge about themselves and their mothers. Infants whose mothers are sensitive to their needs have the most complex knowledge about themselves, whereas those whose mothers are less sensitive in their interactional style generally have less complex knowledge. Neisser (1988, 1991) has suggested that the interpersonal self is directly perceived at birth. While it may be that infants' capacity for self- and mother knowledge influences maternal sensitivity and attachment (and some third capacity such as intelligence or temperament may influence both self-development and attachment classification) the data suggest that individual differences in components of the interpersonal self are subsequently influenced by variations in mother–infant interactions. This may be because the direct perception of these interactions varies. Additionally, with development, representational structures may be constructed from differences in the initial perceptual information, or the construction process itself may differ as a function of different caregiving interactions.

Species characteristics, development, and individual differences

Infants' acquisition of knowledge about self and other is postulated to be a function of species characteristics, developmental advances in cognitive capacity, and individual variations in the quality of the relationship between infants and mothers. The biological structure of our species evolved within the context of the physical characteristics of the earth. Adaptation to the characteristics of the earth resulted in organisms that pick up information from the environment and are also biologically contained. Permeability between self and other is a function of homeostatic regulation and inter-subjectivity. Differences between self and other result from the fact that the self lives in a different body from other. This leads to a structure in which certain physiological characteristics are independent of the other (e.g., digestion) and which forces different perspectives on self than other. The ecological and interpersonal selves are perceived at birth (Neisser, 1988; 1991).

The development of cognitive capacity in infancy serves as a mechanism by which infants transcend the species characteristics inherent in living in separate bodies. A move to the level of symbolic structure marks the addition of a new level of thought. But because sensorimotor components of self and other are the bases out of which interactions and understandings of self and other are built, we do not "develop out of bodies." We remain embedded in the biology given by species characteristics. Symbolic under-standings of self, other, and the interactions between self and others co-occur within the context of sensorimotor interactions.

We postulated that individual differences between newborns are found in the interpersonal self as defined by Neisser (1988, 1991). At birth, these individual differences may be a function of temperament, with some infants more open to affect regulation and attunement than others. Subsequently, however, the interpersonal self is influenced by variations in relationships between infant and mother. Discrete interactive sequences between self and other were hypothesized to become organized into more general characteristics of the relationship with significant others over time and across situations. These general characteristics reflect infants' internal working models of relationships. The complexity of infants' knowledge of self and mother was shown to be differentially related to the four attachment classifications. Internal working models of relationships may guide infants' styles of adaptation to separation from and reunion with mother. These coping styles, in turn, may reflect how infants acquire knowledge about self and other.

ACKNOWLEDGMENTS

The research described in this chapter was supported by a grant from the Foundation for Child Development, Young Scholars in Social and Affective Development and NIH grant 23107. Warm thanks to Scott Brown, Ulric Neisser, and Cliff Siegel for comments on the manuscript. Author's address: Department of Psychology, University of Colorado, Boulder, CO 80309-0345.

REFERENCES

Ainsworth, M. D. S., Bell, S., & Stayton, D. J. (1971). Individual differences in the Strange Situation Behavior of one-year-olds. In H. R. Schaffer (Ed.), *The origins of human social relations* (pp. 17–57). New York: Academic Press.

Ainsworth, M. D. S., Blehar, M. C., Waters, E., & Wall, S. (1978). *Pattern of attachment.* Hillsdale, NJ: Erlbaum.

Ainsworth, M. D. S., & Wittig, A. (1969). Attachment and exploratory behavior in one-year-olds in a stranger situation. In B. M. Foss (Ed.), *Determinants of infant behavior* (pp. 111–136). New York: Wiley.

Amsterdam, B. K. (1972). Mirror self-image reactions before age two. *Developmental Psychology, 5,* 297–305.

Baldwin, J. M. (1899). *Social and ethical interpretations in mental development.* New York: Macmillan.

Bertenthal, B. I., & Fischer, K. W. (1978). Development of self-recognition in the infant. *Developmental Psychology, 14,* 44–50.

Bowlby, J. (1988). *A secure base.* New York: Basic Books.

Bretherton, I. (1985). Attachment theory: Retrospect and prospect. In I. Bretherton & E. Waters (Eds.), *Growing points in attachment theory and research. Monographs of the Society for Research in Child Development, 50*(1–2, Serial No. 209).

Bretherton, I. (1987). New perspectives on attachment relations: Security, communication and internal working models. In J. Osofsky (Ed.), *Handbook of infant psychology.* New York: Wiley.

Bretherton, I, (1988). Open communication and internal working models: Their role in the development of attachment relationships. In R. A. Thompson (Ed.),

& R. A. Eienstbier (Series Ed.), *Socioemotional development.* Nebraska Symposium on Motivation, Vol. 36. Lincoln: University of Nebraska Press.

Bretherton, I., Fritz, J., Zahn-Waxler, C., & Ridgeway, D. (1986). Learning to talk about emotions: A functionalist perspective. *Child Development, 57,* 529–548.

Brownell, C. A., & Kopp, C. B. (1991). Common threads, diverse solutions: Concluding commentary. *Developmental Review, 11,* 288–303.

Carlson, V., Cicchetti, D., Barnett, D., & Braunwald, K. (1989). Disorganized/disoriented attachment relationships in maltreated infants. *Developmental Psychology, 25,* 525–531.

Case, R. (1991). Stages in the development of the young child's first sense of self. *Developmental Review, 11,* 210–230.

Cicchetti, D., & Beeghly, M. (Eds.). (1990). *The self in transition.* Chicago: University of Chicago Press.

Clyman, R. B. (1991). The procedural organization of emotions: A contribution from cognitive science to the psychoanalytic theory of therapeutic action. *Journal of the American Psychoanalytic Association, 39* (Supplement), 349–382.

Crittenden, P. M. (1992). Treatment of anxious attachment in infancy and early childhood. *Development and Psychopathology, 4,* 575–602.

Emde, R. N. (1983). The pre-representational self and its affective core. *Psychoanalytic Study of the Child, 38,* 165–192.

Field, T. (1985). Attachment as biological attunement: Being on the same wavelength. In M. Reite & T. Field (Eds.), *The psychology of attachment and separation.* New York: Academic Press.

Fischer, K. W., & Pipp, S. (1984). Development of the structures of unconscious thought. In K. Bowers & D. Meichenbaum (Eds.), *The unconscious reconsidered* (pp. 88–148). New York: Wiley.

Fivush, R. (1987). Scripts and categories: Interrelationships in development. In U. Neisser (Ed.), *Concepts and conceptual development: Ecological and intellectual factors in categorization.* Cambridge University Press.

Freud, S. (1958). *Formulation on the two principles of mental functioning. Standard Edition* (Vol. 12). London: Hogarth. (Original work published 1911.)

Gibson, J. J. (1950). *The perception of the visual world.* Boston: Houghton Mifflin.

Gibson, J. J. (1966). *The senses considered as perceptual systems.* Boston: Houghton Mifflin.

Hart, D., & Damon, W. (1985). Contrasts between understanding self and understanding others. In R. L. Leary (Ed.), *The development of self.* New York: Academic Press.

Harter, S. (1983). Developmental perspectives on the self system. In P. H. Mussen (Ed.), *Handbook of child psychology: Vol. 4. Socialization, personality, and social development* (pp. 275-385). New York: Wiley.

Hobson, R. P. (1990). On the origins of self and the case of autism. *Development and Psychopathology, 2,* 163–181.

Hofer, M. A. (1984). Relationships as regulators: A psychobiologic perspective on bereavement. *Psychosomatic Medicine, 46,* 183–197.

Hofer, M. A. (1987). Early social relationships: A psychobiologist's view. *Child Development, 58,* 633–647.

Huttenlocher, J., Smiley, P., & Charney, R. (1983). Emergence of action categories in the child: Evidence from verb meanings. *Psychological Review, 90,* 72–93.

James, W. (1890). *Psychology.* New York: Holt.

Kernberg, O. (1976). *Object relations theory and clinical psychoanalysis.* New York: Jason Aronson.

Kohut, H. (1984). *How does analysis cure?* Chicago: University of Chicago Press.

Kopp, C. B., & Brownell, C. A. (Eds.) (1991). The development of self: The first 3 years. *Developmental Review, 11*, 195–303.

Leslie, A. M. (1987). Pretense and representation: The origins of "theory of mind." *Psychological Review, 94*, 412–426.

Lewis, M., & Brooks-Gunn, J. (1979). *Social cognition and the acquisition of self.* New York: Plenum.

Lewis, M., Brooks-Gunn, J., & Jaskir, J. (1985). Individual differences in infant self-recognition as a function of mother–infant attachment relationship. *Developmental Psychology, 21*, 1181–1187.

Mahler, M., Pine, F., & Bergman, A. (1975). *The psychological birth of the human infant.* New York: Basic Books.

Main, M. (1987, May). *Cognitive aspects of the attachment relationship.* Paper presented at the Seventeenth Annual Symposium of the Jean Piaget Society, Philadelphia.

Main, M., Kaplan, K., & Cassidy, J. (1985). Security in infancy, childhood and adulthood: A move to the level of representation. In I. Bretherton & E. Waters (Eds.), *Growing points of attachment theory and research. Monographs of the Society for Research in Child Development, 50*(1–2, Serial No. 209).

Main, M., & Solomon, J. (1986). Discovery of an insecure–disorganized/disoriented attachment pattern. In T. B Brazelton & M. W. Yogman (Eds.), *Affective development in infancy* (pp. 95–124). Norwood, NJ: Ablex.

Neisser, U. (1976). *Cognition and reality.* San Francisco: Freeman.

Neisser, U. (1988). Five kinds of self-knowledge. *Philosophical Psychology, 1*, 35–59.

Neisser, U. (1991). Two perceptually given aspects of the self and their development. *Developmental Review, 11*, 197–209.

Nelson, K., & Gruendel, J. (1981). Generalized event representations: Basic building blocks of cognitive development. In M. E. Lamb & A. L. Brown (Eds.), *Advances in developmental psychology* (Vol. 1, pp. 131–158). New York: Academic Press.

Osofsky, J. D., & Eberhart-Wright, A. (1990). Affective exchanges between high risk mothers and infants. *International Journal of Psychoanalysis, 69*, 221–231.

Perner, J. (1991). *Understanding the representational mind.* Cambridge, MA: MIT Press.

Piaget, J. (1962). *Plays, dreams and imitation in childhood* (C. Gateegno & F. M. Hodgson, Trans.). New York: Norton.

Pipp, S. (1990). Sensorimotor and representational internal working models of self, other and relationship: Mechanisms of connection and separation. In D. Cicchetti & M. Beeghly (Eds.), *The self in transition: Infancy to childhood* (pp. 243–264). Chicago: University of Chicago Press.

Pipp, S., Easterbrooks, M. A., & Brown, S. (1993). Attachment status and complexity of infants' self- and other-knowledge when tested with mother and father. *Social Development, 2*, 1–14.

Pipp, S., Easterbrooks, M. A., Brown, S., & Harmon, R. J. (1992). *Attachment status and infants' knowledge of self and mother: Analysis of the three insecure attachment classifications.* Manuscript submitted for publication.

Pipp., S., Easterbrooks, M. A., & Harmon, R. J. (1992). The relation between attachment and knowledge of self and mother in one- to three-year-old infants. *Child Development, 63*, 738–750.

Pipp, S., Fischer, K. W., & Jennings, S. (1987). Acquisition of self and mother knowledge in infancy. *Developmental Psychology, 23*, 86–96.

Pipp, S., & Foltz, C. (1992). [Knowing self and others: Infants' knowledge of self, mother and inanimate object]. Unpublished raw data.

Pipp, S., & Harmon, R. J. (1987). Attachment as regulation: A commentary. *Child Development, 58*, 648–652.

Pipp, S., Kulkarni, S., & Foltz, C. (1991, April). *Infants' knowledge of self and other.* Poster at the International Conference on Infant Studies, Montreal.

Reite, M., Short, R., Seiler, C., & Pauley, J. D. (1981). Attachment, loss and depression. *Journal of Child Psychology and Psychiatry, 22*, 141–169.

Rogers, S. J., & Pennington, B. F. (1991). A theoretical approach to the deficits in infantile autism. *Development and Psychopathology, 3*, 137–162.

Sagi, A., & Hoffmann, M. L. (1976). Empathic distress in the newborn. *Developmental Psychology, 12*, 175–176.

Sander, L. W. (1975). Infant and caretaking environment: Investigation and conceptualization of adaptive behavior in systems of increasing complexity. In E. J. Anthony (Ed.), *Explorations in child psychiatry.* New York: Plenum.

Schneider-Rosen, K., & Cicchetti, D. (1984). The relation between affect and cognition in maltreated infants: Quality of attachment and the development of self-recognition. *Child Development, 55*, 648–658.

Simner, M. (1971). Newborns' response to the cry of another infant. *Developmental Psychology, 5*, 136–150.

Squire, L. R. (1986). Mechanisms of memory. *Science, 232*, 1612–1619.

Sroufe, L. A. (1989). Relationships, self and individual adaptation. In A. Sameroff & R. Emde (Eds.), *Relationship disturbances in early childhood* (pp. 70–94). New York: Basic Books.

Sroufe, L. A., & Fleeson, J. (1985). Attachment and the construction of relationships. In W. Hartup & Z. Rubin (Eds.), *Relationships and development.* Hillside, NJ: Erlbaum.

Stern, D. N. (1985). *The interpersonal world of the infant.* New York: Basic Books.

Sullivan, H. S. (1953). *The interpersonal theory of psychiatry.* New York: Norton.

Tajima, N. (1984). Infants' temperamental disposition, attachment, and self-recognition in the first 20 months of life. In *Annual report: Research and clinical center for child development* (pp. 71–80). Sapporo, Japan: Hokkaido University, Faculty of Education.

Trevarthen, C. (1988). Universal co-operative motives: How infants begin to know their language and culture of their parents. In. G. Jahoda & I. M. Lewis (Eds.), *Acquiring culture: Cross-cultural studies in child development.* New York: Croom Helm.

Vaughn, B., Egeland, B., Waters, E., & Sroufe, L. A. (1979). Individual differences in infant–mother attachment at 12 and 18 months: Stability and change in families under stress. *Child Development, 50*, 971–975.

Vygotsky, L. (1978). *Mind in society.* Cambridge, MA: Harvard University Press.

Watson, M. W., & Fischer, K. W. (1980). Development of social roles in elicited and spontaneous behavior during the preschool years. *Developmental Psychology, 16*, 483–494.

Winnicott, D. (1965). The theory of the parent–infant relationship. In D. Winnicott (Ed.), *The maturational processes and the facilitating environment.* New York: International Universities Press.

Wolff, P. H. (1969). The natural history of crying and other vocalizations in infancy. In B. M. Foss (Ed.), *Determinants of infant behavior* (Vol. 4). London: Methuen.

11

The role of feelings for an interpersonal self

DANIEL N. STERN

The interpersonal self at issue in this volume is conceived as the result of direct perception of the relationship between the self and another person. It is derived from the ongoing, unreflected, coordinated, social interactions with another human being, which provide objective information that is directly available to the participants (see Neisser in this volume). Thus a major task for exploring the interpersonal self is to specify the perceived nature of the coordinated interaction with another, and how it differs from the interactions we have with inanimate things, ideas, our physical selves, our own mental phenomena (e.g., memories), or other phenomena.

Many specific aspects of the interpersonal situation might lead to the apperception of an interpersonal self, such as contingent responsivity of the partner, specialized gestures that are adapted or have evolved for human communication, sharing human time scales, intentionality, and the like. Other chapters of this volume cover these in some detail. I wish to focus on another aspect of the interpersonal situation – namely, the evoking, the sharing, and the mutual regulation of feelings. In fact, I shall argue that that these specifying aspects of the interpersonal self are perhaps most deeply at its core. Further, I shall discuss some limitations of the notion of the interpersonal self as used in this volume and suggest some directions for expanding the concept.

The feelings to be explored are those that can be evoked by a partner, or shared by a partner, regulated by a partner in a manner that is directly observable and cannot be achieved outside of the interpersonal situation. In this sense they are uniquely interpersonal phenomena. They are events that provide direct subjective evidence of being connected in some inter-active way to a similar other, in the present moment. The crucial event is not only the feeling experienced but also the experience of interpersonal evocation or regulation or sharing. From the point of view of how the infant might categorize experiences as belonging to an interpersonal self, these "interpersonal experiences" include as invariants a feeling quality "within" the self and an ongoing interactive event with another, one which includes some apperception of an evocative or regulating or sharing process. (We assume a self–other differentiation at the "core" level of agency, physical coherence, and continuity, [Stern, 1985], in the same way that Neisser

[1988] assumes the ecological self as a prerequisite for the perception of an interpersonal self.)

First a word about terms and concepts. I have used the word *feelings* as inclusive of affects. By feeling, I want to stress the subjective quality of the experience and I want to include three relatively independent registers or types of feelings. These need to be considered in some detail because they are among the experiences, the evocation, sharing, and mutual regulation of which will help define the interpersonal self.

Types of feeling experience involved

First there are the six or eight Darwinian categorical affects – happiness, sadness, anger, surprise, and so on. Little need be said about them here, as they occupy such a prominent place in current thinking and research.

The second register of feeling concerns what has been called "vitality affects" (Stern, 1985). These feeling qualities are best captured by such kinetic terms as "crescendo," "decrescendo," "fading," "exploding," "bursting," "elongated," "fleeting," "pulsing," "wavering," "effortful," "easy," and so on. The basic ideas for this second register of feeling come from the work of Sylvan Tompkins (1962, 1963) and that of the philosopher Susan Langer (1967), who used the notion of "forms of feeling" to explore some of the emotional impact of the various art forms. The notion of vitality affects developed here (and in more detail elsewhere [Stern, 1985]) is very close to Langer's "forms of feeling" and essentially identical to Tompkins's patterns of neural firing – which I have called "activation contours"– except that Tompkins stresses how different patterns of neural firing give rise to categorical affect. Here we will stress the relative independence between the categorical affects and the vitality affects.

Vitality affects are a broader class of feeling than categorical affects in that they occur with all behavior. They invariably accompany categorical affects. For instance, how many smiles are there? Besides the shades of happiness, a smile can "explode" or "dawn" or "fade." This provides an additional feeling experience alongside? or mixed with? the happiness. (It does not, alone, define the shade of happines.)

Vitality affects are also experienced in other events that are not necessarily associated with categorical affects: how you get out of your chair, button your shirt, walk. Or, how the pieces of a memory tumble (subjectively speaking) into a recollection. Or, how a string of ideas grows and branches. Each will have its own particular vitality affect. For example, a "rush" of anger or of joy (a categorical affect), a rapid flooding of light (a sensation), the resurgence of a musical theme (a perception), an accelerating sequence of thoughts (a cognition), a shot of narcotics (a physiological reaction), can all feel like "rushes." They all share a common activation contour.

Vitality affects are continuously ongoing. We generally think of categorical affects as not being present (as functional communicative signals) until they reach a certain level of manifest intensity. In this sense, categorical affects (as interpersonally effective) seem to appear and disappear for stretches of time. Not so with vitality affects: They are always present. This is important because in the interpersonal situation, vitality affects are continually available for interpersonal coordination via sharing or mutual regulating.

Vitality affects as evokers of feeling in others are exclusively animate and ideally human. If they are to operate between two individuals, the two must share almost identical capacities for temporal discriminations and operate in roughly the same range of intensities in all modalities. This is necessary because vitality affects consist essentially of changes in intensity over time that are directly observable. (In contrast, categorical affects consist essentially of changes in configuration over time). There is now enough evidence to suggest that infants, from the earliest months of life, are sufficiently close to adults in these requisite capacities (De Casper, 1980).

There is a third register of feelings that can operate in parallel with the categorical and vitality affects. These concern the feelings of being loved, esteemed, thought wonderful, special, or hated, and the feelings of being secure, safe, attached, alone, isolated, or separated. These feelings are obvious to all of us in our personal lives and occupy a significant place in clinical discourse and in research on motivation. Nonetheless they represent something of an embarrassment for academic psychologies, because they have proved so hard to operationalize and explore systematically. They clearly cannot be reduced to the categorical and vitality affects, but constitute a third type. I call these feelings the "relational affects" because they are largely about the current feeling status of a relationship. There is much suggestion in the romantic literature, and in some psychoanalytic literature, that quality of visual regard and physical contact (along with categorical affect expression and the performance of certain vitality affects) are among the important observable elements in the relational affects.

This division of feelings into affect registers is not intended as a systematic reconceptualization of the domain of affects. It is simply a way of reordering the domain to clarify the different observable features of the interpersonal sharing and regulation of these feeling states, and to highlight some of the boundary problems with the concept of the interpersonal self.

The interpersonal evocation, sharing, and regulation of feelings

Three main processes of the interpersonal traffic of feelings–affect evocation, affect sharing, and affect regulation by the other–will be considered. These processes are singled out because they provide experiences of the self that can occur only with another human partner. Only other humans have the requisite stimulus and responsive properties. These three processes are different, and involve separate mechanisms. However, from the perspective of the infant's perception of the situation they mix freely, one or another moving to the foreground or background at different times. For instance, when a mother smiles at her baby, a smile is likely to be triggered from the baby. An affect evocation has occurred. At the same moment (or a split second later), the two are smiling at each other. The affect is now being shared. That is directly evident to the infant, who is able to recognize the expression displayed on mother's face and match it to his own proprioceptive configuration. Next, the mother may up the ante and add a vocal component and a more exaggerated, more animated facial variation, thus pushing the infant to a higher level of pleasure – or she may deescalate the process, let her face go bland, and accordingly, bring the baby back down. The infant's affect is now being regulated by the mother. Such regulation is very subtle, fluid, and temporally contoured along parameters unique to human behavior. Whether the infant's subjective experience at any point is more one of affect evocation, or of sharing, or of being regulated depends on developmental considerations (and local context), which will not be discussed here.

To explore further the nature of the feeling exchanges in the interpersonal situation that are available to the infant's direct perception, we examine some examples in each of the three types of feeling experiences.

Categorical affects

Smiling and joy provide a good starting example of categorical affect expression and quality of feeling. At about 8 to 10 weeks of life, the infant starts to smile in return to the face of a partner. It is now clear that the human stimulus for evoking these exogenous smiles is complex and can be greatly degraded or reduced (Sherrod, 1981). Nonetheless, it is also clear that the form of the human face, especially in the configuration of a smile, performing a lively interactive sequence with voice added, is the best evocative stimulus. So, outside of laboratories as well as within, the interacting partner is effectively the sole important natural stimulus.

Several months later the infant will begin to smile at inanimate objects and/or his operations upon them. At that point one could say that the interpersonal interaction is no longer an invariant of his smile-joy experience. However, that would not be wholly the case. The infant's capacity for tolerating and generating higher levels of joy at more intense levels of activation is progressively expanding. During the first year or so of life the experience of these higher, more intense realms of joy remains exclusively interpersonal and interactive. It is only the interactive processes of progressive, mutual escalation of activation and joy that permit the infant to reach these higher levels of feeling. Indeed, it is well documented how natural interpersonal interactions with caregivers achieve just this kind of progressive amplification of experience, both through interpersonal game rituals or the basic theme-and-variation structure of unplanned free play (Stern, 1977). Left on his own with only himself and inanimate objects, an infant cannot boost himself into the higher orbits of joy (the belly laugh and the dynamite smile). In the infant's real world, then, the experience of the higher levels of activated joy remains uniquely interpersonal. One can ask, Does this state of affairs really ever change developmentally? Adults certainly can reach very high levels of joy when alone. The question remains, however. At such moments is there necessarily an imagined other(s) with whom one shares the experience, and whom one uses to amplify and maintain or prolong the feeling? Even if the answer is no (which I would argue), the developmental origins of high-level joy are solidly interpersonal.

No such uniquely interpersonal origin can be ascribed to fear, surprise, or disgust, which clearly apply to all stimuli, whether inanimate or animate, nonhuman or human. The situation with anger and sadness is less clear. In the earliest months, "distress" seems to englobe anger and sadness (Emde, 1980). By the time anger and sadness are clearly differentiated as expressions, an argument can be made that these emotions, like certain kinds or levels of joy, require an interpersonal context – real, remembered, or imagined.

The self-conscious affects (Lewis, Sullivan, Stanger, & Weiss, 1989) of shame, guilt, and embarrassment require (in addition to self-reflection) some experience with and some current element of being in the real or imagined "eyesight" or attention of others. In this sense these "secondary" categorical affects are also rooted in the interpersonal and provide a direct experience of the interpersonal self. As with joy, anger, and sadness, the question arises for shame, embarrassment, and guilt: whether the interacting partners need be actually present, or whether the memory or some unaware "internalized" existence of their presence or function suffices. This issue will be taken up again in a later section.

To summarize, the exercise of some parts of the basic human endowment of categorical affects meets the requirements for interpersonal self-perception; the experience is uniquely interpersonal, and it is manifested and made observable largely in terms of visual and auditory forms or configurations and their temporal and intensity modulation.

Vitality affects

The nature of vitality affects has been described. An example of affect attunement serves to illustrate one way they can function interpersonally.

A ten-month-old girl accomplishes an amusing routine with mother and then looks at her. The girl opens up her face (her mouth opens, her eyes widen, her eyebrows rise) and then closes it back, in a series of changes whose contour can be represented by a smooth arch (⌒⌐). Mother responds by intoning "Yeah," with a pitch line that rises and falls as the volume crescendos and decrescendoes: "Y⁻ᵃ⁻H." The mother's prosodic contour has matched the child's facial-kinetic contour [of a smooth rise and fall]. (Stern, 1985, p.140)

The central interpersonal function of such attunements is to permit the mother (in this example) to signal to the little girl that she knows what the girl must have felt like when she smoothly opened her face up to a peak of expression and then smoothly closed it down. If the mother had performed a faithful imitation with her own face, the infant could only know that the mother knew what the little girl did with her face – not necessarily how she felt at the time. By performing a selective, analogic imitation, the mother refers to the vitality affects experienced by the infant and says the equivalent of "Oh! This is pretty much how you must have felt, and I am showing you I know by matching the temporal contour of my activity to yours." The exact form of the expression is avoided to permit the mother to focus not on the form (the acted expression) but on the feeling (that gave rise to the expression). (For further discussion of affect attunement, see Stern, Hofer, Haft, & Dore, 1983, and Stern, 1985.)

In the case of the vitality affects, the mutually observable – directly perceptible – features are the intensity of a behavior and its temporal changes or contours. In such interpersonal exchanges, the question of what is observable and directly perceptible is complicated. Temporal contours of intensity are observable. The mother and infant in the example given are performing different forms (facial expression vs. vocalization) but similar intensity-temporal contours. Because of the infant's capacities for making cross-modal correspondences, the match between the mother's vocal and the infant's facial behaviors is also directly perceivable by the infant (Meltzoff, 1981).

There is yet a further correspondence involved. We assume in our unreflected perceptions – when in an empathic or identificatory mode – that there is a correspondence between the "inner," subjective qualities of feeling and their manifestations in the form, intensity, and timing of "expressive" displays. The word expressive itself is predicated on just that correspondence. It is in this way that the unobservable subjective qualities of feelings become "observable" (expressed) to each partner and fulfill the essential requirement for the interpersonal self, of being "directly perceived," even if once removed, that is, transformed.

These mechanisms of perceiving and matching feelings between interpersonal partners are an important step toward the establishment of intersubjectivity as it is discussed in this volume by Trevarthen, Hobson, Pipp, and Loveland and originally by Trevarthen (1978, 1980). The concern here is more with interaffectivity than with the other forms of intersubjectivity, such as interattentionality or interintentionality.

The expression of vitality affects is omnipresent because it occurs in essentially all behaviors. As we watch another human behave, the temporal contouring of the neural firing of our perceptual system may essentially copy out a transformed version of the vitality affects manifested in the other's behavior. The intensity contour of the perceptual activity of the observer will correspond to the intensity contour of the behavior of the observed. (This is the central idea behind Tompkins's concept, as applied to observable human behavior. Often, however, some readiness factor permitting affective resonance must be added to direct visual perception.)

Given this scenario, the question becomes: Why are infants or adults not constantly and actively feeling the vitality affects of others? The same question arises for imitation and for phenomena such as "interactional synchrony" (Condon & Sander, 1974), which is claimed (and disputed) to occur all the time between mother and infant. Clinical theorists have asked the same question about empathy, and about the very great individual differences in "permeability" to other people's feeling states (Sandler, 1987). It is clear that more attention needs to be given to the conditions that inhibit or activate these kinds of interpersonal coordination of feelings and to describing how often they actually operate. To the extent that they are operating much of the time (even at a low level, if there is such a thing), one can conceive of these coordinations of feelings as a tonic source of maintenance of the interpersonal self.

Relational affects

The relational affects are particularly interesting because they push the limits of the interpersonal self, and thus help define its boundaries. No one will dispute that feelings of being "attached," "isolated," "alone," "loved," and so on are uniquely interpersonal and that they arise in the course of coordinated interactions – even though the feelings can continue after the interaction is over, when alone, in memory, and so forth, as can any other kind of affect experience. And no one will dispute their personal and clinical importance. In the context of this volume the problem lies in their observability, that is, whether they can be captured by direct perception.

Neisser (this volume) has insisted that the interpersonal coordinations needed for an interpersonal self consist of "objectively existing stimulus information" that can be "perceived." The problem is that relational affects are most often *not* expressed in a manner that is perceivable from the outside. The subjective feeling state of the perceiver is not always "objectively existing stimulus information." It may exist only for him. Only the behaviors of the perceived, which gave rise to the perceiver's feelings, are observable to both of them. Thus, half of the coordinated interpersonal action meets the full criteria. This is very clear in Neisser's description of intersubjectivity: "The mutuality of their behavior exists in fact and can be perceived by the participants themselves. Each of them can see (and hear, and perhaps feel) the appropriate interactive responses of the other. Those responses, in relation to one's own perceived activity, specify the interpersonal self" (1988, p. 8).

Here is an example illustrating the problem. A mother, all of a sudden, looks at her infant very lovingly for a long moment (whatever that means behaviorally). The infant simply looks back at her, with, at most, a slight smile, but with – we assume – a feeling of being loved. Suppose further that the mother's behavior was not triggered by anything the infant did at that moment but rather was brought about by her own reflections or by a third person commenting on her wonderful baby. (This example is construed to best present the problem, but one could imagine many others, such as a feeling of being attached or secure. Many interpersonal experiences with vitality affects and even categorical affects operate like this.) From the infant's subjective point of view, all of the necessary ingredients for the direct perception of her interpersonal self are present: a visible behavior on the part of her mother directed at her (granted, a complex one) and a visible action on her part of looking back at her mother; plus a characteristic feeling response within herself (with or without overt action). Let us assume further that this happens often enough so that the behaviors – a specific overt action by mother and a specific "internal" feeling within the infant – are invariantly linked, so that one can speak of a generalized coordinated social event. For the infant, a direct perception of her interpersonal self will have occurred, but for no one else.

We can resolve this problem by distinguishing two kinds of interpersonal selves, a subjective interpersonal self and an objective interpersonal self. For the *subjective interpersonal self* all of the requisite information must be directly perceived by the subject. For the *objective interpersonal self* all of the requisite information must be directly perceivable by the subject, his interactive partner, and an observer. This distinction permits a close alignment between what Neisser calls the interpersonal self and what I, taking a perspective more rooted in subjectivity, have called, the subjective or intersubjective self (Stern, 1985). More important the distinction allows the notion of an interpersonal self to include a larger range of phenomena and points the way to operationalizing these different forms of interpersonal self.

There is a second problem (besides what is observable and to whom). This problem concerns what is accepted as a social, or interpersonal, interaction. We encountered less this problem earlier with the categorical affects, but the consideration of the vitality and relational affects permits a fuller discussion. The psychoanalytic literature has been rich in describing the influence of persons not actually present, except "in mind," and has evolved several terms and concepts for such phenomena: internalizations (Freud, 1938), introjects (Schafer, 1968), self-objects (Kohut, 1977). These internal agents of influence are conceived of not as persons inside but, rather, as specific interpersonal interactions that have been experienced, remembered, and represented. This emphasis on special interactions or relationship "in the mind" is well captured by such terms as internal object relationship (Sandler, 1987) or experiences of a self-regulating-other (Stern, 1985) or working model of attachment (Bowlby, 1969).

The point is that social, coordinated interactions with a partner exist in a represented form. And such representations can be "activated" so that a form of interpersonal interaction occurs "in the mind." The question is, Do these interactions qualify for the interpersonal self, – or, at best for the subjective interpersonal self as proposed above? No one knows very clearly how such representation of interaction works when activated. There is probably a spectrum from a vivid reliving of the interaction (specific or generalized) in memory or imagination, at one end, to a more automatic influence of the representation in which no reliving of an interaction occurs at all, even in a pale form.

From the point of view of a subjective interpersonal self, where do we draw the line? If we draw the line at actually lived, that is, real, ongoing interactions, and exclude all mentally relived interactions, our scientific task becomes easier, but the domain of the interpersonal self becomes more limited. Many phenomena of clinical (and personal) interest get excluded. If the interaction with the interpersonal partner occurs in vivid memory, that is, it is relived and thereby exerts its influence, would we still be dealing with the interpersonal self, or would we have passed to the domain of the "extended self" (Neisser, 1988). Or, if the interaction has been abstracted into a representation that operates without any subjective experience of reliving, would we be dealing with something closer to Neisser's "conceptual self"? In sum, to what extent does the information that specifies an inter-personal self come from mental operations as well as objectively observable sources, and which mental operations are permissible?

A special role for feelings?

Feelings may have several features that give them a special role in the perception of the interpersonal self. First, feeling interactions are an om-nipresent part of all focused social interactions. Because coordinated feeling exchanges are always (potentially) ongoing, we can dip into them at any time. In this way, they can provide a background source of information that constantly specifies an interpersonal self. For the maintenance of entities such as the interpersonal self, it remains to be seen whether notions of tonic vs. phasic informational input are useful. There is, in fact, a prior question: Is it worth distinguishing the perception (identification) of an interpersonal self from the maintenance of such a percept?

Second, feelings may well occupy the highest place among those features that directly specify the interpersonal self. It is unclear what criteria are to be used to set such priorities. Certainly one would be uniqueness to human social intercourse. In this regard it is interesting that writers of science fiction (who often have explored these questions at a depth equal to that of psychologists) generally conclude that it is relatively easy to simulate (by machine or imagined alien species) the social phenomena of inter-attentionality, interintentionality, and other forms of cognitive coordination, but that a convincing interaffectivity is very difficult to fake. Affect more than cognition seems to determine whether one is engaged with an "it" or another human being (see the chapters by Gustafson and Jopling in this volume).

REFERENCES

Bowlby, J. (1969). *Attachment and loss* (Vol. I). New York: Basic Books.
Condon, W. S., & Sander, L. S. (1974). Neonate movement is synchronized with adult speech. *Science, 183,* 99–101.
De Casper, A. J. (1980, April). *Neonates perceive time just like adults.* Paper presented at the International Conference on Infancy Studies, New Haven, CT.
Emde, R. N. (1980). Levels of meaning for infant emotions: A bisocial view. In W. A. Collins (Ed.), *Development of cognition, affect and social relations.* Hillsdale, NJ: Erlbaum.
Freud, S. (1938). *An outline of psychoanalysis. Standard edition* (Vol. 23; pp. 144–207). London: Hogarth, 1964.
Kohut, H. (1977). *The restoration of the self.* New York: International Universities Press.
Langer, S. K. (1967). *Mind: An essay on human feelings* (Vol. I). Baltimore: Johns Hopkins University Press.
Lewis, M., Sullivan, M. W., Stanger, C., & Weiss, M. (1989). Self-development and self-conscious emotions. *Child Development, 60,* 146–156.
Meltzoff, A. N. (1981). Imitation, intermodal coordination, and representation in early infancy. In G. Butterworth (Ed.), *Infancy and epistemology.* London: Harmester Press.
Neisser, U. (1988). Five kinds of self-knowledge. *Philosophical Psychology, 1,* 35–59.
Sandler, J. (1987). *From safety to superego.* London: Karnac Books.
Schafer, R. (1968). *Aspects of internalization.* New York: International Universities Press.
Sherrod, L. R. (1981). Issues in cognitive-perceptual development: The special case of social stimuli. In M. E. Lamb & L. R. Sherrod (Eds.), *Infant social cognition.* Hillsdale, NJ: Erlbaum.
Stern, D. N. (1977). *The first relationship: Infant and mother.* Cambridge, MA: Harvard University Press.
Stern, D. N. (1985). *The interpersonal world of the infant.* New York: Basic Books.
Stern, D. N., Hofer, L., Haft, W., and Dore, J. (1983). Affect attunement: The sharing of feeling states between mother and infant by means of inter-modal fluency. In T. Field & N. Fox (Eds.), *Social perception in infants.* Norwood, NJ: Ablex.
Tompkins, S. S. (1962). *Affect, imagery and consciousness: Vol. I. The positive affects.* New York: Springer.
Tompkins, S. S. (1963). *Affect, imagery and consciousness: Vol. II. The negative affects.* New York: Springer.

Trevarthan, C. (1980). The foundations of intersubjectivity: Development of interpersonal and cooperative understanding in infants: In D. R. Olson (Ed.), *The
social foundation of language and thought: Essays in honor of Jerome Bruner.* New York:
Norton.
Trevarthan, C., & Haiblerg, P. (1978). Secondary intersubjectivity: Confidence, con-
fiders, and acts of meaning in the first year. In A. Lock (Ed.), *Action, gesture
and symbol.* New York: Academic Press.

12

Spontaneous communication and the foundation of the interpersonal self

ROSS BUCK

Western philosophers often see something puzzling about knowing another person's "inner" meanings when one has access only to behavior: This is the "other minds" problem (Austin, 1959). William James noted: "Our senses only give us acquaintance with facts of the body, and . . . of the mental states of other persons we have only conceptual knowledge" (1890, pp. 222–223); Ludwig Wittgenstein argued: "When we communicate a feeling to someone, something which we can never know happens at the other end. All that we can receive from him is an expression" (1965, p. 185).

This chapter describes a spontaneous communication process in which expressive behaviors constitute "facts of the body" that are veridical signs of motivational–emotional states. Given attention, these expressive behaviors provide *all we need to know* about what has happened at "the other end."[1] It is argued that communication proceeds in two simultaneous streams: a *symbolic* stream, which is learned, intentional, and prepositional; and a *spontaneous* stream which is biologically based, direct, nonpropositional, and based on subcortical and paleocortical brain systems. The chapter presents spontaneous communication as the basis of the interpersonal self, and summarizes relevant research in a variety of subject groups. Also, it suggests how spontaneous communication provides a basis for the conceptualization of a private self through emotional education.

A developmental–interactionist view of motivation, emotion, and cognition

It is first necessary briefly to define motivation, emotion, and cognition. In my view, these represent three aspects of the process of adaptation that has, virtually from the beginning, characterized the evolution of life on earth. Motivation is defined as a potential built into a system of behavior control, and emotion as the actualization, or *readout*, of that potential in the presence of a challenging stimulus (Buck, 1985). Cognition, on the other hand, is knowledge, and it can be knowledge of the physical environment, of other organisms, and of internal bodily processes. These three sources of knowledge are, in my view, related, respectively, to Neisser's (1988) ecological, interpersonal, and private selves.

Developmental–interactionist theory conceives of motivation and emotion in

216

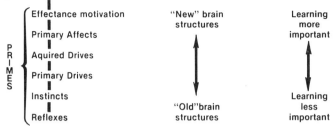

Figure 12.1. The hierarchy of primary motivational–emotional systems (primes). (Reproduced with permission from Buck, 1988a.)

terms of an interaction between special-purpose (SP) and general-purpose (GP) systems over the course of development. SP systems are phylogenetic adaptations – that is, they are structured over the course of evolution to perform a specific function, and they thus serve as the basis of a kind of inherited knowledge. GP systems are systems designed by evolution to be open to influence from experience during ontogeny.

Biological motives and emotions are organized in a hierarchy of SP systems collectively termed primary motivational–emotional systems, or *primes* (Buck, 1985; 1988a). Primes include reflexes, instincts, drives, affects, and effectance motivation (see Figure 12.1). These are organized in progressively higher structures in the nervous system, and they interact increasingly with GP systems of conditioning, learning, and complex information processing at higher levels of the hierarchy: Thus the associated behavior becomes progressively more flexible and open to influence from the individual's experience. This general pattern exists in both human beings and other animals; in humans, linguistic behavior control systems increase greatly this flexibility and openness to experience (Buck, 1988a).

To repeat, emotion is defined as a *readout* of SP systems when activated by a challenging stimulus (Buck, 1985, 1988a). There are three sorts of readout (see Figure 12.2): *Emotion I* is a readout to systems involved directly in bodily adaptation and homeostasis (e.g., the endocrine, immune, and autonomic nervous systems); *Emotion II* is a readout to systems involved in social coordination (e.g., pheromones, facial expressions, postures, vocalizations); and *Emotion III* is a readout to systems involved in direct subjective experience (e.g., neurochemical systems involving peptide neurohormones such as the endorphins). This discussion is most concerned with Emotion II, which involves spontaneous emotional communication and is the basis of the interpersonal self. It also suggests that Emotion III is the basis of the private self, and that spontaneous communication is involved in the conceptualization of the private self.

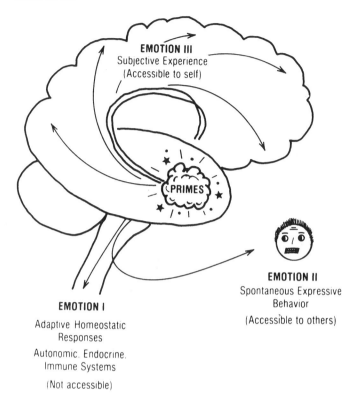

EMOTION III
Subjective Experience
(Accessible to self)

PRIMES

EMOTION II
Spontaneous Expressive
Behavior
(Accessible to others)

EMOTION I
Adaptive Homeostatic
Responses
Autonomic. Endocrine.
Immune Systems
(Not accessible)

Figure 12.2.   The three readouts of the primes and their different accessibilities
to self and others. (Reproduced with permission from Buck, 1991.)

Spontaneous and symbolic communication

Spontaneous communication

There is evidence that expressive displays serve important social functions
in many species. Such displays are useless unless receiving tendencies exist
that (1) are sensitive or preattuned to those displays and (2) alter behavior
tendencies in the receiver accordingly. In the terms of Gibsonian perceptual
theory (Gibson, 1966, 1979), emotional displays can be considered to be
"social affordances" to which the receiver is prepared to respond in certain
biologically determined ways. Thus, displays have coevolved with the perceptual and response apparatus so that the display directly specifies the
receiver's reaction in important ways: Spontaneous communication is
"epistemologically fundamental" (Buck, 1992). The spontaneous communication system, though based on sending and receiving tendencies at the

individual level, constitutes a phylogenetic adaptation at the group level, (Buck & Ginsburg, 1991).

There is compelling evidence that both sending and receiving tendencies are genetically based and participate together in communication processes that are, fundamentally, phylogenetic adaptations. Examples can be cited from widely different levels of the phylogenetic scale. For example, Bentley and Hoy (1974) demonstrated a genetic basis for the songs of crickets. Also, different species of frogs and toads manifest different songs that are responded to preferentially by members of the same species, and hybrids manifest songs that are in turn responded to preferentially by other hybrids (Bogert, 1961; Ryan, 1990). Another example concerns the coydog, which is a cross between a beagle and a coyote. The defensive threat display of the coyote – a U-shaped body posture, wide oral gape, and sibilant hiss – is not shown by the beagle, but in the coydog the displays of both species are present. Normally the coydog shows doglike threat behavior, but around puberty the threat behavior can be switched to that of the coyote by social stress mediated by an elevation in plasma cortisol (Moon & Ginsburg, 1985).

Spontaneous communication is defined as having the following qualities:

1. It is based on *biologically structured sending and receiving mechanisms.* The function of spontaneous communication is social coordination, and it evolves because the transmission of certain kinds of motivationalemotional information between individuals is, on the whole, adaptive.
2. Its elements are *signs,* which are externally accessible aspects of the referent. Pheromones released by an ant, or a human being, are externally accessible aspects of certain important motivational–emotional states. The same is true of spontaneous facial expressions and gestures.
3. Spontaneous communication is *not intentional,* although it can intentionally be suppressed or inhibited.
4. The content of spontaneous communication is *nonpropositional,* because it cannot be false. Propositions must be capable of logical analysis, for example, tests for truth or falsity. Spontaneous communication is composed of signs, and if the sign is present, the referent must be present by definition. The content of spontaneous communication, instead, consists of motivational–emotional states.
5. Spontaneous communication is based on subcortical and paleocortical systems that tend to be right-lateralized in the brain, and it is associated in most persons with right-hemisphere cognitive processing (syncretic cognition or knowledge by acquaintance. (See Buck, 1984; 1990a; Tucker, 1981.)

Spontaneous communication is biologically structured in both its sending and receiving aspects, and it therefore is *direct* in that it requires no intention on the part of the sender or inference on the part of the receiver. This means that the receiver has direct access to the motivational–emotional state of the sender. This statement is meant to be taken in its strongest sense. We directly know certain "inner meanings" in others, certain motivational–

emotional states, because others are constructed to directly express such states and we are constructed so that (when we attend to it) we "pick up" that expression directly and know its meaning directly. This knowledge is based on phylogenetic adaptation and is conferred through inheritance. Therefore, the individuals involved in spontaneous communication literally constitute a biological unit. One's knowledge of the motivational–emotional states of others via spontaneous communication is just as direct and biologically based as one's knowledge of the feel of one's shoe on one's foot. It is in this sense that, to return to Wittgenstein's (1965) terms, with spontaneous communication an expression is *all one needs* to know what has happened on "the other end." Of course, this knowledge is itself not propositional (see note 1).

Symbolic communication

In contrast to spontaneous communication, symbolic communication is defined as being learned and culturally patterned, based on symbols that have an arbitrary relationship with their referent, at some level intentional, and composed of propositions.

The relationship of spontaneous and symbolic communication

Spontaneous and symbolic communication are different kinds of systems that interact with one another. They are *not* at different ends of a continuum but, rather, are related as depicted in Figure 12.3. It is possible to have spontaneous communication without symbolic communication, as in an ant or termite colony. It is not, however, possible to have symbolic without spontaneous communication. Symbolic communication may dominate, as in a dull lecture, but there is always an element of spontaneous communication present mediated by the nuances of gesture, posture, facial expression, and tone of voice.

The abscissa in Figure 12.3 *can* be considered to be a continuum, which can be conceptualized in several ways (Buck, 1984). One could regard it as a continuum of communication situations, ranging from unbridled passion on the left to a preponderance of carefully reasoned argument on the right. Alternatively, one could regard it as a developmental continuum, with the newborn infant on the left and the mature adult on the right. Or it could be a phylogenetic scale with relatively simple organisms – ants, termites, algae, and simple single-celled creatures – on the left and humans on the right. Finally, the continuum could represent the extent to which different primes interact with GP systems of conditioning, learning, and analytic cognition, with reflexes and fixed action patterns to the left and affects and effectance motivation to the right. In more general terms, Figure 12.3 can

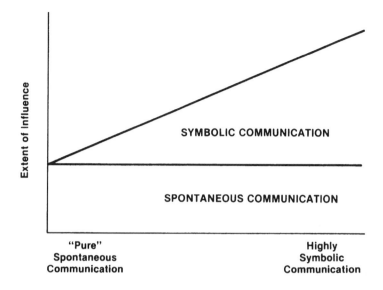

Figure 12.3. The relationship between spontaneous and symbolic communication. (Reproduced with permission from Buck, 1984.)

be considered to reflect the interaction between SP and GP processing systems, reflecting an increasing relative contribution of cortical activity as opposed to the activity of lower neurochemical systems in the determination of behavior (Buck, 1988a).

Nonverbal communication. "Nonverbal" communication can be either spontaneous or symbolic. Symbolic nonverbal communication includes culturally learned gestures that accompany language, including emblems, illustrators, and regulators (Ekman & Friesen, 1969a), as well as sign language and pantomime. There is evidence that much symbolic communication in humans, verbal or nonverbal has a common basis in linguistic competence. For example, we shall see that both verbal and nonverbal symbolic behaviors are associated with left-hemisphere processing in most persons, whereas spontaneous communication appears to be associated with right-hemisphere processing (Buck, 1990b; Buck & Duffy, 1980).

An example: Direct communication via media. The notion of direct communication via media seems to be a contradiction in terms, but there is in fact evidence that direct spontaneous communication occurs via mass communication media (see Buck, 1988b, for a discussion of implications). Studies have used facial EMG to record minute tendencies to smile and frown that are not visible on the face or consciously noticed by the responder.

McHugo and his colleagues (1985) used this technique to record the reactions of viewers to the videotaped smiles and frowns of Ronald Reagan and Walter Mondale during the 1986 presidential election debates. It was found that the facial expressions of Reagan, known as a charismatic "great communicator," elicited tendencies toward similar facial behavior in viewers: When Reagan smiled, the viewer tended to smile; when he frowned, the viewer tended to frown. Mondale's expressions did not have this effect, and the effect was unrelated to the consciously expressed political preferences of the viewers. Apparently Reagan's expressions had a direct impact on the viewer, even via videotape.

Summary

In summary, spontaneous communication is based on a biologically structured hierarchy of SP systems that interact with GP systems involving conditioning, learning, and complex information processing. Symbolic communication, in contrast, is based on these GP systems. Spontaneous communication systems interact with symbolic communication systems in both human beings and in other animals. Any particular communication event involves an interaction of spontaneous and symbolic communication, which is a specific example of the general principle of interaction between SP and GP systems depicted in Figure 12.3.

It should be noted that the notion of spontaneous *communication* is different from that of spontaneous *expression*. Like most concepts in psychology, spontaneous expression is a unitary concept with the individual as the unit of analysis. Spontaneous communication, in contrast, is a dyadic concept that requires for accuracy a sender, receiver, message, and channel. It thus requires spontaneous expression, and we shall see that such expression can be measured by communication scores. However, spontaneous communication in addition requires a similarly innately based process in the receiver with all that implies; for example, the biological unity of sender and receiver based on phylogenetic adaptation, the notion of the direct knowledge of the sender's state on the part of the receiver, and the validity of the concept of display as social affordance.

In humans, an additional level of complexity is added by linguistic competence. In this regard, it can be argued that the essence of the difference between human beings and other animals does not involve cognition or consciousness, per se, but, rather, how cognition and consciousness are organized. Specifically, in human beings cognition and consciousness are organized linguistically, and this is the essence of the difference between human beings and other animals (Buck, 1985, 1988a).

Studying spontaneous communication: The communication of affect paradigm

Having defined spontaneous communication conceptually, we will now define it operationally, that is, specify how it can be measured. The study of communication requires particular measurement techniques that are sensitive to its essentially dyadic nature. As noted, the unit of analysis in communication is inherently dyadic, and this requires a dyadic assessment situation including a sender, receiver, message, and channel. One way to do this is through experimental tasks whose solution requires accurate communication, such as the cooperative conditioning paradigm developed by Robert E. Miller and his colleagues.

The cooperative conditioning paradigm. Miller, Banks, and Ogawa (1962, 1963) developed a procedure in which two rhesus monkeys were taught to press a bar to the presentation of a light to avoid a shock. The animals were then paired so that one, the "sender," could see the light but not press the bar, and the other, the "receiver," could press the bar but not see the light. The receiver could, however, see the sender's response via closed-circuit television. When the light came on, the sender made characteristic facial expressions and postural adjustments that served as signals, for the receiver pressed the bar at the right moment and thus avoided the shock for both animals. The monkeys performed in the paired tests virtually as well as they did individually, and successful communication was apparent from the first paired sessions. Subsequent studies demonstrated that monkeys who had been reared in social isolation for the first year of life could neither send nor receive accurately in the cooperative conditioning situation, although they were able to solve the initial avoidance task (Miller, Caul, & Mirsky, 1967).

The slide-viewing technique. Miller's studies were followed by studies of affective communication in humans. A reliable and flexible way to present emotional stimuli to humans was found with emotionally loaded color slides, resulting in the slide-viewing technique (SVT) (Buck, Miller, & Caul, 1974; Buck, Savin, Miller, & Caul, 1972).

Studies with adults

The first studies were conducted with college-age subjects. The "sender" was told that the purpose of the experiment was to relate physiological responses to the verbal report of subjective emotional experience as one viewed a series of emotionally loaded slides, and heart rate (HR) and skin conductance (SC) electrodes were attached. Senders silently viewed the back-lighted slide until cued by a light, and then verbally described the subjective experience that the slide evoked. They then rated their emotional experience along scales ranging from strong to weak and from pleasant to unpleasant. Unknown to the senders, a camera concealed behind the back-lighted screen televised the sender's initial reaction to the slide, continuing responses for the 10 s while the slide remained on (slide period), and later responses while discussing the emotional experience (talk period).

The following sorts of slides were presented: Sexual slides showed seminude males and females; scenic slides showed pleasant landscapes; pleasant people slides showed happy-looking persons; unpleasant slides showed severe burns and facial injuries; and unusual slides showed strange photographic effects. "Receivers," alone or in groups, viewed the sender's reactions (without audio) and guessed what type of slide was shown, and also how strong or weak, and pleasant or unpleasant, the sender's emotional response was to each slide. This produced two communication accuracy scores: the percentage of slides correctly categorized (percent correct measure) and the correlation between the receiver's and sender's ratings of strength and pleasantness over the slides (strength and pleasantness measures, respectively).

For the percent correct and pleasantness measures, communication accuracy was statistically significant at beyond the .001 level. The average communication scores were well below 100%, but this moderate overall level of communication masked very large individual differences in sending accuracy. Some persons were very accurate senders and others were virtually at chance. Combined data from Buck et al. (1972, 1974) showed that females were significantly better senders on both the percent correct measure (females = 35%; males = 28%; chance = 20%) and the pleasantness measure (female $r = .42$; male $r = .25$). The strength measure showed significant overall communication only for female senders ($r = .22$).

Sending accuracy and physiological responding. One of the most intriguing findings about sending accuracy, or expressiveness, was that, unexpectedly, the pleasantness measure was negatively related (between subjects) to physiological responding: the changes in the number of SC responses and HR acceleration. This was consistent with the results of Lanzetta and Kleck (1970), who were independently working with the Miller procedure, and with other findings on the (negative) relationship of overt and electrodermal responding (Buck, 1979, 1984; Manstead, 1990). SC deflections are indicants of central inhibitory processes (Fowles, 1980), suggesting that a central inhibitory tendency produces both lessened spontaneous expressiveness and a greater number of SC deflections. This "suppression hypothesis" is consistent with Gray's (1982) theorizing on the bases of extraversion–introversion, with Kagan's work on temperament in young children (Kagan & Snidman, 1991), with research on the septal syndrome (Gorenstein &

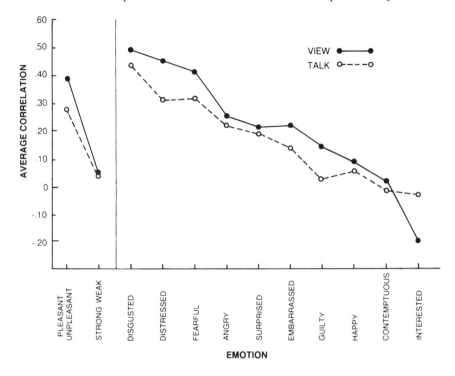

Figure 12.4. Relative "communicability" of 12 emotions. Receivers (British students) saw either the view period (before the senders – American students – described their feelings) or the talk period (as senders described their feelings). Correlations are between receivers' ratings of the sender's feelings and the sender's own ratings of his or her feelings. (From Wagner, Buck & Winterbotham, 1989.)

Newman, 1980), and with other information–relating systems of behavioral inhibition with personality and temperament (Buck, 1979, 1984, 1988a).

The communication of specific emotions. Recently, the range of emotion ratings by senders and receivers has been expanded using Izard's (1977) fundamental emotions and Ekman and Friesen's (1975) primary affects. Thus, Wagner, Buck, and Winterbotham (1989) assessed the ability to communicate the fundamental emotions in addition to pleasantness and strength. Figure 12.4 illustrates the result, showing communication when only the slide period or only the talk period was presented to the receiver.

Studies with preschool children

Studies with preschool children investigated further the sex difference in expressiveness and the relationship between expressiveness and SC responding (Buck, 1975, 1977). These used new categories of slides. Sexual slides were of course omitted, and less upsetting, unpleasant slides (showing a grotesque clown, a crying woman, etc.) were substituted for the originals. The most useful slide category for children was a new "familiar people" category consisting of pictures of the children themselves and their friends and teachers at the preschool. This was a very effective emotional stimulus, yet it was strongly positive. In fact, these slides made the experience of being in the experiment a pleasant one for most of the young subjects.

The children's videotaped expressions were shown to their mothers, and later to groups of undergraduates, who made ratings similar to those made in the adult studies. Results indicated that, as in the study with adults, significant communication occurred with very large variations in communication accuracy suggestive of individual differences in expressiveness. However, there was no evidence of a large sex difference in sending accuracy, although undergraduates were somewhat more accurate with girls than boys on the categorization measure. Most significantly, sending accuracy was related to teachers' ratings on the specially developed Affect Expression Rating Scale (AERS). Expressive children were rated to be active and sociable but also aggressive, bossy, and impulsive; inexpressive children were rated as shy and emotionally inhibited but also cooperative and controlled. Thus the expressiveness in the laboratory was related to the child's behavior in the preschool, giving persuasive evidence of the external validity of the SVT.

Studies in brain-damaged patients

The Buck and Duffy (1977, 1980) study on brain-damaged patients clarified the nature of spontaneous communication and its differences with symbolic communication. The study originated in efforts by Duffy and his colleagues to develop nonverbal techniques for the treatment of aphasia using pantomime (Duffy, Duffy, & Alderdice, 1977). In the process, it was found that patients who could pantomime generally had residual verbal functioning as well.

Pantomimic nonverbal communication is clearly different from the sort of communication measured by the SVT, and indeed the difference parallels a distinction in the aphasia literature between "propositionizing," or using words for the deliberate encoding of a message, and "emotional utterance," which is the use of words (such as expletives) for the expression of a presently existing emotional state. It is commonly observed that emotional utterance may be relatively intact in aphasic patients while propositional speech shows severe deficits (Jenkins, Jimenez-Pabon, Shaw, & Sefer, 1975). Critchley (1975) suggested that a similar distinction can be made for nonverbal behavior, with facial and bodily expression of a present emotional state similar to emotional utterance and intentionally posed expressions or pantomimes similar to propositionizing.

The SVT, by manipulating the emotional state of the viewer, offers a way to measure the nonverbal equivalent of emotional utterance. In a study of patients hospitalized in a Veterans Administration hospital, Buck and Duffy (1980) found that left-hemisphere-damaged (LHD) aphasic patients retained a level of expressiveness (as defined by communication accuracy vis-à-vis groups of college students in the SVT) that was comparable to that of non-brain-damaged patients, whereas right-hemisphere-damaged (RHD) patients (who can use propositional speech) showed significantly less expressiveness that did not differ from the sending accuracy of patients with Parkinson's disease (a disorder long associated clinically with a "masklike" dearth of facial and bodily expressiveness). The general pattern of results suggested that nonverbal emotional utterance is particularly associated with RH activity, and that the LH is involved both in nonverbal propositionizing and in the control of emotional expression via display rules (Buck & Duffy, 1980).

The Buck and Duffy (1977, 1980) sample did not include patients suffering from severe aphasia, and an effort was made to obtain a wider sample from a private hospital. Some of these had been run in the SVT technique in pilot studies prior to the VA sample; others were run after the VA study was completed. The sample of 15 LHD patients permitted correlational analyses of relationships between verbal, pantomimic, and SVT scores (Duffy & Buck, 1979). Verbal and pantomimic measures were highly intercorrelated (mean $r = .93$), whereas the SVT scores were uncorrelated with verbal or pantomimic measures (mean $r = .03$). There was evidence of a curvilinear relationship between the SVT scores and verbal ability (quadratic $r = .50$, $p < .10$), suggesting that patients with moderate verbal ability tended to be more expressive than those with high or low verbal scores. This is consistent with the notion that moderate damage to the left hemisphere is associated with increased expressiveness due to disinhibition, whereas more severe damage – possibly affecting other brain areas – is associated with reduced expressiveness. Critchley (1975), in fact, observed that severe aphasia is associated with deficits in emotional utterance as well as propositionizing.

These studies were replicated and extended by Borod, Koff, Perlman, and Nicholas (1985), who used the SVT with a larger sample and had CAT-scan data available. Employing ratings of facial-gestural and paralinguistic-intonational expressiveness, they found reduced expressiveness in RHD as opposed to LHD patients. Patients with anterior RH damage were particularly lacking in facial-gestural expressiveness, and both anterior and posterior RH damage were associated with a lack in intonational expressiveness. These data are also consistent with the work of Ross (1981; in press), who has found deficits of emotional communication in RHD patients which he terms "aprododias." Furthermore, Mammucari and his colleagues (1988) found that RHD patients show reduced autonomic activity and less of a tendency to look away from a stress-producing film, suggesting that "their negative emotional experience was less intense" (p. 531). These investigators did not, however, find evidence of a difference between RHD and LHD patients in rated expressiveness or in emotional facial expressions as defined by the Ekman and Friesen (1978) Facial Action Coding System (see Buck, 1990b, and Zoccolotti et al., 1990, for discussion of these results). Thus, previous tentative suggestions that the RH may be associated with spontaneous emotional expression and the LH with the learned management of this expression according to display rules still appear to be viable (Buck, 1984, pp. 109–116), although this is clearly an area where important work remains to be done.

Nonverbal Receiving Ability

Sending accuracy and receiving ability. The SVT may assess either sending accuracy (by averaging across receivers) or receiving ability (by averaging across senders). Studies have shown that sending accuracy is more stable than receiving ability, in that communication scores have been more reliably linked to the characteristics of the senders than the receivers (i.e., sex, personality measures of extroversion and self-esteem, and negatively to physiological responding). Receiving ability scores have shown low internal consistency (Buck, 1983, 1984). Sending accuracy scores are much more consistent from receiver to receiver (being responsible for 40% to 50% of the total variance in communication scores) than receiving ability scores are consistent from sender to sender (being responsible for less than 10% of the variance; see Sabatelli, Buck, & Kenny, 1986).

The study of empathy. The measurement of receiving ability is relevant to longstanding questions regarding the measurement of interpersonal sensitivity, or empathy. It would appear at first glance that such sensitivity, or accuracy in person perception, would be an important process in the formation of an interpersonal self. Although the search for a reliable, valid, and useful measure of empathy has been actively pursued in psychology since the 1920s, such a measure has proved elusive. Difficult methodological problems – for example, those involving assumed similarity (Hastorf & Bender, 1952) – have plagued studies of person perception accuracy. With the renaissance in the study of emotion in the 1960s, together with the spread of new videotape technology, it appeared that measures of nonverbal receiving ability might provide such a measure (Buck, 1983; Ekman & Friesen, 1974; Rosenthal, Hall, DiMatteo, Rogers, & Archer, 1979).

The CARAT test. To assess receiving ability systematically, a standard test was constructed using 600 sequences of facial-gestural expressions taken via the SVT as potential items and subjecting them to item analyses. First, items were selected and divided into two 40-item forms that were given to large groups of subjects who judged the type of slide presented. An initial collection of 20 items derived from this procedure was found to have a coefficient alpha of .57. Items from the two 40-item forms that correlated best with the total scores were then combined into a 47-item form and shown to an additional large group. From this, a final 32-item form was constructed that was called the Communication of Affect Receiving Ability Test, or CARAT. CARAT includes both male and female senders – 25 different senders in all – viewing each of four kinds of emotionally loaded slides. Theoretically, this process of item analysis should result in an increase in coefficient alpha. This did not prove to be the case, for the alpha of the final instrument was .56 (Buck, 1976).

There is some evidence for the construct validity of CARAT, in that business and fine arts majors scored higher than science majors (Buck, 1976), and CARAT scores were positively correlated with interpersonal trust (Sabatelli, Buck, & Dreyer, 1983). Overall, however, the results were disappointing. As noted previously, the measures of sending accuracy taken in the SVT studies showed considerable evidence of construct validity – they were significantly related with autonomic responding, personality measures, teachers' ratings, and the like – but the same was not true of measures of receiving ability; which were *not* related strongly with other measures. More importantly, studies relating the new measures of nonverbal receiving ability, such as CARAT and the Rosenthal et al. (1979) Profile of Nonverbal Sensitivity (PONS), found the resulting intercorrelations to be disappointing. Low intercorrelations between tests designed to measure the same thing suggest that there may be a problem with the basic conceptualization of nonverbal receiving ability. It may be that by presenting the videotaped expressions of strangers in a noninteractive setting, and instructing subjects to attend specifically to those expressions, CARAT and similar instruments may miss the most important features of true receiving ability, or empathy (Buck, 1983, 1984, 1990c).

The nature of empathy. This issue takes us back to the foundations of the interpersonal self discussed earlier in this chapter, and specifically to the argument that spontaneous communication is a direct process involving social affordances, analogous to the affordances in Gibson's perceptual theory. If that were the case, important aspects of the receiving process would be direct and biologically based. On that assumption one would not expect important individual differences in receiving ability as operationalized by the CARAT, PONS, and similar instruments. Thus, their failure to detect stable individual differences constitutes indirect evidence for the importance of a direct, Gibsonian interpersonal communication process. Such instruments imply by their design that receiving ability is an individual skill that can be tested like other skills, by accurate performance on a series of items.

The only difference from conventional tests is in the items themselves, which are videotapes or other representations of expressive behavior. Because subjects' attention is specifically drawn to expressive behavior in the instructions, individual differences in the attention to expressive cues are effectively canceled out. Also, there is no way in which subjects can interact with the sender to alter the expressive behavior.

It can be argued that empathy must be measured (1) interactively, so that the subject can affect the display of the other, and (2) in settings where there is a choice of what to attend to (Buck, 1983, 1984, 1990b). Regarding the first point, there is reason to believe that in interactive settings the most controllable way to be an accurate receiver of expressive displays is to be expressive oneself. There is evidence that a lack of expression on the part of one interaction partner is reciprocated by a lack of expression on the part of the other (Krause, Steimer, Sanger-Alt, & Wagner, 1989), and conversely that self-disclosure on the part of one partner tends to be reciprocated. Extending this, one would expect that expressiveness on the part of one interactant would generally be reciprocated by expressiveness on the part of others. Expressive persons would tend to go through life in effect leaving a trail of expressiveness in their wake, and they would have this expressiveness *that they themselves instill in others* to draw on in making attributions about those others. Thus expressiveness may be the single most important individual quality associated with empathy (Buck, 1983, 1984, 1990c).

The second point involves allowing the subject to choose what to attend to. The Gibson analysis of perceptual learning suggests that people become more efficient perceivers because of an "education of attention": They learn what events to attend to in a given situation and what to ignore (Gibson, 1966). The tendency to attend to expressive cues – the spontaneous stream of communication – rather than intentional, symbolic cues may be another important source of individual differences in empathy. In instructing subjects to attend to expressive cues, CARAT and similar instruments fail to assess such individual differences.

Emotional education, emotional competence, and the interpersonal and private selves

I have argued that spontaneous communication is based on SP systems: It has evolved to transmit specific sorts of messages important in adaptation. As with other SP systems, however, there is an interaction with GP systems of learning and, in humans, language. In the case of motivation and emotion, the different aspects of the prime readouts are differentially accessible to the responder and the socialization agent: Subjective experience (Emotion III) is accessible only to the responder, spontaneous expressive behaviors

(Emotion II) are more accessible to the socialization agent, and homeostatic responses (Emotion I) are not very accessible to anyone (see Figure 12.2).

Emotional education

This difference in response accessibility has important implications for the social learning process. The bodily events that provide structured information about the primes to the responder, in the form of subjectively experienced feelings and desires (hunger, sexual desire, anger), are unlike external events (like the color red) that are accessible to all. The child must learn about these internal (Skinner called them "private") events: first, in the education of attention, simply to attend to them and realize they are there; second, to come to terms with them, accept them, label them, and understand what they are; and third, to know what should be done with them. This is the emotion education process, which leads to a greater or lesser degree of emotional competence.

Social biofeedback. It follows that during interaction the other must function in ways analogous to a biofeedback device (Buck, 1988a). If expressive behavior is more accessible to others than it is to the expresser, one way that an individual comes to understand his or her feelings and control his or her expressive displays is by the response to those displays on the part of others.

Ekman and Friesen (1969b) suggested that displays to which others respond quickly and reliably (such as facial expressions in our culture) become controlled by display rules. In contrast, displays that are ignored by others (such as many body movements) are less controlled and thus may "leak" the individual's true feelings. This is equivalent to the Gibsonian process of the education of attention, in that the individual's attention is drawn to those aspects of his or her own display that are responded to by others. Here, an initially less accessible response is rendered more accessible by others' behavior. This interpersonal feedback is analogous to that provided by a biofeedback device, where a relatively inaccessible physiological response is rendered more accessible because of its association with the feedback signal.

Developmental–interactionist theory makes two additions to the Ekman and Friesen (1969b) formulation: first, that the interpersonal feedback process involves spontaneous communication, and second, that one's attention to, understanding of, and ability to deal with one's own subjective feelings and desires are also affected. Interpersonal feedback thus must have important implications for how one labels and interprets one's own feelings and desires: Neisser's (1988) "private self."

Emotional competence. The net result of social biofeedback is that the individual comes to respond more or less effectively in social contexts, to control his or her displays and behaviors more or less appropriately. This occurs in other social animals as well (Harlow & Mears, 1983). In human beings, an additional level of complexity is added by linguistic competence. Human beings use their verbal and logical abilities in the exploration of the external physical environment, a process of cognitive development that has been long acknowledged and much studied (e.g., Piaget, 1971). At the same time, however, they must connect verbal labels and reasoning with the internal environment of their own bodies – the subjectively experienced world of feelings and desires.

Competence in general is the ability to deal effectively with events (White, 1959). Social competence is the ability to deal effectively with other persons; emotional competence is the ability to deal effectively with the internal environment of one's own feelings and desires. Generally, social and emotional competence should be mutually supportive: Accurate emotional communication would foster both the ability to deal with others and with one's own feelings and desires (Buck, 1991).

Personal relationships. Emotional education and the achievement of emotional competence must be, to some extent, specific to particular personal relationships (Buck, 1989). It is axiomatic that as one goes from more impersonal "social" relationships to more intimate "personal" relationships, there are changes in the information used to relate to the other and in the rules governing behavior vis-à-vis the other. Specifically, social relationships use general information about such things as age, sex, and physical attractiveness; personal relationships use information intrinsic to the relationship (Argyle, Henderson, & Furnam, 1985).

Implications: The interpersonal and private selves

It is in this communicative process, based fundamentally on innate spontaneous communication mechanisms and fostered by individual expressiveness, that the interpersonal self is formed. Through it, important aspects of the private self are formed as well. They become differentiated as self-structures – linguistically organized systems of rules, expectations, scripts, and so on – that characterize the individual (Buck, 1988a). In Rogers's (1951, p. 498) definition they come to constitute an "organized, fluid, but consistent conceptual pattern." However, as social psychology has repeatedly demonstrated, these self-structures are very open to influence from the social environment and the situation at hand (e.g., Milgram, 1963). This is because the self-structures are formed from the social environment, are backed up largely by social motives, and are to an extent specific to the personal and social relationships that are salient at the moment.

The view of the self that emerges from this analysis is fundamentally a view of the self as adaptation. The ecological self is an adaptation to the physical environment mediated by basic exteroceptive and proprioceptive perceptual systems. The interpersonal self is an adaptation to the social environment mediated in large part by spontaneous communication. The private self is an adaptation to the internal bodily environment mediated by interoceptive perceptual systems that "pick up" important events in that environment (the Emotion III process) and by the responses of others to one's expressive behaviors (the social biofeedback process). Like any adaptive system, the self tends to become stable as environmental, social, and bodily circumstances become predictable, but it is disrupted by changes in any of these circumstances. The process of therapy may be viewed from this perspective as a process of adaptation or readaptation, of emotional education or reeducation.

NOTE

1. It should be noted that while spontaneous communication is by definition veridical, the message received is not a clearly decodable proposition, like "he is angry," but, rather, is a display that is received as "feeling," "intuition," or "vibes" that may not affect self-reports and indeed may seem to be entirely ignored by the receiver. However, as Rosenthal and his colleagues have demonstrated in many studies, this "covert communication," as he called it (1967), may have quite important effects on the receiver's behavior (Buck, in press).

REFERENCES

Argyle, M., Henderson, M., & Furnam, A. (1985). The rules of social relationships. *British Journal of Social Psychology, 24,* 125–139.

Austin, J. L. (1959). Other minds. In A. G. N. Flew (Ed.), *Logic and language.* Oxford: Blackwell.

Bentley, D. R., & Hoy, R. R. (1974). The neurobiology of cricket song. *Scientific American, 231* (2), 34–44.

Bogert, C. M. (1961). The influence of sound in the behavior of amphibians and reptiles. In W. E. Lanyon & W. N. Tavdga (Eds.), *Animal sounds and communication.* Publication No. 7. Washington, DC: American Institute of Biological Sciences.

Borod, J. C., Koff, E., Perlman, M., & Nicholas, M. (1985). Channels of emotional expression in patients with unilateral brain damage. *Archives of Neurology, 42,* 345–348.

Buck, R. (1975). Nonverbal communication of affect in children. *Journal of Personality and Social Psychology, 31,* 644–653.

Buck, R. (1976). A test of nonverbal receiving ability: Preliminary studies. *Human Communication Research, 2,* 162–171.

Buck, R. (1977). Nonverbal communication accuracy in preschool children: Relationships with personality and skin conductance. *Journal of Personality and Social Psychology, 33,* 225–236.

Buck, R. (1979). Individual differences in nonverbal sending accuracy and electrodermal responding: The externalizing–internalizing dimension. In R. Rosenthal (Ed.), *Skill in nonverbal communication: Individual differences.* Cambridge, MA: Oelgeschlager, Gunn and Hain.

Buck, R. (1983). Recent approaches to the study of nonverbal receiving ability. In J. Weimann & R. Harrison (Eds.), *Nonverbal communication: The social interaction sphere.* New York: Sage.

Buck, R. (1984). *The communication of emotion.* New York: Guilford.

Buck, R. (1985). Prime theory: An integrated view of motivation and emotion. *Psychological Review, 92,* 389–413.

Buck, R. (1988a). *Human motivation and emotion* (2nd ed.). New York: Wiley.

Buck, R. (1988b). Emotional education and mass media: A new view of the global village. In R. Hawkins, J. Weimann, & S. Pingree (Eds.), *Advancing communication science: Merging mass and interpersonal processes* (Vol. 16). Sage Annual Reviews of Communication Research. Beverly Hills, CA: Sage.

Buck, R. (1989). Emotional communication in personal relationships: A developmental–interactionist view. In C. D. Hendrick (Ed.), *Close relationships. Review of personality and social psychology* (Vol. 10). Newbury Park, CA: Sage.

Buck, R. (1990a). William James, the nature of knowledge, and current issues in emotion, cognition, and communication. *Personality and Social Psychology Bulletin, 16,* 612–625.

Buck, R. (1990b). Using FACS versus communication scores to measure the spontaneous facial expression of emotion in brain-damaged patients. *Cortex, 26,* 275–280.

Buck, R. (1990c). Rapport, emotional education, and emotional competence. *Psychological Inquiry, 1*(4), 612–625.

Buck, R. (1991). Temperament, social skills, and the communication of emotion: A developmental–interactionist perspective. In D. Gilbert & J. J. Conley (Eds.), *Personality, social skills, and psychopathology: An individual differences approach.* New York: Plenum.

Buck, R. (1992). Epistemological fundamentals: Knowledge by acquaintance and spontaneous communication. *Journal of pragmatics, 17,* 447–454.

Buck, R. (in press). The spontaneous communication of interpersonal expectations. In P. D. Blanck (Ed.), *Interpersonal expectations: Theory, research, and applications.* Cambridge University Press.

Buck, R. (1977). Nonverbal communication of affect in brain-damaged patients. Presented at the American Psychological Association Convention, San Francisco.

Buck, R., & Duffy, R. (1977). Nonverbal communication of affect in brain-damaged patients. *Cortex, 16,* 351–362.

Buck, R., & Ginsburg, B. (1991). Emotional communication and altruism: The communicative gene hypothesis. In M. Clark (Ed.), *Altruism. Review of personality and social psychology* (Vol. II). Newbury Park, CA: Sage.

Buck, R. W., Miller, R. E., & Caul, W. F. (1974). Sex, personality and physiological variables in the communication of emotion via facial expression. *Journal of Personality and Social Psychology, 30,* 587–596.

Buck, R., Savin, V. J., Miller, R. E., & Caul, W. F. (1972). Nonverbal communication of affect in humans. *Journal of Personality and Social Psychology, 23,* 362–371.

Critchley, M. (1975). *Silent language.* London: Butterworths.

Duffy, R., & Buck, R. (1979). A study of the relationship between propositional (pantomime) and subpropositional (facial expression) extraverbal behavior in aphasics. *Folia Phoniatrica, 31,* 129–136.

Duffy, R. J., Duffy, J. R., & Alderdice, M. (1977). Limb apraxia and gestural impairment in aphasia. Paper presented at the convention of the American Speech and Hearing Association, Chicago.

Ekman, P., & Friesen, W. V. (1969a). The repertoire of nonverbal behavior: Categories, origins, usage and coding. *Semiotica, 1,* 49–98.

Ekman, P., & Friesen, W. V. (1969b). Nonverbal leakage and clues to deception. *Psychiatry, 32,* 88–105.

Ekman, P., & Friesen, W. V. (1974). Nonverbal behavior and psychopathology. In R. J. Friedman & H. M. Katz (Eds.), *The psychology of depression: Contemporary theory and research.* New York: Wiley.

Ekman, P., & Friesen, W. V. (1975). *Unmasking the face.* Englewood Cliffs, NJ: Prentice Hall.

Ekman, P., & Friesen, W. V. (1978). *The Facial Action Coding System (FACS): A technique for the measurement of facial action.* Palto Alto, CA: Consulting Psychologists Press.

Fowles, D. C. (1980). The three arousal model: Implications of Gray's two-factor learning theory for heart rate, electrodermal activity, and psychotherapy. *Psychophysiology, 17,* 87–104.

Gibson, J. J. (1966). *The senses considered as perceptual systems.* Boston: Houghton Mifflin.

Gibson, J. J. (1979). *An ecological approach to visual perception.* Boston: Houghton Mifflin.

Gorenstein, E. E., & Newman, J. P. (1980). Disinhibitory psychopathology: A new perspective and a model for research. *Psychological Review, 87,* 301–315.

Gray, J. A. (1982). Precis of *"The neuropsychology of anxiety."* With commentaries. *Behavioral and Brain Sciences, 5,* 469–534.

Harlow, H. F., & Mears, C. E. (1983). Emotional sequences and consequences. In R. Plutchik & H. Kellerman (Eds.), *Emotion: Theory, research and experiences: Vol. 2, Emotions in early development.* New York: Academic Press.

Hastorf, A. H., & Bender, I. E. (1952). A caution respecting the measurement of empathic ability. *Journal of Abnormal and Social Psychology, 47,* 574–576.

Izard, C. E. (1977). *Human emotions.* New York: Plenum.

James, W. (1890). *The principles of psychology* (Vol. 1). New York: Holt.

Jenkins, J., Jimenez-Pabon, E., Shaw, R., & Sefer, J. (1975). *Schuell's aphasia in adults,* New York: Harper & Row.

Kagan, J., & Snidman, N. (1991). Temperamental factors in human development. *American Psychologist, 46(8),* 856–862.

Krause, R., Steimer, E., Sanger-Alt, C., & Wagner, G. (1989). Facial expression of schizophrenic patients and their interaction partners. *Psychiatry, 52,* 1–12.

Lanzetta, J. T., & Kleck, R. E. (1970). Encoding and decoding of nonverbal affect in humans. *Journal of Personality and Social Psychology, 16,* 12–19.

McHugo, G. J., Lanzetta, J. T., Sullivan, D. G., Masters, R. D., & Englis, B. G. (1985). Emotional reactions to a political leader's expressive displays. *Journal of Personality and Social Psychology, 49,* 1513–1529.

Manstead, A. S. R. (1990). Expressiveness as an individual difference. In R. S. Feldman & B. Rime (Eds.), *Fundamentals of nonverbal behavior.* Cambridge University Press.

Mammucari, A., Caltagirone, C., Ekman, P., Friesen, W., Gainotti, G., Pizzamiglio, L., & Zoccolotti, P. (1988). Spontaneous expression of emotions in brain-damaged patients. *Cortex, 24,* 521–533.

Milgram, S. (1963). Behavioral study of obedience. *Journal of Abnormal and Social Psychology, 67,* 371–378.

Miller, R. E., Banks, J., & Ogawa, N. (1962). Communication of affect in "cooperative conditioning" of rhesus monkeys. *Journal of Abnormal and Social Psychology, 64,* 343–348.

Miller, R. E., Banks, J., & Ogawa, N. (1963). Role of facial expression in "cooperative-avoidance conditioning" in monkeys. *Journal of Abnormal and Social Psychology, 67,* 24–30.

Miller, R. E., Caul, W. F., & Mirsky, I. A. (1967). Communication of affects between feral and socially isolated monkeys. *Journal of Personality and Social Psychology, 7,* 231–239.

Moon, A., & Ginsburg, B. E. (1985, August). Genetic factors in the selective expression of species typical behavior of coyote x beagle hybrids. Invited paper presented at the Nineteenth International Ethological Conference, Toulouse, France.

Neisser, U. (1988). Five kinds of self-knowledge. *Philosophical Psychology, 1*(1), 35–59.

Piaget, J. (1971). Piaget's theory. In P. Mussen (Ed.), *Handbook of child development* (Vol. 1). New York: Wiley.

Rogers, C. R. (1951). *Client-centered therapy.* Boston: Houghton Mifflin.

Rosenthal, R. (1967). Covert communication in the psychological experiment. *Psychological Bulletin, 67,* 356–367.

Rosenthal, R., Hall, J. A., DiMatteo, M. R., Rogers, P. L., & Archer, D. (1979). *Sensitivity to nonverbal communication: The PONS test.* Baltimore: Johns Hopkins University Press.

Ross, E. D. (1981). The aprosodias: Functional-anatomic organization of the affective components of language in the right hemisphere. *Archives of neurology, 37,* 561–569.

Ross, E. D. (in press). Right hemisphere's role in language, affective behaviors, and emotions: Implications for diagnosing depression in brain injured persons. In W. G. Gordon (Ed.), *Advances in stroke rehabilitation.* New York: Andover.

Ryan, M. J. (1990). Signals, species, and sexual selection. *American Scientist, 78,* 46–52.

Sabatelli, R., Buck, R., & Dreyer, A. (1983). Locus of control, interpersonal trust, and nonverbal communication accuracy. *Journal of Personality and Social Psychology, 44,* 399–409.

Sabatelli, R., Buck, R., & Kenny, D. (1986). Nonverbal communication in married couples: A social relations analysis. *Journal of Personality, 54*(3), 513–527.

Tucker, D. M. (1981). Lateral brain function, emotion, and conceptualization. *Psychological Bulletin, 89,* 19–46.

Wagner, H., Buck, R., & Winterbotham, M. (1989). *Sex differences in the communication of specific emotions.* Unpublished paper, University of Manchester.

White, R. W. (1959). Motivation reconsidered: The concept of competence. *Psychological Review, 66,* 297–333.

Wittgenstein, L. (1965). *The blue and the brown books.* New York: Philosophical Library Edition.

Zoccolotti, P., Caltagirone, C., Ekman, P., Friesen, W., Gainotti, G., Mammucari, A., & Pizzamiglio, L. (1990). Methodological questions on the study of spontaneous emotional responding as compared to nonverbal communication in brain damaged patients: Comments on Buck's reply (1989). *Cortex, 26,* 281–289.

13

Autism, affordances, and the self

KATHERINE A. LOVELAND

In his paper "Five Kinds of Self-Knowledge," Neisser (1988) reminds us of J. J. Gibson's (1979) argument that the self and environment are always coperceived. Gibson's discussion was mainly about what Neisser calls the *ecological self,* which is directly perceived. However, if, as Neisser has argued, the *interpersonal self* is also directly perceived, then the coperception of self and environment should occur on this level as well as on the level of the ecological self. If so, then while we engage in interactions with other persons, we perceive not only the other person but ourselves. What do we learn about the self in this way? I believe we learn about the self as actor in an environment inhabited by other humans: We learn how others react to us, how our actions influence the course of events, and whether our assumptions about the world, including ourselves, are correct.

Neisser makes the further, and very important, point that the perception of the interpersonal self must be in species-specific terms: "The successful achievement of intersubjectivity depends not only on the operation of the perceptual and motor systems, but on some additional, specifically human mechanism that permits us to relate to members of our own species" (1988, p. 12). One way to talk about these species-specific mechanisms that provide information about the self and other is in terms of Gibson's (1979) concept of *affordances.* The theory of affordances is part of Gibson's larger theory of perception, which embodies what he termed an *ecological* approach to perception. I shall briefly review some relevant points of Gibson's theory and explain how the concept of affordances might apply to the interpersonal self.

J. J. Gibson's ecological approach to perception asserts among other things that:

1. Perception of the world is direct rather than mediated by mental representations, because the information specifying the invariant structure of the world is available in the light (or sound, or other stimulation).
2. Perception and action form one integrated system: Perception guides action, action provides opportunities for perception. Human activity can be described in terms of perception–action systems.
3. We perceive a *meaningful* world. This meaningfulness resides neither in the organism (person) nor in the environment, but derives from the interaction of the two. Gibson described meaning in terms of affordances, that is, what the environment offers us. For example, some surfaces offer me support .

for walking, whereas others do not. What the environment affords you depends on what kind of animal you are, not only in terms of physical effectivities but also in terms of your level of cognitive and behavioral development (Goldfield, 1983; Goldfield & Shaw, 1984). Thus, all affordances are in this sense both species-specific and individual-specific.

4. Meaning, in the form of affordances, can be perceived directly, because it is based on available information to specify real relations between the perceiver and environment. The meaning of what we perceive does not need to be added through association, processing, or other transformations of "raw" data.

5. Not only inanimate objects, events, and places have affordances but also people and other animals. These "social affordances" have to do with the meaning of other people's activities for the perceiver (cf. Loveland, 1990; McArthur & Baron, 1983; Reed, 1988; Van Acker & Valenti, 1989).

In these terms, one could say that from earliest infancy we begin to perceive the affordances of other people – that is, what they, their activities, their affective expressions, and so on, offer us. Other people and their activities are meaningful to us in species-specific ways. If in fact the inter-personal self reflects the perception of the self as actor in a human social world, then its development must depend on an adequate grasp of the social affordances present in that world. That is, without some understanding of the meaning of other people's actions and reactions toward the self, the kind of self-knowledge Neisser calls the interpersonal self would be absent or impaired.

Can such a state of affairs come about? What would a person with such a disability be like? As the reader will have deduced from the title of this chapter, I believe that people with autism display such a disability. My thoughts about autism come from 10 years of clinical and research work with autistic people. Before making my argument about the interpersonal self in autism, I shall review briefly what autism is and how it is manifested.

Autism and the interpersonal self

Autism is a severe developmental disorder that afflicts a small number of people. Though it has doubtless been present in the human population for a very long time, it was only in the 1940s that it was first described as a syndrome by Leo Kanner (1943). Autistic people are interesting, because, among other things, they seem to lack the normal person's natural interest in and ability for establishing interpersonal relatedness. (This seems to be a deficiency in the "immediate, unreflective" social relatedness that Neisser writes about in his discussion of the interpersonal self.) Despite the name given to the syndrome, autism is not a form of emotional withdrawal in response to trauma or poor parenting. Though there are few reliable accounts of autistic children's earliest development, it is believed that their disability is present from birth, and that it affects all subsequent development. The result is a syndrome that includes severely deficient social behavior and social awareness, language deficits (especially social use of language), and rigidity of thought or "preservation of sameness," often appearing as stereotyped movements or ritualized activity.

The DSM III-R criteria for pervasive developmental disorders, including autism, are as follows:

1. Qualitative impairment of reciprocal social interaction
2. Qualitative impairment in verbal and nonverbal communication and im-aginative activity
3. Markedly restricted repertoire of activities and interests

Other symptoms often associated with autism, but not always present, include abnormalities of gait (e.g., toe walking), stereotyped movements such as rocking or flapping, echolalia, and sensory abnormalities (e.g., apparent indifference to pain, overreaction to noises). Current thinking (Cohen, Paul, & Volkmar, 1987) places autism along a spectrum of disorder (Pervasive Developmental Disorders) such that an individual may be more or less impaired in any of several areas while still exhibiting a disorder of this type.

Cognitive impairment. Most autistic persons are mentally retarded, many severely so. A few have intelligence within normal limits, at least in some areas. Commonly, autistic people have uneven intellectual profiles; very often they are more able in nonverbal than verbal skills, though in the highest functioning individuals, the two may be more evenly matched.

Language impairment. Many autistic people have no language at all; most have very little. Among those who do, such symptoms as echolalia and pronoun reversals are often observed. Even where a great deal of language is acquired, the *use* of language is significantly impaired; thus verbal autistic people frequently have trouble managing simple aspects of conversations such as making requests, introducing and ending topics, and the like. They are particularly poor at determining the social implications of their own and other people's communications; they often understand things literally and concretely, and their grasp of meaning is apt to be idiosyncratic. Gestural communication is also notably impaired.

Repetitive, stereotyped behaviors. Autistic people prefer to spend much of their time engaged in stereotyped or repetitive activities, ranging from such motor activities as rocking, hand flapping, or banging to repetitive play to elaborate fixations such as continually watching the Weather Channel and devising weather maps. A hallmark of autistic repetitive behaviors is that they are idiosyncratic; that is, they seem to have special meaning for the autistic individual that is not shared with others (cf. Frith, 1989; Loveland, 1990).

Social impairment. Social impairment is thought to be the most characteristic symptom of autism (Fein, Pennington, Markowitz, Braverman, & Waterhouse, 1986). Note that just as people with autism can have a wide range of intellectual levels, they can also be impaired in social skills to varying degrees. The main criterion, diagnostically, is that the level of social development be very discrepant with the level of intellectual development. The social impairment can be manifested as a general unresponsiveness, in the severest form, or can appear as inappropriate behavior of either a gross or subtle nature. Although the social impairment is often said to be the main or essential deficit in autism, I think it is actually a symptom of a larger deficit in the ability to perceive a fully meaningful environment in human terms – to share in what might be called the human point of view.

Given that autistic people do have an impaired ability to relate socially to others, what are the implications of this impairment for the development of self-awareness?

1. The *ecological self* would most likely remain intact. Autistic people do get around in the world on physical terms without any special problems, for the most part. (They do not characteristically fall down stairs or try to fit through spaces that are obviously too small, for example.) Thus there is no reason to suppose they have any particular trouble perceiving such things as the location and extent of their own bodies.

2. The *interpersonal self*, by contrast, might be seriously affected. If the interpersonal self is learned about through interactions with others, then an impaired ability to perceive the meaning of other people and their activity (social affordances) would certainly lead to distortions in the awareness of the self as social actor.

Is there evidence about the development of self-awareness in people with autism, particularly with respect to the interpersonal self? In the sections to follow, I examine some areas of research that bear on the question of self-awareness in autism and the perception of social affordances.

The meaning of the mirror

The mirror has long been regarded as a means of examining awareness of or knowledge about the self. Mirror tasks are said to provide an index of self-recognition, self-awareness, self-concept and so on. Several studies have sought to examine whether autistic persons, who are notably deficient in social skills of all kinds, might not also be deficient in understanding the self, as shown in mirror self-recognition tasks (Dawson & McKissick, 1984; Ferrari & Matthews., 1983; Spiker & Ricks, 1984). In general, it has been found that autistic people are able to succeed at conventional mirror self-recognition tasks, provided they reach a mental age level comparable to that of most normal children who succeed. From this it has been concluded that autistic people are not deficient in sense of self, self-image, and the like. But what, exactly, can mirror tasks actually tell us about the self-awareness of a subject?

The most common mirror self-recognition procedure is what might be called the "marked-face task." The marked-face task, of which several versions exist, consists essentially of a situation in which the subject's face is unobtrusively marked with a colorful substance (cf. Dixon, 1957; Gallup, 1977, 1979; Lewis & Brooks-Gunn, 1979, 1984; Loveland, 1987a, 1987b). The subject is then placed before the mirror, and the observer looks for signs that the subject notices the mark and can locate it on the self, usually by touching. Finding the mark is taken as evidence that the subject recognizes the self-image.

What exactly does it mean to *recognize* the self? It seems to mean different things, depending on the investigator. For some, it means that the subject must have a kind of template (mental representation) to which the mirror image was compared, in order that the discrepant mark might be detected. To recognize the self, then, is to connect the mirror image to the template. For others, it seems to mean that the subject has a reasonably elaborated self-concept, including such knowledge as "what I usually look like" and even that the self may be the object of another's regard (cf. Baron-Cohen, 1988). It is the ability to reflect upon the self, both literally and figuratively. Sometimes this achievement is viewed as a special kind of consciousness that may or may not be unique to humans (Gallup, 1986).

But does the mirror task actually provide any evidence of such constructs as self-image or self-concept? It seems to me to provide very little, if any. The mental representation hypothesized by most investigators is nowhere measured in this task; rather, it is inferred, after the fact, as an explanation of the underlying processes that bring about success in the marked-face task. Thus, the mirror is at best only an indirect index of the presence of what Neisser (1988) terms a *conceptual self.*

I have offered explanations elsewhere to show that mental representations, whether of self or of other things, do not need to be invoked in order to explain what is happening as children or animals learn to solve mirror tasks (Loveland, 1986). The mirror can be understood as a perceptual phenomenon, and much of the early mirror behavior observed in young children and animals can be explained as resulting from a process of exploration involving perceptual learning. In this view, the mirror is a kind of tool for mediated perception of things (including the self) that are not ordinarily visible from the observer's standpoint in the environment. Through a process of perceptual learning, the observer gradually learns what the mirror affords (seeing things not located where you are looking) and how to use one accurately (i.e., how to tell where the reflected thing is actually located and how to relate its location or movements to one's own).

Evidence from several studies shows that children learning to use a mirror make inconsistent progress, commit errors in some situations and are correct in others, contradict themselves, and sometimes fail tasks they had previously passed (e.g., Loveland, 1986, 1987a, 1987b; Zazzo, 1979). Their performance suggests that the properties of mirrors are gradually being worked out. This is what one would expect if a process of perceptual learning is taking place that depends on exploration as well as on the developmental maturity of the learner.

What, then, does success at the marked-face task tell us about a person with autism? It indicates that the individual has learned what mirrors are for (i.e., their affordances) and how to use mirrors to see things not otherwise visible. But does an understanding of the mirror as it applies to the marked-face task presuppose the existence of a "self"? Yes, it does. The self it presupposes is the ecological self, the self-who-is-located-here. The ecological self is probably unimpaired in an autistic individual who can perform the marked-face task, because in order to use the mirror to examine the self, one must be able to perceive one's body on the level of the ecological self.

Does the mirror also provide evidence about the development of an interpersonal self? It could, but not necessarily through the marked-face task. Human infants commonly behave in front of the mirror in a way described as "social"; so do many other animals. That is, they are said to react toward the mirror as they would toward another person: smile, laugh, kiss, pat, make faces. Is this behavior the result of a perception that another person is located at or in the mirror? In some cases, it may be. Some animals (fighting fish, for example) respond to the mirror self-image with threat displays (Thompson & Sturm, 1965). Their behavior gives us no reason to think that the mirror image is distinguished from another animal. Rather, the animal seems to notice only information for the social affordances of another animal; thus, the meaning of the mirror image for the fish may be the same as the meaning of another animal. Some of the earliest behavior of human infants before the mirror might be explained in this way.

In other cases, however, an infant or other animal seems to detect the fact that the mirror self-image does not really behave like a separate individual, and so it *does not really afford what another individual affords.* Zazzo and colleagues (1979) found that German shepherd dogs tended to bark and to appear distressed before the mirror; his explanation was that the dog's mirror image *looks* in some ways like a conspecific, but it does not *behave* like one. Its behavior lacks the reciprocity, the rhythmic structure, and the species-specific intersubjectivity characteristic of a real interaction between dogs. The virtual dog's behavior is therefore disturbing to the real dog.

Similarly, there is reason to think that 1-year-olds, at least, can tell that the mirror self-image does not afford what a real playmate affords. Their playful behavior before the mirror seems to be mirror-specific; that is, infants do not normally pat, kiss, or make faces at each other at close range. It seems more likely that this kind of behavior represents exploration in the mirror situation (Loveland, 1987a). On the other hand, the ability to distinguish the mirror self-image from another, real person, if demonstrated in different behavior toward each, would suggest that the observer *is* indeed aware of the meaning of social interactions. This would imply that some awareness of the interpersonal self – the self who takes part in such reciprocal inter-actions – is present.

We do not know much about the behavior of autistic people in front of mirrors, apart from investigations of the marked-face task. Thus it is hard to say whether they can distinguish the social affordances of a real person from the pseudo-social affordances of the self-image (cf. Loveland, 1986). I suspect that many of them can, though not necessarily with the facility of normal individuals. I have often seen autistic people observing themselves in mirrors, making faces, touching the mirror, or behaving in other ways that suggest they do not perceive it to be another person.

It is sometimes reported that autistic people do not respond in a self-conscious way before the mirror, and that they also do not evidence em-barrassment. Baron-Cohen (1988) has suggested that the non-self-conscious behavior of the autistic person before the mirror represents "an inability to conceive of oneself as the object of another person's thoughts" (p. 393). However, I have frequently observed autistic persons (adolescents, very often) who are aware of their appearance, are concerned about being observed during testing (we have a two-way mirror in the lab), and who attribute social intentions to others that relate to themselves (e.g., he's watching me). Of course, these perceptions of self and other are often wrong; for example, no one is watching. What this demonstrates is not that autistic people have no idea that others can have mental states but, rather, that they are poor at interpreting the meaning of other people's social behavior toward themselves, as well as the implications of their own actions for other persons.

I–you pronouns and the self

Autistic people are well known for having difficulty in using I–you pronouns (Fay & Schuler, 1980). Only some autistic persons reach a language level at which the use of pronouns would normally be expected. In these cases the autistic person may substitute names for I and you ("Give Jon a cracker" = "Give *me* a cracker"), or may confuse I and you receptively and expressively (e.g., "You want to go outside" for "*I* want to go outside").

Despite a tendency to reverse first and second person pronouns, they do not, in general, have trouble with third person pronouns or with names. What can account for a deficit of this nature? Some of the possible explanations are as follows:

1. *Autistic people have a specific language delay in this area.* One way to look at this is to say that the I–you deficit only means that autistic people are stuck in a phase of language development that normal young children pass through rapidly (Oshima-Takane & Benaroya, 1989). This idea has the virtue of acknowledging that autistic children do develop, and that not all aspects of their development need be abnormal. However, it does not explain why such a specific deficit is present, and why the autistic child's pronoun errors are typically so out of keeping with his or her overall level of language development. It also does not explain why autistic pronoun errors persist as long as they do, or why they do not really resemble pronoun usage of young normal children (most of whom make few reversals). A suggested explanation has been that autistic people only make I–you errors because they are echoing the adult's speech – Adult: "Do you want a cookie?" Child: "You want a cookie." It seems likely that some pronoun reversals arise this way, but reversal errors can be seen in individuals who rarely if ever echo. Some individuals who make reversal errors then self-correct or show confusion, suggesting that their use of the pronoun is more than just an echo. Moreover, not only production but comprehension of pronouns by autistic people is impaired. Thus, a deeper explanation seems to be required.

2. *Autistic people lack a sense of self.* On this view, autistic people cannot easily distinguish self and other, and so cannot talk about self and other consistently. In light of Neisser's theory, this is a rather vague idea. The earlier discussion of the mirror suggests that autistic people do have some awareness of the self. There is no evidence at all that the ecological self is impaired in autism, so the ability to distinguish self from other in this basic sense must be present very early. Thus it cannot be a simple matter of failing to know who is who.

If not on the level of the ecological self, then, is there any reason to think that a deficiency in the interpersonal self might be at the root of pronoun problems? I believe this explanation, though incomplete, is on the right track. As was shown earlier, there is good reason to think that autistic people are deficient in the awareness of the interpersonal self, because their ability to perceive the meaning of other persons' behavior is impaired. However, it remains to be explained how awareness of the interpersonal self (as opposed to something else) might underlie the acquisition of I–you pronouns.

3. *Autistic people have difficulty acquiring the developmental basis for use of I–you.* That is, they are deficient in knowing that others have a different point of view. Versions of this idea have been espoused by several investigators (e.g., Fay, 1979; Fay & Schuler, 1980; Frith, 1989; Ricks & Wing, 1975; and cf. Loveland, 1984). Because I–you pronouns "move around" in a reciprocal

fashion (I am "I" to myself; you are "I" to yourself) rather than remaining in a constant relationship to particular referents (as names do), their use is difficult. To disambiguate this situation, the child must be able to perceive that each person has a unique point of view both ecologically (visually) and socially (Gibson, 1976; Loveland, 1984). On the most basic level, the child must perceive that other persons exist at other station points in the environment, that they are in different orientations relative to that environment, and that these differences in orientation have meaningful implications for the child and others.

In a set of studies some years ago I sought to examine the relationship between understanding visual points of view and the acquisition of I–you pronouns (Loveland, 1984). In young normal children, acquisition of I–you pronouns begins in the second year of life and may extend to about 36 months of age. Early, one-sided uses ("Mine!") tend to have a fixed point of reference, the child's own. Gradually, the child shows evidence of appreciating that such words mean different things when uttered by different speakers. This process, like so much else in development, is lumpy, irregular, full of inconsistencies, and backsliding. A few children seem to make consistent reversal errors for periods of time (Clark, 1977), but most do not. Eventually, errors drop out altogether.

As a realist who believes that meaning derives from real relations between perceiver and environment, I hypothesized that progress in the understanding of visual points of view would be reflected in parallel progress in correctly using I–you pronouns (cf. Dent, 1989). I proposed that points of view would not be understood until the child was fully aware of the following possibilities:

1. That she or he may adopt any number of differing points of view on the environment.
2. That because other perceivers occupy different points of observation, their points of view must differ in some way from the child's own. In particular.
   a. Someone else may see something not visible to the child, and
   b. The child may see something not visible to someone else.

The theory is that awareness of others' points of view in a larger, social sense begins with an appreciation of differences in visual point of view. Using an ordered series of tasks, I examined young children's awareness of these points and compared it to the occurrence of errors in using I–you pronouns over about a year. Results showed that the mastery of points of view was closely followed by a final mastery of pronouns, and that no child used I and you without errors until points of view were first understood.

Results of this study clearly supported the interpretation that understanding the ways in which human viewpoints can differ is a necessary, though by no means sufficient, prerequisite to sorting out the reciprocal use of I and you. What this implies for autistic children is that they, too, should have trouble using I–you without errors until visual points of view have been sorted out. However, this hypothesis has never actually been tested. The studies of perspective taking in autistic children (e.g., Dawson & Fernald, 1987; Hobson, 1984; Oswald & Ollendick, 1989) have shown that some autistic children can determine whether another person can see something based on observation of the direction of their gaze and that some can even solve Piagetian coordination of perspective tasks. However, because of the verbal and intellectual demands of the tasks used, these studies have dealt with high-functioning verbal autistic children whose development was well past the point at which I–you pronouns would likely have been mastered. Thus, we cannot tell what these children may have been like in earlier phases of development, when points of view were still being sorted out. In particular, we do not know the relationship between this discovery and the mastery of I–you pronouns in these children.

Some have argued that visual points of view, in the sense I have been discussing, are "merely perceptual" – that is, one need not understand anything about other people, only about the geometry of spatial relations. When some autistic people succeed at this type of task, the conclusion is that they only understand physical (socially meaningless?) relationships, not the social relationships between people. This goes along with the idea that autistic people are primarily impaired on interpersonal factors but have an otherwise normal perceptual substrate. This position assumes that the perceived world is initially without meaning, and that meaning must be added. It could be argued, instead, that the kind of basic perspective taking that is represented by gaze following involves the perception of social affordances, and is an outgrowth of the early, species-specific intersubjectivity discussed earlier. What do we know about early interpersonal skills such as gaze following in autistic children?

Fortunately, a number of studies of *joint attention* in autism shed some light on this issue. Joint attention (Bruner, 1975) is established when two persons attend to the same thing. Gestural joint attention mechanisms such as gaze following, pointing, and showing are part of parent–child interactions by the latter part of the first year of life (Tomasello, 1988, and in this volume). There is much reason to believe that gestural joint attention mechanisms are based on some appreciation of differences in points of view (see, e.g., Butterworth & Cochran, 1980). The reason is that, ordinarily, one attempts to direct someone's attention to something only if one can determine that the person is not already attending to that thing.

Research in autism has shown that autistic people have a great deal of trouble both using and understanding joint attention gestures (Landry & Loveland, 1988; Loveland & Landry, 1986; Mundy, Sigman, Ungerer, & Sherman 1986). Young autistic children with little or no language, unlike preverbal normal or language-delayed children, rarely initiate joint attention interactions and are less likely than other children to respond correctly to others' gestures.

Why should autistic people be impaired in joint attention skills such as gaze following? Most likely they have no special trouble detecting the direction of gaze. Rather, they have trouble understanding its *meaning*, that in the indicated direction there is something to be looked at. The ability to manage joint attention gestures implies that one perceives the social affordances of such gestures – their meaning – both for the self and for others. I would argue that the autistic child's deficient use of gestural joint attention mechanisms reflects a deficient appreciation of social affordances more generally (Loveland, 1990).

What does this deficit in joint attention mean for the use of I–you pronouns by autistic people? One might predict that given an adequate overall language level, an autistic child could use I and you without errors, provided a basic understanding of points of view was first acquired. One would also predict, on the basis of the close relation between joint attention and understanding points of view, that awareness of the meaning of joint attention gestures should precede understanding of I and you.

The pertinent research in this area is not conclusive. Just as mainly high-functioning autistic individuals have been studied in perspective-taking research, so mainly low-functioning or very young individuals have been studied in joint attention research. Many of these individuals have not had enough language to make the study of pronoun use possible. Nevertheless, Susan Landry and I found that for young verbal autistic children, correct expressive use of I–you pronouns was positively related to the number of kinds of joint attention gestures used, the developmental sophistication of the gestures used, and the likelihood of responding appropriately to attention-directing gestures by others (Landry & Loveland, 1988; Loveland & Landry, 1986). These relationships were not present for young normal children. We concluded that the autistic subjects were still struggling to understand the basis of I and you in points of view, and that for most of them, this was the primary obstacle to correct use of I–you. This issue should be examined further using a longitudinal methodology.

The interpersonal self in conversation

Thus far I have discussed the manifestations of autism on a basic level of development. If there is a general impairment of the perception of social affordances, it should be manifested even in the most developmentally advanced individuals and in more sophisticated activity. What might such a deficit look like in a high-functioning, verbally adept person with autism, and what might its implications be for the self?

Some evidence comes from clinical observation. Verbal people with autism are notoriously poor communicators, not from a lack of the means to express themselves (language) but because they seem to ignore what most people recognize as the rules of conversation. They are inadvertently rude, they are repetitious, they are unclear, they stick to favorite topics that interest no one else, they adopt idiosyncratic meanings for words and expressions, they fail to start and end conversations appropriately (cf. Frith, 1989, for some interesting observations). These problems could be characterized as failures in language pragmatics, that is, the use of language in social context.

In the past several years Belgin Tunali and I and our colleagues at the University of Texas Medical School have done a series of studies examining the behavior of verbal autistic persons in situations that place relatively high demands on their verbal and social skills. Our purpose has been in part to determine the nature of these pragmatic deficits under controlled conditions and in part to determine what conditions facilitate appropriate language use in autistic people.

Referential communication. In one study we examined the autistic person's ability to teach a simple board game to a naive listener (Loveland, Tunali, Kelley, & McEvoy, 1989). Subjects were taught a game much like Candyland, and only those who demonstrated ability to play by the rules were asked to teach it to another person. The naive listener was actually an experimenter who began by asking, "I don't know how to play this game. Tell me how to play this game." The listener noted down how many of 10 pieces of "target" information were conveyed. When no more were given, the listener asked more specific questions, such as, "What are these things over here [gesturing to game props]? What do we do with them? If necessary, she became even more specific, asking about particular items or places on the board. Compared to language-matched subjects with Down syndrome (DS), autistic subjects were equally likely to remember and produce all the target information. However, they needed a far greater degree of specific prompting to do it. When prompting was most general, DS subjects' responses were clearer, more informative, and more elaborated than those of autistic subjects.

This result suggested to us that even when autistic people know the information to be communicated, they still need help selecting it and organizing it into a response. It appears that our subjects lacked awareness of the listener's needs and their implications for the subject's communication. Other studies, not dealing with language, have also found that autistic people frequently fail to determine accurately what others know or believe in situations where not all knowledge is shared (e.g., Baron-Cohen, 1988, 1989a, 1989b; Baron-Cohen, Leslie, & Frith, 1985).

Social scripts in conversation. Another study (Loveland & Tunali, 1990) examined autistic people's appreciation of "social scripts," or expected regularities in the way human behavioral events occur (Fibush & Slackman, 1986; Nelson, 1986). We set up a situation in which an examiner described a sad personal experience (e.g., a sick pet) to the subject and another examiner. Ordinarily, one would react to such a telling with sympathy or an attempt to be helpful. Although DS subjects usually offered an appropriate response, autistic subjects rarely did; more often they requested food or said something else not relevant to the topic of conversation. After the second examiner modeled an appropriate response, a few of the autistic subjects produced their own appropriate responses.

The difference between the DS and autism groups in this study was striking. Several factors may have been at work. There may have been lack of awareness of the affect expressed by the first examiner (cf. Hobson, 1989a,b), as well as a lack of appreciation for culturally accepted modes of responding to it. In terms of social scripts, the situation may not have been identified as an example of the type of situation in which one expresses sympathy. Thus, in some sense, the meaning of the examiner's behavior – its social affordances – was lost to the autistic subject.

Narrative storytelling. A third study dealt with the ability of autistic subjects to tell the story of a puppet show or video script they had just seen enacted (Loveland, McEvoy, Tunali, & Kelley, 1990). Autistic subjects, surprisingly, were able to perform this task. Considered from the standpoint of structural characteristics, their narratives were not different from those of DS subjects. However, the groups' narratives differed in several other ways:

1. Autistic subjects produced much more bizarre speech – that is, intrusive, irrelevant, or purely idiosyncratic speech that did not contribute to telling the story.
2. Autistic subjects who saw the puppet show sometimes produced narratives that did not reflect awareness that the puppets represented characters in a story. Rather, they were treated as moving objects without meaning. No DS subjects did this.
3. Whereas, DS subjects often enhanced their narration with gesture, autistic subjects instead often used vague gestures that resembled the handpuppet moving its mouth (the "talking hand" gesture), but without coordinating this gesture with any part of the narration.

These differences suggested to us that the puppet show was not meaningful to the autistic subjects in the ways one would normally expect. Failure to understand what the puppets represent might mean that the social affordances for characters' actions were not perceived; thus the puppet was only a piece of cloth moving up and down. Moreover, the broader cultural context of puppet shows and storytelling – the representation of events by means of symbols or by means of other events – may have been lost as well. The results also suggest again that the autistic narrator has a poor appreciation of the listener's needs, as demonstrated by the frequent use of bizarre language, which reflected idiosyncratic meanings not shared with the listener.

Taken together these studies show that even high-functioning people with autism have serious deficits in the ability to interact and communicate effectively with others. The nature of these deficits suggests that autistic people have an impaired appreciation of the meaning of social interactions in which they engage. If so, then Neisser's theory would predict that their awareness and understanding of themselves based on information available through such interactions would be impoverished as well.

Concluding comments

The areas of research examined in this chapter provide evidence about self-awareness in persons with autism. The diversity of the research areas reflects the diversity of approaches taken to investigating the self: Not only do different investigators define the self differently, but not all the potentially relevant research would be defined by its authors as having to do with issues of self. This state of affairs results from a lack of consensus about the proper object of study in such investigations. Neisser's theory makes a unique contribution in focusing on modes of self-knowledge rather than on a reified self while still encompassing most of the explicit and implicit selves postulated or assumed by earlier theorists. This approach makes it appropriate to draw evidence from a wide variety of research areas with different methodologies (e.g., perception, child language, clinical psychology) that reflect upon different sources of information about the self.

Despite their diversity, all of the findings discussed here suggest that the autistic person's problems in interacting and communicating with others illustrate the serious developmental consequences of an impaired appreciation for the species-specific meanings of human activity. If so, they also demonstrate that where an understanding of other people is limited, so also is an understanding of the self.

REFERENCES

Baron-Cohen, S. (1988). Social and pragmatic deficits in autism: Cognitive or affective? *Journal of Autism and Developmental Disorders, 18,* 379–402.

Baron-Cohen, S. (1989a). Joint-attention deficits in autism: Towards a cognitive analysis. *Development and Psychopathology, 1,* 185–189.

Baron-Cohen, S. (1989b). Perceptual role-taking and protodeclarative pointing in autism. *British Journal of Developmental Psychology, 7,* 113–127.

Baron-Cohen, S., Leslie, A. M., & Frith, U. (1985). Does the autistic child have a "theory of mind"? *Cognition, 21,* 37–46.

Bruner, J. (1975). The ontogenesis of speech acts. *Journal of Child Language, 2*, 1–20.

Butterworth, G., & Cochran, E. (1980). Towards a mechanism of joint visual attention in human infancy. *International Journal of Behavioral Development, 3*, 253–272.

Clark, E. V. (1977). From gesture to word: On the natural history of deixis in language acquisition. In J. S. Bruner & A. Garton (Eds.), *Human growth and development*. Wolfson College Lectures, 1976. London: Oxford University Press.

Cohen, D. J., Paul, R., & Volkmar, F. R. (1987). Issues in the classification of Pervasive Developmental Disorders and associated conditions. In D. J. Cohen & A. M. Donellen (Eds.), *Handbook of Autism and Pervasive Developmental Disorders*. (pp. 20–40). New York: Wiley.

Dawson, G., & McKissick, F. C. (1984). Self-recognition in autistic children. *Journal of Autism and Developmental Disorders, 14*(4), 383–394.

Dawson, G., & Fernald, M. (1987). Perspective-taking ability and its relationship to the social behavior of autistic children. *Journal of Autism and Developmental Disorders, 17*(4), 487–498.

Dent, C. (1989, December). An ecological approach to language development: An alternative functionalism. In C. Dent & P. Zukow (Eds.), *The idea of innateness: Effects on language and communication research*. Special issue of *Developmental Psychobiology*.

Dixon, J. C. (1957). Development of self-recognition. *Journal of Genetics Bulletin, 91*, 251–256.

Fay, W. H. (1979). Personal pronouns and the autistic child. *Journal of Autism and Developmental Disorders, 9*, 247–260.

Fay, W. H., & Schuler, A. L. (1980). *Emerging language in autistic children*. Baltimore: University Park Press.

Fein, D., Pennington, B., Markowitz, P., Braverman, M., & Waterhouse, L. (1986). Toward a neuropsychological model of infantile autism: Are the social deficits primary? *Journal of the American Academy of Child Psychiatry, 25*, 198–212.

Fivush, R., & Slackman, E. (1986). The acquisition and development of scripts. In K. Nelson (Ed.), *Event knowledge: Structure and function in development* (pp. 71–96). Hillsdale, NJ: Erlbaum.

Ferrari, M., & Matthews, W. S. (1983). Self-recognition deficits in autism: Syndrome-specific or general developmental delay? *Journal of Autism and Developmental Disorders, 13*, 317–324.

Frith, U. (1989). *Autism: Explaining the enigma*. Oxford: Blackwell.

Gallup, G. G., Jr. (1977). Self-recognition in primates: A comparative approach to the bi-directional properties of consciousness. *American Psychologist, 32*, 329–338.

Gallup, G. G., Jr. (1979). Self-recognition in chimpanzees and man: A developmental and comparative perspective. In M. Lewis & L. Rosenblum (Eds.), *The child and its family* (pp. 107–126). New York: Plenum.

Gallup, G. G., Jr. (1985). Do minds exist in species other than our own? *Neuroscience and Biobehavioral Reviews, 9*, 631–641.

Gallup, G. G., Jr. (1986). Self-awareness and the emergence of mind in humans and other primates. In J. Suls & A. G. Greenwald (Eds.), *Psychological perspectives on the self* (pp. 3–26). Hillsdale, NJ: Erlbaum.

Gibson, E. J. (1969). *Principles of perceptual learning and development*. New York: Appleton-Century-Crofts.

Gibson, E. J. (1976). *A few thoughts inspired by the papers of Fraiberg, Bellugi, and Sinclair*. Lenneberg Symposium, Cornell University, Ithaca. NY.

Gibson, J. J. (1979). *The ecological approach to visual perception*. Boston: Houghton Mifflin.

Goldfield, E. C. (1983). The ecological approach to perceiving as a foundation for understanding the development of knowing in infancy. *Developmental Review, 3,* 371–404.

Goldfield, E. C., & Shaw, R. (1984). Affordances and infant learning. *Developmental Review, 4,* 376–378.

Hobson, R. P. (1984). Early childhood autism and the question of egocentrism. *Journal of Autism and Developmental Disorders, 14,* 85–104.

Hobson, R. P. (1989a). Beyond cognition: A theory of autism. In G. Dawson (Ed.), *Autism: Nature, diagnosis, and treatment* (pp. 22–48). New York: Guilford.

Hobson, R. P. (1989b). Emotion-related and abstract concepts in autistic people: Evidence from the British Picture Vocabulary Scale. *Journal of Autism and Developmental Disorders, 19,* 601–623.

Kenner, L. (1943). Autistic disturbances of affective contact. *Nervous Child, 2,* 217–250.

Landry, S., & Loveland, K. (1988). Communication behaviors in autism and developmental language delay. *Journal of Child Psychiatry and Psychology, 29,* 621–634.

Lewis, M., & Brooks-Gunn, J. (1979). *Social cognition and the acquisition of self.* New York: Plenum.

Lewis, M. & Brooks-Gunn, J. (1984). The development of early visual self-recognition. *Developmental Review, 4,* 215–239.

Loveland, K., (1984). Learning about points of view: Spatial perspective and the acquisition of "I/you." *Journal of Child Language, 11,* 535–556.

Loveland, K., (1986). Discovering the affordances of a reflecting surface. *Developmental Review, 6,* 1–24.

Loveland, K., (1987a). Behavior of young children with Down syndrome before the mirror: Exploration. *Child development, 58,* 768–778.

Loveland, K., (1987b). Behavior of young children with Down syndrome before the mirror: finding things reflected. *Child Development, 58,* 928–936.

Loveland, K., (1990, July). *The affordances of the human environment: Theory and applications.* Manuscript based on presentation to the fifth International Conference Event on Perception and Action, Miami, OH.

Loveland, K., & Landry, S. (1986). Joint attention and communication in autism and language delay. *Journal of Autism and Developmental Disorders, 16,* 335–349.

Loveland, K., McEvoy, R., Tunali, B., & Kelley, M. L. (1990). Narrative story-telling in autism and Down syndrome. *British Journal of Developmental Psychology, 8,* 9–23.

Loveland, K., & Tunai, B. (1990, March). *Social scripts for conversational interactions in autism and Down syndrome.* Paper presented at conference on Human Development, Richmond, VA.

Loveland, K., Tunali, B., Kelley, M., & McEvoy, R. (1989). Referential communication and response adequacy in autism and Down syndrome. *Applied Psycholinguistics, 10,* 401–413.

McArthur, L. Z., & Baron, R. M. (1983). Toward an ecological psychology of social perception. *Psychological Review, 90,* 215–238.

Mundy, P., & Sigman, M. (1989). Specifying the nature of the social impairment in autism. In G. Dawson (Ed.), *Autism: Nature, diagnosis, and treatment* (pp. 3–21). New York: Guilford.

Mundy, P., Sigman, M., Ungerer, J., & Sherman, T. (1986). Defining the social deficits of autism: The contribution of non-verbal communication measures. *Journal of Child Psychology and Psychiatry, 27,* 657–669.

Neisser, U. (1988). Five kinds of self-knowledge. *Philosophical Psychology, 1,* 35–59.

Nelson, K. (Ed.) (1986). *Event knowledge: Structure and function in development.* Hillsdale, NJ: Erlbaum.

Nelson, K., & Gruendel, J. (1986). Children's scripts. In K. Nelson (Ed.), *Event knowledge: Structure and function in development* (pp. 21–46). Hillsdale, NJ: Erlbaum.

Oshima-Takane, Y., & Benaroya, S. (1989). An alternative view of pronominal errors in autistic children. *Journal of Autism and Developmental Disorders, 19,* 73–85.

Oswald, D. P., & Ollendick, T. H. (1989). Role taking and social competence in autism and mental retardation. *Journal of Autism and Developmental Disorders, 19,* 119–127.

Perner, J., Frith, U., Leslie, A. M., & Leekham, S. R. (1989). Exploration of the autistic child's theory of mind: Knowledge, belief, and communication. *Child Development, 60,* 689–700.

Reed, E. S. (1988). The affordances of the animate environment: Social sciences from the ecological point of view. In T. Ingold (Ed.), *What is an animal?* London: Allen & Unwin.

Ricks, D., & Wing, L. (1975). Language, communication, and the use of symbols in normal and autistic children. *Journal of Autism and Childhood Schizophrenia, 5,* 191–221.

Spiker, D., & Ricks, M. (1984). Visual self-recognition in autistic children: Developmental relationships. *Child Development, 55,* 214–225.

Thompson, T., & Sturm, T. (1965). Classical conditioning of aggressive display in Siamese fighting fish. *Journal of the Experimental Analysis of Behavior, 8,* 397–403.

Tomasello, M. (1988). The role of joint attentional processes in early language development. *Language Sciences, 10,* 69–88.

Van Acker, R., & Valenti, S. S. (1989). Perception of social affordances by children with mild handicapping conditions: Implications for social skills research and training. *Ecological Psychology, 1,* 383–405.

Weeks, S. J., & Hobson, R. P. (1987). The salience of facial expression for autistic children. *Journal of Child Psychology and Psychiatry, 28,* 137–152.

Zazzo, R. (1979). Des enfants, des singes, et des chiens devant le miroir. *Revue de Psychologie Appliquée, 29,* 235–246.

14

Through feeling and sight to self and symbol

R. PETER HOBSON

To know oneself is to know oneself as a person among others. In order to acquire a developed concept of self, therefore, children need to appreciate the nature of persons and to recognize the existence of other selves with whom they have much in common but from whom they are differentiated. A principal concern of this chapter is to consider how very young children come to apprehend their commonality with other people and grasp the ways in which different selves occupy distinct psychological orientations toward an objectively existing world. I shall emphasize how interpersonal communication of feeling is especially important for individuals' experience of connectedness with others, and suggest that vision plays a special but not indispensable role in enabling young children to discover the fact that different people have different attitudes and points of view vis-à-vis a shared environment that includes the children themselves.

My second concern is with young children's developing capacity to symbolize. To symbolize is to treat one thing in such a way that it stands for another. This statement is a crude oversimplification, but let that be. In order to acquire a capacity to symbolize, children need to connect symbol and referent in the act of symbolizing, while at the same time maintaining an awareness of how symbol and referent are differentiated. Following the leads of Werner and Kaplan (1963) and Mead (1934), I shall explore the possibility that young children develop the capacity for creative symbolic play along with and in relation to their acquiring a concept of self.

Perhaps I might restate these themes from a different vantage point. My thesis is that we need to consider infants' capacities for feeling and seeing if we are to understand how they develop from a relatively fragmented state of being to one in which they can not only reflect on their own and other selves but also exercise the capacity to symbolize. In concert with Michael Tomasello (this volume), I take the view that an essential pivot for cognitive as well as social development is the infant's evolving awareness of the nature of persons with their own subjective mental life, and I argue that such awareness is heavily dependent on the infant's affectively charged and perceptually anchored experiences of interpersonal relations (see also Hobson, 1989a, 1989b, 1990a, 1990b, 1990c). Pursuing Martin Buber's (1950/1984) distinction between I–Thou and I–It relatedness, and joining with J. M. Baldwin (1902), J. J. Gibson (1979), Ulric Neisser (1988), and Katherine Loveland (this volume) in stresssing the significance of innately determined meaning-perceiving faculties, I attempt to trace the social developmental pathway by which a normal 1-year-old becomes aware of the forms of connectedness that exist not only between herself and other selves but also among herself, her symbols, and their referents. On the other hand, a child's self needs to be differentiated both from the inanimate world and from other selves; a child's symbols need to be differentiated from the self who employs them *as* symbols and from that which they symbolize. In order to complement an account of the different forms of connectedness between young children and their social and nonsocial environment, therefore, I offer a further account of how children accomplish the processes of differentiation that self-reflection and symbolization require.

I shall be adopting the perspective of developmental psychopathology. I begin by presenting four clinical vignettes distilled from published case descriptions. The first three concern autistic individuals, and the fourth concerns a congenitally blind child. I hope that the descriptions of autistic individuals will complement Loveland's overview of autism as a syndrome. My purpose is to illustrate the intriguing coincidence of impairments in self-conceptualization and symbolization that characterize many young autistic and perhaps congenitally blind children. We face a major challenge in explaining the cluster of clinical features that are common to these two apparently disparate conditions. I believe that in order to meet this challenge, we require an adequate view of the processes of normal early social–affective and cognitive development. For this reason, I follow my clinical examples with an attempt to provide a partial account of the normal development of self-awareness and suggest how this dovetails with an account of the developing capacity to symbolize. Finally, I return to autism and congenital blindness. I suggest that autistic children's deficient capacity for affectively grounded interpersonal relations seriously constrains both their connectedness to and differentiation from other people, and for this reason impairs their capacity to symbolize. I further suggest that blind children's lack of vision may not only limit their comprehension of self–other differentiation but also by this very fact may hamper their development of the ability to symbolize flexibly.

The picture of autism

It is appropriate to begin by drawing on the classic description of autistic children: Kanner's (1943) original account of "autistic disturbances of affective contact." Here are some edited excerpts, more or less verbatim from Kanner's paper, which apply to one of the 11 autistic children he described:

Donald was first seen at just over 5 years of age. Before he was 2 years old, his father reported, Donald had shown an unusual memory for faces and names, and soon he had learned the Twenty-third Psalm and 25 questions and answers of the Presbyterian catechism. On the other hand, he rarely asked questions or gave answers. He was happiest when left alone, almost never cried to go with his mother, did not seem to notice his father's homecomings, and was indifferent to visiting relatives.

When examined at home at the age of 5, Donald was observed to wander about smiling, making stereotyped movements with his fingers, crossing them about in the air. He shook his head from side to side, whispering or humming the same three-note tune. Most of his actions were repetitions. He always seemed to be parroting what he had heard said to him. He used the personal pronouns for the persons he was quoting, even imitating the intonation. When he wanted his mother to pull his shoe off, he said: "Pull off your shoe." When he wanted a bath he said: "Do you want a bath?" For Donald, words had a specifically literal, inflexible meaning. The colloquial request to "Put that down" meant to him that he was to put the thing on the floor.

Kanner wrote:

He paid no attention to persons around him. When taken into a room, he completely disregarded the people and instantly went for objects, preferably those that could be spun. Commands or actions that could not possibly be disregarded were resented as unwelcome intrusions. But he was never angry at the interfering *person*. He angrily shoved the *hand* that was in his way or the *foot* that stepped on one of his blocks. Once the obstacle was removed, he forgot the whole affair. He gave no heed to the presence of other children.

Two years after Kanner's paper, Scheerer, Rothmann, and Goldstein (1945) published an account of an idiot savant who they called L.

L first presented at the age of 11 as an inattentive person rubbing the four fingers of each hand in a drumbeat against his thumbs. On Binet's test, he had an IQ of 50. Yet L was capable of telling the day of the week for any given date between about 1880 and 1950. He could also recount the day and date of his first visit to a place, and could usually give the names and birthdays of all the people he met there. He could spell forwards and backwards. He could play melodies by ear.

L's background history included the fact that in his fourth and fifth years he rarely offered spontaneous observations or reasons for any action or perceived event. Nor would he imitate an action of others spontaneously. He was unable to understand or create an imaginary situation. He did not play with toys, nor did he show any conception of make-believe games. He was unable to converse in give-and-take language. He frequently displayed laughter out of keeping with the situation. He barely noticed the presence of other children, and appeared emotionally indifferent to others if they cried or if they took away his toys. He was, however, very attached to his mother. He was said to have "little emotionality of normal depth and coherence" (p. 4). On the other hand, he would run up and down in a stereotyped manner, slapping his sides and waving his hands.

Up to 15 years of age, L was unable to define the properties of objects except in terms of egocentred and situational use. For example, he defined orange as "That I squeeze with." At the age of 15, he defined the difference between a stone and an egg as "I eat an egg and I throw a stone." Once, when the doctor said, "Goodbye my son," L replied: "I am not your son." When asked, "What would happen if you shot a person?" L replied: "He goes to the hospital." He showed no shame in parading naked through the house. Even at 15, his emotional responses and human attachments remained shallow and perfunctory.

The third autistic person I shall describe is a man called Gerry, who was diagnosed by Kanner at the age of 4 and interviewed 27 years later at the age of 31 (Bemporad, 1979).

In his late childhood and early adolescence, Gerry demonstrated a marked social naïveté despite average performance on IQ tests. For example, he completely disregarded his appearance and had to be reminded to change his clothes, comb his hair, and so on. He had no grasp of table manners, nor any sense of propriety; for example, he openly picked his nose. Gerry was happiest when he could be alone doing arithmetic or studying maths. From about the age of 11, he gradually came to perceive that he was different from other youngsters. He now expressed the desire to be with other children, but his behavior was so inappropriate that he was either rejected or ignored. On one occasion, when he was 14, the family took a trip to a Mexican border town. Gerry suddenly disappeared. The family searched frantically for him all day, and finally found him at their motel, 10 miles away. He had walked all the way back because he disliked the smell of the market where they had been shopping. He did not understand that his family might be concerned about his disappearance and so had not told anyone he was leaving. He simply could not appreciate how other people felt.

When interviewed at 31 years of age, Gerry had no ability to make small talk. He simply could not empathize with others, and could not predict what they would do. He did not mention any relationship with family members when reconstructing his childhood; they seemed of little importance. He said that he realized that he was now a burden to his family, but he attributed this to his stuttering.

To conclude these clinical descriptions of autism, I quote one further intelligent young autistic adult, Ronald, who was interviewed by Cohen (1980), and who spoke of how the first years of his life were devoid of people."

I really didn't know there were people until I was seven years old. I then suddenly realized that there were people. But not like you do. I still have to remind myself that there are people. . . . I never could have a friend. I really don't know what to do with other people, really.

Before I turn to the case of the congenitally blind child, it may help if I review some of the phenomena of autism that bear on my thesis about the development of self-reflection and the capacity to symbolize. The first thing to note is autistic children's impaired capacity for personal relatedness with others, an impairment that finds expression in nonverbal as well as verbal communication. Immediately we are led to reflect on what this impairment might mean for autistic children's experience of interpersonal relations, and more specifically, to question whether they experience such relations *as* "interpersonal." Kanner indicated how, in the presence of autistic children, he felt that he himself was being treated like a piece of furniture. It seems to have been partly for this reason that he chose to characterize the children's primary deficit as one that involved "disturbances of affective contact" with others. We all know what Kanner meant by this metaphorical use of the word contact, and it is precisely in the domain of intersubjective connectedness that there seems to be a striking deficit in autistic children's interpersonal relations. Believing that disruption in these children's capacity for reciprocal, affective relatedness with others is somewhere at the core of "autism," colleagues and I embarked on a series of experimental studies of emotion perception and understanding in autistic individuals. Because the role of affective perception and communication is pivotal for my argument, I shall discuss our work in this area.

The first experiment I shall describe is one that a colleague Jane Weeks and I designed to test the hypothesis that autistic children are abnormal in their relative lack of attentiveness to facial expressions of emotion (Weeks & Hobson, 1987). We pairwise matched 15 autistic and 15 nonautistic retarded children and young adolescents for chronological age, sex, and peformance on three subtests of the Verbal Scale of the WISC-R. Given that autistic children's verbal abilities are among the most impaired of their intellectual capacities, these represent stringent matching procedures for investigating deficits specific to autism. Subjects were given a task of sorting photographs to go with one or other of a pair of target photographs showing the head and shoulders of individuals who differed in three, two, or one of the following respects: sex, age, facial expression of emotion, and the type of hat they were wearing. The principal statistically significant finding was that the majority of nonautistic children sorted according to people's facial expression (happy versus sad or nonhappy) before they sorted according to type of hat (floppy versus woollen), but most autistic children gave priority to sorting by type of hat. Moreover, when in the course of the experiment the number of contrasting features in the target photographs was progressively reduced, all 15 nonautistic children sooner or later sorted by emotional expression without being told to do so, but only 6 of the 15 autistic children did this. Finally, 5 of the 15 autistic children but none of the 15 nonautistic children failed to sort consistently by facial expression when given explicit instructions to do so. Only after we had completed this experiment did we discover that Jennings (1973) had conducted a similar but not identical unpublished study that yielded results comparable to our own.

In a second study, colleagues and myself focused on autistic individuals' capacity to discriminate among standardized photographs of happy, unhappy, angry, and afraid faces (Hobson, Ouston, & Lee, 1988a). Once again autistic and nonautistic retarded subjects were matched for age and verbal ability. The "emotions" task was to match the same expressions displayed by different people (i.e., to match the faces for emotion across changes in identity), and the control task was to match the faces for identity across changes in emotional expression. A match-to-sample procedure was employed, first using full faces, then faces with blanked-out mouths, and then faces with blank mouths and foreheads. The materials were designed so that even the latter photographs retained some feel of the emotions in the faces. The results included a significant second-order interaction of diagnosis by condition (emotion, identity) by form of face (full-face, blank-mouth, blank-mouth-and-forehead). On the identities task the performance of the two groups showed a similar steady decline as the photographs became increasingly blanked-out, but on the emotions task the performance of autistic subjects worsened more abruptly than that of control subjects as cues to emotion were progressively reduced. The autistic subjects seemed relatively unable to use the "feel" in the faces to guide performance. Not only this, but correlations between individual subjects' scores on the identity and emotion tasks were higher for autistic than for nonautistic subjects, suggesting that autistic subjects might have been sorting the expressive faces by nonemotional perceptual strategies.

A third study was designed to examine autistic subjects' understanding of emotion-related concepts (Hobson & Lee, 1989). We took two groups of autistic and nonautistic retarded adolescents and young adults who were pairwise matched for age and *overall* scores on the British Picture Vocabulary Scale (BPVS; Dunn, Dunn, & Whetton, 1982), a British version of the Peabody Picture Vocabulary Test (Dunn, 1965). In this test, individuals are presented with a series of plates in which drawings are arranged in groups of four. Subjects are given instructions such as "Point to . . . dentist" or "Show me . . . surprise," and they respond by indicating the appropriate picture. We then asked independent raters to select the items of the BPVS that were emotion-related – these included word-picture combinations in which the words to be judged were delighted, disagreement, greeting, and snarling, as well as more obviously emotional words such as horror and surprise – and compared subjects' scores on these items with their scores on nonemotion items of BPVS that are equally difficult for normal children. Sure enough, nonautistic retarded subjects achieved similar scores on the selected emotion-related and emotion-unrelated items, but autistic subjects with almost identical overall BPVS scores were specifically impaired on the emotion-related vis-à-vis emotion-unrelated items. Moreover, the results could not be attributed to the abstract nature of such concepts, as autistic and nonautistic subjects were equally able to judge non-emotion-related abstract words vis-à-vis equally difficult concrete words. Once again, therefore, this time at a conceptual level, significant group differences between autistic and nonautistic subjects were demonstrable specifically in the realm of emotional understanding.

Elsewhere I have reviewed these studies and additional evidence for (or, occasionally, against) specific emotion recognition deficits in autistic individuals (e.g., Braverman, Fein, Lucci, & Waterhouse, 1989; Hobson, 1986a, 1986b; Hobson, Ouston, & Lee, 1988b, 1989; Macdonald et al., 1989; Ozonoff, Pennington, & Rogers, 1990, 1991; Prior, Dahlstrom, & Squires, 1990;

Tantam, Monaghan, Nicholson, and Stirling, 1989; see also Hobson 1991a). It is also important to note that autistic children's emotional expressiveness is frequently muted or idiosyncratic and often uncoordinated with the expressive behaviour of others (e.g., Dawson, Hill, Spencer, Galpert, & Watson, 1990; Hertzig, Snow, & Sherman, 1989; Macdonald et al., 1989; Ricks, 1975; Snow, Hertzig, & Shapiro, 1987; Yirmiya, Kasari, Sigman, & Mundy, 1989). There is, therefore, growing evidence for deficits in autistic children's capacities and propensities for the perception, understanding, and communication of emotion, deficits that might well underpin and/or reflect impairments in their experience of affective contact with others.

The next thing to observe is that at least some autistic children seem hardly aware of other persons as subjects of experience with whom things can be shared (Hobson, 1989b). This lack of social understanding does not simply reflect cognitive disabilities of a general kind. When young autistic children have been compared with nonautistic retarded and developmentally language-delayed children matched for chronological and mental age, as well as with normal children aged about 2 years, they have been found to exhibit few indicating gestures, such as pointing to or showing objects to others, gestures that have the aim of sharing experiences (Curcio, 1978; Landry & Loveland, 1988; Mundy, Sigman, Ungerer, & Sherman, 1986; Sigman, Mundy, Sherman, & Ungerer, 1986). They are similarly unusual in their relative failure to respond to (and, in the case of older children, to explain the meaning of) other people's indicating gestures (Baron-Cohen, 1989). Moreover, autistic children's relative incapacity to share may prove to be responsible for at least some of their characteristic difficulties with language. Mundy, Sigman, and Kasari (1990) found that within their sample of young autistic children, language development was predicted by a measure of gestural nonverbal joint attention 1 year previously but not by measures of initial language score or IQ. So, too, Landry and Loveland (1988) reported that young autistic children's joint attention skills in social contexts were significantly correlated with the children's language abilities, including proficiency in the use of personal pronouns such as "I" and "you" or "mine" and "yours."

In fact, autistic children are frequently delayed in coming to use personal pronouns in the fully correct, adult manner (e.g., Fay, 1979; Kanner, 1943; Loveland, this volume; Silberg, 1978). The cause or causes of this phenomenon are still in dispute, but they are likely to include autistic children's impairment in recognizing the complementarity of self-other roles (e.g., Charney, 1981; Hobson, 1990a; Tager-Flusberg, 1989). Two investigations may serve by way of illustration. When Jordan (1989) tested autistic, mentally retarded, and normal children matched for verbal mental age (between 3 and 10 years) on simple tasks such as "Make the doll kiss you/me," most subjects were able to comprehend these personal pronouns. On the other hand, the majority of autistic children were unusual in responding to such prompts as "Now the puppet's tickling . . . ?" by giving proper names to themselves or the experimenter rather than using "me" or "you," or else they used incorrect pronouns or unusual forms of pronoun. Or, again, Tager-Flusberg (1989) has been recording young autistic and language (MLU)–matched Down syndrome children's conversations with their mothers, and has found that only among autistic children have there been pronoun reversal errors. Such errors have occurred in about 12% of instances of pronoun use, for example, where the child might have been asking a question through a form of utterance that would have been appropriate had the mother rather than the child been speaking.

Then there is the matter of autistic children's relative lack of self-consciousness. The classic technique to test bodily self-consciousness in primates and young children is to mark surreptitiously the face of an individual and see how that individual reacts when confronted with her own reflection in a mirror (e.g., Gallup, 1982; Lewis & Brooks-Gunn, 1979). When done with autistic children who are not severely cognitively impaired, the result has been that the children have tended to act toward the mark on their own bodies rather than to touch the reflected image, per se. But what, characteristically, they have *not* done is to manifest the signs of coyness that are very common among young normal and nonautistic retarded children (Dawson & McKissik, 1984; Neuman & Hill, 1978; Spiker & Ricks, 1984).

Finally, I would note that there is substantial experimental evidence that autistic children are both delayed and often lastingly impaired in the development of flexible, creative symbolic play (e.g., Baron-Cohen, 1987; Riguet, Taylor, Benaroya & Klein, 1981; Ungerer & Sigman, 1981; Wing, Gould, Yeates, & Brierley, 1977; Wulff, 1985). I have already illustrated how there are also aspects of autistic children's language, not least their so-called concrete thinking, which seem to reflect specific forms of abnormality in symbolic functioning.

Thus autistic children have impairments in affectively coordinated personal relatedness with others, in their concept of persons *as* persons with mental life, in their recognition of the complementarity of self–other roles, in their degree of self-consciousness, and in their capacity for flexible symbolic functioning. Before I attempt to link these clinical phenomena in a developmental nexus, I shall turn to consider the congenitally blind child.

The congenitally blind child

Kathie was a healthy, very bright blind child who was followed by Selma Fraiberg and Edna Adelson from the age of 6 months to 6 years (Fraiberg & Adelson, 1977).

Kathie had been born 3 months premature with retrolental fibroplasia, but was said to have no other sensory defects and to be neurologically intact. It is worth stressing that by 6 years of age, she had become inventive in imaginative play, mischievous and fun-loving, independent and responsible, as well as sociable and linguistically accomplished. In many respects, therefore, she was emphatically *non*autistic.

When Kathie was 2 years 1 month old, her speech was sampled and analyzed by Eric Lenneberg. Lenneberg was said to have considered that her language competence compared favorably with that of a sighted child of the same age. On the other hand, Kathie's confusions in personal pronoun use were unusually marked – "Want me carry you?" she said to her mother when she herself wanted to be carried; "My hair," she said when referring to another person's hair – and she seemed to have a remarkable lack of interest in stories. She was also noted to employ parental admonitions to inhibit forbidden actions: "Don't put your finger in your eye," she would say in her mother's voice when she pressed her eye, sometimes managing to stop herself. Then between 2 ½ and 3 years of age, it became clear that Kathie "could not represent herself through a doll or a toy. She could not recreate or invent a situation in play. She could not attend to a story or answer questions regarding a story or tell a story herself. She could not spontaneously report an experience. Between the ages of three and four, she still continued to confuse and reverse pronouns" (Fraiberg & Adelson, 1977, p. 256). When tested at the age of just over 3 years, for instance, Kathie could neither pretend that playdough was a cookie nor understand personal pronouns; when the interviewer asked: "Can I have a bite of the cookie, Kathie?" Kathie put the playdough in her own mouth and said, "This cookie different." She was unable to endow a doll with human characteristics, and when it was suggested that she give the doll a bath, Kathie herself climbed into the tiny bathtub and pretended to be bathing, conducting a dialogue as if one voice belonged to Kathie and the other to her mother. It was not until after she reached the age of 4 that Kathie began to represent herself in doll play and, in parallel with this, to master the use of personal pronouns, to report dreams, and to reconstruct from memory events of the previous day.

Fraiberg and Adelson (1977) considered that Kathie's difficulties arose from the delayed development of a certain level of mental representation, one in which the self can be taken as an object and other objects can be used for symbolic representation of the self. However, it was only in passing that these authors noted how at the time of her pronoun difficulties, Kathie could not yet "see herself as an object to *others*" (p. 260, my italics).

I have emphasized some important respects in which the description of Kathie was markedly unlike that of autistic children, particularly in relation to her sociability and many aspects of her advanced language skills. On the other hand, the pattern of her psychological handicaps was strikingly reminiscent of that seen in many autistic individuals. It was this clinical picture that has led my colleagues Maggie Minter and Rachel Brown and myself to investigate the possibility that during certain phases of their development, congenitally blind as well as autistic children may present with a constellation of clinical features that includes confusions in the comprehension and use of personal pronouns; echolalia and the use of "situational phrases" like the parental admonitions employed by Kathie; impaired symbolic play; impaired ability to produce and follow stories or accounts of people's experiences; lack of self-consciousness; a relative lack of evidence of sharing experiences and possibly of competitiveness and possessiveness; and delays in language onset and use in communication, perhaps including more specific delay in using "no" and "yes" as signs of refusal or agreement. I should emphasize that such a picture is not yet established as one that characterizes blind children, but there is already evidence that at least in certain populations of congenitally blind or partially blind and partially deaf children, autisticlike symptoms such as these are surprisingly common (Blank, 1975; Chase, 1972; Freedman, 1971; Keeler, 1958; Wing, 1969). The question is: Why?

One possibility is that the clinical phenomena are a direct manifestation of neurological dysfunction that is coincidental with, but relatively independent of, whatever damage has occurred to the children's visual system. Yet the picture seems to apply to at least some blind children such as Kathie who show little evidence of neurological impairment. An alternative possibility is that the cited constellation of symptoms and signs is (at least in part) the expression of some underlying psychological impairment that is the developmental outcome of "autistic disturbances of affective contact" on the one hand and congenital blindness on the other. It is this latter possibility that I wish to explore. In order to do so, I shall now try to chart some stretches of the normal developmental pathway to self-reflective awareness and the capacity for symbolic play.

The origins of reflective self-awareness

In order to understand the development of reflective self-awareness, it would be well to consider what we mean by the self and to characterize whatever prereflective modes of self-experience there might be (Hobson, 1990a). Thus William James (1980) emphasized the distinction between a subject that thinks or knows an object and a subject that thinks that it thinks, or knows that it knows, and he criticized associationist writers such as Hume (1739/1888) for failing to address the problem of how the self comes to be aware of itself or its mental contents. James also stressed how the capacity to think of subjectivity as such, to think of ourselves as thinkers, is bound up with the capacity to distinguish between thought itself and what the thought is of or about. The latter capacity is essential to a person's understanding of the relation between the mind and a mind-independent reality. Thus we might begin by considering how an infant comes to distinguish self from nonself, but then as a partly separate undertaking examine how an infant or young child acquires the capacity for reflective self-awareness, including consciousness of the self's own mental states. I shall be concentrating on this latter, more developed form of self-awareness.

To reflect on oneself is to reflect on oneself as a person. The young child's concept of persons is pivotal for my account (Hobson, 1989a). Strawson (1962) analyzed the concept thus:

What we have to acknowledge . . . is the *primitiveness* of the concept of a person. What I mean by the concept of a person is the concept of a type of entity such that *both* predicates ascribing states of a consciousness *and* predicates ascribing corporeal characteristics, a physical situation, etc. are equally applicable to a single individual of that single type . . . The concept of a person is logically prior to that of an individual consciousness. The concept of a person is not to be analyzed as that of an animated body or of an embodied anima. (pp. 135–137).

I quote this passage because it brings home the essential connectedness that exists between body and mind, as encompassed within the concept of a person. The question I want to ask is: How does a child acquire the concept of persons who have both bodies and minds? One might even pose the more searching epistemological question: How is it possible for a child to acquire the concept of persons?

In order to answer this question, I shall make a brief digression. Recall how the autistic adult Ronald did not realize there were people until he was 7, and felt that he could never have a friend. I vividly remember an autistic man whom I cared for as an in-patient when I was a junior psychiatrist. This man had high advanced placement test scores in English and German, yet he could not grasp what a "friend" *is*. He would pester the hospital staff with endlessly repetitive questions of various kinds, but foremost among these were questions like: "Are you a friend?" "Is he a friend?" and so on. The staff even organized a "befriender" to visit this man and accompany him on walks, but to no avail. He still could not fathom the meaning of "friend." The reason is that in order to know what a friend is, one needs to have had friends and been a friend and shared with friends the kinds of thing that are the stuff of friendship. In Wittgenstein's (1958) phrase, one needs to have enjoyed a "form of life" in which friends, and the language of friendship, find a place. It is just not possible to teach the meaning of the word friend from the outside, as it were. The person being taught needs to have experienced at least the kind of "thing" that friendship is. So it is with the concept of persons. As Hamlyn (1974) has argued, a part of what is involved in having the concept of a person is that one should understand what it is to stand in personal relations with another person. This understanding must be based on "natural reactions of persons to persons" (p. 5) – that is, on biologically founded emotional attitudes and reactions to other people. I have not space to argue against alternative accounts of the origins of a young child's concept of persons, for example, the suggestion that he "infers" the existence of other people's mental states on the basis of analogy with his own subjective experiences (see, e.g., Malcolm, 1962; Hobson, 1990b, 1990c). Instead, I shall say something about the biologically based capacities for personal relatedness.

As a preliminary remark, it is pertinent to note that "personal relatedness" is to be contrasted with another kind of relatedness, let us say "thing-relatedness," that exists between an infant and her world. This distinction corresponds with Martin Buber's (1937/1984) famous dichotomy between I–Thou and I–It attitudes (see James Gustafson's account in this volume). For Charles Cooley (1902) and James Baldwin (1902) writing at the turn of the century, as for Charles Darwin (1877) some 25 years earlier, an initial demarcation of the personal and nonpersonal spheres of experience is accomplished through an infant's more or less innate perceptual–affective propensities. For example, Baldwin (1902) suggested that the child is endowed with an "organic" capacity for sympathy with others, and can differentiate persons from things by responding to "suggestions of personality" in other people. In recent times, of course, it is J. J. Gibson (e.g., 1979) who has been most influential in highlighting the importance of "meaning-sensitive" perceptual faculties. According to Gibson, meanings in the form of "affordances" are what the infant begins by noticing. For instance, "the other animals of the environment afford, above all, a rich and complex set of interactions, sexual, predatory, nurturing, fighting, play, cooperating and communicating" (Gibson, 1977, p. 68). It is clear that the organism might need to have sexual inclinations in order to perceive others *as* "sexual," propensities to flee and to feel threatened in order to perceive others *as* "predatory," and so on, so that any such perceptual capacities would need to be understood with reference to action and feeling tendencies that establish the relations between organism and environment. This does not alter the crux of the matter, which is that infants might have innate capacities to perceive meaning in other people's bodily actions and expressions.

Such a suggestion finds support in the results from a range of experiments with normal infants. In the domain of emotion recognition and responsiveness, for example, these include studies of neonatal imitation (Field, Woodson, Greenberg, & Cohen, 1982; Field et al., 1983), of neonatal contagion of affect through distressed vocalizations (Sagi & Hoffman, 1976; Simner, 1971), of 10-week-olds' emotional responsiveness to mothers' face-plus-voice affective expressions (Haviland & Lelwica, 1987), and of 2- or 3-month-olds' affectively patterned responses to mother's depressed or blank-faced behavior (Cohn & Tronick, 1983; Murray & Trevarthen, 1985).

I would make three points here. The first is to acknowledge the formative influence of less obviously perceptual but nonetheless critical aspects of personal relatedness, such as the temporal patterning and activation contours of interpersonal events that Stern (1985) has emphasized, or the representational structures that may serve to organize early experience and have been explored by "object-relations" psychoanalytic theorists such as Fairbairn (1952) and Isaacs (1948). The second point concerns the nature of the meanings that infants perceive in (for example) the emotional expressions of others. I suggest that in becoming attuned to other people's bodily expressions and behaviour, infants are already becoming aware that such expressions are indeed expressive of personal, subjective life. As Scheler (1954) has written, our knowledge of others' experiences "is given for us *in* expressive phenomena – again, not by inference, but directly, as a sort of primary 'perception.' It is *in* the blush that we perceive shame, in the laughter joy" (p. 10). Wittgenstein (1980) has outlined a similar argument. The third, related, point is that affective communication establishes a form of connectedness between the infant and others, what Trevarthen (1979) has called "primary intersubjectivity," a commonality of body and mind through which the infant may come to distill out more sophisticated awareness of self and other as separable yet related centers of consciousness.

I have emphasized the importance of innate perceptual–affective sensibilities for an infant's developing capacity for personal relatedness. I have also stated that such personal relatedness is a necessary prerequisite for the infant to arrive at a concept of persons with their own subjective experiences. What I have referred to only in passing is the need for the infant to *differentiate* his own and others' psychological orientations vis-à-vis a commonly experienced world. I shall not discuss the earliest, possibly innately determined forms of self–other differentiation but shall focus instead on the manifestations of what Trevarthen and Hubley (1978) have called secondary intersubjectivity, or what Stern (1985) has conceived to be the expressions of an intersubjective self, which first become evident when an infant reaches the age of about 9 months.

The final quarter of the first year of life is a period of dramatic change in the quality of the infant's social relatedness. It is now that the infant comes to give, show, and point things out to others, often looking back and forth between an object and the other's eyes; the infant requests help to obtain objects, initiates games such as peekaboo, imitates household activities and conventional actions, and manifests a range of additional social accomplishments (e.g., Bretherton & Bates, 1979; Bretherton, McNew, & Beeghly-Smith, 1981; Harding & Golinkoff, 1979; Trevarthen & Hubley). They may also be observed to "tease" adults (Reddy, 1990). Infants at this stage seem to perceive others as subjects of experience with their own psychological orientations toward the world and toward themselves, and to understand that human beings are persons with whom things can be shared (Hobson, 1989b). It is also at this time that infants engage in social referencing (Campos & Stenberg, 1981; Feinman, 1982; Feinman and Lewis, 1983; Klinnert, 1984; Klinnert, Campos, Sorce, Emde, & Svejda, 1983; Walden & Ogan, 1988). In the study conducted by Sorce, Emde, Campos, and Klinnert (1985), for example, infants of 12 months who were confronted with a disconcerting "visual cliff" often looked to the facial expression of their watching mother; if the mother posed a happy face, the majority crossed to the deep side of the cliff, whereas if the mother posed a fearful expression, none did so. Thus the infants appeared to recognize that another person's visually perceived affective expressions had meaning with reference to an environment common to themselves and the other person.

In this range of phenomena we can observe how infants have some grasp of the commonality that exists between themselves and others, but also how they grasp the fact that others' experiences may differ from, as well as be aligned with, their own. Of particular interest are situations such as those of social referencing and teasing by infants, in that here we can discern a point of entry for an infants' understanding that a given object or event can have meaning for self and a different meaning for other. I would suggest that a child's awareness of persons who have distinct but coordinated psychological orientations vis-à-vis the world heralds the discovery that given objects or events are pregnant with meanings. The meanings in question depend on the meaning-conferring nature of people's minds. Correspondingly, a child's awareness of the multiple-meanings potential of objects and events may depend heavily if not exclusively on her having become aware of people with minds and thus of her own potential as a person to adopt more than one mental attitude at any given moment. That is, a child's capacity to entertain the dual attitude of taking an object both as itself and also as a "something else" may arise out of a prior awareness that different people may have different attitudes toward a given state of affairs. Once the child understands the nature of individuals' subjective, egocentric points of view, moreover, she can begin to abstract away from such particular viewpoints in order to arrive at a conception of the world that is not the view from anywhere within it, and thereby achieve objectivity (Nagel 1979).

It will be apparent that I join with a number of other authors, including Neisser, Loveland, and Tomasello (see their chapters in this volume), who follow Bruner (1975), Trevarthen and Hubley (1978), and more recent writers (e.g., Adamson & Bakeman, 1982) in emphasizing the significance of "joint attention" for an infant's experience of a coreferenced world. I believe that our concept of joint attention needs further analysis, however (Hobson, 1989b). While it is impressive that an infant can follow another person's line of regard (e.g., Butterworth & Cochran, 1980; Scaife & Bruner, 1975) more than this is involved when the infant comes to perceive the focus of another person's attention *as* a focus of that person's attention. In such a situation, the infant appreciates that the other person is a locus of psychological attitudes toward the world, that the other person is "attending" in such a way that *shared* experiences are possible. Indeed, one important source of motivation for infants to follow another person's line of sight is precisely such awareness that the other is a being with experiences that can be coordinated with the infant's own experiences. According to this account, there are two partly separable components to the child's participation in joint attention: the child's awareness of another person as having attitudes and experiences, and the child's awareness of the *directedness* of the other person's behavior – and often, the person's corresponding psychological orientations – toward the world.

It is now possible to trace the origins of reflective self-awareness. Such awareness entails that an individual adopts a psychological orientation to herself as a person with her own mental states. Only when the child has arrived at a concept of persons with minds can she "disembed" from her own immediate apprehension of the world, and – by adopting a perspective "as if" of another person – entertain a psychological orientation vis-à-vis her own feelings, thoughts, and attitudes. As Baldwin (1902) expressed it, reflection is "just a relation of separateness created between the ego-self and the alter-self. If there were no alter thought, there would be no reflection," (p. 233). The point is that in order for a child to adopt a psychological perspective vis-à-vis her own self and her own mental life, she needs to appreciate the potential existence of appropriate kinds of alternative perspective. A child's capacity to reflect by abstracting away from her own particular subjective orientation may depend on her becoming aware of other persons as centers of their own subjective experience, such that she can take the role of the other (Mead, 1934). I should add that this account is intended to indicate certain necessary but not sufficient conditions for the emergence of a normal quality of self-consciousness and self-reflective awareness, so that such awareness may not be evident until some time after the child has grasped the nature of persons.

It is also from the time around her first birthday that a child gives the first indications of being able to play symbolically. Although it is not for some months that she will be able to represent absent objects or absent properties of objects by means of arbitrary signifiers, she is already coming to see that one object or event can stand for another. I shall now offer some comments on this new development.

The capacity to symbolize

It is hazardous to enter the intellectual jungle that is known as semiotics, the science of signs. As Edmund Leach has observed, the "most frequently cited "authorities" . . . ring the changes with the terms sign, symbol, index, signal, icon, with very little agreement as to how the categories should be related but with ever increasing complexity of argument" (1976, p. 10). I shall follow Charles Morris (1938/1971), for whom a sign referred to something for someone. Signs may then be subdivided into symbols and signals. Susanne Langer stressed the contrast thus: "A term which is used symbolically and not signally does *not* evoke action appropriate to the presence of its object. . . . Symbols are not proxy for their objects, but are vehicles for the conception of objects" (1957, pp. 60–61). Thus, according to Langer, the commonest form of symbolism, denotation, has four essential terms:

subject, symbol, conception, and object. I would stress that to have a conception is to have a particular way of thinking about an object, such that one may conceive of the object in a number of *different* ways.

Thus far I have focused on what might be called the "signal-dependent," nonverbal communication that forms that scaffolding for interpersonal relations and thus for a child's knowledge of persons. I suggest that the capacity to symbolize in a creative, flexible manner develops in the following way. Given his capacity for personal relations, the infant finds, in and through his caretaker, patterns of action and feeling in which he himself can participate. Alongside this commonality and connectedness with others, the infant also discovers that other people may have a current psychological orientation toward the world that differs from his own. There would seem to be two prerequisites for this discovery. The first has to do with the infant's increasingly sophisticated awareness that bodily expressions and behavior are indeed "expressive" of subjective mental life. The second has to do with the realization that people's minds are "oriented," and that mental states not only have a source (the person whose mental states they are) but also objects to which they are directed. It may be said that such objects are objects only in a formal sense – they have what Brentano (1874/1973) called "intentional inexistence" – in that a person can have thoughts, feelings, and so on about things that do not actually exist. Or again, thoughts and feelings are about objects that fall under a particular description for the individual: There is a "perspectival" quality to mental contents (Perner, 1990). None of this alters the fact that an infant might first apprehend the directedness of other people's physical and psychological orientation toward objects perceived to be "out there" in the perceptible world. Once a child understands that a single object or event can have meaning for self and meaning for other, then the stage is set for the child to realize its own potential for holding more than one orientation to a given object or event at any one time.

My thesis, then, is that a child acquires the capacity for symbolic play by "interiorizing" a configuration of attitudes that is first experienced in interpersonal settings (Vygotsky, 1962). The child first relates to perceptible forms of other people's psychological relatedness (including affective relatedness) to the surroundings – and for this, other persons must be recognized as such – and through such experience, he grasps something of the nature of psychological relations and attitudes vis-à-vis a "stable" external world. It is by this route that the child comes to relate to his own manner of relating to the world. Only now can an object be taken for what it is – a block of wood is a block of wood – but at the same time be "taken" in play as if it were something else, for example, a house. Indeed, the child seems conscious of his newfound capacity to "pretend-take" the block as a house – witness his knowing looks in such contexts. He can now relate to an object both as it is *and* as it is pretended to be (see also Leslie, 1987), both as he apprehends the object *and* as a "someone else" might be apprehending the object with a different meaning.

It is at this point that we see how intimately the capacity for self-reflective awareness conjoins with the capacity to symbolize in play, in that each requires the ability to adopt more than one psychological orientation to a given set of events at any one time. It should also be clear how an individual's capacity to appreciate the perspectival, meaning-conferring nature of minds might be related to his ability to recognize and use symbols as the vehicles for various conceptions of their referents.

I should like to add two details to this account, each pertaining to the connectedness between symbols and their referents. The first point is that one form of linkage among symbols and their referents is forged by an individual's emotional attitudes. This contribution to symbolism has been emphasized not only by psychologists such as Werner (1948) but also by psychoanalysts such as Ferenczi (1913/1952) and Rycroft (1956), who have referred to the different affective conceptions embodied in so-called unconscious symbolism. The second point has more to do with a child's ultimate grasp of how, in one sense, a symbol (as well as a person) "symbolizes." A child's understanding that the meaning of an object has to do with a person's orientation to that object may promote his understanding that the meaning of a symbol (for a person) has to do with the way the symbol can be oriented toward that which it symbolizes. Once the child recognizes that a person is a being whose experiences are "about" things, he may then see how one object or event can also be "about" another. An individual who understands symbols is able to orient himself to a symbol in a way that encompasses the symbol's orientation to (yet separateness from) its referent.

Autism, blindness, and "self"-development

An obvious question presents itself: What is the evidence for or against all this speculation? I shall not be able to make an adequate response to the question, for this would require a detailed appraisal of each step in the argument, and the need for a more fine-grained analysis would become apparent (for example, about the various kinds of symbolism, to only some of which the present description applies). Broadly speaking, however, I think there is evidence for the thesis in the constellation of symptoms observed in autistic and perhaps in congenitally blind children.

I shall take autism first. In oversimplified outline, the story goes as follows. Autistic children have an impairment in biologically based capacities for personal relatedness, and especially affective relatedness, with others. This severely compromises the degree to which they acquire a concept of persons and of themselves and others *as* persons who share the property of having a subjective mental life but who may hold separate and at times contrasting psychological orientations vis-à-vis the world (Baron-Cohen, Leslie, & Frith, 1985, 1986; Hobson, 1982, 1989a, 1990c, 1990d; Leslie & Frith, 1988; Trevarthen, 1989). As Neisser (1988) has expressed it, autism is a disorder of the interpersonal self. Autistic children's failure to recognize the commonality yet differentiation between self and other leads to difficulty in identifying with the other person who says "I" or "my" when engaged in action or when expressing attitudes, and further difficulty in recognizing reciprocal roles in dialogue.

As Charney (1981) has pointed out, autistic children are prone to lift out words or phrases that are associated with their own experiences (rather than the other person's experiences) in circumstances when another person uses personal pronouns. When, subsequently, the children themselves use such words or phrases in appropriate settings but in speech forms that are unmodified according to speaker–listener roles, the result is that they produce echolalic utterances and/or pronoun reversals. By learning to use proper names instead of personal pronouns, however, some autistic children seem to circumvent their difficulties in this domain. My divergence from Loveland (chapter 14) is that whereas she focuses on possible deficits in autistic individuals' comprehension of visual points of view, my emphasis is on their relative failure to understand the nature of persons with their own *psychological* (and, especially, affective and experiential) points of view. In autism, that failure derives from impairments in social perception that antedate and give rise to deficient joint attention skills.

When it comes to considering self-consciousness, autistic children seem to understand the geometric properties of vision (Hobson, 1984; Leslie & Frith, 1988), and even relate their mirror reflection to their own bodies, but what they relatively (not absolutely) lack is the kind of *evaluative* "self-reflection" that has its origins in the experience and/or conception of being evaluated in the minds of others. So, too, in the more conventionally cognitive sphere, autistic children can but partially disembed from their own immediate, concrete apprehension of the world in order to adopt an external orientation on themselves, in order to adopt other people's (or indeed "objective") attitudes to things or events, or in order to entertain multiple "coorientations" to objects as in creative symbolic play. As Scheerer et al. (1945) concluded about their autistic patient L, his grasp and use of language were restricted to "a concrete, situationally determined and ego-centered sense. This handicap in abstract capacity of holding in mind simultaneously two different aspects . . . [means] his performance cannot be lifted out of its concrete context for reflection and verbalization" (pp. 27–29). According to the present account, unlike that of Scheerer et al. (1945), such autism-specific impairments in creative symbolic play and language are rooted in autistic children's primary social–affective abnormalities.

If this account is broadly correct, autism provides a powerful case for the need to relate matters of the heart (the capacity for affective contact with others) to matters of the head (the children's capacities to understand the nature of persons, to reflect on themselves, to symbolize and even think creatively, and much else besides). Autism also indicates the need to acknowledge the essential contribution of social experience to an individual's early cognitive development.

Congenital blindness may be teaching some of the same lessons but from a different perspective. Once again, the congenitally blind child appears to have difficulty in arriving at a concept of other persons with minds that are differentiated from her own *and also* directed toward objects and events that are held in common among people. The real multiple-meanings, coreferenced world is therefore late to become established in the child's understanding. The reason for the blind child's lack of coorientation with others is not so much a failure to establish commonality with people as a limitation in recognizing the differentiation and coordination of people's psychological perspectives.

My thesis is that vision not only plays a role in enabling an infant to perceive and thereby understand the emotional reactions of other people, but more particularly it affords a wealth of opportunity for infants to follow other people's lines of gaze, to discern the targets of their actions, and to apprehend the objects of their feelings and attitudes (cf. social referencing). There is some experimental evidence that blind children encounter difficulty in recognizing and/or understanding emotions. Hobson, Minter, and Pring (1991) tested eight congenitally blind children and eight individually matched sighted children for their ability to name six vocally expressed emotions recorded on audiotape. The control task was to name the recorded sounds of six types of vehicle, six kinds of bird, and six kinds of garden implement in use. Although the children of each group achieved similar scores overall, the blind children were specifically impaired on the emotion vis-à-vis the nonemotion naming tasks. Potentially more damaging than the effects of such "emotion recognition" deficits is the way that congenital blindness may restrict an infant's perception of the directedness of people's actions and attitudes, and more specifically, may limit the infant's experience of having shared or contrasting psychological orientations toward a visually shared world (Mulford, 1983; Rowland, 1983). I suggest that blind children's problems with psychological and visual perspective-taking tasks (Andersen, Dunlea, & Kekelis, 1984; see also E. Gibson, 1977; Loveland, 1984) are causally related to their echolalia and difficulties with personal pronouns, to their relative lack of self-consciousness and reflective self-awareness, and to their delays or impairments in acquiring flexible symbolic play with objects. What congenitally blind and autistic children may have in common is difficulty in developing a full awareness of self and others as persons with subjective orientations that have qualities and directedness common to all normal individuals but that may also differ in their particulars vis-à-vis any given situation or event.

To recapitulate: Autistic children seem to have a form of social imperception toward the bodily expressiveness of other people that severely restricts their understanding of what it means to have a psychological attitude, a mental state, at all (Hobson, 1991b). Congenitally blind children have a specifically visual inability to perceive the directedness of other people's attitudes toward an objectively existing world. In each case the affected children may be slow to understand the nature of different people's psychological coorientations to the world and therefore be delayed in grasping reversible speech roles, in becoming self-conscious, and in engaging in creative symbolic play. For a nonautistic sighted child, the world as perceived by self and other is in one sense a common world – the object that I see is the object that you see – and yet this shared world may be seen to prompt different attitudes, feelings, and judgments in self and other. The normal child soon comes to grasp that a given object may have different significance for self and other. The relations between people's attitudes and the objects of those attitudes, between thoughts and what those thoughts are of, and between things and what those things are taken as (including what they may symbolize) are partly apprehended through the young child's visual perception of other people's bodily-cum-mental attitudes to a visually shared world. In order to comprehend speech roles, to become self-reflective, and ultimately to use symbolic materials creatively, a child may need to experience the world and herself in the minds of others as well as in the mind of herself, and thus to constitute "an own and common world" (Bosch, 1970, p. 115). If these achievements rely heavily on the child's perceptually anchored and especially visually provided awareness of other people as people, with their own affective attitudes and orientations to the world, then it is not surprising that congenitally blind and autistic children may be delayed or deficient in acquiring reflective self-awareness and the capacity for creative symbolic play.

Connectedness and differentiation, feeling and sight, heart and head: The account I have offered will not be correct in all its particulars, but perhaps it will illuminate the route by which a normal infant's affectively patterned and visually enriched experience of interpersonal relations yields both self-reflective awareness and the capacity to symbolize flexibly.

REFERENCES

Adamson, L., & Bakeman, R. (1982). Affectivity and reference: Concepts, methods, and techniques in the study of communication development of 6- to 18-month-old infants. In T. Field & A. Fogel (Eds.), *Emotion and early interaction* (pp. 213–236). Hillsdale, NJ: Erlbaum.

Andersen, E. S., Dunlea, A., & Kekelis, L. S. (1984). Blind children's language: Resolving some differences. *Journal of Child Language, 11,* 645–664.

Baldwin, J. M. (1902). *Social and ethical interpretations in mental development.* New York: Macmillan.

Baron-Cohen, S. (1987). Autism and symbolic play. *British Journal of Developmental Psychology, 5,* 139–148.

Baron-Cohen, S. (1989), Perceptual role-taking and protodeclarative pointing in autism. *British Journal of Developmental Psychology, 7,* 113–127.

Baron-Cohen, S., Leslie, A. M., & Frith, U. (1985). Does the autistic child have a "theory of mind"? *Cognition, 21,* 37–46.

Baron-Cohen, S., Leslie, A. M., & Frith, U. (1986). Mechanical, behavioural and intentional understanding of picture stories in autistic children. *British Journal of Developmental Psychology, 4,* 113–125.

Bemporad, J. R. (1979). Adult recollections of a formerly autistic child. *Journal of Autism and Developmental Disorders, 9,* 179–197.

Blank, H. R. (1975). Reflection on the special senses in relation to the development of affect with special emphasis on blindness. *Journal of the American Psychoanalytic Association, 23,* 32–50.

Bosch, G. (1970). *Infantile autism* (D. Jordan & I. Jordan, Trans). New York: Springer-Verlag.

Braverman, M., Fein, D., Lucci, D., & Waterhouse, L. (1989). Affect comprehension in children with pervasive developmental disorders. *Journal of Autism and Developmental Disorders, 19,* 301–316.

Brentano, F. (1874/1973). *Psychology from an empirical standpoint* (A. C. Rancurello, D. B. Terrell, & L. L. McAlister, Trans.). London: Routledge & Kegan Paul.

Bretherton, I., & Bates, E. (1979). The emergence of intentional communication. In I. C. Uzgiris (Ed.), *Social interaction and communication during infancy: New directions for child development* (No. 4, pp. 81–100). San Francisco: Jossey-Bass.

Bretherton, I., McNew, S., & Beeghly-Smith, M. (1981). Early person knowledge as expressed in gestural and verbal communication: When do infants acquire a "theory of mind"? In M. E. Lamb & L. R. Sherrod (Eds.), *Infant social cognition: Empirical and theoretical considerations* (pp. 333–373). Hillsdale, NJ: Erlbaum.

Bruner, J. (1975). From communication to language – a psychological perspective. *Cognition, 3,* 255–287.

Buber, M. (1937/1984). *I and Thou* (2nd ed., R. G. Smith, Trans.). Edinburgh: T. and T. Clark.

Butterworth, G., & Cochran, E. (1980). Towards a mechanism of joint visual attention in human infancy. *International Journal of Behavioral Development, 3,* 253–272.

Campos, J. J., & Stenberg, C. R. (1981). Perception, appraisal and emotion: The onset of social referencing. In M. E. Lamb & L. R. Sherrod (Eds.), *Infant social cognition* (pp. 273–314). Hillsdale, NJ: Erlbaum.

Charney, R. (1981). Pronoun errors in autistic children: Support for a social explanation. *British Journal of Disorders of Communication, 15,* 39–43.

Chase, J. B. (1972). *Retrolental fibroplasia and autistic symptomatology.* New York: American Foundation for the Blind.

Cohen, D. J. (1980). The pathology of the self in primary childhood autism and Gilles de la Tourette syndrome. *Psychiatric Clinics of North America, 3,* 383–403.

Cohen, J. F., & Tronick, E. (1983). Three-month-old infants' reaction to simulated maternal depression. *Child Development, 54,* 185–193.

Colmer, J. (1975). *E. M. Forster: The personal voice.* London: Routledge & Kegan Paul.

Cooley, C. H. (1902). *Human nature and the social order.* New York: Scribner.

Curcio, F. (1978). Sensorimotor functioning and communication in mute autistic children. *Journal of Autism and Childhood Schizophrenia, 8,* 281–292.

Darwin, C. (1877). A biographical sketch of an infant. *Mind, 2,* 285–294.

Dawson, G., Hill, D., Spencer, A., Galpert, L., & Watson, L. (1990). Affective exchanges between young autistic children and their mothers. *Journal of Abnormal Child Psychology, 18,* 335–345.

Dawson, G., & McKissick, F. C. (1984). Self-recognition in autistic children. *Journal of Autism and Developmental Disorders, 14,* 383–394.

Dunn, L. M. (1965). *Expanded manual for the Peabody Picture Vocabulary Test.* Circle Pines, MN: American Guidance Service.

Dunn, L. M., Dunn, L. M., & Whetton, C. (1982). *British Picture Vocabulary Scale.* Windsor: NFER-Nelson.

Fairbairn, W. R. D. (1952, 1946). Object-relationships and dynamic structure. In Psychoanalytic studies of the personality. (pp. 137–151). London: Routledge & Kegan Paul.

Fay, W. H. (1979). Personal pronouns and the autistic child. *Journal of Autism and Developmental Disorders, 9,* 247–260.

Feinman, S. (1982). Social referencing in infancy. *Merrill-Palmer Quarterly, 28,* 445–470.

Feinman, S., & Lewis, M. (1983). Social referencing at ten months: A second-order effect on infants' responses to strangers. *Child Development, 54,* 878–887.

Ferenczi, S. (1913/1952). The ontogenesis of symbols. In *First contributions to psychoanalysis* (E. Jones, Trans.) (pp. 276–281). London: Maresfield Reprints.

Field, T. M., Woodson, R., Cohen, D., Greenberg, R., Garcia, R., & Collins, K. (1983). Discrimination and imitation of facial expressions by term and preterm neonates. *Infant Behavior and Development, 6,* 485–489.

Field, T. M., Woodson, R., Greenberg, R., & Cohen, D. (1982). Discrimination and imitation of facial expressions by neonates. *Science, 218,* 179–181.

Fraiberg, S., & Adelson, E. (1977). Self-representation in language and play. In S. Fraiberg, *Insights from the blind* (pp. 248–270). London: Souvenir Press.

Freedman, D. A. (1971). Congenital and perinatal sensory deprivation: Some studies in early development. *American Journal of Psychiatry, 127,* 1539–1545.

Gallup, G. G. (1982). Self-awareness and the emergence of mind in primates. *American Journal of Primatology, 2,* 237–248.

Gibson, E. J. (1977, June). *Thoughts inspired by the paper of Selma Fraiberg.* Unpublished manuscript prepared for the Lenneberg Memorial Symposium, Cornell University, Ithaca, NY.

Gibson, J. J. (1977). The theory of affordances. In R. Shaw & J. Bransford (Eds.), *Perceiving, acting and knowing* (pp. 67–82). Hillsdale, NJ: Erlbaum.

Gibson, J. J. (1979). *The ecological approach to visual perception.* Boston: Houghton Mifflin.

Hamlyn, D. W. (1974). Person-perception and our understanding of others. In T. Mischel (Ed.), *Understanding other persons,* (pp. 1–36). Oxford: Blackwell.

Harding, C. G., & Golinkoff, R. M. (1979). The origins of intentional vocalizations in prelinguistic infants. *Child Development, 50,* 33–40.

Haviland, J. M., & Lelwica, M. (1987). The induced affect response: 10-week-old infants' responses to three emotion expressions. *Developmental Psychology, 23,* 97–104.

Hertzig, M. E., Snow, M. E., & Sherman, M. (1989). Affect and cognition in autism. *Journal of the American Academy of Child Psychiatry, 28,* 195–199.

Hobson, R. P. (1982). The autistic child's concept of persons. In D. Park (Ed.), *Proceedings of the 1981 International Conference on Autism, Boston, U.S.A* (pp. 97–102). Washington, DC: National Society for Children and Adults with Autism.

Hobson, R. P. (1984). Early childhood autism and the question of egocentrism. *Journal of Autism and Developmental Disorders, 14,* 85–104.

Hobson, R. P. (1986a). The autistic child's appraisal of expressions of emotion. *Journal of Child Psychology and Psychiatry, 27,* 321–342.

Hobson, R. P. (1986b). The autistic child's appraisal of expressions of emotion: A further study. *Journal of Child Psychology and Psychiatry, 27,* 671–680.

Hobson, R. P. (1989a). Beyond cognition: A theory of autism. In G. Dawson (Ed.), *Autism: Nature, diagnosis, and treatment* (pp. 22–48). New York: Guilford.

Hobson, R. P. (1989b). On sharing experiences. *Development and Psychopathology, 1,* 197–203.

Hobson, R. P. (1990a). On the origins of self and the case of autism. *Development and Psychopathology, 2,* 163–181.

Hobson, R. P. (1990b). On acquiring knowledge about people and the capacity to pretend: Response to Leslie. *Psychological Review, 97,* 114–121.

Hobson, R. P. (1990c). Concerning knowledge of mental states. *British Journal of Medical Psychology, 63,* 199–213.

Hobson, R. P. (1990d). On psychoanalytic approaches to autism. *American Journal of Orthopsychiatry. 60.* 324–336.

Hobson, R. P. (1991a). Methodological issues for experiments on autistic individuals' perception and understanding of emotion. *Journal of Child Psychology and Psychiatry, 32,* 1135–1158.

Hobson, R. P. (1991b). Social perception in high-level autism. In E. Schopler & G. Mesibov (Eds.), *High-functioning autism.* New York: Plenum.

Hobson, R. P., & Lee, A. (1989). Emotion-related and abstract concepts in autistic people: Evidence from the British Picture Vocabulary Scale. *Journal of Autism and Developmental Disorders, 19,* 601–623.

Hobson, R. P., Minter, M., & Pring, L. (1991). Recognition of vocally expressed emotion by congenitally blind children. *Journal of Visual Impairment and Blindness, 85,* 411–415.

Hobson, R. P., Ouston, J., & Lee, A (1988a). What's in a face? The case of autism. *British Journal of Psychology, 79,* 441–453.

Hobson, R. P., Ouston, J., & Lee, A (1988b). Emotion recognition in autism: Coordinating faces and voices. *Psychological Medicine, 18,* 911–923.

Hobson, R. P., Ouston, J., & Lee, A (1989). Naming emotion in faces and voices: Abilities and disabilities in autism and mental retardation. *British Journal of Developmental Psychology, 7,* 237–250.

Hume, D. (1739/1888). *A treatise of human nature* (L. A. Selby-Bigge, Ed.). Oxford: Clarendon.

Isaacs, S. (1948). The nature and function of phantasy. *International Journal of Psycho-Analysis, 29,* 73–97.

James, W. (1890). The principles of psychology (Vol. 1). New York: Dover.

Jennings, W. B. (1973). *A study of the preference for affective cues in autistic children.* Unpublished Ph.D. thesis, Memphis State University.

Jordan, R. R. (1989). An experimental comparison of the understanding and use of speaker-addressee personal pronouns in autistic children. *British Journal of Disorders of Communication, 24,* 169–179.

Kanner, L. (1943). Autistic disturbances of affective contact. *Nervous Child, 2,* 217–250.

Keeler, W. R. (1958). Autistic patterns and defective communication in blind children with retrolental fibroplasia. In P. H. Hoch & J. Zubin (Eds.), *Psychopathology of communication.* New York: Grune & Stratton.

Klinnert, M. (1984). The regulation of infant behavior by maternal facial expression. *Infant Behavior and Development, 7,* 447–465.

Klinnert, M. D., Campos, J. J., Sorce, J. F., Emde, R. N., & Svejda, M. (1983). Emotions as behavior regulators: Social referencing in infancy. In R. Plutchik, & H. Kellerman (Eds.), *Emotion: Theory, research and experience, Vol. 2. Emotions in early development* (pp. 57–86). New York: Academic Press.

Landry, S. H., & Loveland, K. A. (1988). Communication behaviors in autism and development language delay. *Journal of Child Psychology and Psychiatry, 29*, 621–634.

Langer, S. K. (1957). *Philosophy in a new key* (3rd ed.). Cambridge, MA: Harvard University Press.

Leach, E. (1976). *Culture and communication.* Cambridge University Press.

Leslie, A. M. (1987). Pretense and representation: The origins of "theory of mind." *Psychological Review, 94*, 412–426.

Leslie, A. M., & Frith, U. (1988). Autistic children's understanding of seeing, knowing and believing. *British Journal of Developmental Psychology, 6*, 315–324.

Lewis, M., & Brooks-Gunn, J. (1979). *Social cognition and the acquisition of self.* New York: Plenum.

Loveland, K. A. (1984). Learning about points of view: Spatial perspective and the acquisition of "I/you." *Journal of Child Language, 11*, 535–556.

Macdonald, H., Rutter, M., Howlin, P., Rios, P., LeCouteur, A., Evered, C., & Folstein, S. (1989). Recognition and expression of emotional cues by autistic and normal adults. *Journal of Child Psychology and Psychiatry, 30*, 865–877.

Malcolm, N. (1962, 1958). Knowledge of other minds. In V. C. Chappell (Ed.), *The philosophy of mind* (pp. 151–159). Englewood Cliffs, NJ: Prentice Hall.

Mead, G. H. (1934). *Mind, self, and society* (C. W. Morris, Ed.). Chicago: University of Chicago Press.

Morris, C. W. (1938). *Foundations of the theory of signs* (International Encyclopedia of Unified Science, Vol. 1). Chicago: University of Chicago Press. Reprinted in C. Morris (1971). Writings on the general theory of signs. In T. A. Sebeok (Ed.), *Approaches to semiotics.* The Hague: Mouton.

Mulford, R. (1983). Referential development in blind children. In A. E. Mills (Ed.), *Language acquisition in the blind child: Normal and deficient* (pp. 89–107). London: Croom Helm.

Mundy, P., Sigman, M., & Kasari, C. (1990). A longitudinal study of joint attention and language development in autistic children. *Journal of Autism and Developmental Disorders, 20*, 115–128.

Mundy, P., Sigman, M., Ungerer, J., & Sherman, T. (1986). Defining the social deficits of autism: The contribution of non-verbal communication measures. *Journal of Child Psychology and Psychiatry, 27*, 657–669.

Murray, L., & Trevarthen, C. (1985). Emotional regulation of interactions between two-month-olds and their mothers. In T. M. Field & N. A. Fox (Eds.), *Social perception in infants* (pp. 177–197). Norwood, NJ: Ablex.

Nagel, T. (1979). *Mortal questions.* Cambridge University Press.

Neisser, U. (1988). Five kinds of self-knowledge. *Philosophical Psychology, 1*, 35–59.

Neuman, C. J., & Hill, S. D. (1978). Self-recognition and stimulus preference in autistic children. *Developmental Psychobiology, 11*, 571–578.

Ozonoff, S., Pennington, B. F., & Rogers, S. J. (1990). Are there emotion perception deficits in young autistic children? *Journal of Child Psychology and Psychiatry, 3*, 343–361.

Ozonoff, S., Pennington, B. F., & Rogers, S. J. (1991). Executive function deficits in high-functioning autistic children: Relationship to theory of mind. *Journal of Child Psychology and Psychiatry, 32*, 1081–1105.

Perner, J. (1990). *Understanding the representational mind.* Cambridge, MA: MIT/Bradford.

Prior, M. R., Dahlstrom, B., & Squires, T.-L. (1990). Autistic children's knowledge

R. PETER HOBSON

of thinking and feeling states in other people. *Journal of Child Psychology and Psychiatry, 31,* 587–601.

Reddy, V. (1990). Playing with others' expectations: Teasing and mucking about in the first year. In A. Whiten (Ed.), *The emergence of mindreading: Evolution, development and simulation of second order representations.* Oxford: Blackwell.

Ricks, D. M. (1975). Vocal communication in pre-verbal normal and autistic children. In N. O'Connor (Ed.), *Language, cognitive deficits, and retardation* (pp. 75–80). London: Butterworths.

Riguet, C. B., Taylor, N. D., Benaroya, S., & Klein, L. S. (1981). Symbolic play in autistic, Down's, and normal children of equivalent mental age. *Journal of Autism and Developmental Disorders, 11,* 439–448.

Rowland, C. (1983). Patterns of interaction between three blind infants and their mothers. In A. E. Mills (Ed.), *Language acquisition in the blind child: Normal and deficient* (pp. 114–132). London: Croom Helm.

Rycroft, C. (1956). Symbolism and its relationship to the primary and secondary processes. *International Journal of Psycho-Analysis, 37,* 137–146.

Sagi, A., & Hoffman, M. L. (1976). Empathic distress in the newborn. *Developmental Psychology, 12,* 175–176.

Scaife, M., & Bruner, J. S. (1975). The capacity for joint visual attention in the infant. *Nature, 253,* 265–266.

Scheerer, M., Rothmann, E., & Goldstein, K. (1945). A case of "idiot savant": An experimental study of personality organization. *Psychological Monographs, 58* (whole No. 269), 1–63.

Scheler, M. (1954). *The nature of sympathy* (P. Heath, trans.). London: Routledge & Kegan Paul.

Sigman, M., Mundy, P., Sherman, T., & Ungerer, J. (1986). Social interactions of autistic, mentally retarded and normal children and their caregivers. *Journal of Child Psychology and Psychiatry, 27,* 647–656

Silberg, J. L. (1978). The development of pronoun usage in the psychotic child. *Journal of Autism and Childhood Schizophrenia, 8,* 413–425

Simner, M. L. (1971). Newborn's response to the cry of another infant. *Developmental Psychology, 5,* 136–150.

Snow, M. E., Hertzig, M. E., & Shapiro, T. (1987). Expression of emotion in young autistic children. *American Academy of Child and Adolescent Psychiatry, 26,* 836–838.

Sorce, J. F., Emde, R. N., Campos, J., & Klinnert, M. D. (1985). Maternal emotional signaling: Its effect on the visual cliff behavior of 1-year-olds. *Developmental Psychology, 21,* 195–200.

Spiker, D., & Ricks, M. (1984). Visual self-recognition in autistic children: Developmental relationships. *Child Development, 55,* 214–225.

Stern, D. N. (1985). *The interpersonal world of the infant.* New York: Basic Books.

Strawson, P. F. (1962/1958). Persons. In V. C. Chappell (Ed.), *The philosophy of mind* (pp. 127–146). Englewood Cliffs, NJ: Prentice Hall.

Tager-Flusberg, H. (1989). *An analysis of discourse ability and internal state lexicons in a longitudinal study of autistic children.* Paper presented at the biennial meeting of the Society for Research in Child Development, Kansas City.

Tantam, D., Monaghan, L., Nicholson, H., & Stirling, J. (1989). Autistic children's ability to interpret faces: A research note. *Journal of Child-Psychology and Psychiatry, 30,* 623–630.

Trevarthen, C. (1979). Communication and cooperation in early infancy: A description of primary intersubjectivity. In M. Bullowa (Ed.), *Before speech* (pp. 321–347). Cambridge University Press.

Trevarthen, C. (1989). The relation of autism to normal socio-cultural development: The case for a primary disorder in regulation of cognitive growth by emotions. [Unpublished English translation of the French edition.] In G. Lelord, J. P. Muk, M. Petit, & D. Sauvage (Eds.), *Autisme et troubles du developpement global de l'enfant.* Paris: Expansion Scientifique Française.

Trevarthen, C., & Hubley, P. (1978). Secondary intersubjectivity: Confidence, confiding and acts of meaning in the first year. In A. Lock (Ed.), *Action, gesture and symbol: The emergence of language* (pp. 183–229). London: Academic Press.

Ungerer, J. A., & Sigman, M. (1981). Symbolic play and language comprehension in autistic children. *Journal of the American Academy of Child Psychiatry, 20*, 318–337.

Vygotsky, L. S. (1962). *Thought and language* (E. Hanfmann & G. Vakar, Trans.). Cambridge, MA: MIT Press.

Walden, T. A., & Ogan, T. A. (1988). The development of social referencing. *Child Development, 59*, 1230–1240.

Weeks, S. J., & Hobson, R. P. (1987). The salience of facial expression for autistic children. *Journal of Child Psychology and Psychiatry, 28*, 137–152.

Werner, H. (1948). *Comparative psychology of mental development.* Chicago: Follett.

Werner, H., & Kaplan, B. (1963). *Symbol formation.* New York: Wiley.

Wing, L. (1969). The handicaps of autistic children – a comparative study. *Journal of Child Psychology and Psychiatry, 10*, 1–40.

Wing, L., Gould, J., Yeates, S. R., & Brierley, L. M. (1977). Symbolic play in severely mentally retarded and in autistic children. *Journal of Child Psychology and Psychiatry, 18*, 167–178.

Wittgenstein, L. (1958). *Philosophical investigations* (G. E. M. Anscombe, Trans.). Oxford: Blackwell.

Wittgenstein, L. (1980). *Remarks on the philosophy of psychology* (Vol. 2). Eds., G. H. von Wright & H. Nyman (C. G. Luckhardt & M. A. E. Aue, Trans.). Oxford: Blackwell.

Wulff, S. B. (1985). The symbolic and object play of children with autism: A review. *Journal of Autism and Developmental Disorders, 15*, 139–148.

Yirmiya, N., Kasari, C., Sigman, M., & Mundy, P. (1989). Facial expressions of affect in autistic, mentally retarded and normal children. *Journal of Child Psychology and Psychiatry, 30*, 725–735.

15

G. H. Mead and Martin Buber on the interpersonal self

JAMES M. GUSTAFSON

This volume is devoted to Ulric Neisser's first two kinds of self-knowledge: ecological and interpersonal. My focus here is on the second of these, interpersonal knowledge. Pertinent writings by G. H. Mead and Martin Buber will be considered, then, in terms of how their writings contribute to, or differ from, Neisser's view (1988; see also this volume). At the risk of some redundancy, I begin by summarizing the main features of Neisser's account of the interpersonal self (1988, pp. 41–46).

Neisser opens by stating that this self is "engaged in immediate unreflective social interaction with another person." When the actions of one person "mesh appropriately" with the actions of another, they create an occasion of intersubjectivity. This mutuality can be perceived both by the external observer and by the participants. Direct perception rather than inference is the basis of this mutuality or intersubjectivity. As studies of infants indicate, the interpersonal self is specifically oriented by and through expressive gestures; communication through gestures develops the interpersonal self. This process is "an emotional business: the two partners are obviously sharing an affect" (p. 44). It is not cognitive or inferential at its early stage of formation. But it becomes supplemented by forms of cognition; the participant learns that others have beliefs and intentions and feelings of their own.

Neisser cautions, however, that the inferential process can be manipulated by the other and that the self can make incorrect inferences. He argues that, in contrast to this more cognitive and inferential process, "the *perception* of ongoing intersubjectivity is necessarily veridical." "Intersubjectivity is defined by an appropriate match between the nature/direction/timing/ intensities of two people's activities; it either occurs or it does not. When it does occur, two distinct and yet closely related interpersonal selves are brought into existence along with it" (p. 45). He closes with a warning that by excessive focus on intersubjective experience, one can miss other kinds of information that specify the self. In a sense, it seems to me that Neisser could more appropriately distinguish between the ecological and interpersonal aspects of the self rather than between different selves.

Why is it appropriate to examine writings of G. H. Mead and Martin Buber in relation to Neisser's account?[1] Mead's work is cited and taken into account by Neisser, and most North Americans trained in pragmatic philosophy, sociological theory, and social psychology have at least secondary knowledge of Mead's *Mind, Self, and Society* (1934). Even though the form in which we have this book (produced from notes by students) is unsatisfactory in many respects, its seminal qualities have grown to affect a variety of disciplines and fields of study. Martin Buber is not cited by Neisser in his 1988 paper (but see this volume). The work of this Jewish social philosopher and religious thinker has, however, profoundly affected the reflections of both Jewish and Christian religious thinkers, and of some philosophers. Among readers of English, his best-known work is probably *I and Thou* (1937). Three general contrasts can be drawn between these two authors.

First, whereas Mead takes a basic stance that is "scientific" in a modern North American sense – the external observer seeking to provide a genetic or causal explanation of the emergence of self and mind – Buber's stance is more expressive than analytical, more aphoristic and narrative than argumentative, perhaps more concerned to show a valued quality of human life from within than to account for it from without. Yet Buber's work is descriptive of self in relations, in dialogue, and thus one can ask what evidences would support its truthfulness.

One sharp distinction between Mead and Buber is that Mead desires to provide a theory that explains a wide range of information – biological evolution, the central nervous system, how children learn, the use of gestures and language, and so on – whereas Buber invites the reader to self-reflection or empathic participation, and anticipates that the reader's own life is understood at a deeper level in the process. Buber "shows" rather more than he "explains"; presumably the reader recognizes himself or herself in the account. Buber's work has religious dimensions not only with reference to the Eternal Thou, God, but to one's interpersonal relations with others.

Indeed, becoming aware of oneself does not necessarily require another person. "It can be an animal, a plant, a stone. No kind of appearance or event is fundamentally excluded from the series of things through which from time to time something is said to me. Nothing can refuse to be the vessel for the Word. The limits of the possibility of dialogue are the limits of awareness" (Buber, 1947, p. 10). Buber seems to invite us to share in the mystery of being a self in relation to others and the Other; he might agree with Neisser that intersubjectivity "either occurs or it does not." Any speech about it is reductionistic to some extent; aphorisms and narratives are more adequate than externally objective scientific efforts. Mead, in contrast, intends to expel the mystery with a theory – one that can be made into hypotheses for experiments. (He did not do the experiments, but they can be done). In the methodological controversy over the natural sciences and the human sciences (Dilthey's Naturwissenschaften and Geisteswissenschaften) Mead is clearly in the camp of those who applied natural science methods to the study of the human, and Buber in the camp of those who believed that such methods could not fully account for human experience.

Where Mead explicitly emphasizes that the "primary structure of the self ... is ... essentially a cognitive rather than an emotional phenomenon." Buber stresses more affective aspects of the self. Mead wrote, "The thinking or intellectual process – the internalization and inner dramatization, by the individual, of the external conversation of significant gestures which constitutes his chief mode of interaction with other individuals belonging to the same society – is the earliest phase in the genesis and development of the self" (1934, p. 173). He differentiates his position from that of Charles Horton Cooley and William James, whom he interprets to find the basis of the self in "reflexive affective experiences." The formation of mind, in a sense, precedes the formation of self. "The essence of the self ... is cognitive, it lies in the internalized conversation of gestures which constitutes thinking, or in terms of which thought or reflection proceeds. And hence the origin and foundations of the self, like those of thinking, are social" (ibid).

One notes that Neisser, following evidence he cites from experimental data with infants and young children, says that intersubjectivity is an emotional business; there is what Daniel Stern (1985) calls *affect attunement*. One difficulty in relating Mead's cognitive orientation to Neisser's account is whether both use the term cognitive in the same way. Does Mead's interpretation come closer to Neisser's "conceptual self" than it does to his "interpersonal self"? One notes that Mead's extended discussion of gestures comes in his interpretation of the development of "mind." Mead also uses the language of "social act" prominently in his discussion. His distinction between a significant and a nonsignificant gesture or symbol has to be noted: "Gestures may be either conscious (significant) or unconscious (nonsignificant)." He writes that below the human level the conversation of gestures "is not significant because it is not self-conscious" (1934, p. 81). Through the process of taking the attitudes of others involved in one's conduct, one becomes an object to oneself – that is, one becomes "self-conscious" (1932, p. 184).

The function of the gesture is to make adjustment possible among the individuals implicated in any given social act with reference to the object or objects with which that act is concerned; and the significant gesture or significant symbol affords far greater facilities for such adjustment and readjustment than does the non-significant gesture, because it calls out in the individual making it the same attitude toward it (or toward its meaning) that is called out in other individuals participating with him in the given social act, and thus makes him conscious of their attitude toward it (as a component of his behavior) and enables him to adjust his subsequent behavior to theirs in the light of that attitude. (1934, p. 46).

Mead, more than Neisser, wishes to move quickly to the emergence of thinking. Significant gestures make possible "the existence of mind or intelligence"; only in terms of significant symbols can "thinking" take place. Neisser says "that intersubjectivity is based on direct perception rather than inference" (p. 42). One can possibly interpret Mead as introducing rather earlier in his account a kind of inferential process. Indeed, Neisser explicitly differentiates his account from Mead's on this point in his one citation: "Such inferences are certainly not the primary basis of self-knowledge" (p. 45).

In contrast to Mead's emphasis on the cognitive processes of interpersonal selfhood, I have suggested that Buber stresses the affective aspects of the self. The term *affective* is not present in Buber's work, and may not be quite appropriate. I use it with hesitation to make possible a way of relating Buber to some of Neisser's points and to distinguish Buber from Mead in terms more common to what I know about contemporary psychology.

Neisser, as I previously quoted, states that the interpersonal self is "engaged in immediate unreflective social interaction with another person." The process is "an emotional business." "The perception of ongoing intersubjectivity is necessarily veridical." "Perception" in this last sentence is not confined to cognitive or inferential processes. Is there some defensible affinity between Neisser and at least some insights depicted by Buber? To answer this question even with hesitation is to embark on some treacherous verbal shoals, for even Buber's most discursive discussions are illustrated by aphorisms and narratives. The truthfulness of Buber's account to the reader depends not on data from experiments but on a kind of intuitive and affective recognition of one's relations to others, as the self becomes an *I* in meeting another. As I said, Buber seems to show, not argue. The response of the reader is either, "Yes, the reality of the self in relation is really like what he says," or "No, it is not like that at all." And, because Buber's larger purpose is a prophetic, moral one – a critique of culture in which thingification and causal explanations erode the meaning of what it is to be a person – this purpose directs his analysis more intimately than Mead's moral concerns direct his.

Buber's concentration on the meeting of I and Thou is not denial of the relations between I and It. I–It relations are relations to objects, they are relations of utility value in the ongoing processes of life. "The primary relation of man to the world of *It* is comprised in *experiencing*, which continually reconstitutes the world, and *using*, which leads the world to its manifold aim, the sustaining, relieving, and equipping of human life" (1937, p. 38). The world, including other individuals, is more and more reduced to specialized utilization. Even individuals are treated as means to ends only, and not also as ends in themselves, to recall one of Kant's statements of the categorical imperative. "Causality has an unlimited reign in the world of *It* (p. 51). Ordinary life "swings by nature between Thou and It" (p. 52).

Buber clearly recognizes the necessity of objectifications, of more depersonalized relations, of institutions. This leads inevitably to a divided self, to "two tidily circled-off provinces, one of institutions and the other of feelings – the province of *It* and the province of *I*." "Institutions are 'outside,' where all sorts of aims are pursued, where a man works, negotiates, bears influence, undertakes, concurs, organizes business, officiates, preaches." They tolerably order, with the help of human brains and hands, the process of human affairs. The moral problem is the erosive effect of I–It relations when there is no return to the realm of that elusive reality he calls "spirit," which includes feelings. "Feelings are 'within,' where life is lived and man recovers from institutions. Here the spectrum of emotions dances before the interested glance. . . . Here he is at home, and stretches himself out in his rocking-chair" (p. 43). Indeed, the Thou is bound to become an It when a relational event runs its course, and an It, by "entering the relational event, *may* become a *Thou*" (p. 33).

Mead's account of the emergence of self has made the self an It; the self is explainable in causal terms. And insofar as the self is a cognitive phenomenon, in Mead's sense, something has been reduced out of Buber's I. Mead's interpretation of the I in his distinction between the I and the me might approach but hardly gets to what Buber attempts to express about the I. Mead's I is always a self in a discrete present moment; it names what we are never fully aware of, and what causes us to be surprised by our own action. It is "the response of the organism to the attitudes of others; the 'me' is the organized set of attitudes of others which one . . . assumes" (1934, p. 175). The response of the I is something more or less uncertain; "the 'I' gives the sense of freedom, of initiative" (p. 177). For Mead, perhaps the I is a remainder concept; it points to what is, at least for the present, inexplicable. It represents what Mead does not call, but others might, *agency* – though consistent with his overall framework he uses the word *response* to name its function. Response, for Mead, however, is perhaps more like a reaction of the organism; I think it does not carry the connotations of response and responsiveness that Buber's description of life as meeting does.

"All real living is meeting," writes Buber (1937, p. 11). Does the word *real* here refer to what describes the essence of human living, or is it almost totally value-laden? My view is that, for Buber, the descriptive is the basis of the value, but the descriptive refers to what be believes to be unique to the human and not the conditions it shares with other creatures.

"If I face a human being as *Thou*, and say the primary word *I–Thou* to him, he is not a thing among things, and does not consist of things" (1937, p. 8). Human life is not passed in transitive verbs alone; it is not just perceiving, sensing, imaging, willing, thinking. These terms establish an I–It relationship. Things have bounds; "*Thou* has no bounds." Is this boundless Thou present in all relations? Is it what some since Buber have called the horizon of all relations? Relations, he says arise in three spheres: the world of nature and creatures which we can address as Thou, but when we do we only cling to the threshold of speech; our life with other persons where the world is open and we can give and accept the Thou; and our life with "intelligible forms" where speech is not used but begotten and where we perceive no Thou but feel we are being addressed and answer by thinking and acting. In all three "we look out toward the fringe of the eternal *Thou*; in each we are aware of a breath from the eternal *Thou*; in each Thou we address the eternal *Thou*" (p. 6). But we do not *experience* Thou; we meet the Thou. "The relation to the *Thou* is direct" (p. 11), and the relation is mutual: "My *Thou* affects me, as I affect it" (p. 15). Buber has moved us into the religious dimensions of his writing. "Every sphere is compassed in the eternal *Thou*, but it [the eternal Thou] is not compassed in them" (p. 101).

This is not the place for an apologetic defense of Buber's religious dimensions, even if one were desirable. Mead, one can note parenthetically, does aspire to a set of significant symbols that would have a universal meaning, to a potential universality in the process of communication, but this certainly does not get at the mystery of Buber's eternal Thou. Our interest, I take it, is in whether there are any affinities at all between Buber's account and Neisser's.

The interpersonal self, Neisser states, is "engaged in immediate unreflective social interaction with another person." Certainly for Buber the meeting of the I and the Thou is immediate and unreflective. I do not know whether Buber would say that "the *perception* of ongoing intersubjectivity is necessarily veridical," as Neisser does, but he does have confidence that in meeting a Thou there is a kind of recognition of oneself as an I. "The *I* of the primary word *I–Thou* makes its appearance as person and becomes conscious of itself as subjectivity" (1937, p. 62). The word *person* is used by Neisser but with different overtones than one finds in Buber. Buber distinguishes between individuality and person: "Individuality makes its appearance by being differentiated from other individualities. A person makes his appearance by entering into relations with other persons." Persons have the "spiritual form of natural solidarity and connexion." Individuality (for which he uses the pronoun it) takes the form of detachment, of self-differentiation (p. 62). "The person becomes conscious of himself as sharing in being, as co-existing, and thus as being." Person and subjectivity for Buber resonate with the elusive quality of spirit. I find it hard to think that Neisser would use that word, any more than he would affirm the reality of the Eternal Thou.

I suggest that a meeting point between Neisser and Buber might be the recognition of affective qualities in interpersonal relations, and in the sense of being a self in relations. Both would clearly find Mead's cognitive emphasis to be reductionistic. One might explore Neisser's use of affect attunement as a phenomenon that has some affinity with Buber's I–Thou relation. But this is not to claim that Buber's work could make substantive contributions to Neisser's view of the interpersonal self. Maybe those it could make are already in Neisser – that is, that the other person is never merely an It in the interpersonal relations that form the self. But for Buber, these distinctions are in the service of a profoundly prophetic critique of modern culture, as well as affirmations of what is "really" the case.

A final contrast between Mead and Buber is their very different delineations of the proper context in which to understand the interpersonal self. For Mead, it is a society; for Buber, it is ultimately the Eternal Thou, the mystery of God.

Mead writes, "Any self is a social self, but it is restricted to the group whose roles it assumes, and it will never abandon this self until it finds itself entering into the larger society and maintaining itself there (1932, p. 194). In *Mind, Self and Society* he writes, "The organized community or social group which gives to the individual his unity of self may be called 'the generalized other.' The attitude of the generalized other is the attitude of the whole community." The development of an identifiable self does not occur fully in a person taking the attitudes of *other individuals* toward oneself. The individual takes the attitudes of others toward their common social activity and undertakings. This is what integrates the individual into the social group, and this is part of developing "a complete self" (pp. 154, 155). One's behavior is directed according to one's generalized other.

This, in effect, is a proposal about moral development and about a theory of "conscience." One's attitudes and acts are socialized in a community to some significant degree of conformity with its expectations and attitudes, and one judges one's action with the generalized other looking over a shoulder. Communication is the essence of this process; indeed, it involves one's "participation in the other. This requires the appearance of the other in the self, the identification of the other with the self, the reaching of self-consciousness through the other" (1934, p. 253). Interestingly, the social control exercised in this way seems to be rather benign. "Social control, so far from tending to crush out the human individual or to obliterate his self-conscious individuality, is, on the contrary, actually constitutive of and inextricably associated with that individuality; for the individual is what he is, as a conscious and individual personality, just in so far as he is a member of society, involved in the social process of experience and activity, and thereby socially controlled in his conduct" (1934, p. 255).

Mead, the moralist, recognizes the limits of such a view, but if it is descriptively and analytically correct, any social ideal has to be consonant with his theory. He echoes, in sense, his teacher Royce's ideal of a beloved universal community. Mead writes:

The human social ideal – the ideal or ultimate goal of human social progress – is the attainment of a universal human society in which all human individuals would possess a perfected social intelligence, such that all social meanings would each be similarly reflected in their respective individual consciousnesses – such that the meanings of any one individual's act or gestures . . . would be the same as any other individual whatever who responded to them. (p. 310)

There is no mystery of an Eternal Thou here, but there is an ideal of a universal human community, and Mead is very aware of the impediments to its achievement.

The context for Buber, as I have already had to introduce, is the Eternal Thou – and that is a mystery, in a nonpejorative sense. Buber is not given to arguing for the attributes of God as these have been developed in Western theology, nor is he given to speculative metaphysics that become theologically significant as one finds in classical theism or process theology. Nor, I think, is the Eternal Thou only a remainder concept, a way of saying what is on the fringe of experience but cannot be fully known. For Buber, the Eternal Thou is responsive to the I, just as a human Thou is responsive to the I. Nor is God what taking a step or two beyond Mead might lead to theologically, namely, the beloved universal community. As I have already said, one meets the Thou, and the Thou meets oneself. Maybe one has a direct veridical perception of it, or one does not. Mead would probably account for it as the result of a process of becoming a self in relation to the other through a set of significant symbols. Another set of symbols would lead to a different construal; living in a different community would lead to a different language about what Buber wants his readers to see and to feel.

Buber, the moralist, provides a different understanding of the locus of the fault in the fulfillment of the human. Mead's locus, I believe, is the absence of the universal generalized other made necessary by the fact that our social locations are always limited and specific. For Buber, what impedes human well-being is the encroaching dominance of I–It relationships, the thingification of relationships, which depersonalize the human. His concern is for a quality of life, life in relations, which fulfills the human spirit. This has to be realized from within and between more than through manipulative utilitarian reforms, though reforms (as in his work on education) can provide conditions for it.

Neisser, the scientist (which is not the whole Neisser by any means), to my knowledge has not provided any social and moral ideal based on his work like Mead has, nor can one claim that a profound moral concern, as in Buber's case, predisposes him to (or even correlates with) his account of the interpersonal self. I think, however, that one could readily draw inferences from his discussion of the interpersonal self about the necessary conditions that have to be met if that self is to have a decent measure of human fulfillment and well-being. But this volume is not on ethics.

To recapitulate a bit: I have attempted to show three general contrasts between Mead and Buber, and in the course of those contrasts relate them somewhat to Neisser's work. In that analysis I have not always pointed explicitly to how each of them answers three questions: One, *How does an identifiable self come to exist,* or what is the genesis of the self? This has been attended to more than the other two questions I shall ask. Two, *How does a self understand itself?* This, I believe, is a different question from the explanation of how a self comes into being in interpersonal relations. It suggests, I think, that a person's understanding of himself or herself in relations affects a sense of self-worth, the kinds of actions engaged in, and so on. This is not part of Neisser's project in this volume. Third, *What does it mean to be a self, a person?* This is obliquely addressed in my third contrast. Different contexts frame different possibilities of the meaning of being a human person, and they describe the meaning in different ways.

Since my first conversations with Neisser about this project, I have kept a memo on which I have written five words that are related but might be distinguishable when thinking about the self, and particularly the interpersonal self: knowledge, explanation, understanding, meaning, and interpretation. I close these remarks with some reflections about how these five words might be used to compare Mead, Buber, and Neisser.

All three claim that there is self-knowledge that develops in interpersonal relations. Mead is clearly most interested in providing a complete and coherent explanatory account of how the self comes into being in relations; Neisser, I think, is as well. An adequate explanation of how the self comes into being in interpersonal relations is what gives us self-knowledge. Self-understanding for Mead, and probably for Neisser, comes with the causal or explanatory account; Mead introduces his "I" as a heuristic device for self-understanding basically as a remainder concept, as that which as yet his theory does not fully explain. For Buber, understanding the self is to understand its dimensions as spirit, something that the It language of the sciences cannot explain. The meaning of being a self in relations for Buber is a kind of indicator about the mystery of human life; that meaning seems to be veridical and profoundly experiential to him and to those who are guided by his meditations, aphorisms, and narratives. Meaning of the interpersonal self for Mead seems to focus on one's participation in a particular community of significant symbols. Meaning, for Neisser, I think, is not exhausted by Mead's more cognitive–social interactionist account; his subjectivity and intersubjectivity might be ways of warding off a Meadian reductionism, though they do not fully resonate with Buber's view of intersubjectivity. All three accounts are interpretations. My analysis, by implication at least, points to the features each thinks are the salient guides in that process and to what each believes to be the evidences that back his views.

NOTE

1. George Herbert Mead (1863–1931) graduated from Harvard College in 1888, where he studied with William James and Josiah Royce. For 3 years he studied in Germany at Berlin and Leipzig. From 1891 to 1894 he taught philosophy at the University of Michigan, and from 1894 until his death at the University of Chicago.

Martin Buber (1878–1965) was born in Vienna and raised in Lvov, Galicia, where he came to know both the Enlightenment tradition and Hasidism. He studied at the University of Vienna and at Leipzig and Zurich. In 1938 he left the professorship of Jewish theology and history at Frankfurt to become professor of social philosophy at the Hebrew University in Jerusalem.

REFERENCES

Buber, M. (1937). *I and Thou.* Edinburgh: T. and T. Clark.
Buber, M. (1947). *Between mind and man.* London: Routledge & Kegan Paul.
Mead, G. H. (1932). *The philosophy of the present.* Chicago: Open Court.
Mead, G. H. (1934). *Mind, self and society.* Chicago: University of Chicago Press.
Neisser, U. (1988). Five kinds of self-knowledge. *Philosophical Psychology,* 1, 35–59.
Stern, D. N. (1985). *The interpersonal world of the infant.* New York: Basic Books.

16

Cognitive science, other minds, and the philosophy of dialogue

DAVID JOPLING

> The single man for himself possesses the essence of man neither in himself as a moral being nor in himself as a thinking being. The essence of man is contained only in the community and unity of man with man; it is a unity, however, which rests only on the reality of the distinction between I and Thou.
>
> – Feuerbach (1843, p. 71)

Philosophy may not tell us how galaxies are born, or what it is that makes squealing and babbling infants squeal and babble. One thing it does well, however, is show us how to question the questions that we begin with whenever we investigate something. And one thing it has tended to reveal over many years of practicing this questionable art is that the form in which we cast our original questions, and the assumptions and models these questions conceal, consistently determine the form in which we frame our answers. Starting points have a tendency to haunt us all the way through to our theoretical conclusions.

In this chapter I shall examine two widely divergent ways to frame epistemological and metaphysical questions about the nature of social and interpersonal relations. One way, what I call the philosophy of subjectivity, has representatives as varied as Descartes, Locke, Husserl, and a number of cognitive scientists. The other way of framing these questions, the philosophy of intersubjectivity, has representatives as varied as Wittgenstein, Habermas, Mead, Buber, and Levinas. These ways are fundamentally at odds with each other. I shall argue that the philosophy of subjectivity encounters intractable problems and requires deep revisions.

What are some of the epistemological and metaphysical questions to be asked about interpersonal relations? We must begin with the fact that most of us manage quite successfully in everyday life in perceiving, understanding, and getting along with such infinitely complex cognitive–behavioral creatures as other people. We are adept at these sophisticated and highly tuned interactions even in situations we have never before encountered or observed. How is this near-miraculous feat possible? What is going on here?

One way to interpret these questions is to ask: What is going on *inside the mind* when this happens? What sorts of internal mental processes best explain the phenomena of social and interpersonal relations: mental representation, information processing at a subpersonal (or nonconscious) level, analogy or modeling from our own case, inferences to the best explanation? Are we adopting an "intentional stance" to other creatures (Dennett, 1989)? Are we making sense of others in terms of a "theory of mind," that is, a "framework of abstract laws or principles concerning the dynamic relations holding between causal circumstances, psychological states, and overt behaviour" (Churchland, 1979, p. 92)? These are typical of the questions framed by the philosophy of subjectivity.

The move from "What is going on here?" to "What is going on inside the mind?" is critical, for it conceals a number of assumptions that constrain subsequent theory construction. But it is not the only possible move. A less "head-oriented" way of framing the question is to ask: What is going on *between two people* when this happens? What kinds of relations are occurring, and what sorts of objectively existing information make these relations possible? Are interpersonal relations intelligible, smooth, and workable because cognition, representation, theory construction, or the intentional stance allows us to impute minds to other creatures? Or are they possible because of a more primitive set of properties that makes cognition, representation, or the knowledge of other minds possible? More to the point, are interpersonal relations direct and unmediated or indirect and cognitively mediated? These are the sorts of questions framed by the philosophy of intersubjectivity.

The philosophy of subjectivity, as we shall see, tends to be cognitivist, atomist, and internalist. It conceives social and interpersonal relations as relations between minds – or subjects of experience, with all the epistemological baggage that such talk tends to carry about internal mental processes, representation, privacy, and privileged access. The same difficulties that plague its attempt to explain how the cognizing subject emerges from its inner sphere into one that is external (What relates internal representations to the world?) also plague its attempts to explain interpersonal relations (How is the cognizing subject rescued from the oblivion of solipsism?). And the solutions are similar: The same kinds of internal mental processes (e.g., cognition, inference, representation, theory construction) explaining how the mind relates to the world also explain how it relates to other minds.

Whatever particular story a philosophy of subjectivity tells about what is going on in the mind, it typically begins with the first-person perspective as the paradigm of mindedness. Whether the existence of other minds is inferred, imputed, represented, or theorized, we always begin by taking ourselves as the touchstone of whether others can be said to house a mind. The knowledge of other minds is parasitic on our knowledge of our own mind. Thus one cognitive scientist writes: "Every member of the human species [has] both the power and inclination *to use a privileged picture of his own self as a model for what it is like to be another person*" (Humphrey, 1983, p. 6).

Three serious problems afflict the view that interpersonal relations are best explained as relations between minds. First, it leads to the unwanted "problem of other minds" (or the "egocentric predicament"), from which there are no philosophically convincing escape routes. How do I know with certainty that other creatures really have minds, when all I perceive is overt behavior? Second, it is unfaithful to our ordinary experience of human relationships: We encounter persons, not minds. Third, it models interpersonal relations exclusively on the first-person point of view. This is misleading. In modeling the other person as a "re-edition" of the first person (Theunissen, 1977) – as an alien I – the difference and otherness of the other person are overlooked. I shall argue that the other whom the self encounters in interpersonal relations is better characterized as the *second person*. The first-person point of view is only half of the story.

The philosophy of intersubjectivity escapes these problems. It defends the view that social and interpersonal relations are best explained as relations between persons, not minds, or bodies-with-minds; personhood is more fundamental than mindedness. It begins by affirming the equiprimordiality of self and other, and by emphasizing that the reality of interpersonal relations is a given rather than a cognitive achievement. Community, reciprocity, and sharing are fundamental realities; they are not ontologically and epistemologically secondary. Because one is a self only in relation to other selves, and in relation to a community of interlocutors, it is not necessary to postulate internal mental processes to do the work required by the self to reach the other. The self is always and already in relation with the other. This is a direct and immediate relation, not an indirect and cognitively mediated one.

To understand how the problem of other minds has come to haunt cognitive science, and how it might be overcome, it is important to begin at the beginning: with seventeenth-century rationalism, the often-overlooked birthdate of the mind's new science.

The philosophy of subjectivity

One of the primary goals of seventeenth-century rationalism was to show how reality could be made fully intelligible to human reason, without the aid of faith or revelation. The central idea was that the mind itself is a source of knowledge. Truths provided by the intellect are fundamentally different from truths based on sense experience. As truths of reason, they are unchanging and necessary; they are immune from the error that infects knowledge based on observation.

Like Archimedes, Descartes felt that he could "hope for great things if I manage to find just one thing, however slight, that is certain and unshakeable" (1641, p. 149). His foundationalist aspirations were finally satisfied by appealing to internal mental processes. The absolutely certain foundations on which to build the entire edifice of human knowledge are to be found in interiority, in the self-conscious thinking mind. *Cogito ergo sum:* The very fact of thinking, which the thinker cannot doubt, implies the reality of the cognizing subject. The guiding insight here is that we know ourselves directly and apodictically from within, as the unitary subjects of experience. Thinking is our essence, and self-consciousness is our lot. We are immediately aware of the contents of our minds, and unshakably certain of them.

Descartes argued that because of the fallibility of the senses he might be mistaken about things in the external world, but he could not be wrong about the contents of his mind at the present moment. "I know plainly that I can achieve an easier and more evident perception of my own mind than of anything else" (1641, p. 157). To be a cognizing subject is to be directly aware of the immediate data of conscious experience, even if not in a fully explicit or propositionalizable way; and to be conscious is to enjoy what phenomenologists call a "translucency" and "presence" (Sartre, 1943) with respect to one's mental states. This Cartesian (and later the cognitivist) assumption, that the mind can be understood independently of its immediate physical and social world, places deep and mostly unwanted constraints on theorizing about interpersonal relations.

The notion of privileged access has an air of familiarity about it. There are a number of reasons for this. Commonsense psychology (and natural grammar) divides up the contents of the world into subjects and objects. We think of ourselves as subjects of experience – thinkers of thoughts, sufferers of pain, and perceivers of situations. We do not view ourselves as a mere series of experiences but rather as something that *has* these experiences. Rocks, clouds, and wardrobes do not have experiences; there is nothing that it is like to be a rock. But there is something that it is like to be us, something it is like *for* us (Nagel, 1974). We are subjectivities, or êtres-pour-soi, as Sartre (1943) would say.

Also, commonsense psychology leads us to think that each cognizing subject has a privileged window on his or her own mind. We know from the inside what it's like to be us and what we are experiencing. If I have a pain in my foot, no one knows it better than I do; and sense cannot be attached to the claim that I might be mistaken about being in pain. How things experiential seem is how they are: The reality–appearance distinction does not count in matters subjective and conscious.

This contrasts with the way we know about external physical objects. Trees and stars and paramecia can be observed from a number of different viewpoints. The relevant information can be picked up by anyone with the appropriate perceptual capacities; and our perceptual judgments are sometimes wrong. Conscious mental states are not similarly observable from external points of view. In commonsense psychology, we think that they are private. Only the subject having them can know them directly, without having to resort to inductive inference, observation, or other potentially corrigible means.

The inner–outer dualism

Further, commonsense psychology tends to map the dualism of subjectivity and objectivity onto the dualism of inner and outer. The operations of the mind are inner and privately accessible, whereas the operations of the body are outer and publicly accessible. Conscious mental states are known from the inside only by their subject; everyone else knows them from the outside. Collapsing these two dualisms, the history of a person comes to be pictured as a history of two things that are in some peculiar way meshed together – an inside and an outside, a private mental life and an overt behavioral life.

The dualism of inner and outer is obviously metaphorical and misleading. Because minds are not (ex hypothesi) spatial or extended, they cannot properly be described as being "inside" anything else (i.e., inside a head) or as having "contents." Despite its metaphorical character, however, the spatialization of mind pervades both commonsense and scientific psychology. Whatever its heuristic value, cognitivism's use of diagrams, arrows, black boxes, and flowcharts to model the path of information through the cognizing system only deepens the fallacy of spatialization.

Just as commonsense psychology talks unhesitatingly about the "inner world of subjective experience," as if this had a different kind of accessibility and epistemic status from the things of the "outer," observable world, so certain kinds of scientific psychology postulate that we can never "really" know the subjective world that others (e.g., prelinguistic infants) inhabit. Stern, for instance, writes: "Because we cannot know the subjective world that infants inhabit, we must invent it" (1985, p. 4). Again, commonsense psychology (as well as the psychology prevalent in the nineteenth-century novels of Stendhal, James, and Proust) tends to view the inner life as definitive of who a person really is in a way that the history of their overt behavior does not; it is somehow truer, more essential, and closer to the real person than the "outer life."

The problem of other minds

If minds are pictured as containers of private, inner, mental episodes or representations, then a problem arises in explaining relations between minds. All persons enjoy privileged access to their own conscious mental lives, but they do not enjoy a similar access to the mental lives of others. They can see, hear, and touch other *bodies*, but the subjective experiences of others are forever closed to them. All that they can experience is their own experience: They feel a pain in their own leg, but they cannot feel the pain in another's leg. The force of this "cannot" is logical, and not merely empirical. In the inner life, then, each person is pictured as a kind of Robinson Crusoe (Ryle, 1949).

But this leads to the slippery slope to solipsism, which right-thinking Cartesians and cognitivists alike wish to deny. For if overt behavior is the only basis on which to ascribe mental predicates to other creatures, then how can I know with certainty that other creatures are minded? The strongest prima facie evidence would cite overt indicators like facial expressions, gestures, autobiographical reports, and intelligent behavior. When my friend knits her brow, stares intently at a chess board, and mutters something about protecting the bishop, I take this as evidence that she is thinking about chess tactics. But evidence of this kind is not sufficient to quell doubts about the presence or absence of mind. Gestures, behaviors, and the like are still overt and objective indicators; they are not of the same nature as the inner states with which they are putatively associated. After all, similar external behavioral indicators might be convincingly reproduced by "mindless" robots or Turing machines.

Faced with the overt antics of such infinitely complex creatures as other people, how can I be sure that there really are subjectivity and mind here? How do I know that other people are not merely complex mindless objects, or automata? Despite visibly intelligent overt behavior, there may be nobody home. Even more worryingly, I may be altogether alone in the universe and utterly unique in being minded. This is the "problem of other minds."

One solution, adopted by philosophers from Thomas Hobbes and John Stuart Mill to the present day, is to suggest that the existence of other minds is modeled on the basis of the first-person perspective (Hampshire, 1952; Hyslop, 1979; Hyslop & Jackson, 1972; Levin, 1984; Mill, 1865; Price, 1938). Each person uses a privileged picture of the contents of his or her own mind as a model for what it is like to be another person. Hobbes writes:

[Given] the similitude of the thoughts and passions of one man, to the thoughts and passions of another, whosoever looketh into himself, and considereth what he doth, when he does *think, opine, reason, hope, fear* & c. and upon what grounds; he shall thereby read and know, what are the thoughts and passions of all other men upon the like occasions (1651, p. 82)

When we are confronted with a human body displaying coherent behavior, we draw an analogy from our case to the other person's case. Because we know how our own conscious experience (e.g., a feeling of pain) is regularly manifested in our own external behavior (e.g., writhing and groaning), we can reasonably infer that the other person's behaviour is a manifestation of a similar internal mental state. Inference is the stuff of which interpersonal relations are made.

Problematic assumptions in the problem of other minds

There are a number of difficulties with this solution to the problem of other minds; more importantly, there are a number of difficulties with the very formulation of the problem.

Clearly, the weakest link in the theory is the notion of inference. In this instance, it is an inductive generalization resting on only one case – my own. Inference from a single case is the weakest and most fallible kind of induction. Nevertheless, it seems perverse to suppose that *this* inference might be radically mistaken, or that the existence of other minds is at best a probablistic affair. Ryle (1949), a vociferous critic of Cartesianism, sums up the inference theory neatly and disturbingly: Only our bodies can really meet; the rest is merely inferential.

The real weakness in the problem of other minds lies not in these heroic but unconvincing attempts to save us from solipsism; it is to be found in the form in which we cast the original problem, and the assumptions it conceals. When these are examined closely, the problem of other minds begins to look suspiciously like a pseudoproblem.

First, the starting point of the other minds theorist is a picture of the self as alienated and socially detached. The assumption is that the self interacts with things or material objects (i.e., human bodies), not with persons. To overcome its alienation, it must read into these bodies, through some sophisticated internal cognitive process, a mental life that is modeled on its own case. But in countenancing the possibility that another human's behavior might be nothing more than the brute mechanical workings of an electrochemical mechanism, the self's alienation is taken to implausible and dehumanized lengths.

Second, the picture of the self–other relation that is suggested by this formulation is altogether too top-heavy and first-personal. Given the masses of internal mental processing that are required to model the other person as a "re-edition" of oneself, it is questionable whether the self really *encounters* anything that is genuinely other than itself. It seems to be trapped in the web of its own mental life, unaware of the difference and otherness of the other. To rework a phrase that was once directed against overly cognitive theories of rat behavior, this view leaves the other person lost in the maze of the self's own thought. The interpersonal relation begins and ends in the head.

Finally, these doubts about the existence of other minds simply do not arise in our ordinary experience. Except in extreme or pathological cases, we do not actually ask ourselves, sotto voce, whether a *mind* animates another's behavioral display. We do not actually construct theories about the existence of other minds or make analogical inferences about them. The grounds for doubt are not to be found in the fabric of everyday life. Wittgenstein noted this: "'I believe that he is suffering.' – Do I also *believe* that he isn't an automaton? It would go against the grain to use the word in both connexions. . . . My attitude towards him is an attitude towards a soul. I am not of the *opinion* that he has a soul"(1953, p. 178).

In ordinary interpersonal relations, others are encountered directly and immediately. We address them, engage them in conversation, and stand in a practical, moral, or evaluative relation with them. Meeting them as *persons* is prior to treating them as bodies or minds or bodies-with-minds.

This is not to deny that certain interpersonal contexts may require constructing a theory of other minds, or inferring mindedness, or adopting the intentional stance. But we do not treat other humans as minded (rather than as objects or mindless automata) because we first have a theory of other minds (or because we infer they are minded); rather, we have a theory of other minds only because we first *encounter* others as persons. A theory of other minds is an abstraction and idealization from this primary fact of human experience.

Cognitive science and other minds

Fodor once remarked that everything goes round twice, first as philosophy, then later as cognitive science. Unwanted philosophical problems and pseudoproblems also get recycled. As the child of the marriage of Cartesian representationalism and Kantian constructivism, cognitivist (or information processing) versions of cognitive science have unfortunately inherited the problem of other minds. Although they have rightly disburdened themselves of the Cartesian theory of privileged access (and of the theory that consciousness is coextensive with the mental), they have inherited the language of internal mental processes, the inner–outer dualism, the atomistic spirit, and the tendency toward methodological solipsism.

The classical cognitivism of Turing, McCarthy, Newell, and Simon treats the organism as if it could be understood independently of its immediate social world and ecological niche. Cognitivist explanations target processes internal to the individual cognizing subject, and pay only lip service to the constraints of environment, society, biology, and phenomenology. The strategy of "opportunistic oversimplification" is defended on grounds of plausible neglect: "Things that are horribly complicated may be usefully and revealingly approximated by partitionings, averagings, idealizations, and other deliberate over-simplifications, in the hope that some molar behaviour of the complex phenomenon will prove to be relatively independent of all the myriad micro-details, and hence will be reproduced in a model that glosses over those microdetails" (Dennett, 1990, p. 48).

Neglect of things messy and complex is designed to establish a new level of analysis, a pure science of structure and function itself (Pylyshyn, 1984). But the high price of oversimplification is not always justified (Neisser, 1976), for it too often conflicts with the fundamental commitment of all theories:

to save the phenomena. Cognitivist explanations of social and interpersonal relations have paid too little attention to how humans are embedded in an information-rich social, interpersonal and natural world. The strategy of explaining interpersonal relations by appeal to internal mental processes has the effect of cramming into the modeled head what nature leaves to society and the world. Cognizing subjects are pictured as encapsulated entities: disembodied, historyless, asocial thinkers, housed in a self-contained subjectivity, consciousness, or mind.

If a moral is to be drawn here, it is that any attempt to theorize about social and interpersonal relationships should be faithful to what people actually feel and think and to what it is actually like to be involved in interpersonal relationships. Before engaging in theory construction and model building, it is essential to attend to the phenomena in question and to describe them as accurately as possible. Without this preliminary empirical work, and the ecological and phenomenological validity it assures, the questions with which we begin our investigations will be theory-driven and our solutions will be implausible abstractions with little bearing on reality. It is from such skewed starting points that pseudoproblems arise.

Persons are as inseparable from their environmental niche as from their social network and their place in the interpersonal dyad; each term implies the other. The mutuality of animal and environment described by Gibson (1979) parallels the mutuality of self and other in interpersonal relations. Some of these ideas will now be developed.

The philosophy of intersubjectivity

The twentieth-century reaction to Cartesianism

The twentieth century has witnessed a number of philosophical reactions to the philosophy of subjectivity: Mead's (1934) social behaviorism, Buber's (1923) and Levinas's (1961) philosophy of dialogue, Wittgenstein's (1953) linguistic behaviorism, Heidegger's existential phenomenology, Habermas's critical theory, Vygotsky's theory of the social origin of mind, Rorty's (1980) neopragmatism, and feminist philosophy's ethics of care (Baier, 1985; Code, 1987; Gilligan, 1982; Noddings 1984).

If anything unites such diverse theories, it is the view that what makes a person a person is not "inside the head." Rather it is outside, in relations between persons, in "webs of interlocution" (Taylor, 1990). Persons cannot be described adequately without reference to social relationality and interpersonal mutuality. The shared theme of the philosophy of intersubjectivity is that the condition of possibility for selfhood and personhood is recognition by other persons. There is no self or cognizing subject prior to the interpersonal dyad.

Let us take just Wittgenstein, Mead, and the philosophers of dialogue as representatives of the philosophy of intersubjectivity. We can see that despite profound theoretical differences, all are engaged in developing an ontology of the social, in contrast to an ontology of the private, atomistic, cognizing subject. The central focus of this ontology is language and communication, and the constitutive role of language in the formation of personhood and selfhood. In defending the idea of the simultaneous genesis of self and other through social encounter, Wittgenstein, Mead, and the philosophers of dialogue develop an unconventional way of philosophizing – one that requires thinking in terms of relations and reciprocities rather than inner–outer dichotomies. This way of thinking is faithful to the particularities of our ordinary experience of relationship. (Critical of the "craving for generality" that drives philosophers to reduce the complex to the simple, Wittgenstein (1965, p. 18) writes: "I want to say here that it can never be our job to reduce anything to anything.")

Yet another strand uniting Wittgenstein, Mead, and the philosophers of dialogue is the notion that the ground of meaningful behavior is to be found in shared forms of life. Meaning is not "in the head," the exclusive function of representations, mental content, or Kantian constitution. Meaning is a function of the complex networks of social practices that make up the shared and largely tacit background for human action. The meanings that certain central concepts have for a given person are those that they have for the whole linguistic community. It is sharing that makes sense (Trevarthen, 1987).

The idea that shared forms of life are essentially linguistic in nature, and that they consist of practices like language games, conversations of gestures, and interpersonal dialogue, is familiar to developmental psychology. In identifying and describing something, an infant and its caregiver make it a common object of reference. It is established in a public space (Tomasello, see this volume). We learn a whole range of interconnected moral, emotional, and psychological concepts through this experience of common reference and joint attention.

Without engaging at this stage in some basic exposition of both Levinas's and Buber's philosophy of dialogue, the uniqueness of their vision and its distance from the philosophy of subjectivity would not be appreciated. Afterward, an interpretation that brings the philosophy of dialogue into closer proximity with the conceptual framework of the cognitive sciences will be developed.

The philosophy of dialogue

The distinction between persons and things is the most fundamental way of dividing up the furniture of the world. We think of ourselves as essentially persons and only contingently as things, material objects, minds, mammals, reasoners, scientists, taxpayers, and so forth. Similarly, we think of other humans as essentially persons and only contingently as things, material objects, minds, and so forth. We do this because we stand in a unique set of moral and practical relations to others: They are the primary objects of love, friendship, responsibility, care, and moral concern. We learn the distinction between persons and things at our mother's knee and rarely stray from it; it is part of the general framework of human life.

The distinction between persons and things is rooted in the depths of prehistory and folk metaphysics. In philosophy, it has roots in Platonist and Christian metaphysics, Jewish philosophy, Kantianism, and the nineteenth-century interplay between the human sciences and the natural sciences (*Geisteswissenschaften* and *Naturwissenschaften*) from which the cognitive sciences emerged). Buber's and Levinas's philosophy of dialogue is yet another appropriation of this fundamental distinction.

Levinas's philosophy of dialogue

Emmanuel Levinas, curiously, is both a transcendental philosopher in the tradition of Kant and Husserl and a postmodern philosopher in the tradition of Derrida and Foucault. He is a critic of Western philosophy's excessive rationalism and theoretism and its unceasing attempts from Plato onward to underpin human knowledge and practice with indubitable and lasting foundations. But he is an atypical postmodern in his resistance to the antirealism, relativism, and antihumanism that often accompany the critique of foundationalism and philosophical totalization. Rather than deploying the essentially negative method of deconstruction, he develops a positive and original view of the ethical conditions of human life – one that departs radically from the major traditions of ethical thought represented by Kantian deontology, utilitarianism, virtue ethics, and situation ethics. He does this through a detailed and wide-ranging analysis of the self–other relation.

The central claim in Levinas's "humanism of the other person" – a claim that is made at the level of transcendental rather than empirical explanation – is that the form or framework of human life is irreducibly ethical. We are ethical creatures "all the way down." In limning the true nature of the human, then, ethics (as a transcendental inquiry) has priority over ontology, epistemology, psychology, and the other human sciences.

To be a person is to stand in a special set of relations to other persons. Levinas conceives these relations as first and foremost ethical; they involve responsiveness, responsibility, respect, desire, and interest. Higher-order cognitive relations between self and other are possible because of these first-order ethical relations. The event at the heart of the self–other relation is the face-to-face dialogical encounter, in which the other person is given to the self directly and fully and immediately. In this encounter, Levinas argues, the other is not a source of information, is not something that is represented, interpreted, or known. In some sense, the other is *beyond* the mediation and commensuration afforded by cognitive relations. The "otherness" (or alterity, or transcendence) of the other is one of the most important features of the self–other relation and a central clue to understanding how ethics lies at the heart of the human.

The otherness of the other person, however, is easily overlooked. When we think about another person – for instance, a colleague or friend – we tend to think of them in our own terms and from our own finite and parochial perspective. The descriptions and interpretations under which we view them are scaled to the dimensions of the self. Typically, we view them as other selves. Subsequent higher-order theorizing about the nature of self–other relations is also biased by the first-person perspective.

The otherness that Levinas argues is a central feature of the self–other relation resembles the otherness that is ascribed to God, who cannot be fully known or comprehended. God is uncontainable, and beyond every idea that we might formulate, and yet we still manage to stand in relation to God. But how is the relation to God to serve as an appropriate model for the self–other relation? Without ideas, concepts, theories, or categories, how is it possible for the self to be related to something so remote and uncontainable?

Levinas argues that it is dialogue – address and response – that holds the self-other relation together. Dialogue allows both terms of the relation to remain separate and autonomous, and yet it also allows a kind of community to be established. Dialogue is not a union, a mystical at-oneness, or a blending of the self with the other into a harmonious whole: It is a relation between separated terms (Levinas, 1961). Dialogue is the most receptive soil for radical pluralism. The face-to-face encounter is essentially a relation of interlocutors. It is a relation of two people responding to each other and, at a deeper level, being responsible for each other. To live is to engage in dialogue, to listen, to answer, to be open to the other.

Buber's philosophy of dialogue

Martin Buber develops his ideas by a method of "indirectness," which moves forward by means of metaphor, aphorism, narrative, and phenomenological description rather than through analysis and logical argument. Avoiding the cool, distanced style of most contemporary philosophers, he appeals to our experience of what it's like to be in interpersonal relationships. We are asked to search our own experience for moments that will illustrate the relationships he describes. Though unorthodox and sometimes mischievous, this method is valuable. Philosophical thought takes many forms, and flourishes in widely different ways; a priori straitjackets about what constitutes "genuine" philosophy too often serve as camouflage for dogma and narrow-mindedness.

To spell out the difference between persons and things, Buber makes two central claims. The first is that we are creatures of relation. To do justice to this fact, any ontology must be a relational ontology; substance-based and entity-based ontologies are inadequate. The second claim is that of all the myriad kinds of social relations in which persons are implicated at any one moment – historical, economic, linguistic, cognitive, psychological, and sexual – there are ultimately two basic kinds: I–Thou relations and I–It relations (Buber, 1923).

To *encounter* another person, in the sense of addressing them and re-sponding to them fully and spontaneously, is to be related to them as a Thou. The other person is not a thing among things. The other is not viewed under a certain description or in light of certain concepts, rules, representations, and other-directed psychological attributions. This is a special relation: It is direct, unmediated, and fully involving. It is beyond information.

Buber describes it as a relation that has a deeply ethical character. (The conceptual and etymological similarities between the words *respond* and *responsible* also suggest this.) Buber calls this the I–Thou relation:

> The relation to the Thou is direct. No system of ideas, no foreknowledge, and no fancy intervene between I and Thou. The memory itself is transformed. . . . No aim, no lust, and no anticipation intervene between I and Thou. (1923, p. 11)

By contrast, to *experience* another person, in the sense of adopting a theoretical, technical, aesthetic, or practical stance to them, is to be related to them as an It. This occurs when the primary focus of the relation involves treating the other person as predictable, explainable, manageable, or in-telligible. The other person is information-bearing. As such, the other is the appropriate subject of what might broadly be called the objective attitude (Strawson, 1974). Buber calls this the I–It relation. (Interestingly, the Latin derivation of the word *experience – experientia –* is experiment, trial, proof.)

The fate of human beings, Buber writes, is to oscillate between these two fundamental ways of relatedness. There is no permanent condition in one or the other. What was at one moment an I–Thou relation is at the next moment an I–It relation, and this must always be the case. Still, "all real living is meeting."

The relation of I to Thou is characterized by mutuality, presentness, exclusiveness, and intensity. It is a nonobjectifying relation; the relation is *lived*, not known or described. To try to identify and describe it, Buber writes, is to be outside it. Our ordinary descriptive and conceptual apparatus is intrinsically incapable of capturing the full reality of the Thou. The I–Thou relation is nonobjectifying in yet another sense: It cannot be willed into being or controlled. It is not the object of an intentional act. The Thou cannot be sought out, Buber writes, for one meets the Thou through grace.

The relation between I and It, by contrast, lacks mutuality. To relate to a person as an It is to relate to that person as ordered, intelligible, and predictable. In this mode of relatedness, the world is characterized by "causal texture" and affordances, with all the advantages that these bring for using, managing, and assimilating things. The "It-world," Buber writes, sustains humans materially, but not ethically or spiritually. The It is an object of cognition, perception, or action. To infer or theorize that another person is "minded" is to stand in an I–It relation to that person.

It is difficult to describe the I–Thou encounter without distorting it with the objectifying categories appropriate to the I–It world. Buber tries, however, to indicate what the I–Thou encounter is not. First, it is misleading (though very common) to characterize it as a mystical experience. Mysticism implies absorption into the Absolute and the annihilation of personal identity. It is also misleading to characterize it as a "feel-good-at-oneness" with an other person or as a rosy state of inner well-being. The I-Thou relation is not to be confused with a *psychological* relation of intimacy, closeness, or empathy. Buber emphasizes the other's otherness and independence with respect to the self.

It is also misleading to explain the I-Thou relation by appeal to internal mental processes. It is not inside the head (or inside two heads); it is what lies *between* self and other. Because we are so prone to thinking in terms of the inside–outside and subject–object dualisms, it is difficult to grasp this non-thing-like realm of the "between."

If we think of true intercourse, each person talking with the other with a spontaneity that gives it an unpredictable character; or of a true class session which goes beyond the routine framework, or of a veritable embrace and the like, we note that in all of these situations the encounter does not take place in each of the participants, or in a neutral unity encompassing them, but *between* them in the most exact sense, in a dimension accessible to them alone. (Marcel, 1967, p. 43)

Finally, it is misleading to characterize the other person to whom the self is related as a Thou as an *other self,* or as a like-minded subjectivity who differs from the self by virtue of a distinct spatial or psychological perspective. This would be to make the mistake made by the philosophy of subjectivity. We relate to others as essentially persons and only contingently as minds, subjectivities, bodies-with-minds, or material objects. The concept of a person is a logically primitive category; it is more basic than these other concepts (Strawson, 1959).

The ideas of Buber and Levinas are unusual and elusive, couched in a philosophical terminology that resists facile assimilation and naturalization. Can they be cashed out and creatively transformed, so that they are open to boundary bridging with other fields of inquiry? Might the cognitive sciences benefit from establishing interfield connections (Darden & Maull, 1977) with the philosophy of intersubjectivity, with the ultimate goal not of reducing one field to the other (or imposing one on the other) but rather of facilitating inquiries that were not previously possible from within one theoretical framework? The remaining discussion sketches out affirmative answers to these questions. Everything, after all, goes round twice.

An interpretation of the philosophy of dialogue

Even if we learn about the fundamental distinction between persons and things at our mother's knee, how do we come to know that some creature is a person? Is this a decision? An empirical discovery? Is there some set of necessary and sufficient conditions that the creature must meet? The central claim made by the philosophy of dialogue is that we do *not* first establish as objective fact (and by empirical means) that some creature is a person – because, for instance, it satisfies certain conditions of rationality, intentionality, or self-consciousness – and then relate to it in an appropriate way. Rather, our treating it and responding to it in a certain way is somehow *constitutive* of its being a person. This fundamental idea is shared by philosophers across a number of different traditions (Dennett, 1978; Putnam, 1964; Rorty, 1962; Sellars, 1966, 1968; Strawson, 1974).

The distinction between persons and things is indissolubly tied to the nature of social or dialogic encounter. Outside the context of a shared form of life, and the linguistic community and the face-to-face interaction that it affords, there are, properly speaking, no persons. Dialogue not only opens one person to another; it is by means of dialogue that we are, as it were, "talked into" personhood (Pfuetze, 1967).

In the philosophy of dialogue, the appropriate person-engendering way of relating to a creature consists of address and response. The sense attributed to these concepts is quite specific and needs to be spelled out. First, address and response is not to be confused with the exchange of information or the weaving of narratives. It is the spontaneous and direct face-to-face dialogue between two speakers who are in each other's presence. This aspect of language is easily overlooked because of its pervasiveness and familiarity. Spoken language is often modeled as the enunciation of propositions, as the exchange of information, or as the vehicle for referential statements. These models are too abstract. One of the most common events of everyday life is the act of addressing and responding to someone face to face and engaging that person in a way that is frank, unrehearsed, and responsive. Language would be a rootless, shifting, and impersonal system of signs if it were not anchored in the direct face-to-face confrontation of interlocutors. This event, Buber and Levinas argue, is at the root of our social institutions and moral practices.

Second, engaging another person in face-to-face dialogue is closely tied to a whole range of other-directed emotions, mutually responsive attitudes, and feelings of participation – for example, care, compassion, gratitude, sympathy, resentment, forgiveness, love, hurt feelings, respect, dislike, shame, desire (Strawson, 1974). To engage others in this way – say, to feel shame before them or to cause them to be ashamed – is to engage them as persons and moral agents. We cannot feel shame before an inanimate object (Sartre, 1943). It is only once we are in a certain interpersonal environment that the phenomenon of shame exists. A whole range of other-directed emotions and attitudes would not exist without the public space opened up by face-to-face dialogical encounters.

Third, the precise propositional content of dialogue is not important for its person-engendering capacities. Nothing may be said, yet a person may be addressed. A clear example of this is the situation of a caregiver speaking "motherese" to an infant (during the stage Trevarthen [1980, 1987; Murray & Trevarthen 1985] calls primary intersubjectivity). Here the nominative second person pronoun "you" plays a critical role. The infant's first sense of itself is as the referent of the address "you," spoken by a caregiver whom it too will eventually address as "you." The pronoun you has an elicitative locutionary force: As the pronoun of mutual recognition and response, it calls a person forth and situates the person in a space where the first person and third person pronouns also become appropriate (Baier, 1985; Code, 1987). This might be called an elicitative speech act. Buber (1923) calls it a "primary word."

Finally, it is not possible to address another person with elicitative locutionary force while maintaining a detached and objective stance. A person being addressed is not being observed, studied, or analyzed. The person is not the object of a certain stance. Of course, it is always possible to size up others, to interpret their actions according to psychodynamic theory, to form judgments about their character, and to admire the beauty of their face. And it is always possible to view others under such descriptions as "brilliant," "beautiful," or "neurotic." But in so doing, the other person is not being engaged as a genuine interlocutor in a social relationship.

The theoretical, technical, or aesthetic *stance* to the other is fundamentally different from the dialogical *encounter* with the other. These are not simply different versions of the same self–other relation. It is not a matter of seeing a person in a different way, as we see the duck-rabbit reversible figure first as a duck, then as a rabbit. Nor is it a matter of adopting a different attitude toward a person: that is, same person, different attitude. The person addressed face to face is not part of the same information-yielding world that is the object of the theoretical, technical, or aesthetic stances. To address someone in the specific sense of the term established by Buber and Levinas is to stand in a relation that *constitutes* their personhood. And to be addressed by someone is to be called into a conversation through which we acquire a sense of moral and social identity. It is this original dialogical situation that provides the context for an answer to the question "Who am I?" (Taylor, 1990).

Knowledge, cognition, and the other

The most ambitious and contentious claim made by the philosophy of dialogue is that the relation between self and other is not explained by appeal to internal mental processes – for instance, inference, representation, or information processing. Rather, it is explained by something that in turn explains how cognitively mediated social relations are possible: namely, the social and ethical relation of addressing and responding. Openness and moral responsiveness to the other are the heart of human experience (Gilligan, 1982; Levinas, 1961; Noddings, 1984). Without this logically prior responsiveness, cognitive and representation-mediated interpersonal relations would not be possible.

The philosophy of dialogue does not deny that many ordinary interpersonal relations are shaped by representations, theories, and beliefs. We may, for instance, describe a friend as "acting out an unresolved childhood complex," thereby relating to the friend in light of psychodynamic theory, one of the primary purposes of which is explanation and prediction. But such an approach does not characterize the original sense of the self–other relation. The other person is not first an object of representation, cognition, or explanation and afterward an interlocutor; the other is "neither initially nor ultimately what we grasp or thematize" (Levinas, 1961).

The specific cognitive skills that we exercise as knowers and theory builders presuppose our everyday shared social and ethical encounters. It is in terms of this shared background that such activities as knowing, theorizing, and inquiring make sense. Insofar as it is logically dependent, the whole range of cognitive and epistemic skills bears the mark of the social and interpersonal. There is no cognition independent of a social and normatively guided context. To be a knower is to be responsive to criticism and to participate in a responsible way in the practice of mutual criticism and affirmation (Baier, 1985). The condition for this is membership in a community of mutually aware interlocutors.

Conclusion

Levinas offers a telling metaphor to summarize the differences between the philosophy of dialogue and the philosophy of subjectivity. The general orientation and spirit of the former resembles that of Abraham; the orientation of the latter resembles that of the Greek hero Odysseus. However numerous his wanderings, however far from his homeland he may travel, Odysseus still returns to his point of origin. He never suffers the fate of the refugee, the truly homeless. Abraham, by contrast, obeys a divine command and leaves his home searching for an unknown country. When he starts out he knows that he will never return.

The philosophy of subjectivity tends to privilege the model of return and coincidence represented by Odysseus' journey: It is constantly striving for original unity and self-sameness. This way of thinking pervades the entire Western philosophical tradition – a tradition that models itself on the recursive and reflexive unfolding of the cognizing subject (or consciousness, mind, spirit, or transcendental ego) by that *same* subject. This recursive movement occurs in different forms, as Socratic midwifery, as Cartesian reflection, as Kantian critique, as Hegelian totalization, as Husserlian transcendental description, and as cognitive science's inquiry into the mind. Like the travels of Odysseus, it is essentially a reflexive movement, *from* the self *to* the self *by* the self. Alterity, the other, is only a stage on the way of the self-unfolding and self-realizing activity of the self.

This kind of self-dominated philosophy is unable to conceive otherness and transcendence in any radical sense – transcendence as *scandere trans*, meaning "to go across," to leave oneself, to go toward the other, like Abraham leaving his home never to return.

REFERENCES

Baier, A. (1985). *Postures of the mind: Essays on mind and morals.* Minneapolis: University of Minnesota Press.

Buber, M. (1923, 1958). *I and Thou* (R. G. Smith, Trans.). New York: Scribners.

Churchland, P. M. (1979). Scientific realism and the plasticity of mind. Cambridge University Press.

Code, L. (1987). Second persons. In M. Hanen & K. Nielsen (Eds.), *Science, morality and feminist theory* (supplementary Vol. 13. *Canadian Journal of Philosophy*).

Darden, L., & Maull, N. (1977). Interfield theories. *Philosophy of Science, 43.*

Dennett, D. (1978). *Brainstorms.* Cambridge, MA: MIT Press.

Dennett, D. (1989). *The intentional stance.* Cambridge, MA: MIT Press.

Dennett D. (1990). The myth of original intentionality. In K. A. Mohyeldin Said, W. H. Newton-Smith, R. Viale, & K. V. Wilkes (Eds.), *Modeling the mind.* Oxford: Clarendon.

Descartes, R. (1641/1968). *Meditations.* In *The philosophical works of Descartes* (E. Haldane & G. Ross, Eds., Vol. 1 and 2). Cambridge University Press.

Feuerbach, L. (1843/1966). *Principles of the philosophy of the future.* (M. Vogel, Trans.). Indianapolis, IN: Bobbs-Merrill.

Gibson, J. J. (1979). *The ecological approach to visual perception.* Hillsdale, NJ: Erlbaum.

Gilligan, C. (1982). *In a different voice.* Cambridge, MA: Harvard University Press.

Hampshire, S. (1952). The analogy of feeling. *Mind, 61.*

Hobbes, T. (1651, 1946). *Leviathan* (M. Oakeshott, Ed.). Oxford: Oxford University Press.

Humphrey, N. (1983). *Consciousness regained.* New York: Oxford University Press.

Hyslop, A. (1979). A multiple case inference and other minds. *Australasian Journal of Philosophy, 57*(4).

Hyslop, A., & Jackson, F. (1972). The analogical inference to other minds. *American Philosophical Quarterly, 9*(2).

Levin, M. (1984). Why we believe in other minds. *Philosophy and Phenomenological Research, 44*(3).

Levinas, E. (1961/1969). *Totality and infinity* (A. Lingis, Trans.). Pittsburgh: Duquesne University Press.

Marcel, A. J., & Bisiach, E. (Eds.). (1988). *Consciousness in contemporary science.* Oxford: Clarendon.

Marcel, G. (1967). I and Thou. In P. A. Schilpp & M. Friedman (Eds.), *The philosophy of Martin Buber.* La Salle, IL: Open Court.

Mead, G. H. (1934). *Mind, self and society* (C. Morris, Ed.). Chicago: University of Chicago Press.

Mill, J. S. (1865). *An examination of Sir William Hamilton's philosophy.* London.

Murray, L., & Trevarthen, C. (1985). Emotional regulation of interactions between two-month olds and their mothers. In T. M. Field & N. A. Fox (Eds.), *Social perception in infants.* Norwood, NJ: Ablex.

Nagel, T. (1974). What is it like to be a bat? *Philosophical Review, 83,* 435–450.

Neisser, U. (1976). *Cognition and reality.* New York: Freeman.

Neisser, U. (1988). Five kinds of self-knowledge. *Philosophical Psychology, 1,* 35–59.

Noddings, N. (1984). *Caring: A feminine approach to ethics and moral education.* Berkeley: University of California Press.

Overall, C. (1988). Feminism, ontology and "other minds." In L. Code, S. Mullett, & C. Overall (Eds.), *Feminist perspectives: Philosophical essays on method and morals.* Toronto: University of Toronto Press.

Pfuetze, P. (1967). Martin Buber and American pragmatism. In P. A. Schilpp & M. Friedman (Eds.), *The philosophy of Martin Buber.* La Salle, IL: Open Court.

Price, H. H. (1938). Our evidence for the existence of other minds. *Philosophy, 13.*

Putnam, H. (1964). Robots: Machines or artificially created life? *Journal of Philosophy, 61.*

Putnam, H. (1975). *Mind, language and reality.* Cambridge University Press.

Pylyshyn, Z. (1984). *Computation and cognition.* Cambridge, MA: MIT Press.

Rorty, A. O. (1962). Slaves and machines. *Analysis, 22*(5), 118–120.

Rorty, R. (1980). *Philosophy and the mirror of nature.* Princeton, NJ: Princeton University Press.

Ryle, G. (1949). *The concept of mind.* Harmondsworth, U. K.: Penguin.

Sartre, J. P. (1943/1969). *Being and nothingness* (H. Barnes, Trans.). London: Methuen.

Sellars, W. (1956). Empiricism and the philosophy of mind. In H. Feigl & M. Scriven (Eds.), *Minnesota studies in the philosophy of science.* Minneapolis: University of Minnesota Press.

Sellars, W. (1963). *Science, perception and reality.* London: Routledge & Kegan Paul.

Sellars, W. (1966). Fatalism and determinism. In K. Lehrer (Ed.), *Freedom and determinism.* New York: Random House.

Sellars, W. (1968). *Science and metaphysics.* London: Routledge & Kegan Paul.

Strawson, P. F. (1959). *Individuals.* London: Methuen.

Strawson, P. F. (1974). *Freedom and resentment and other essays.* London: Methuen.

Stern, D. N. (1985). *The interpersonal world of the infant.* New York: Basic Books.

Taylor, C. (1990). *Sources of the self.* Cambridge, MA: Harvard University Press.

Theunissen, M. (1977, 1984). *The other: Studies in the social ontology of Husserl, Heidegger, Sartre and Buber* (C. MacAnn, Trans.). Cambridge, MA: MIT Press.

Trevarthen, C. (1980). The foundations of intersubjectivity: Development of interpersonal and cooperative understanding in infants. In D. Olson (Ed.), *The social foundations of language and thought: Essays in honor of Jerome S. Bruner.* New York: Norton.

Trevarthen, C. (1987). Sharing makes sense: Intersubjectivity and the making of an infant's meaning. R. Steele & T. Threadgold (Eds.), *Language topics: Essays in honour of Michael Halliday.* Amsterdam: John Benjamins.

Wittgenstein, L. (1953/1968). *Philosophical investigations* (G. E. M. Anscombe, Trans.). Oxford: Blackwell.

Wittgenstein, L. (1965). *The blue and brown books.* New York: Harper & Row.

Author index

Subject index